SIXTH EDITION

CONTACTS

Langue et culture françaises

Cahier d'activités

Workbook
Lab Manual

Jean-Paul Valette
Rebecca M. Valette
Boston College

Video Workbook

Rick Altman
University of Iowa

HOUGHTON MIFFLIN COMPANY BOSTON NEW YORK

CREDITS

Videocassette produced by special arrangement with Video Publishing Group, Inc.

Senior Sponsoring Editor: E. Kristina Baer
Development Editor: Cécile Strugnell
Project Editor: Nicole Ng
Associate Production/Design Coordinator: Deborah Frydman
Electronic Production: Esther Marshall
Senior Manufacturing Coordinator: Priscilla Bailey
Editorial Assistant: Hélène de Portu
Marketing Manager: Elaine Uzan Leary

Printed in the U.S.A.

ISBN: 0-395-79795-0

5 6 7 8 9 - PO - 00 99

Contents

WORKBOOK

LAB MANUAL

VIDEO WORKBOOK

ANSWER KEYS

To the Student

The three parts of the *Cahier d'activités* have been designed to accompany **CONTACTS, Sixth Edition.** Each part is coordinated with the 33 lessons and the **Vivre en France** sections of the student text.

1. The WORKBOOK contains exercises that reinforce reading and writing skills and supplement vocabulary practice. For easy review, the exercises are keyed to correspond to the **Structure** and **Vocabulaire** sections of the student text. Each workbook lesson ends with a personalized **Communication** activity that encourages students to express their opinions or to answer personal questions using the vocabulary and structures presented in the lesson.

   The WORKBOOK also contains four self-tests, or **Révisions,** which appear after lessons 9, 18, 27, and 33. These self-tests help students prepare for midterm and final examinations.

2. The LAB MANUAL provides written activities keyed to the audiocassettes. In order to increase students' ability to link pronunciation and comprehension to visual stimuli, many art-based activities are included. Phonetic exercises are also included; the phonetic explanations are highlighted for easy reference.

   At the end of each unit is a **Vivre en France** section, corresponding to the **Vivre en France** sections in the student text. These task-oriented activities help students build proficiency in listening comprehension. Students first listen to a series of questions and choose the best response to each from the possibilities listed. They then listen to a short conversation. Finally, they complete items such as a map or a hotel registration form based on what they hear.

3. The VIDEO WORKBOOK is intended to be used in conjunction with the *Pas de problème!* video. *Pas de problème!* consists of twelve modules of video material, shot on location in France. The VIDEO WORKBOOK offers students a variety of pre-viewing, viewing, and post-viewing activities designed to guide the student through each video segment. The video program has a problem solving format. Students learn about daily life in France and are then challenged to apply what they have learned to realistic situations that they might actually encounter while in France or other French-speaking countries.

At the end of the *Cahier d'activités,* the student will find answer keys for the WORKBOOK exercises, the four **Révisions,** and the texts for the **Dictée** sections of the lab program.

WORKBOOK

Jean-Paul Valette
Rebecca M. Valette

NOM ______________________ DATE ______________

UNITÉ 1. BONJOUR, LES FRANÇAIS!

Leçon 1. Bonjour!

1. Au club international. Students from different countries often meet at the international club of the Université François-Rabelais. At each table there are *two* students with traditional French names. Circle these names. *[Section A, p. 2*]*

❖	Olga	(Françoise)	Karen	(Marie-Christine)
1.	Bill	André	Philippe	Steven
2.	Thérèse	Colleen	Carmen	Suzanne
3.	Carlos	Wolfgang	Pierre	Jacques
4.	Hélène	Linda	Jérôme	Erika
5.	Karl	Luc	Pedro	Jean-Louis
6.	Monique	Heidi	Michiko	Cécile
7.	Mary	Véronique	Brigitte	Pamela
8.	Henri	Tatsuo	Antoine	Mikhail

2. Dans le foyer *(student lounge)* **de la cité universitaire.** You are meeting your new French-speaking classmates at the university residence. Give a logical answer to each of the statements or questions below. There may be more than one correct answer. *[Section A, p. 6]*

1. Salut! Ça va?

   Ça va bien

2. Ça va bien. Et toi?

   Ça va mal

3. Bonjour. Je m'appelle Iris. Comment vous appelez-vous?

   Je m'appelle Cary

4. Au revoir.

   Au revoir. À demain

5. Marc, je te présente mon ami Mourad. Mourad, Marc.

   Je enchanté

* Refers to corresponding section and page number from your textbook.

6. Bonjour!

Bonjour Comment allez vous?

7. À tout à l'heure.

À bientôt

3. Rencontres *(Encounters).* Look at the drawings below and write a two- or three-line conversation that might take place between the people pictured. *[Section A, p. 6]*

Salut Jean.
Salut Thérèsa Ça va?
Ça va bien. A Bientôt

Comment ~~allez~~ vas tu Marie
Pas mal ajourdui. Ça va?
Ça va bien, merci

Bonjour. Comment vous appelez vous.
~~Je m'appelle~~
Je m'appelle Cary.

- Salut Marc. Je te presente mon ami Charles.
- Bonjour. Enchanté. Ça va?
- Merci, Ça va bien.

Bonjour Harriet.
Bonjour. À tout a l'heure
A bientôt

NOM ________________________________ DATE ____________________

COMMUNICATION

Imagine that you are in a French-speaking country. Write what you would say in the following circumstances.

❖ Say hello to your friend Caroline.

Bonjour, Caroline!

1. Say good-bye to your friend Jean-Marc.

   À tout a l'heure Jean Marc

2. Tell Monique that you will see her soon.

   À bientôt Monqiue

3. Ask your roommate how things are going.

   Ça va?

4. You are at a rehearsal of your university orchestra. Ask your new stand partner his or her name.

   Comment t'appelles-ten?

5. Give a bank teller your name.

   Bonjour, ~~je~~ m'appelle Charles

6. Introduce your friend Élise to your mother **(Maman).**

   Maman, jete presenté mon ami Élise

7. Your neighbor asks you how things are. You're in the middle of exam week. Your answer is not too enthusiastic.

   Comme çi, Comme ça

NOM ______________________________ DATE ____________________

Leçon 2. Comment vas-tu?

1. Mon quartier *(My neighborhood).* You meet the following people in the street. Write down the exchange you have with each of them as you ask them how they are doing and they respond. Don't forget to include their responses. *[Section A, p. 15]*

1. some old school friends of yours

   ____

   ____

   ____

2. the butcher and his wife

   ____

   ____

   ____

3. your ten-year-old neighbor

   ____

   ____

   ____

4. the retired director of your primary school

   ____

   ____

   ____

5. your sister

   ____

   ____

   ____

2. Rencontres *(Encounters).* Complete the following conversations with a logical phrase or sentence. *[Section A, p. 15]*

1. ______________________________

   Pas mal.

2. Merci.

   ____

3. ______________________________

   Il n'y a pas de quoi.

4. Comment allez-vous?

   ____

5. ______________________________

   Ça va très bien, et toi?

   ____

3. Ça va? How would you answer the question **"Ça va?"** in each of the following circumstances? *[Section A, p. 15]*

❖ (You got a "B" on your French exam, when you expected a "C.")
Ça va (très) bien.

1. (You got a "B," but you expected an "A.")

   ____

2. (You received a letter from your best friend.)

   ____

3. (You have a bad headache.)

   ____

4. (You have just won 1,000 francs in the French lottery.)

   ____

5. (You have had a bad case of the flu and are now recovering slowly.)

   ____

NOM ______________________ DATE ______________________

4. Au café. Look at the drawings below and write short conversations that might be taking place between the people shown. (You may add lines if you wish.) *[Présentations, p. 10]*

Serveur: ______________________

Client: ______________________

Serveur: ______________________

Serveur: ______________________

Client(e) #1: ______________________

Serveur: ______________________

Client(e) #2: ______________________

5. Présentations *(Introductions).* Imagine that you are the president of the International Club. You will be introducing the following new members and want to be sure that you pronounce their names correctly. Cross out all silent letters and circle final consonants that are pronounced. *[Section B, p. 17]*

❖ Albert̸ Duro(c)

1. Nicolas Duval
2. Daniel Renard
3. Élisabeth Aveline
4. Michèle Camus
5. Louis Beaufort
6. Bruno Maréchal
7. Bernard Colas
8. Denise Martinot
9. Rémi Andrieux
10. Charles Malec

6. Les accents. The following names have been typed without accent marks. The nature of the missing accent is given in parentheses. Rewrite the name, putting the accent mark where it belongs. *[Section C, p. 18]*

❖ (accent grave) Daniele ***Danièle***

1. (accent aigu) Andre ________________
2. (accent aigu) Felix ________________
3. (accent grave) Michele ________________
4. (accent grave) Marlene ________________
5. (tréma) Joel ________________
6. (cédille) François ________________
7. (tréma) Raphael ________________

NOM ______________________ DATE ______________________

COMMUNICATION

Imagine that you are in France. Write out what you would say in the following situations.

❖ You meet Mlle Boulanger, your French teacher, on the street.
Say hello and ask her how she is.

Bonjour, Mademoiselle! Comment allez-vous?

1. On the bus you meet M. Arnaud, the father of a classmate. Say hello to him and ask him how he is.

____

2. At the Café de l'Univers, you meet Corinne, a classmate. Say hi and ask her how she is.

____

3. Corinne has helped you with your homework. Thank her.

____

4. You are in a restaurant. Ask the waiter to please bring you a cup of coffee.

____

5. You are working part-time in a record shop. You have just informed a customer about the records that are popular in the United States. She thanks you for your information. Tell her she is welcome.

____

NOM ______________________ DATE ______________

Leçon 3. Qui est-ce?

1. Qui est-ce? At the International House you point out certain friends and classmates to a new student just arrived from Québec. Describe them in complete sentences following the model below. *[Section A, p. 26]*

❖ voici Zineb / copine / algérien

Voici Zineb, une copine algérienne.

1. voilà Tuyen / copine / vietnamien

____

2. voilà Roger / copain / suisse

____

3. voici France / copine / québécois

____

4. voici Léopold / poète / sénégalais

____

5. voilà Ricardo / architecte / mexicain

____

6. voici Raïssa / amie / marocain

____

2. Mais non! Answer the following questions with complete sentences. Note in parentheses the real places of origin of these people. *[Section A, p. 26]*

❖ Shaquille O'Neal est canadien? (États-Unis d'Amérique)

Non, il est américain.

Céline Dion est sénégalaise? (Québec)

Non, elle est québécoise.

1. Jeanne Moreau est marocaine? (France)

____

2. Le prince Charles est suisse? (Angleterre)

____

3. Aimé Césaire est mexicain? (Martinique)

____

4. Frieda Kahlo est québécoise? (Mexique)

____

5. Jean Calvin est vietnamien? (Suisse)

____

6. Jean Chrétien est américain? (Canada)

____

7. Hillary Rodham Clinton est anglaise? (États-Unis d'Amérique)

____

NOM ______________________________ DATE ______________________

3. Une rue en ville *(A city street).* You're showing a photo of Main Street in your town to some French-speaking visitors. Point out some of the places shown. Write your answers in the same form as the model. *[Section B, p. 28]*

❖ Et le numéro 7?

Voilà (Voici) le musée.

1. ______________________________

2. ______________________________

3. ______________________________

4. ______________________________

5. ______________________________

6. ______________________________

4. À Paris! The following actions take place in Paris. Show your understanding of each sentence by writing its English equivalent. *[Section B, p. 28]*

❖ Paul téléphone à Jacqueline.

Paul is phoning Jacqueline.

1. Le docteur téléphone à l'hôpital.

___

2. Thomas dîne au restaurant.

___

3. Daniel invite Monique au cinéma.

___

4. Les touristes visitent le musée.

___

5. Le taxi arrive à l'aéroport.

___

6. L'autobus passe dans l'avenue Victor-Hugo.

___

5. Préférences. Choose elements from both columns below to create eight sentences that tell what you like and what you don't like. *[Section B, p. 28]*

A	B	
J'adore...	la télévision	l'université
J'aime...	la musique	le cinéma
Je n'aime pas tellement...	le café	le dessert
Je déteste...	le jogging	les brocoli
Je préfère...	la violence	le sport

1. ___
2. ___
3. ___
4. ___
5. ___
6. ___
7. ___
8. ___

NOM ____________________ DATE ____________________

Communication

Write what you would need to say in the following situations.

1. You are sitting in a café when a student whom you don't know walks by. Ask a friend who he or she is.

   ____

2. A friend asks you who the teacher in the blue suit is. Tell him that is it Mme Leblanc.

   ____

3. You and a friend from southern France are visiting Paris by bus. As you approach the cathedral of Paris, you tell her that here is Notre-Dame.

   ____

4. As your bus continues along the Seine River, tell your friend that there is the Orsay Museum **(le musée d'Orsay).**

   ____

5. At the restaurant, you mention that you hate spaghetti **(les spaghetti)** and that you prefer salad **(la salade).**

   ____

6. After dinner, you and your friend discuss what to do. Tell her that you like the movies and you love to dance.

   ____

7. At a club, you introduce your companion to Hassan, an Algerian friend.

   ____

Comunicación

[illegible]

1. [illegible]

2. [illegible]

3. [illegible]

4. [illegible]

5. [illegible]

6. [illegible]

7. [illegible]

NOM ______________________ DATE ______________________

UNITÉ 2. QUI PARLE FRANÇAIS?

Leçon 4. Au Canada

1. Au travail *(At work).* Say where the people in parentheses are working. Complete the sentences below with the corresponding subject pronouns and the appropriate forms of the present tense of the verb **travailler.** *[Section A, p. 43]*

❖ (Mlle Moreau) *Elle travaille* à Montréal.

1. (Guy et François) ______________________ à Québec.
2. (vous) ______________________ à l'hôtel Frontenac.
3. (tu) ______________________ à l'hôtel Méridien.
4. (nous) ______________________ à Paris.
5. (M. et Mme Leblanc) ______________________ à Genève.
6. (M. Michaud) ______________________ à l'hôpital Saint-Jacques.
7. (je) ______________________ au Café de l'Univers.
8. (Thérèse et Annie) ______________________ à l'Université François-Rabelais.

2. Activités. Within the parentheses, write the infinitives of the activities suggested by the illustrations. Then complete the sentences with the appropriate forms of these verbs. *[Section A, p. 43]*

❖ (*parler*)

Mlle Marchand *parle* français.

1. (______________)

Nous ______________ au tennis.

2. (______________)

M. et Mme Moreau ______________ la télévision.

3. (____________________)

Vous ____________________ au restaurant.

4. (____________________)

Tu ____________________ à Caroline.

5. (____________________)

M. Tremblay ____________________ au Canada.

6. (____________________)

Les touristes ____________________ Paris.

3. Dialogues. Complete the following dialogues according to the model. First complete each question with the appropriate present-tense form of the verb suggested by the illustration. Then use this verb to answer the question in the negative. *[Section B, p. 48]*

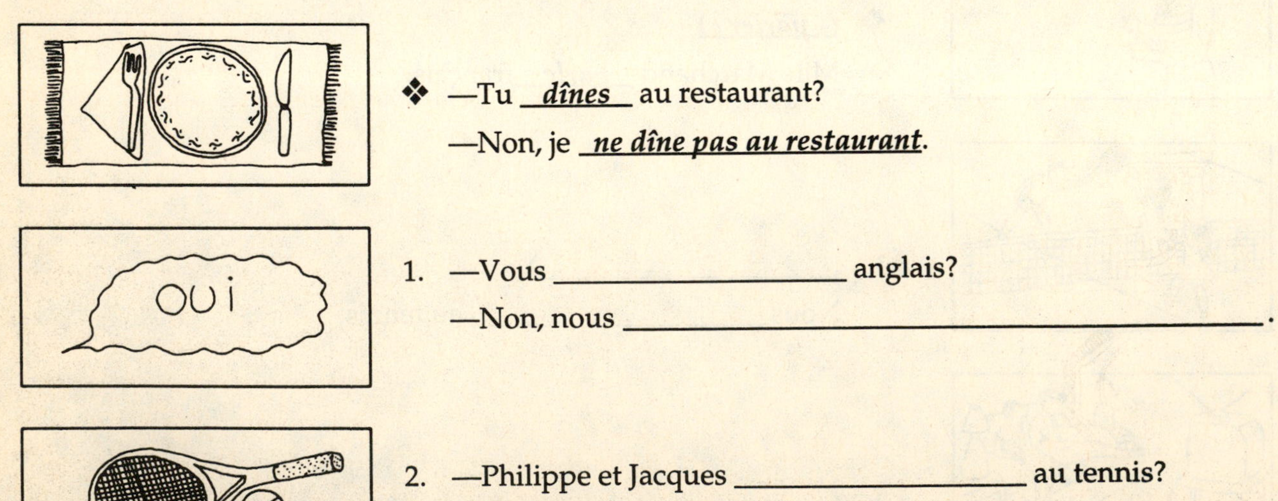

❖ —Tu *dînes* au restaurant?

—Non, je *ne dîne pas au restaurant*.

1. —Vous ____________________ anglais?

—Non, nous ____.

2. —Philippe et Jacques ____________________ au tennis?

—Non, ils ____.

NOM ______________________ DATE ______________________

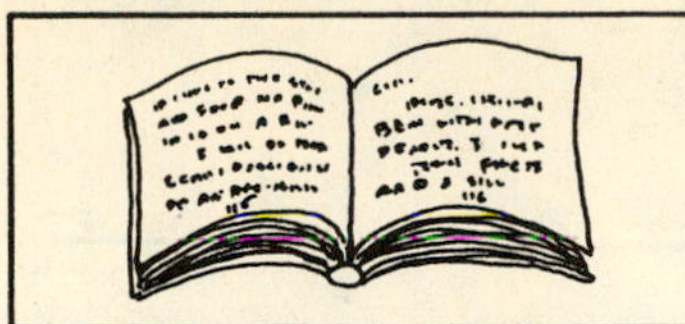

3. —Vous ______________ la géographie?
—Non, nous ______________________________.

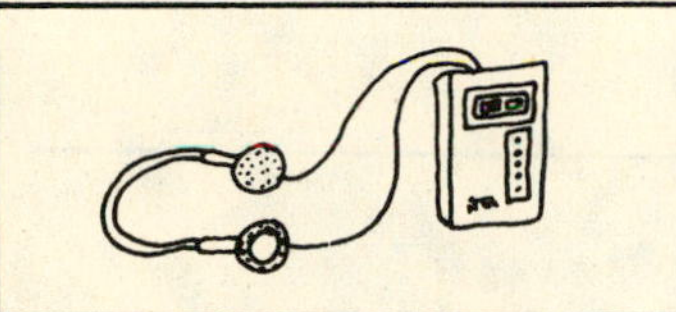

4. —Charles ______________ la radio?
—Non, il ______________________________.

5. —Monique et Suzanne ______________ Paul?
—Non, elles ______________________________.

6. —Tu ______________ à Caroline?
—Non, je ______________________________.

4. Les maths. Write out the results of the following arithmetic problems. *[Section C, p. 49]*

❖ 6 – 2 = *quatre*

1. 3 x 3 = ______________
2. 8 + 4 = ______________
3. (5 x 2) + 1 = ______________
4. (6 - 3) x 2 = ______________
5. (4 x 2) - 1 = ______________
6. (3 x 4) - 7 = ______________
7. 8 - (2 x 2) = ______________
8. 9 - 3 = ______________

5. La ponctualité. Write out the times indicated on the clocks below. *[Section C, p. 49]*

1. Il est ______________________________

2. Il est ______________________________

3. Il est ______________________________

4. Il est ______________________________

5. Il est ______________________________

6. Il est ______________________________

Communication

Imagine that you are studying at the Alliance française in Paris. Another student wants to get to know you better. Answer her questions with affirmative or negative sentences.

1. Tu parles anglais?

____

2. Tu parles italien?

____

3. Tu habites à San Francisco?

____

4. Tu regardes la télé française *(French TV)*?

____

5. Tu joues au bridge?

____

6. Tu étudies la biologie?

____

7. Tu aimes Paris?

____

NOM ______________________ DATE ______________________

Leçon 5. À Dakar

1. Où? *(Where?)* Read the sentences below and then say where the people are. In your statements, use subject pronouns, the appropriate forms of **être à,** and the cities in italics. *[Section A, p. 57]*

❖ Philippe aime *New York.* ***Il est à New York.***

1. Nous visitons *Montréal.* ______________________
2. Vous travaillez à *Genève.* ______________________
3. M. et Mme Lambert habitent à *Tours.* ______________________
4. Jacqueline étudie à *Paris.* ______________________
5. J'arrive à *Dakar.* ______________________
6. Tu travailles à *Québec.* ______________________

2. Préférences. Read what the following people do or don't do, and then say that they like or don't like these things. Study the two models. *[Section B, p. 58]*

❖ Philippe joue au tennis. ***Il aime jouer au tennis.***

❖ Carole ne joue pas au tennis. ***Elle n'aime pas jouer au tennis.***

1. Vous voyagez.

____

2. Tu ne voyages pas.

____

3. Je nage.

____

4. Isabelle ne téléphone pas.

____

5. Nous dansons.

____

6. Paul et Louis n'étudient pas.

____

7. Vous n'écoutez pas la radio.

____

3. Rencontres. A French student is asking you the following questions. Answer him or her affirmatively or negatively. *[Section C, p. 59]*

❖ Est-ce que tu habites à Boston? ***Oui, j'habite à Boston.***

ou: ***Non, je n'habite pas à Boston.***

1. Est-ce que tu es en cours maintenant? ______________________
2. Est-ce que tu étudies beaucoup? ______________________
3. Est-ce que tu voyages souvent? ______________________
4. Est-ce que tu nages? ______________________
5. Est-ce que tu nages bien? ______________________
6. Est-ce que tu chantes bien? ______________________
7. Est-ce que tu aimes voyager? ______________________
8. Est-ce que tu aimes danser? ______________________

4. Questions. Complete the following dialogues. First complete each question using the subject in parentheses and the verb suggested by the illustration. Then complete the answer affirmatively or negatively as suggested. *[Section C, p. 59]*

❖ (tu)

—***Est-ce que tu joues*** bien au tennis?

—Non, je ***ne joue pas bien au tennis.***

1. (Robert)

—______________________ souvent?

—Oui, il ______________________.

2. (tu)

—______________________ bien?

—Non, je ______________________.

NOM ________________________ DATE ________________

3. (Paul et André)

—________________ beaucoup?

—Oui, ils ________________________.

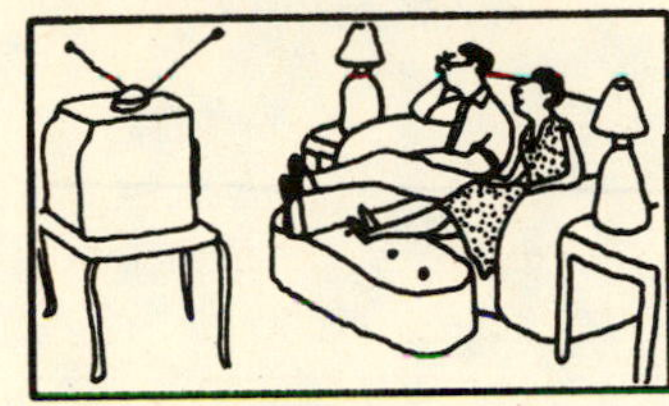

4. (vous)

—________________ souvent la télévision?

—Non, nous________________________.

5. Les nombres. Read the following numbers and write them in digits. *[Section D, p. 63]*

❖ *54* cinquante-quatre

1. ______ vingt-huit
2. ______ trente et un
3. ______ cinquante-deux
4. ______ quatre-vingt-cinq
5. ______ quinze
6. ______ soixante et onze
7. ______ quatre-vingt-douze
8. ______ soixante-six
9. ______ quarante-trois
10. ______ quatorze
11. ______ quatre-vingts
12. ______ cinquante-sept

6. À quelle heure? Say at what time the following events are taking place. Complete the sentences with the times indicated on the clocks. *[Section D, p. 63]*

❖ Le concert est à *huit heures cinq*.

1. La classe est à ________________________.

2. Le film est à ________________________.

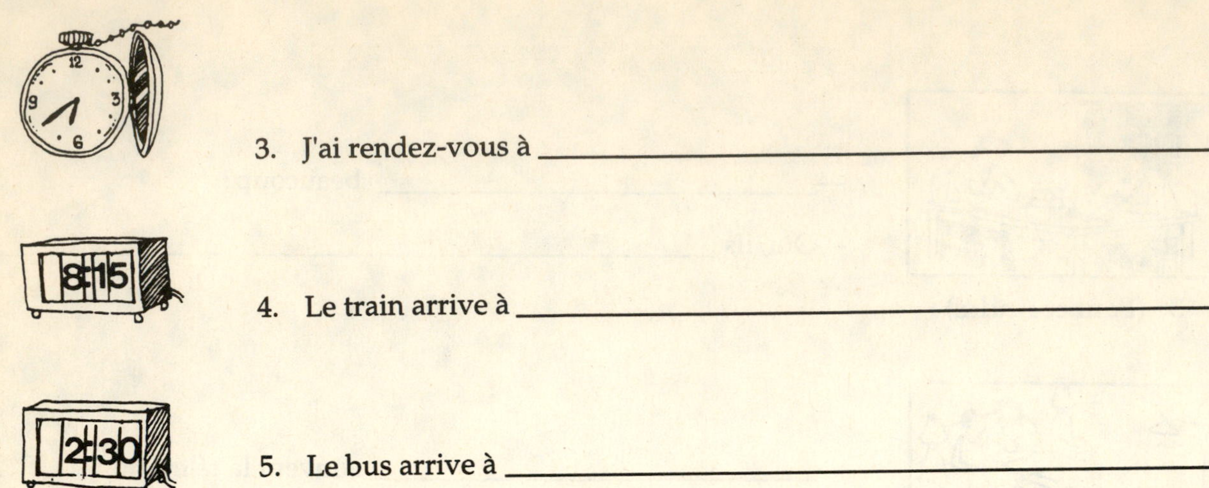

3. J'ai rendez-vous à ______________________________.

4. Le train arrive à ______________________________.

5. Le bus arrive à ______________________________.

6. Je rentre à ______________________________.

COMMUNICATION

Imagine that you are at a sports club with your French friends. Write out what you would say in the following situations.

❖ Ask Jean-Pierre if he likes to swim.
Est-ce que tu aimes nager?

1. Ask Béatrice and Nicole if they swim often.

____

2. Ask Robert if he wants to play tennis.

____

3. Ask Suzanne and Catherine if they want to play golf..

______________________________au golf?

4. Ask Denise if she can phone François.

____

5. Tell your friends that you cannot have dinner with them.

____

6. Tell them that you must study.

____

NOM ____________________ DATE ____________________

Leçon 6. À Bruxelles, à l'Alliance française

1. Quand on est étudiant. Say whether or not students at your university generally do the following things. Use **on** in affirmative or negative sentences. *[Section A, p. 72]*

❖ étudier beaucoup? *Oui, on étudie beaucoup.*
ou: *Non, on n'étudie pas beaucoup.*

1. regarder souvent la télé?

____

2. dîner souvent au restaurant?

____

3. être idéaliste?

____

4. être toujours d'accord avec les professeurs?

____

2. Rencontres. Imagine that a French student is asking you the questions below. Write out your answers in complete sentences. *[Section B, p. 73]*

1. Où est-ce que tu habites?

____

2. Où est-ce que tu études?

____

3. À quelle heure est-ce que tu regardes la télé?

____

4. Avec qui est-ce que tu parles français?

____

3. Une interview. Imagine that you are transcribing an interview with Anne Marchand, a Canadian student who is visiting your campus. Use the information in her answers to decide which questions were asked. In your questions, use **est-ce que** and address Anne as **tu.**

❖ VOUS: ***Où est-ce que tu habites?***

ANNE: J'habite à Québec.

1. VOUS: ______________________________

   ANNE: J'étudie à l'Université Laval.

2. VOUS: ______________________________

   ANNE: J'étudie les sciences sociales.

3. VOUS: ______________________________

   ANNE: Je voyage avec mon amie *(my friend)* Pauline.

4. VOUS: ______________________________

   ANNE: Je voyage en bus.

5. VOUS: ______________________________

   ANNE: Je rentre au Canada le 10 septembre.

6. VOUS: ______________________________

   ANNE: Je visite les États-Unis parce que j'aime voyager.

4. Vraiment? *(Really?)* Bernard talks to Pierre about his friends. Pierre seems surprised. Write what Pierre says, using the appropriate subject and stress pronouns to replace the names of people Bernard mentions. *[Section C, p. 76]*

	Bernard	Pierre
❖	Sylvie est avec Jacques.	Vraiment? ***Elle est avec lui?***
1.	Brigitte est avec Paul.	Vraiment? ______________
2.	Louise habite avec Hélène et Anne.	Vraiment? ______________
3.	Paul étudie avec Isabelle.	Vraiment? ______________
4.	Françoise travaille pour M. Moreau.	Vraiment? ______________
5.	Nicole est avec Philippe et Thomas.	Vraiment? ______________
6.	Henri voyage avec Albert et Nicolas.	Vraiment? ______________

NOM ______________________ DATE ______________________

5. Réciprocité. Rewrite each sentence so that the person indicated by the stress pronoun becomes the subject and vice versa. Use the appropriate pronouns, and make sure that the verb agrees with the new subject. *[Section C, p. 76]*

❖ Il travaille avec moi. ***Je travaille avec lui.***

1. J'étudie avec eux.

____

2. Tu danses avec elle.

____

3. Vous travaillez pour lui.

____

4. Ils étudient avec nous.

____

5. Elles rentrent avec toi.

____

6. Nous habitons avec elles.

____

6. Quand? Write out when the following actions are taking place. Use complete sentences. Remember that in French, dates are abbreviated as follows: day / month. *[Section D, p. 78]*

❖ Paul / arriver / à Paris (10/5) ***Paul arrive à Paris le dix mai.***

1. nous / arriver / à Genève (2/9)

____

2. vous / rentrer / à Québec (15/2)

____

3. Jean-Pierre / inviter / Suzanne (21/8)

____

4. je / dîner au restaurant (1/6)

____

COMMUNICATION

Imagine you are spending your summer vacation in France. At the youth hostel you meet other young people. Since you want to become better acquainted, ask each of them two questions in French.

1. Nathalie is from Lausanne, Switzerland. Ask her if she speaks French. Ask her if people speak French in Lausanne.

   ____?

   ____ à Lausanne?

2. Luisa is a Spanish student. Ask her what she studies. Ask her if one studies a lot in Spanish universities.

   ____?

   ______________________________ dans les universités espagnoles?

3. Robert is listening to his radio. Ask him what he is listening to. Ask him if you can listen to the radio with him.

   ____?

   ____?

4. You want to go out to dinner with Isabelle. Ask her at what time she has dinner. Ask her if she wants to have dinner with you tomorrow.

   ____?

   ____?

NOM ______________________ DATE le ~~le~~ 25 Mars ______

UNITÉ 3. IMAGES DE LA VIE

Leçon 7. La vie est belle!

1. *Être* et *avoir*. Complete the sentences below. Fill in the first blank with the appropriate form of **être** and the second blank with the appropriate form of **avoir.** *[Section A, p. 88]*

1. Marc Richard est ______ millionnaire. Il ______ une Rolls Royce.
2. Vous ______ pianiste. Vous ______ un piano.
3. Je ______ en France. J' ______ un ami à Paris.
4. Nous ______ à l'université. Nous ______ un examen à neuf heures.
5. Paul et David ______ musiciens. Ils ______ une guitare.
6. Tu ______ avec Hélène. Tu ______ rendez-vous avec elle.

2. Présentations. Introduce the following people, using the appropriate indefinite articles. *[Sections B, C, pp. 89, 94]*

❖ Paul / copain *Paul est un copain.*

1. Philippe / cousin ______
2. Louise / cousine ______
3. Jacqueline / amie ______
4. Nicolas et Paul / copains ______
5. Thomas et Denis / amis ______
6. Anne et Véronique / copines ______

3. Est-ce que ça marche? *(Does it work?)* Point out the following objects and say whether or not they work. *[Sections B, C, pp. 89, 94]*

❖ *Voici une bicyclette. Elle ne marche pas.*

1. ______

2. ______________________________

3. ______________________________

4. ______________________________

4. On ne peut pas tout avoir. *(You can't have everything.)* Say that the following people have the first item listed, but not the second one. Be sure to use the appropriate indefinite articles. *[Sections B–D, pp. 89–96]*

❖ Paul (caméra, téléviseur) ***Paul a une caméra, mais il n'a pas de téléviseur.***

1. Marie (machine à écrire, ordinateur)

____

2. Jean-Jacques (VTT, voiture)

____

3. nous (chaîne stéréo, disques)

____

4. Louise et Marc (caméscope, magnétophone)

____

5. je (moto, vélomoteur)

____

6. tu (ordinateur, imprimante)

____

NOM ______________________________ DATE ______________________

5. La chambre de Caroline. Describe Caroline's room at the **Cité universitaire** by indicating whether or not she has the following objects. Use the appropriate articles. *[Sections C–E, pp. 94–98]*

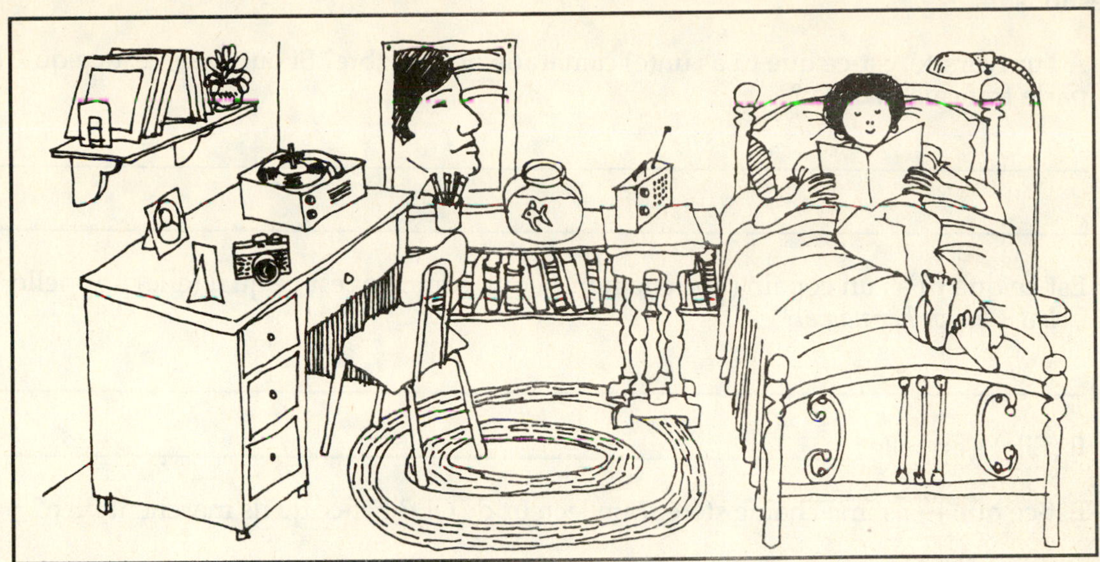

❖ crayons? *Non, il n'y a pas de crayons.*

❖ radio? *Oui, il y a une radio.*

1. téléviseur? ______________________________
2. sac à dos? ______________________________
3. compact disques? ______________________________
4. appareil-photo? ______________________________
5. ordinateur? ______________________________
6. cassettes? ______________________________

6. Expression personnelle. Complete the following sentences with an expression of your choice. Be sure to use the appropriate articles. *[Sections B–E, pp. 89–98]*

1. J'ai ______________________________
2. Je n'ai pas ______________________________
3. J'ai un ami qui *(who)* a ______________________________
4. J'ai des amis qui ont ______________________________
5. Dans ma chambre *(In my room)*, il y a ______________________________

   ____
6. Il n'y a pas ______________________________

COMMUNICATION

Imagine that you are in France. You have met Nicolas, who wants to know you better. Answer his questions.

1. À l'université, est-ce que tu as un(e) camarade de chambre? Si oui *(If so)*, est-ce qu'il (elle) parle français avec toi?

   ____

   ____

2. Est-ce que tu as un copain (une copine)? Si oui, comment est-ce qu'il (elle) s'appelle *(what's his or her name)?*

   ____

   Il (Elle) s'appelle ______________________________.

3. Est-ce que tu as une chaîne stéréo? un lecteur de CD? Est-ce qu'ils marchent bien?

   ____

   ____

4. Est-ce que tu utilises un lecteur de CD-ROM?

   ____

5. Est-ce que tes parents ont une voiture?

   ________, ils ______________________________.

6. Est-ce qu'il y a un magnétoscope chez toi *(in your home)?*

   ______________________________ chez moi *(at my house).*

NOM ______________________ DATE ______________________

Leçon 8. Dans la rue

1. Shopping. You and your friend are shopping. Tell your friend to look at the following objects. Be sure to use the appropriate definite articles. (If you are not sure of the gender of these nouns, see page 91 in your textbook.) *[Section A, p. 102]*

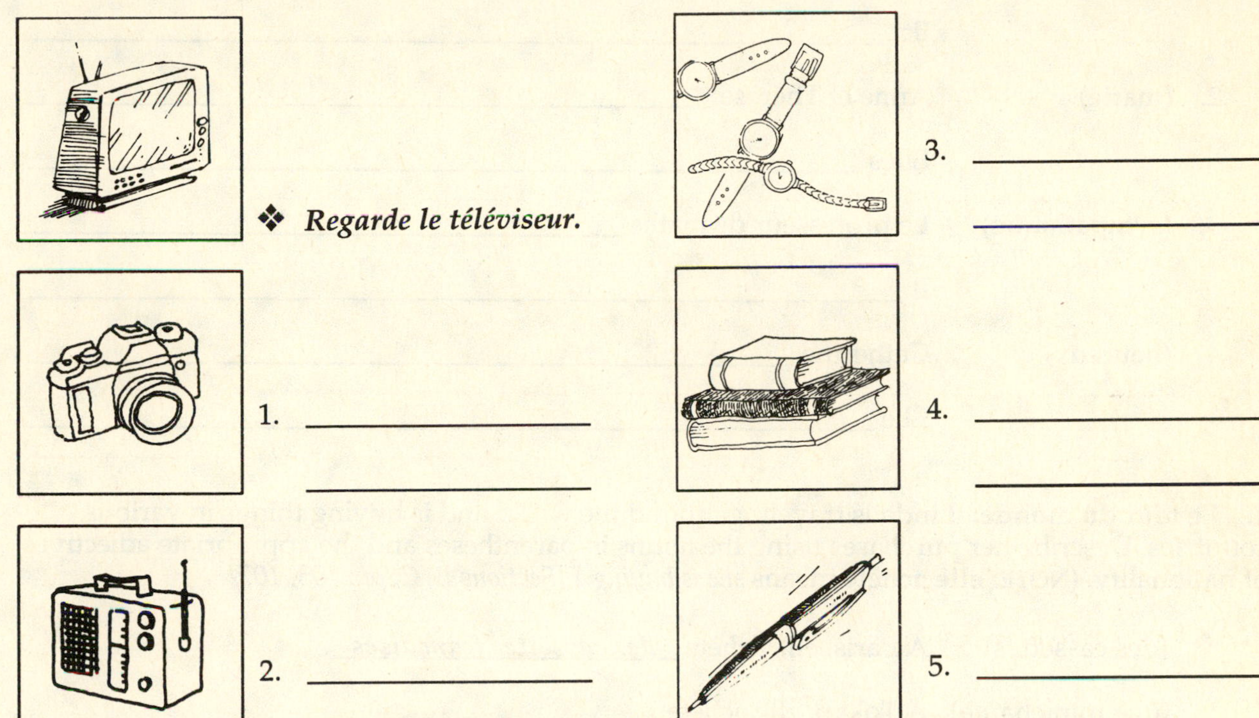

❖ ***Regarde le téléviseur.***

1. ______________________
2. ______________________
3. ______________________
4. ______________________
5. ______________________

2. Mes amis *(My friends).* Describe your two best friends, male and female, using the adjectives in parentheses in affirmative or negative sentences. Be sure to use the appropriate forms of the adjectives. *[Section B, p. 103]*

		Mon meilleur ami	Ma meilleure amie
1.	(blond?)	Il (n')est (pas) ______	Elle (n')est (pas) ______
2.	(grand?)	______	______
3.	(optimiste?)	______	______
4.	(indépendant?)	______	______
5.	(réservé?)	______	______
6.	(égoïste?)	______	______
7.	(poli?)	______	______

3. Non! The following people do not have the characteristics in parentheses. Express this in two sentences, one negative, the other affirmative. Use the appropriate corresponding adjectives. (See page 106 of your textbook.) *[Section B, p. 103]*

❖ (brun) Janine *n'est pas brune.*
Elle *est blonde.*

1. (petit) Marc et Thomas ______.
   Ils ______.
2. (marié) Anne et Thérèse ______.
   Elles ______.
3. (sympathique) Le professeur de maths ______.
   Il ______.
4. (heureux) Catherine ______.
   Elle ______.

4. Le tour du monde. Linda is traveling around the world and is buying things in various countries. Describe her purchases using the nouns in parentheses and the appropriate adjectives of nationality. (NOTE: **elle achète** means *she is buying.) [Sections B, C, pp. 103, 107]*

❖ (des cassettes) À Paris, elle achète *des cassettes françaises*.

1. (une minichaîne) À Tokyo, elle achète ______.
2. (une guitare) À Madrid, elle achète ______.
3. (des montres) À Genève, elle achète ______.
4. (des disques) À Berlin, elle achète ______.
5. (un vélo) À Londres *(London)*, elle achète ______.
6. (des CD) À Tours, elle achète ______.

NOM ______________________ DATE ______________________

5. Une question de personnalité *(A matter of personality).* Describe the following people, using the appropriate form of the suggested adjective. Then say that they have friends or possessions with the same characteristics. Study the model carefully. *[Sections B, C, pp. 103, 107)*

❖ Jacqueline (intéressant) — ***Jacqueline est intéressante.***
(des livres) — ***Elle a des livres intéressants.***

1. Paul (amusant) ______________________
   (des amies) ______________________
2. Annie (petit) ______________________
   (une auto) ______________________
3. Sylvie et Catherine (français) ______________________
   (une voiture) ______________________
4. Pauline (grand) ______________________
   (un appartement) ______________________
5. Mme Lenoir (compétent) ______________________
   (un assistant) ______________________
6. Le professeur (brillant) ______________________
   (des étudiants) ______________________

6. Descriptions. Nathalie describes various people and things. Complete her descriptions with the appropriate form of **il est** or **c'est.** *[Section D, p. 109]*

1. J'ai un copain.
   __________ canadien.
   __________ un garçon sympathique.
   __________ photographe.

2. J'ai une camarade de chambre.
   __________ une fille brillante.
   __________ sympathique.
   __________ une bonne étudiante.

3. J'ai une voiture.
   __________ une Renault.
   __________ une voiture française.
   __________ très rapide.

4. J'ai un magnétoscope.
   __________ japonais.
   __________ un Sony.
   __________ très bon.

COMMUNICATION

A. Vos amis. Describe two friends of yours, a man and a woman. Write a short paragraph in which you describe each friend's physical appearance and personality traits. Use both affirmative and negative sentences.

1. J'ai un copain. Il s'appelle *(His name is)* ______________________________
____
____
______________________________.

2. J'ai une copine. Elle s'appelle ______________________________
____
____
______________________________.

B. Vos possessions. Name three things that you own. Describe each one in a short paragraph.

❖ ***J'ai une voiture. C'est une Toyota. Elle est japonaise. C'est une petite voiture. Elle n'est pas très rapide, mais elle est assez confortable. C'est une bonne voiture.***

1. ______________________________
____
____

2. ______________________________
____
____

3. ______________________________
____
____

NOM ______________________ DATE ______________

Leçon 9. Le temps libre

1. Généralisations. Make general statements, affirmative or negative, using the elements below. (NOTE: Nouns with an asterisk are feminine. The others are masculine.) *[Section A, p. 114]*

❖ Américains / aimer / musique* classique *Les Américains aiment la musique classique.* ou: *Les Américains n'aiment pas la musique classique.*

1. étudiants / respecter / professeurs
____
2. étudiants américains / aimer / cinéma
____
3. Américains / détester / violence*
____
4. personnes* indépendantes / être pour / autorité*
____

2. Qu'est-ce qu'ils font? Describe what the following people are doing. In your sentences, use the suggested elements. *[Section B, p. 116]*

❖ Éric / arriver à / le stade *Éric arrive au stade.*

1. je / rester à / l'université
____
2. on / parler de / le match de tennis
____
3. vous / jouer de / le piano
____
4. tu / téléphoner à / l'étudiante canadienne
____
5. le président / parler à / les journalistes
____
6. vous / rentrer de / les magasins
____

3. Le verbe exact. Complete the following sentences with the appropriate forms of **être, avoir,** or **aller.** Be sure that your sentences are logical. *[Section C, p. 119]*

1. Nous ____________________ étudiants.
   Nous ____________________ rendez-vous avec des amies.
   Nous ____________________ danser dans une discothèque.
2. Jacques ____________________ une raquette de tennis.
   Il ____________________ souvent jouer au tennis.
   Il ____________________ très athlétique.
3. Pierre et Sylvie ____________________ français.
   En septembre, ils ____________________ visiter Québec.
   Ils ____________________ des cousins là-bas.
4. Vous ____________________ parisiens, n'est-ce pas?
   ____________________-vous une voiture?
   ____________________-vous souvent en Normandie?

4. Activités. Say where the following people are going by completing the sentences below with the appropriate forms of **aller** and of **à** + definite article. Then say what each person is going to do there, using the construction **aller** + a verb from the box. *[Sections B, C, pp. 116, 119]*

voyager **nager** **travailler** **étudier** **regarder des tableaux** **jouer au football**

❖ Catherine *va à la* plage.
Elle va nager.

1. Nous ____________________ bibliothèque.
   ____
2. Tu ____________________ stade.
   ____
3. Mme Dupin ____________________ bureau.
   ____
4. Vous ____________________ piscine.
   ____
5. Je ____________________ aéroport.
   ____
6. Les touristes ____________________ musée.
   ____

NOM ______________________________ DATE ____________________

5. Samedi soir. On Saturday night, some people go out and others stay home. Read what the following people do and say whether or not they stay home. Use the verb **rester** in affirmative or negative sentences and **chez +** the appropriate form of the corresponding stress pronoun. *[Section D, p. 121]*

❖ Nous dînons au restaurant.

Nous ne restons pas chez nous.

1. Je regarde la télé.

____

2. Tu écoutes tes *(your)* cassettes.

____

3. Nous allons au théâtre.

____

4. M. et Mme Durand invitent des amis.

____

5. Jean-François va à la discothèque.

____

6. Questions. You want to know more about the following people. Complete the questions below using inversion and the appropriate subject pronouns. *[Section E, p. 123]*

❖ Jacques va au musée.

Avec qui ***va-t-il au musée***?

1. Catherine téléphone.

À qui ____?

2. Les étudiants travaillent.

Pourquoi ____?

3. Mlle Moreau voyage.

Quand ____?

4. Antoine est au restaurant.

Avec qui ____?

5. Florence et Sophie jouent au tennis.

Comment ____?

6. On va à la piscine.

À quelle heure ____?

COMMUNICATION

Imagine you have met Alexandre at the **"Maison des Jeunes."** You want to know more about his leisure-time activities. Write out the questions you ask him. Use inversion and the **tu** form.

❖ Ask him if he likes music. ***Aimes-tu la musique?***

1. Ask him if he likes sports.

   ____?

2. Ask him if he plays chess.

   ____?

3. Ask him if he plays the guitar **(la guitare).**

   ____?

4. Ask him if he often goes to the movies.

   ____?

5. Ask him if he is going out to the theater on Saturday.

   ____?

6. Ask him if he wants to go to the restaurant with you on Sunday.

   ____?

NOM ______________________________ DATE ____________________

Révision 1: Leçons 1–9

By completing this series of short tests, you will be able to check your progress in French. Correct your work using the Answer Key at the back of the *Cahier d'activités.* If you make any mistakes on these tests, you may want to review the lesson sections indicated in brackets.

PARTIE A. STRUCTURES

Test 1. Les pronoms sujets et les pronoms accentués. Read the following sentences carefully and fill in the blanks with the appropriate subject or stress pronouns. *[1–A; 3–C]*

1. __________ habites à Québec, n'est-ce pas?
2. Où est-ce que __________ travaillez?
3. J'admire Paul, mais je ne suis pas toujours d'accord avec __________.
4. Philippe et Robert habitent à Versailles. Demain nous allons dîner chez __________.
5. Toi et __________, nous jouons bien au tennis, n'est-ce pas?
6. Nous allons à la piscine. Est-ce que tu veux nager avec __________?
7. Est-ce que c'est Mélanie là-bas? Oui, c'est __________!
8. Robert aime Monique. Il pense souvent à __________.

Test 2. La forme des adjectifs. Complete the following sentences with the appropriate forms of the adjectives in parentheses. *[5–B]*

1. (brillant) Pauline et Suzanne sont très ____________________.
2. (bon) Janine est très ____________________ en espagnol.
3. (canadien) Christine et Monique sont ____________________, n'est-ce pas?
4. (mauvais) François et Charles sont ____________________ en maths.
5. (individualiste) Le frère d'Annie est très ____________________.
6. (marié) Sylvie et Thérèse ne sont pas ____________________.
7. (poli) Les étudiants sont toujours ____________________ avec le professeur.
8. (égoïste) Denis et Pierre sont ____________________.

Test 3. L'article défini: formes simples et formes contractées. Complete the following sentences with the verbs in parentheses and the appropriate forms of the definite articles. Use contracted forms where necessary. *[5–A; 6–B]*

1. (parler à) Je vais ______________________ professeur.
2. (inviter) Je vais ______________________ amies de Claudine.
3. (utiliser) Je vais ______________________ caméscope de Philippe.
4. (arriver à) Le train va ______________________ gare dans dix minutes.
5. (jouer à) Nathalie va ______________________ tennis avec nous.
6. (parler à) Le professeur va ______________________ étudiants.
7. (arriver de) Les étudiants vont ______________________ laboratoire.
8. (parler de) Jeanne aime ______________________ copains de Michèle.

Test 4. La négation. Answer the following questions in the negative. *[1–B; 4–D]*

1. Est-ce que Paul regarde la télévision?

   ____

2. Est-ce que Sylvie a des compact disques?

   ____

3. Est-ce que Christine aime parler français?

   ____

4. Est-ce que Georges va aller à Paris?

   ____

Test 5. Descriptions. Describe the following people and things, using the appropriate indefinite articles and the appropriate forms of the nouns and adjectives in parentheses. (The nouns are given in the singular. The adjectives are given in the masculine singular.) *[5–B, C]*

❖ Suzanne (fille / intelligent) *Suzanne est une fille intelligente.*

1. Paul et Antoine (garçon / sympathique) ______________________
2. Jacqueline et Hélène (amie / français) ______________________
3. Les Rolling Stones (musicien / anglais) ______________________
4. Jane Fonda (actrice / américain) ______________________
5. Les Ford et les Chevrolet (voiture / américain) ______________________
6. Les Renault (voiture / bon) ______________________
7. M. Dupont (professeur / intéressant) ______________________
8. Christine et Florence (amie / vrai) ______________________

NOM ________________________________ DATE ______________________

Test 6. Autres structures. Decide which of the four options suggested correctly completes each sentence. Circle the corresponding letter.

❖ Voici ____ voiture française.

a. un (b.) une c. le d. l'

1. ____ Philippe.

   a. Il y a b. C'est c. Il est d. Elle est

2. Regarde la voiture rouge. ____ est rapide.

   a. C' b. Il c. Elle d. Voici

3. ____ parle français à Québec, n'est-ce pas?

   a. On b. Les gens c. Les Canadiens d. Tu

4. Émile est un ____ étudiant.

   a. timide b. intelligent c. mauvais d. canadien

5. Tu es un copain ____.

   a. bon b. grand c. vrai d. sympathique

6. Combien d'étudiants est-ce que (qu') ____ dans la classe?

   a. c'est b. ils sont c. il est d. il y a

7. Mlle Leblanc n'a pas ____ voiture.

   a. un b. une c. de d. d'

8. En général, les jeunes Français aiment ____ cinéma.

   a. un b. le c. au d. *(no word needed)*

9. Est-ce que tu veux dîner chez ____?

   a. tu b. je c. il d. nous

10. Est-ce que tu veux ____

    a. joue au ping-pong? b. regardez la télé? c. rester ici? d. visites le musée avec moi?

PARTIE B. VERBES

Test 7. Les verbes en *-er*. Complete the sentences below with the appropriate present-tense forms of the verbs in the box. Be logical in your choice of verbs. *[1–A]*

danser	**dîner**	**étudier**	**habiter**	**inviter**	**visiter**

1. Nous ____________________ dans *(in)* une maison moderne.
2. Je ____________________ le musée d'Orsay.
3. À quelle heure est-ce que tu ____________________ au restaurant?
4. Vous ____________________ le français, n'est-ce pas?
5. À la discothèque, François ____________________ avec Denise.
6. Alain et Jacqueline ____________________ des amis à dîner.

Test 8. Les verbes *être, avoir* et *aller*. Complete each set of sentences with the appropriate present-tense forms of **être, avoir,** and **aller,** in that order. *[2–A; 4–A; 6–C]*

1. Nous ____________________ étudiants. Nous ____________________ une classe à une heure. Après *(afterward)*, nous ____________________ passer à la bibliothèque.
2. Vous ____________________ français. Vous ____________________ des camarades sympathiques. Vous ____________________ souvent au café avec eux.
3. Nancy et Janet ____________________ américaines. Elles ____________________ un cousin à Paris. Elles ____________________ à Paris en octobre.
4. Tu ____________________ athlétique *(athletic)*. Tu ____________________ une raquette de tennis. Tu ____________________ jouer au tennis avec un copain.

Test 9. Verbes. Fill in the blanks with the French verbs that correspond to the English words in parentheses. Be sure to use the appropriate present-tense form and construction for each verb.

❖ *(plays)* Jacques *joue au* football.

1. *(plays)* Sylvie ____________________ tennis.
2. *(plays)* Jacques ____________________ piano.
3. *(listens to)* Paul ____________________ un CD.
4. *(looks at)* Marie ____________________ Pierre.
5. *(phones)* Thomas ____________________ Michèle.
6. *(thinks of)* Antoine ____________________ Sophie.
7. *(enters)* Albert ____________________ sa chambre.
8. *(spends)* Gisèle ____________________ deux mois à Québec.

NOM ______________________ DATE ______________________

PARTIE C. VOCABULAIRE

Test 10. Qu'est-ce que c'est? Identify each object by writing the corresponding noun with its appropriate indefinite article **(un, une).**

1. ______________________

2. ______________________

3. ______________________

4. ______________________

5. ______________________

6. ______________________

7. ______________________

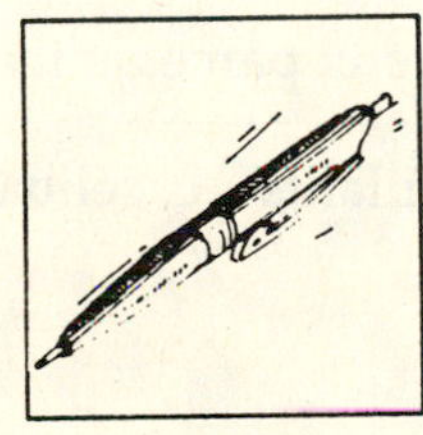

8. ______________________

Test 11. Les contraires. Write the adjectives that have the opposite meaning of those given below. *[5–B]*

1. bon ≠ ______________________
2. faible ≠ ______________________
3. rapide ≠ ______________________
4. marié ≠ ______________________
5. blond ≠ ______________________
6. triste ≠ ______________________

Test 12. Logique! For each item, select the option that logically completes the sentence. Circle the corresponding letter.

1. Ça va ____!

   a. bon b. mauvais c. petit d. mal

2. J'aime beaucoup Béatrice. C'est une fille ____.

   a. triste b. sympathique c. faible d. pénible

3. L'ordinateur ne ____ pas.

   a. travaille b. marche c. va d. rentre

4. Je vais à la piscine parce que j'aime ____.

   a. chanter b. voyager c. marcher d. nager

5. Thomas est mon *(my)* camarade de chambre. Il ____ avec moi.

   a. habite b. est d'accord c. visite d. marche

6. Je n'ai pas de ____. Quelle heure est-il?

   a. cahier b. magnétoscope c. montre d. lecteur de CD

7. Regarde ____ là-bas! Qu'est-ce que c'est?

   a. la chose b. le jeune homme c. la femme d. une copine

8. Le professeur est heureux parce qu'il a des étudiants ____.

   a. désagréables b. brillants c. célibataires d. mauvais

NOM ________________________________ DATE ________________________

UNITÉ 4. PROBLÈMES D'ARGENT

Leçon 10. Le budget de Martin

1. Combien? Give the prices of the following items by filling in the blanks with the corresponding numbers. *[Section A, p. 134]*

❖ 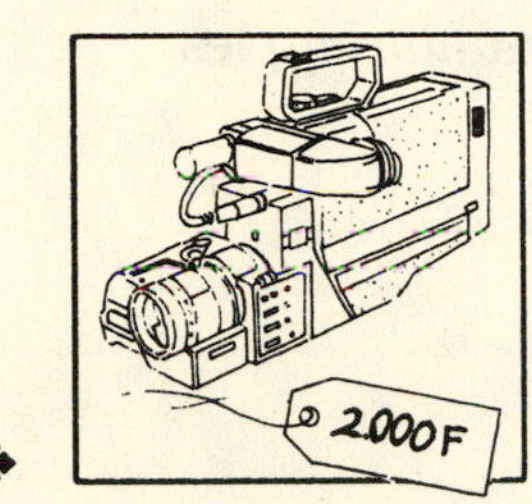

1. 

2. 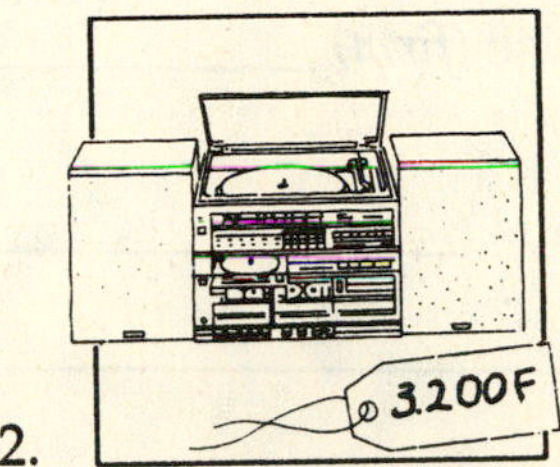

3. 

4. 

5. 

❖ La caméra coûte *deux mille* francs.

1. La bicyclette coûte ________________________ francs.
2. La chaîne stéréo coûte ________________________ francs.
3. La mobylette coûte ________________________ francs.
4. La voiture coûte ________________________ francs.
5. La maison coûte ________________________ francs.

2. Activités. Describe what the following people are doing by filling in the blanks with the appropriate forms of the verbs in the box. Be logical! *[Section B, p. 136]*

employer **envoyer** **nettoyer** **payer**

❖ Mme Dulac *envoie* une lettre à un client.

1. Nous ____________________ un télégramme à Daniel.
2. Je ____________________ l'appartement.
3. Les touristes ____________________ l'hôtel avec des chèques de voyage.
4. Cette entreprise *(firm)* ____________________ des étudiants pendant *(during)* les vacances.
5. Est-ce que vous ____________________ le restaurant avec une carte de crédit?
6. M. Durand ____________________ le garage.
7. Est-ce que tu ____________________ un dictionnaire?
8. Je ____________________ le loyer *(rent)* le premier octobre.

3. À qui est-ce? Read what the following people do. Use this information to decide to whom the objects belong. Use the expression **être à.** *[Section C, p. 138]*

Annette joue au tennis.
Tu étudies les maths.
Nous regardons la télé.
Mme Moreau voyage en voiture.
Je suis photographe.
Éric écoute des CD.
Les étudiants voyagent à bicyclette.
Vous prenez *(take)* des notes.

❖ La voiture *est à Mme Moreau*.

1. Le lecteur de compact disques ____.
2. Le téléviseur ____.
3. La raquette ____.
4. Le stylo ____.
5. L'appareil-photo ____.
6. Le livre d'algèbre ____.
7. Les vélos ____.

4. Emprunts *(Borrowed items).* Sometimes we use things that belong to other people. Express this by completing the sentences according to the model. *[Section D, p. 139]*

❖ Jacques a une raquette.
Paul joue au tennis avec *la raquette de Jacques.*

1. Philippe a un vélo. Nathalie utilise ____.
2. Sylvie a une machine à écrire. Charles utilise ____.

NOM ______________________________ DATE ______________________

3. Élisabeth a une mobylette. Brigitte emploie souvent ______________________.

4. Le professeur a des livres. Nous regardons ______________________.

5. Les étudiants anglais ont des cassettes. Vous écoutez ______________________.

6. Les voisins ont un ordinateur. J'utilise ______________________.

7. Le copain de Janine prépare un budget. J'étudie ______________________.

5. Les relations familiales. Express the family relationships that exist among the people in the family tree below. *[Section D, p. 139 and Vocabulary, p. 142]*

❖ Alain Vasseur *est le frère de* Jacques Vasseur.

1. Robert ______________________ Alain Vasseur.
2. Jacques Vasseur ______________________ Éliane.
3. Monique Vasseur ______________________ Suzanne.
4. Robert ______________________ Suzanne.
5. Suzanne ______________________ Robert.
6. Éliane ______________________ Suzanne.
7. Robert ______________________ Éliane.
8. Robert et Suzanne ______________________ M. Dumas.
9. Mme Dumas ______________________ M. Dumas.
10. Jacques Vasseur ______________________ Monique Vasseur.

6. À l'aéroport. The following students are going to spend a year in France. They have come to the airport with friends and family. Complete the sentences with the appropriate possessive adjectives. *[Section E, p. 140]*

❖ Tu arrives avec __*ta*__ cousine.

1. Linda arrive avec __________ frère et __________ ami Charles.
2. Suzanne arrive avec __________ père, __________ ami Georges et __________ amie Lili.
3. Paul arrive avec __________ oncle et __________ tante.
4. Robert arrive avec __________ parents et __________ frère.
5. Sylvia et Barbara arrivent avec __________ amies et __________ frère.
6. Henry et Roger arrivent avec __________ amies et __________ sœur.
7. Tu arrives avec __________ ami Marc et __________ parents.
8. Nous arrivons avec __________ amis et __________ professeur de français.
9. Vous arrivez avec __________ amies et __________ cousine Donna.

COMMUNICATION

Imagine that you are in France. Caroline wants to know more about you and your life in the United States. Answer her questions.

1. Est-ce que tu vas travailler pendant *(during)* les vacances? Combien d'argent est-ce que tu vas gagner? ______________________________

   ____

2. Combien sont les frais de scolarité à ton université? ______________________________

   ____

3. Est-ce que tu habites chez tes parents? Si non *(If not)*, combien paies-tu par mois pour ton logement? ______________________________

   ____

4. As-tu une voiture? Combien te coûte-t-elle? Si tu n'as pas de voiture, est-ce que tu empruntes *(borrow)* la voiture de tes parents? Est-ce que tu empruntes la voitures de tes copains? ______________________________

   ____

5. Est-ce que tu prépares un budget? Quelles sont tes dépenses régulières?

   ____

   ____

6. As-tu des dettes à payer pour tes études? ______________________________

   ____

NOM ______________________ DATE ______________________

Leçon 11. Un tee-shirt qui coûte cher

1. Quels vêtements? Read what the following people are going to do. Then describe what they are wearing for these occasions. Give the colors of the items of clothing.

1. Pierre va jouer au tennis. Il porte ______________________

   ____

2. Sylvie va danser dans une discothèque très élégante. Elle porte ______________________

   ____

3. M. Thomas a un rendez-vous professionnel avec le président d'IBM. Il porte ______________________

   ____

4. Je vais à la plage. Je porte ______________________

   ____

5. Tu vas skier. Tu portes ______________________

   ____

2. Activités. Complete the sentences below with the appropriate present-tense forms of the verbs in the box. Be logical! *[Section A, p. 148]*

acheter	**amener**	**célébrer**	**espérer**	**posséder**	**préférer**	**répéter**

❖ Pauline *achète* une robe à Mod'Shop.

1. Jacques et André ______________ des chaussures chez Bally.
2. Tu ______________ une amie au concert.
3. M. et Mme Lamblet ______________ leur anniversaire de mariage le 24 juillet.
4. Mlle Lasalle est riche. Elle ______________ une Rolls Royce.
5. Nous étudions beaucoup. Nous ______________ avoir un «A» à l'examen.
6. Le professeur ______________ toujours la même *(same)* question!
7. J'aime le cinéma, mais je ______________ le théâtre!

3. La publicité. Imagine that you are working in a French department store. Advertise the following products by indicating their qualities. Use the appropriate form of the demonstrative adjective and the suggested descriptive adjective. *[Section C, p. 151]*

❖ les cravates / joli *Ces cravates sont jolies.*

1. les chaussures / joli ________________________________
2. le livre / intéressant ________________________________
3. l'anorak / bon marché ________________________________
4. les disques / bon ________________________________
5. l'appareil-photo / excellent ________________________________
6. la veste / élégant ________________________________
7. les raquettes de tennis / cher ________________________________

4. Dialogues. Complete the following dialogues according to the model. *[Sections B, C, pp. 150, 151]*

❖ —*Quel tee-shirt* est-ce que tu préfères?

—Je *préfère ce tee-shirt-ci*.

1. —________________ est-ce que tu achètes?

   —J' ________________________________.

2. —________________ est-ce que Pauline va acheter?

   —Elle ________________________________.

3. —________________ est-ce que Jacques va porter?

   —Il ________________________________.

NOM ______________________ DATE ______________________

4. —__________est-ce que vous préférez?

—Nous ______________________.

5. Comparaisons. Read the descriptions below. On the basis of the information, make comparisons using the appropriate present-tense form of **être** and the adjectives in parentheses. *[Section D, p. 152]*

❖ La robe bleue coûte 800 francs. La robe rouge coûte 1.000 francs.
(cher) La robe bleue ***est moins chère que*** la robe rouge.

1. M. Simon a 500.000 francs. Mme Dumas a un million de francs.

   (riche) M. Simon ______________________ Mme Dumas.

2. La Ferrari roule *(goes)* à 200 kilomètres à l'heure. L'Alfa Roméo roule à 180 kilomètres à l'heure.

   (rapide) La Ferrari ______________________ l'Alfa Roméo.

3. L'imperméable coûte 1.200 francs. Le costume coûte 1.200 francs.

   (cher) L'imperméable ______________________ le costume.

4. À l'examen de français, Robert a un «A». Paul a un «C».

   (bon) En français, Robert ______________________ Paul.

5. Jacqueline a dix-huit ans *(is 18 years old)*. Sa cousine a dix-huit ans aussi.

   (jeune) Jacqueline ______________________ sa cousine.

6. Les Yankees jouent bien. Les Red Sox jouent mal.

   (bon) Les Yankees ______________________ les Red Sox.

6. À votre avis *(In your opinion)*. Compare the following people and things. Express your own opinions. *[Section D, p. 152]*

❖ les jeunes / leurs parents (idéaliste?)
Les jeunes sont plus (moins, aussi) idéalistes que leurs parents.

1. les Américains / les Français (individualiste?)

   ____

2. les Américaines / les Françaises (élégant?)

   ____

3. les femmes / les hommes (indépendant?)

____

4. les voitures américaines / les voitures japonaises (économique?)

____

5. la cuisine française / la cuisine américaine (bon?)

____

COMMUNICATION

Andrée, a French friend, will ask you a few questions about American clothing and cars. Answer her questions.

1. Quels vêtements portes-tu quand tu vas à une fête? (Indique *[Give]* aussi leur couleur, s'il te plaît.)

____

____

2. Quels vêtements est-ce que tu vas acheter pour cet été?

____

____

3. Dans quel magasin achètes-tu tes vêtements? Pourquoi est-ce que tu préfères ce magasin? (Est-ce que les vêtements sont moins chers? plus élégants? de meilleure qualité?)

____

____

4. De quelle couleur est la voiture de tes voisins? Et la voiture de tes parents? Est-ce que la voiture de tes parents est plus grande que la voiture de tes voisins?

____

____

____

NOM ______________________ DATE ______________________

Leçon 12. Le rêve et la réalité

1. Attention! Read what the people below are doing during French class and say whether or not they are paying attention. Use the expression **faire attention** in affirmative or negative sentences. *[Section A, p. 158]*

❖ André parle à Caroline. ***Il ne fait pas attention.***

1. Nous écoutons le professeur. ______________________
2. Tu penses à tes copines. ______________________
3. Vous êtes attentifs. ______________________
4. Ces étudiants regardent par la fenêtre *(out the window)*. ______________________
5. Je pose *(ask)* une question au professeur. ______________________
6. Alice joue avec sa calculatrice. ______________________

2. Qu'est-ce qu'ils font? Read what the following people are doing. Describe their activities by using an expression with the appropriate present-tense form of the verb **faire.** (If necessary, review these expressions on page 158 of your textbook.) *[Section A, p. 158]*

❖ Jacqueline joue au tennis.
Elle fait un match.

1. Nous nettoyons notre appartement.
____
2. Les étudiants préparent les leçons.
____
3. Je nettoie les assiettes *(plates)*.
____
4. Vous ne dépensez pas votre argent.
____
5. Tu marches dans la campagne *(country)*.
____
6. M. Broussard n'est pas chez lui. Il est au Japon.
____

3. Où est-ce? Indicate where one place or thing is in relation to the other.

❖ Le magasin de sport est ___*dans*___ la rue de la République.

1. La voiture est ____________________ hôtel de France.
2. L'hôtel de France est ____________________ café des Artistes et le cinéma Vox.
3. Le restaurant «Chez Jean» est ____________________ magasin de sport.
4. Le parking est ____________________ bibliothèque municipale.
5. La bibliothèque municipale est ____________________ magasin de sport.
6. Le café des Artistes est ____________________ hôtel de France.

4. Descriptions. Complete the sentences below with the appropriate forms of the adjectives in parentheses *[Section B, p. 164]*

1. (nouveau) M. Thibaud va moderniser son bureau. Il va acheter un _______________ ordinateur et une _______________ imprimante.
2. (vieux) Oh là là, notre appartement est très ancien! Il y a de _______________ meubles: un _______________ sofa dans le salon et de _______________ chaises dans la cuisine.
3. (beau) Jacques va aller à une entrevue *(interview)* professionnelle très importante. Il va porter une _______________ cravate et un _______________ costume.
4. (beau) Mlle Dupont est toujours très élégante. Aujourd'hui, elle porte une _______________ robe rouge et de _______________ chaussures noires.
5. (nouveau) Nous allons redécorer notre maison. Nous allons mettre une _______________ table et de _______________ fauteuils dans notre _______________ salon.
6. (vieux) M. Bertrand aime les choses anciennes. Il y a beaucoup de _______________ livres dans son _______________ appartement.

NOM ________________________________ DATE ____________________

5. Les Oscars. Below are several categories of people or things. Indicate who or what in your opinion is the best in each category. Use the superlative form of the italicized adjectives. *[Section C, p. 165]*

❖ un acteur *intelligent* — ***L'acteur le plus intelligent est [Anthony Hopkins].***
❖ une *bonne* saison — ***La meilleure saison est [le printemps].***

1. un(e) comédien(ne) *drôle* ____________________
2. un professeur *intéressant* ____________________
3. un *bon* film ____________________
4. une *jolie* ville ____________________
5. des voitures *confortables* ____________________
6. un *bon* restaurant ____________________

6. Quel temps fait-il? For each of the following scenes, write three sentences to describe the weather. Your sentences may be affirmative or negative. *[Section D, p. 167]*

1. ____________________
____
____

2. ____________________
____
____

3. ____________________
____
____

COMMUNICATION

Jean-Philippe wants to know about your home. Answer his questions.

1. Est-ce que tes parents louent ou est-ce qu'ils possèdent la maison (l'appartement) où ils habitent?

2. Combien de pièces est-ce qu'il y a dans ta maison?

3. Quelle est la plus grande pièce de la maison? Quelle est la plus petite pièce?

4. Est-ce que la cuisine est moderne? Est-ce qu'elle est grande? De quelle couleur est-elle?

5. Combien de chambres y a-t-il? Est-ce que chaque *(each)* chambre a un cabinet de toilette?

6. Quels meubles est-ce qu'il y a dans ta chambre?

7. Quels meubles est-ce qu'il y a dans le salon?

NOM ______________________________ DATE ______________________

UNITÉ 5. CHEZ LES FRANÇAIS

Leçon 13. Ma vision du bonheur

1. Pourquoi? Read about the following people. Explain their activities by completing the sentences below with an expression using the appropriate present-tense form of **avoir.** *[Section A, p. 178]*

❖ Nous allons au restaurant.
Nous *avons faim.*

1. Jacqueline regarde le thermomètre. Il fait 30° C. Jacqueline ouvre *(opens)* la fenêtre.

   Elle ______________________________

2. Tu achètes une limonade.

   Tu ______________________________

3. Paul célèbre son anniversaire. Maintenant il peut *(can)* voter.

   Il ______________________________

4. Il est une heure et demie du matin. J'ai envie d'aller au lit.

   J' ______________________________

5. Vous allez dans la cuisine et vous faites des sandwiches.

   Vous ______________________________

6. Alain pense que New York est la capitale des États-Unis *(des USA).*

   Il ______________________________

7. Il fait moins dix degrés (-10° C). Je n'ai pas mon manteau. Je veux rentrer chez moi.

   J' ______________________________

2. Activités. Read about the following people. Then complete the sentences with the appropriate present-tense forms of the verbs in the box. *[Section B, p. 181]*

choisir **finir** **grossir** **maigrir** **réfléchir** **réussir**

❖ Janine va au supermarché. Elle *choisit* des oranges pour le pique-nique.

1. Robert et Pierre vont dans un magasin de disques. Ils __________________ un nouveau CD pour l'anniversaire de leur sœur.
2. Vous êtes d'excellents étudiants. Vous __________________ toujours à vos examens.
3. Quand est-ce que les employés __________________ leur travail? À cinq heures ou à six heures?
4. Vous faites des erreurs *(mistakes)* dans vos exercices. C'est parce que vous ne __________________ pas.
5. M. Lebeau mange *(eats)* beaucoup et il ne fait pas d'exercice. Voilà pourquoi il __________________!
6. Moi, au contraire *(on the contrary)*, je nage, je joue au tennis, je fais de l'exercice et je fais attention aux calories. Voilà pourquoi je __________________.

3. D'autres activités (*Other activities).* Read about the following people. Then complete the sentences with the appropriate present-tense forms of the verbs in the box. *[Section C, p. 182]*

attendre **entendre** **perdre** **rendre** **répondre** **vendre**

❖ Marc est au café. Il *attend* ses amis.

1. Les touristes sont à l'aéroport. Ils __________________ leur avion.
2. Janine est à Québec. Elle __________________ visite à ses cousins canadiens.
3. Aujourd'hui, vous ne jouez pas bien. Vous __________________ tous *(all)* vos matchs!
4. Ma tante a un magasin de vêtements. Elle __________________ des jupes et des robes.
5. Répétez votre question à M. Thibaud. Il est vieux. Il n' __________________ pas très bien.
6. J'utilise ma machine à écrire. Je __________________ à la lettre de mon oncle.
7. Les étudiants vont à la bibliothèque. Là, ils __________________ les livres dont *(which)* ils n'ont pas besoin.

4. Des conseils *(Advice).* Tell your roommate to do the following things. Complete the sentences with the **tu** form of the imperative. *[Section D, p. 184]*

❖ (étudier) ***Étudie*** tes leçons!

1. (aller) ______________ à la bibliothèque!
2. (nettoyer) ______________ l'appartement!
3. (faire) ______________ des économies pour les vacances!
4. (finir) ______________ tes devoirs avant *(before)* le week-end!
5. (répondre) ______________ à la lettre de ton cousin!
6. (être) ______________ patient(e) avec tes amis!
7. (avoir) ______________ le courage de tes opinions!
8. (choisir) ______________ tes classes pour le semestre prochain *(next)!*

5. Le club de théâtre. You are coaching several French students for the school play. Tell them what to do and what not to do, using the affirmative or negative **vous** forms of the imperative of the verbs in parentheses. **Soyez logique!** *[Section D, p. 184]*

❖ (parler) ***Parlez*** distinctement!
❖ (être) ***Ne soyez pas*** timides!

1. (rester) ______________ calmes!
2. (faire) ______________ attention à votre prononciation!
3. (réfléchir) ______________ à votre texte!
4. (répéter) ______________ le dialogue!
5. (répondre) ______________ à vos partenaires *(partners)!*
6. (perdre) ______________ votre concentration!
7. (être) ______________ nerveux *(nervous)!*
8. (avoir) ______________ peur!

COMMUNICATION

A. Le week-end. Imagine that some of your French friends are visiting you this weekend. Suggest things to do using the **nous** form of the imperative in affirmative or negative sentences. You may want to use some of the verbs from the box.

aller	**faire**	**visiter**	**jouer**	**acheter**	**rendre visite**
choisir	**dîner**	**organiser**	**inviter**	**regarder**	**rentrer**

❖ *Ne restons pas à la maison.*
Dînons au restaurant.
Choisissons un restaurant italien.

____

____

____

____

____

____

B. Économies (*Savings*). Your French friend Michel wants to put aside money to pay for a trip to the United States. Advise him about what to do and what not to do using the **tu** form of the imperative in affirmative or negative sentences. You may want to use some of the verbs from the box.

aller	**faire**	**attendre**	**vendre**	**dépenser**
travailler	**payer**	**utiliser**	**choisir**	**acheter**

❖ *Fais des économies.*
N'achète pas de vêtements chers.

____

____

____

____

____

____

NOM ______________________________ DATE ______________________

Leçon 14. Un mois à Paris

1. Le week-end. Describe what the following people did last weekend by completing the sentences below with the appropriate passé composé forms of the verbs suggested by the illustrations. Use the same verb in each of the two sentences. *[Section A, p. 190]*

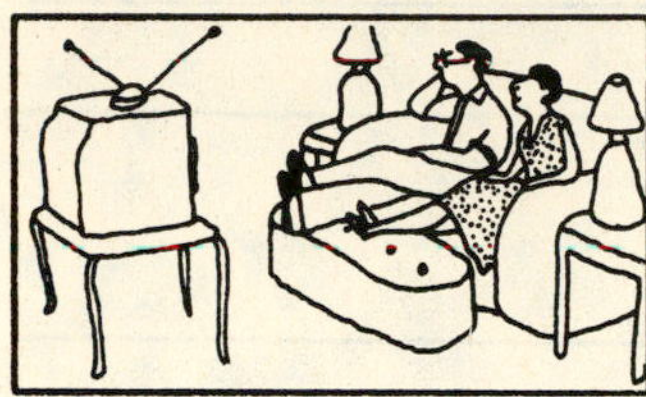

1. Nous ______________________ un match de football.

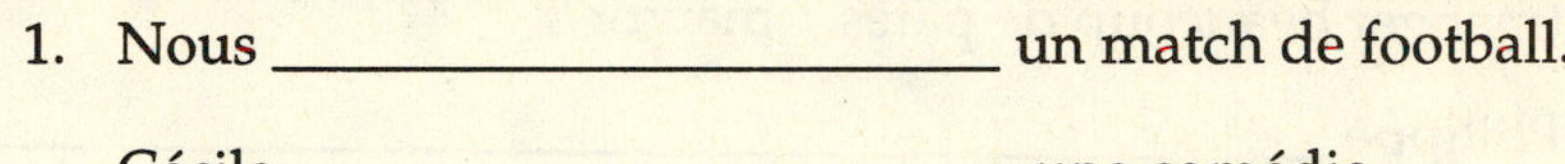

Cécile ______________________ une comédie.

2. Vous ______________________ à la piscine.

J' ______________________ à la plage.

3. Patrick ______________________ à la bibliothèque.

Tu ______________________ chez toi.

4. Jean et Claire ______________________ avec leurs amis.

Vous ______________________ dans un restaurant chinois.

5. Corinne et Jérôme ______________________ au tennis.

On ______________________ au tennis avec nos amis.

2. Oui ou non? Describe what the following people did, using the first expression in parentheses. Then say whether or not they did the second thing. Use the passé composé in both sentences. *[Sections A, B, pp. 190, 193]*

❖ (travailler / perdre son temps?)
Paul ***a travaillé. Il n'a pas perdu son temps.***

1. (visiter Paris / rendre visite à nos amis français?)

   Nous ____

   ____

2. (manger beaucoup de pâtes / maigrir?)

   Philippe ____

   ____

3. (maigrir / grossir?)

   Tu ____

   ____

4. (perdre patience / attendre mes amis?)

   J' ____

   ____

5. (gagner le match / perdre?)

   Vous ____

   ____

6. (étudier / rendre visite à leur oncle?)

   Hélène et Suzanne ____

   ____

3. En vacances. You want to know whether the people in parentheses did certain things during the vacation. Ask the appropriate questions, using the passé composé with **est-ce que.** *[Section C, p. 194]*

❖ (tu) visiter Paris? ***Est-ce que tu as visité Paris?***

1. (ces étudiants) travailler?

   ____

2. (vous) rendre visite à vos grands-parents?

   ____

3. (M. Lamblet) maigrir?

   ____

4. (tu) voyager en train?

   ____

NOM ________________________ DATE ________________

4. Précisions *(Additional details).* Read what the following people have done. Then request additional details by asking inverted questions in the passé composé. Use the interrogative expression in parentheses and the appropriate subject pronoun. *[Section C, p. 194]*

❖ Monique a téléphoné. (pourquoi?)
Pourquoi a-t-elle téléphoné?

1. Robert et Paul ont dîné au restaurant. (avec qui?)

   ____

2. Janine a acheté une robe. (dans quel magasin?)

   ____

3. Philippe a vendu sa mobylette. (à qui?)

   ____

4. Stéphanie et Thérèse ont nagé. (où?)

   ____

5. Les étudiants ont rendu les livres. (quand?)

   ____

5. Le mois dernier. Say whether or not you did the following things during the past month. Use the passé composé. *[Section D, p. 198]*

❖ faire un voyage? ***Oui, j'ai fait un voyage.***
ou: ***Non, je n'ai pas fait de voyage.***

1. être malade *(sick)?*

   ____

2. être invité(e) chez des amis?

   ____

3. avoir un accident?

   ____

4. avoir une aventure extraordinaire?

   ____

5. faire des économies?

   ____

6. faire une promenade à bicyclette?

   ____

6. **Zut alors!** *(Too bad!)* Several bad things happened yesterday. Explain what the following people did or did not do by putting the verbs in parentheses into the appropriate forms of the affirmative or negative passé composé. *[Sections B, D, pp. 193, 198]*

❖ (perdre) Ce touriste ***a perdu*** son passeport.

❖ (réussir) Tu ***n'as pas réussi à*** ton examen.

1. (gagner) Nous ______________________ le match de foot.
2. (répondre) Je ______________________ correctement à la question du professeur.
3. (faire) Caroline ______________________ des erreurs dans sa composition.
4. (être) Ces enfants ______________________ polis avec le professeur.
5. (avoir) M. Bellamy ______________________ un accident avec sa nouvelle voiture.

COMMUNICATION

Your friend Stéphanie is asking you a few questions about past events and your recent activities. Answer each set of questions with at least two sentences. (Do *not* use the verb **aller** in your answers.)

1. Est-ce que tu as voyagé l'été dernier? À qui as-tu rendu visite?

____

____

2. Est-ce que tu as travaillé pendant les vacances? Qu'est-ce que tu as fait?

____

____

3. Quand est-ce que tu as célébré ton anniversaire? Comment?

____

____

4. As-tu invité des amis récemment *(recently)*? Qu'est-ce que vous avez fait?

____

____

5. Quel temps a-t-il fait l'hiver dernier? Quel temps a-t-il fait l'été dernier? Quel temps a-t-il fait hier? ____

____

NOM ______________________________ DATE ______________________

Leçon 15. Séjour en France

1. Activités. Read about the following people and say what they do. Complete the sentences with the appropriate form of a verb from the box. *[Section A, p. 203]*

dormir **partir** **sentir** **sortir**

❖ Jacqueline va au cinéma. Elle *sort* avec ses amies.

1. Nous allons à Nice demain matin. Nous ________________ à huit heures.
2. Non merci, je n'ai pas besoin de somnifères *(sleeping pills)*. Je ________________ très bien.
3. Il y a des roses dans le jardin. Est-ce que vous ________________ leur odeur *(fragrance)?*
4. Nathalie et Florence ne vont pas étudier ce soir. Elles ________________ avec des étudiants anglais!
5. Je vais aller en vacances à Québec. Je ________________ le 2 juillet.
6. Je n'ai pas réussi à l'examen. Je ________________ que je vais avoir une mauvaise note *(grade)*.
7. Cet enfant a des cauchemars *(nightmares)*. Il ________________ mal.

2. Hier soir. Read about the weekend activities of the following people and say whether or not they stayed home. Use the passé composé of the verb **rester** in affirmative or negative sentences. *[Section B, p. 205]*

❖ Claire a étudié. *Elle est restée chez elle.*

1. Nous avons nettoyé notre appartement. ______________________________
2. Alice a fait une promenade. ______________________________
3. J'ai regardé la télé. ______________________________
4. Paul et André ont fait leurs devoirs. ______________________________
5. Tu as retrouvé tes amis au café. ______________________________
6. Hélène et Anne ont dîné au restaurant. ______________________________
7. M. Vallon a fait le ménage. ______________________________
8. Vous avez rendu visite à vos amis. ______________________________

3. Questions et réponses. Complete the sentences below with the appropriate passé composé form of a verb from the box. Be logical! *[Section B, p. 205]*

arriver	**descendre**	**entrer**	**monter**	**mourir**	**naître**	**partir**	**rester**	**sortir**	**tomber**

❖ —Jacqueline est canadienne?

—Oui, elle *est née* à Québec.

1. —Alain et Jean-Claude sont français?

   —Oui, ils ____________________ à Paris.

2. —Tes cousins sont chez toi?

   —Oui, ils ____________________ hier après-midi.

3. —Claudine a habité en Italie?

   —Oui, elle ____________________ trois ans à Rome.

4. —Ta sœur a eu un accident cet été?

   —Oui, elle ____________________ de bicyclette.

5. —Ton grand-père est vivant *(alive)?*

   —Non, il ____________________ d'un cancer l'année dernière.

6. —Les touristes ont visité la Tour Eiffel?

   —Oui, ils ____________________ au deuxième étage *(second landing).*

7. —Les touristes anglais sont encore (*still*) dans le train?

   —Non, ils ____________________ du train à Lyon.

8. —Mme Florent a quitté son bureau?

   —Oui, elle ____________________ à cinq heures.

9. —Florence et Christine sont chez elles?

   —Non, elles ____________________ avec des amis.

10. —Les cambrioleurs *(burglars)* sont passés par la porte?

    —Non, ils ____________________ dans mon appartement par la fenêtre.

4. En vacances. Say what the following people did during their vacation by completing the sentences with the passé composé of the verbs in parentheses. Be careful with the use of **être** or **avoir,** as appropriate.

1. (aller) Mélanie ______________________ à Paris.

   (visiter) Elle ______________________ le musée d'Orsay.

2. (faire) Paul ______________________ la connaissance d'une étudiante italienne.

   (sortir) Il ______________________ avec elle.

3. (avoir) Mes cousins ______________ un accident d'auto.
   (rester) Ils ______________ une semaine à l'hôpital.
4. (descendre) Nous ______________ sur la Côte d'Azur *(French Riviera).*
   (voyager) Nous ______________ en train.
5. (quitter) Tu ______________ l'université.
   (partir) Tu ______________ pour l'Australie.

5. Dates de naissance *(Birth dates).* Give the birth dates of the following people. *[Section C, p. 209]*

1. Je suis né(e) ______________________.
2. Mon père est né ______________________.
3. Ma mère est née ______________________.
4. Mon meilleur ami est né ______________________.
5. Ma meilleure amie est née ______________________.

6. Quand? Say when you did the following things, using the passé composé and the expression **il y a.** *[Section D, p. 210]*

❖ téléphoner à mon cousin?
J'ai téléphoné à mon cousin il y a deux jours (il y a trois semaines...).

1. nager?

____

2. aller à la bibliothèque?

____

3. rendre visite à mes amis?

____

4. envoyer une lettre à mes grands-parents?

____

5. nettoyer ma chambre?

____

7. La belle vie (*The good life).* Hélène writes to Marc about her current stay in France. Marc, who spent some time there a year ago, replies that he did the same things. *[Section E, p. 210]*

Hélène:	Marc:
❖ Je sors beaucoup.	***Moi aussi, je suis beaucoup sorti.***
1. J'étudie peu.	Moi aussi, ______________
2. Je nage beaucoup.	Moi aussi, ______________

3. Je vais souvent au cinéma. Moi aussi, ______________________

4. Je dors trop. Moi aussi, ______________________

5. Je joue bien au tennis. Moi aussi, ______________________

6. Je voyage très souvent. Moi aussi, ______________________

7. Je reste rarement chez moi. Moi aussi, ______________________

8. J'aime vraiment mon voyage. Moi aussi, ______________________

COMMUNICATION

Describe a recent trip (real or imagined) by answering the following questions.

1. Où es-tu allé(e)? Comment as-tu voyagé? Avec qui?

____

____

____

2. Quand es-tu arrivé(e) là-bas? Combien de temps es-tu resté(e)? Où est-ce que tu es resté(e)?

____

____

____

3. Qui as-tu rencontré? À qui as-tu rendu visite?

____

____

____

4. Qu'est-ce que tu as fait pendant le voyage?

____

____

____

5. Quel cadeau *(gift)* est-ce que tu as acheté pour tes parents ou tes amis?

____

____

6. Quand es-tu rentré(e) chez toi?

____

NOM ______________________________ DATE ______________________

UNITÉ 6. POURQUOI LA FRANCE?

Leçon 16. Pourquoi la France?

1. Activités. Complete the following sentences with the appropriate forms of the verbs in the box. Note that in items 1 to 4 the verbs are in the present tense, and in items 5 to 8 the verbs are in the passé composé. *[Section A, p. 230]*

venir devenir revenir

Présent

1. Nous étudions à l'Alliance française.

   Vraiment, nous ____________________ très compétents en français.

2. Quand est-ce que tu vas à Paris?

   Quand est-ce que tu ____________________?

3. J'ai des billets *(tickets)* pour le concert.

   Est-ce que vous ____________________ avec nous?

4. Albert n'aime pas attendre.

   Il ____________________ très impatient quand ses amis ne sont pas à l'heure *(on time)*.

Passé composé

5. Philippe et Denis sont sortis hier soir.

   Ils ________________________ au cinéma avec nous.

6. Ma cousine a gagné le gros lot *(grand prize)* à la loterie.

   Elle ________________________ millionnaire!

7. Paul est allé en France cet été.

   Il ________________________ avec des cadeaux pour ses copains.

8. Gisèle et Anne-Marie ont étudié l'espagnol à l'université.

   Après l'université, elles ________________________ professeurs d'espagnol.

2. D'où viennent-ils? The following people are coming back from certain places. Express this by using the appropriate forms of the present tense of **revenir.** Then say what they have just done, using the construction **venir de** + infinitive. Use your imagination, but be logical! *[Sections A, B, pp. 230, 232]*

❖ Robert *revient* de la plage. ***Il vient de nager.***

ou: ***Il vient de faire une promenade.***

ou: ***Il vient de jouer au Frisbee.***

1. Anne et Sophie ____________________ du café.

____

2. Tu ____________________ d'un magasin de vêtements.

____

3. Les étudiants ____________________ de la bibliothèque.

____

4. Nous ____________________ de la discothèque.

____

3. Un peu de géographie? Locate these twelve countries by continent: **Allemagne, Algérie, Canada, Chine, Vietnam, États-Unis, France, Japon, Luxembourg, Maroc, Sénégal, Venezuela.** Do not forget the definite articles. *[Section C, p. 233]*

1. La Chine, ____ sont des pays d'Asie.

2. ____ sont des pays d'Afrique.

3. ____ sont des pays d'Amérique.

4. ____ sont des pays d'Europe.

NOM ________________________________ DATE ________________________

4. Quel pays? Answer the following questions in the affirmative, replacing the name of the city with the name of the country or state in which it is located. Be sure to use the appropriate prepositions. *[Section D, p. 236]*

❖ Jacques revient de Tokyo, n'est-ce pas?

Oui, il ***revient du Japon.***

1. Catherine passe l'été à San Francisco, n'est-ce pas?

   Oui, elle ____.

2. Tu rentres de Pékin, n'est-ce pas?

   Oui, je ____.

3. Joséphine étudie à Genève, n'est-ce pas?

   Oui, elle ____.

4. Ces touristes reviennent de Rio de Janeiro, n'est-ce pas?

   Oui, ils ____.

5. Vous arrivez de Madrid, n'est-ce pas?

   Oui, nous ____.

5. Depuis combien de temps? Say for how long the following people have been doing certain things. In parentheses you will note the time at which the activities began and the time at which the statement is being made. Calculate the elapsed time, as in the model. *[Section E, p. 237]*

❖ Pauline / attendre Robert / minutes (10h00 → 10h25)

Pauline attend Robert depuis 25 minutes.

1. tu / téléphoner / minutes (8h00 → 8h45)

   ____

2. vous / être à la bibliothèque / heures (5h00 → 8h00)

   ____

3. je / avoir la grippe *(flu)* / jours (lundi → vendredi)

   ____

4. nous / étudier le français / mois (septembre → janvier)

   ____

5. M. Rimbaud / habiter à Paris / ans (1980 → 1990)

   ____

6. **Depuis quand?** Say since when you have been doing the following things. Use the present tense and **depuis.** *[Section E, p. 237]*

❖ étudier le français

J'étudie le français depuis septembre (janvier...).

1. aller à cette université

___

2. habiter dans cette ville

___

3. jouer au tennis

___

4. faire mes devoirs

___

COMMUNICATION

Michèle, a French friend, has spent her summer on a trip around the world. Ask her eight questions about her trip, focusing especially on the countries she visited. You may want to use some of the verbs in the box. Put your questions in the passé composé.

aller	**partir**	**rester**	**arriver**	**quitter**	**visiter**
voyager	**acheter**	**faire**	**rencontrer**	**trouver**	

❖ *As-tu visité le Japon?*

❖ *Comment as-tu voyagé en Chine?*

___

___

___

___

___

___

___

___

___

___

NOM ________________________________ DATE ________________________

Leçon 17. Pour garder la ligne

1. Activités. Explain what the following people do or did by filling in the blanks with the appropriate forms of the verbs in the box. Note that in items 1 to 3 the verbs are in the present tense, and in items 4 to 6 the verbs are in the passé composé. *[Section A, p. 242]*

apprendre **comprendre** **prendre**

Présent

1. À l'université, Thomas ____________________ le japonais.

   Ses amis ____________________ l'italien.

2. Comment allez-vous à Paris? Est-ce que vous ____________________ l'avion?

   Nous, nous ____________________ le train.

3. Est-ce que tu ____________________ pourquoi le professeur est furieux?

   Moi, je ne ____________________ pas!

Passé composé

4. Philippe est allé à l'Institut britannique et il ____________________ l'anglais.

   Moi, je suis allé(e) à l'Alliance française et j' ____________________ le français.

5. Est-ce que vous ____________________ quand le guide a parlé de l'histoire de ce monument?

   Nous, nous ____________________!

6. Est-ce que tu ____________________ des photos pendant les dernières vacances?

   Moi, j' ____________________ beaucoup de photos.

2. Le menu. For each course, say which of the two possibilities you will have. (If you are uncertain of gender, check the Vocabulaire sections on pages 245 and 246 of your textbook; **quiche** *[f.]*.) *[Section B, p. 243]*

MENU

① *Saucisson ou Melon*

....

② *Quiche ou Thon*

....

③ *Poulet ou Pâtes*

....

④ *Salade ou Fromage*

....

⑤ *Glace ou Gâteau*

....

⑥ *Vin ou Eau minérale*

⑦ *Thé ou café*

1. ______________________________
2. ______________________________
3. ______________________________
4. ______________________________
5. ______________________________
6. ______________________________
7. ______________________________

3. Au régime *(On a diet)*. The following people are on a special diet that excludes milk products. However, they can eat or drink anything that does not contain milk. Say whether or not they will select the following items. *[Sections A–C, pp. 242–247]*

❖ Jacques *ne prend pas de beurre.*

1. Vous ______________________________

2. Tu ______________________________

3. Anne et Denise ______________________________

NOM ______________________ DATE ______________________

4. Mme Mirault ______________________

5. Nous ______________________

6. Je ______________________

4. À la fête. Complete the following conversation, overheard at a party, with the appropriate forms of the present tense of the verb **boire.** *[Section D, p. 248]*

—__________-vous de la bière?

—Non, merci, je ne __________ pas de bière.

—Et vos amies?

—Annie __________ du café et Thérèse et François __________ de la limonade.

—Nous, nous __________ du vin.

5. Qu'est-ce qu'ils font? Read about the following people and say what each one does. Complete the sentences using the appropriate form of the present tense of **faire** and one of the expressions in the box. *[Section E, p. 250]*

la photo	**le français**	**le camping**	**le théâtre**
l'espagnol	**la gymnastique**	**les maths**	

❖ Paul a un nouvel appareil-photo. Il *fait de la photo.*

1. Nous aimons beaucoup la nature. Pendant les vacances, nous ______________________
2. Anne et Gisèle ont l'intention d'être ingénieurs. Elles ______________________
3. Vous voulez maigrir. Vous ______________________
4. Les étudiants vont à l'Alliance française. Ils ______________________
5. Je voudrais être acteur. À l'université, je ______________________
6. Ma cousine va passer un an au Mexique. C'est pourquoi elle ______________________

6. **Chez le médecin.** M. Legros, a 60-year-old businessman, is quite overweight. He asks his doctor whether he can do the following things. Write out the doctor's answers, using the affirmative or negative imperative. Use the **vous** form to address the patient. *[Sections A–E, pp. 242–250]*

❖ faire du sport? — ***Oui, faites du sport.***

❖ boire du vin? — ***Non, ne buvez pas de vin!***

1. faire du ski? ____________________
2. boire de la bière? ____________________
3. boire de l'eau minérale? ____________________
4. manger de la glace? ____________________
5. manger du yaourt? ____________________
6. prendre de la crème avec le café? ____________________
7. prendre du thé? ____________________
8. manger des pâtes? ____________________

COMMUNICATION

Your friend Christine wants to get to know you better. She is asking you about your eating preferences and extracurricular activities. Answer her questions.

1. Est-ce qu'il y a des choses que tu ne manges pas? Quoi? ____________________

   ____
2. En général, qu'est-ce que tu manges au petit déjeuner *(breakfast)?* Qu'est-ce que tu bois?

   ____
3. En général, qu'est-ce que tu bois quand tu es à la cafétéria de ton université? Et quand tu vas à une fête? ____________________

   ____
4. Comment est-ce que tu restes en forme *(shape)?* Est-ce que tu fais du jogging? de la gymnastique? Où et quand? Quelles sont tes autres activités sportives?

   ____

   ____
5. Est-ce que tu as déjà fait du camping? Où, quand et avec qui? ____________________

   ____
6. Est-ce que tu fais du théâtre maintenant? Est-ce que tu as déjà fait du théâtre? Si oui, quel rôle est-ce que tu as joué? ____________________

   ____

NOM ______________________ DATE ______________________

Leçon 18. Bon appétit!

1. Les vêtements. Say what the following people wear in the indicated situations. Use the verb **mettre** and the appropriate items of clothing. (You may refer to the Vocabulaire on page 146 [Leçon 11] of your textbook.) Note that in items 1 to 4 the verbs are in the present tense, in items 5 and 6 the verbs are in the passé composé. *[Section A, p. 256]*

Présent

1. Quand il fait froid, je ______________________
2. Quand il pleut, nous ______________________
3. Mes amis vont au concert. Ils ______________________
4. Tu vas à la plage. Tu ______________________

Passé composé

5. Paul a joué au tennis. Il ______________________
6. Vous avez fait du ski. Vous ______________________

____

2. Préférences personnelles. Say whether or not you like the following dishes or drinks. Then say whether you often have them. Use the suggested verbs. *[Section B, 258]*

❖ lait (boire) *J'aime le lait. Je bois souvent du lait.*
ou: *Je n'aime pas le lait. Je ne bois pas (souvent) de lait.*

1. riz (manger) ______________________
2. bière (boire) ______________________
3. vin (acheter) ______________________
4. glace (prendre) ______________________
5. pain (manger) ______________________
6. eau minérale (commander) ______________________

3. Au restaurant français. The following remarks were heard in a French restaurant. Complete them with the appropriate definite, indefinite, or partitive articles. (If you do not remember the genders of the nouns, check the Vocabulaire on pages 245, 248, and 262 of your textbook.) *[Section B, p. 258]*

1. Est-ce que vous prenez _______ vin ou _________bière avec votre repas?
2. Aimez-vous _________roquefort *(m.)?* C'est ________ excellent fromage français.
3. J'aime beaucoup ________ poisson. Je vais commander ________ sole!
4. S'il vous plaît, est-ce que vous pouvez *(can)* passer ________ moutarde et ________ sel?
5. Regarde ________ gâteau sur la table! C'est ________ tarte au chocolat.
6. Est-ce qu'il y a _______ mayonnaise dans ________ salade?
7. ________ café est servi. Allez-vous prendre ________ sucre?
8. Comme dessert, je vais prendre ________ pomme et Caroline va prendre ________ poire.

4. À l'université. Answer the following questions affirmatively or negatively, using **beaucoup** or **beaucoup de,** as appropriate. *[Section C, p. 262]*

❖ Vous travaillez? ***Oui, je travaille beaucoup.***
ou: ***Non, je ne travaille pas beaucoup.***

❖ Vous faites du sport? ***Oui, je fais beaucoup de sport.***
ou: ***Non, je ne fais pas beaucoup de sport.***

1. Vous étudiez? ____
2. Vous avez des examens? ____
3. Il y a des étudiants français à votre université? ____________________
4. Vous voyagez? ____
5. Les étudiants ont des vacances? _________________________________
6. Vous faites du jogging? ____

NOM ________________________________ DATE ____________________

5. Des plaintes! *(Complaints!)* Robert is always complaining about his life. Express his complaints in affirmative or negative sentences using an expression of quantity. *[Section C, p. 262]*

❖ travailler *Je travaille trop.*

❖ avoir de l'argent *Je n'ai pas assez d'argent.*

1. fumer ______________________________
2. maigrir ______________________________
3. avoir des loisirs ______________________________
4. dépenser de l'argent ______________________________
5. faire des économies ______________________________
6. gagner de l'argent ______________________________

6. Comparaisons. Compare the following people using the expressions in parentheses and the appropriate comparative constructions. *[Section C, p. 262]*

❖ Jacques a 500 francs. Isabelle a 1.000 francs.

(avoir de l'argent) *Jacques a moins d'argent qu'Isabelle.*

1. Roland joue au tennis et fait du jogging. Henri joue seulement *(only)* au tennis.

   (faire du sport) ______________________________

2. M. Martin gagne 10.000 francs par mois. Son frère gagne aussi 10.000 francs.

   (gagner de l'argent) ______________________________

3. Marthe achète une robe et deux pantalons. Sylvie achète seulement une robe.

   (acheter des vêtements) ______________________________

4. Philippe commande un verre *(glass)* d'eau minérale. Charles commande une bouteille *(bottle).*

   (boire de l'eau minérale) ______________________________

COMMUNICATION

Your friend Christophe wants to know more about your eating habits. Answer his questions.

1. Est-ce que tu aimes le café noir? Si non, qu'est-ce que tu mets dans ton café?

2. Est-ce que tu manges des toasts au petit déjeuner? Qu'est-ce que tu mets dessus *(on them)?*

3. Est-ce que tu manges souvent des fruits? Quels fruits préfères-tu?

4. À quelle heure est-ce que tu prends tes différents repas?

5. Quel est ton repas favori? Pourquoi?

6. Est-ce que tu aimes la cuisine de la cafétéria de ton université? Pourquoi ou pourquoi pas?

7. Quelles boissons est-ce qu'on sert à la cafétéria de ton université?

8. Quand tu es invité(e) à un pique-nique, est-ce que tu apportes quelque chose? Quoi?

9. Est-ce que tu as fait des courses récemment *(recently)?* Où? Qu'est-ce que tu as acheté?

NOM ______________________________ DATE ____________________

Révision 2: Leçons 10–18

By completing this series of short tests, you will be able to check your progress in French. Correct your work using the Answer Key at the back of the *Cahier d'activités.* If you make any mistakes on these tests, you may want to review the lesson sections indicated in brackets.

PARTIE A. STRUCTURES

Test 1. Les adjectifs possessifs. Complete the following sentences with the possessive adjectives that correspond to the subject of each sentence. *[10–E]*

❖ Gérard écoute _ses_ disques.

1. Nous invitons ________ amis au restaurant.
2. Je ne trouve pas ________ cravate.
3. Est-ce que tu vas mettre ________ chaussures noires?
4. Ces étudiants n'écoutent pas ________ professeur.
5. Quand est-ce que vous allez vendre ________ voiture?
6. François et Olivier vont en vacances avec ________ copains.
7. Marguerite va téléphoner à ________ amie Catherine.
8. Quand as-tu acheté ________ auto?
9. Est-ce que vous êtes toujours d'accord avec ________ parents?
10. Nous allons rendre visite à ________ tante Jacqueline.

Test 2. L'article partitif: formes et emplois. Complete the following sentences with the noun in parentheses. Be sure to use the correct forms of the definite or partitive articles, as appropriate. *[17–B; 18–B]*

❖ (le vin, la bière) Marc achète *du vin* parce qu'il n'aime pas *la bière.*

1. (le lait, la limonade) Dans le réfrigérateur, il y a ____________________ et ____________________.
2. (l'eau minérale, le jus d'orange) J'ai acheté ____________________ parce que je n'aime pas ____________________.
3. (les pâtes, la salade) Si tu veux maigrir, ne mange pas ____________________! Mange ____________________!
4. (le sucre, la crème) Est-ce que tu prends ____________________ et ____________________ dans ton café?
5. (le poisson, la sole) J'aime beaucoup ____________________. Je mange souvent ____________________.
6. (l'ambition, le courage) Jacques a ____________________, mais il n'a pas ____________________.
7. (le pain, le fromage) Où est ____________________? Où est ____________________?
8. (le champagne, le vin) Ne bois pas ____________________! ____________________ n'est pas bon pour toi!

Test 3. Les articles et les prépositions avec les pays. Complete the following sentences with the appropriate articles or prepositions. *[16–C, D]*

1. Quel pays préfères-tu? ________ France, ________ Italie ou ________ Portugal?
2. Marc ne travaille pas ________ États-Unis. Il travaille ________ Canada.
3. Mon père revient ________ Japon le 8 octobre. En novembre, il va aller ________ Venezuela et ________ Argentine.

Test 4. Autres structures. Decide which of the four suggested options correctly completes the sentence. Circle the corresponding letter.

❖ ____ travailles en France.

a. Je (b.) Tu c. Nous d. Vous

1. Regarde cette voiture bleue. Elle est ____ ma cousine Jeannette.

   a. à b. de c. avec d. *(no word needed)*

2. C'est l'anorak ____ Charles, n'est-ce pas?

   a. a b. de c. son d. leur

3. Est-ce que tu vas acheter ____ veste-ci?

   a. la b. une c. sa d. cette

4. Nous habitons dans cette maison ____ 1980.

   a. depuis b. pour c. pendant d. il y a

5. Nous sommes allés au Brésil ____ deux ans.

   a. depuis b. pour c. avant d. il y a

6. Marc n'étudie pas l'italien. Il ____ de l'espagnol.

   a. apprend b. fait c. étudie d. a une classe

7. Christophe n'est pas là. Il ____ partir.

   a. est b. va c. vient d. vient de

8. François a un ____ appareil-photo.

   a. nouveau b. vieux c. bel d. japonaise

9. Ma cousine a une ____ voiture.

   a. vieil b. nouvelle c. nouveau d. nouvel

PARTIE B. VERBES

Test 5. Le présent des verbes comme *payer, acheter* et *préférer;* le présent des verbes réguliers en *-ir* et *-re*. Read the following sentences carefully. Then fill in the blanks with the appropriate present-tense forms of the verbs in the box. Be logical. *[10–B; 11–A; 13–B, C]*

acheter	**amener**	**attendre**	**célébrer**	**envoyer**
finir	**posséder**	**répondre**	**réussir**	**vendre**

1. Julien est à la poste. Il ____________________ une lettre à sa cousine.
2. Les vacances commencent en juin et ____________________ en septembre.
3. Nous ____________________ à nos examens parce que nous étudions beaucoup.
4. Hélène est au café. Elle ____________________ son copain André.
5. Ma tante est très riche. Elle ____________________ un yacht.
6. Je travaille dans une boutique. Je ____________________ des chaînes stéréo.
7. Où va le taxi? Il ____________________ les touristes au musée d'Orsay.
8. Tu es dans un magasin de vêtements. Tu ____________________ des chemises.
9. Pourquoi est-ce que vous ne ____________________ pas à ma question?
10. Anne-Marie ____________________ son anniversaire le 8 décembre.

Test 6. Le présent des verbes irréguliers. Read the following sentences carefully. Then fill in the blanks with the appropriate present-tense forms of the verbs in the box. Be logical. *[12–A; 15–A; 16–A; 17–A; 17–D; 18–A]*

apprendre	**boire**	**comprendre**	**faire**
mettre	**partir**	**revenir**	**sortir**	**venir**

1. Ce soir, je ne reste pas chez moi. Je ____________________ avec mes copains.
2. À quelle heure ____________________ le train de Marseille?
3. Qu'est-ce que vous ____________________? Du thé ou du café?
4. Mes amis ne ____________________ pas ta question. Répète, s'il te plaît!
5. Qu'est-ce que vous ____________________ le week-end prochain? Nous, nous allons à la campagne.
6. Tu ____________________ à la fête que *(that)* j'organise pour mon anniversaire, n'est-ce pas?
7. Lucile et Stéphanie étudient à l'Institut Linguistique. Elles ____________________ l'italien.
8. Je ____________________ un pull parce que j'ai froid.
9. Gilbert et Raymond sont en vacances au Canada. Ils ____________________ chez eux le 12 septembre.

Test 7. Le passé composé avec *avoir:* verbes réguliers. Complete the following sentences with the appropriate passé composé forms of the verbs in parentheses. (Note that these verbs are in the affirmative in the odd-numbered items, and in the negative in the even-numbered items.) *[14–A, B]*

1. (téléphoner) Oui, Jacques __________________________ à Béatrice.
2. (téléphoner) Non, je __________________________ à Henri.
3. (jouer) Oui, mes cousins __________________________ au tennis avec moi.
4. (visiter) Non, nous __________________________ Montréal.
5. (acheter) Vous __________________________ une Renault, n'est-ce pas?
6. (vendre) Non, Charles __________________________ sa bicyclette.
7. (rendre) Bien sûr, nous __________________________ visite à nos amis hier.
8. (finir) Non, les étudiants __________________________ l'examen.
9. (maigrir) Oui, tu __________________________ un peu!
10. (perdre) Non, je __________________________ mon temps ce matin.

NOM ______________________ DATE ______________________

Test 8. Les participes passés irréguliers. Complete the following sentences with the appropriate passé composé forms of the verbs in parentheses. Note that these verbs have irregular past participles. *[14–D; 15-A; 17–A, D; 18–A]*

1. (avoir) Henri ______________ un accident de voiture.
2. (être) Paul ______________ au cinéma avec des copains.
3. (boire) Jacqueline ______________ du champagne pour son anniversaire.
4. (faire) Antoine ______________ une promenade en auto.
5. (prendre) Charles ______________ les disques de Juliette.
6. (apprendre) Alice ______________ quelque chose d'intéressant.
7. (mettre) Jean-François ______________ une cassette de jazz.
8. (dormir) Béatrice ______________ dix heures.
9. (servir) Robert ______________ du café à ses amis.

Test 9. *Être* ou *avoir?* Complete the following sentences with the appropriate passé composé forms of the verbs in parentheses. Be careful, as some of the verbs are conjugated with **avoir** and others with **être.** *[15–B; 16–A]*

1. (visiter, aller) Jacqueline ______________ Québec.

   Après, elle ______________ à Montréal.
2. (sortir, aller) Pierre et Jacques ______________ avec des copains.

   Ils ______________ au cinéma.
3. (aller, rentrer) Nous ______________ au cinéma.

   Nous ______________ à dix heures.
4. (inviter, venir) J' ______________ Jacques.

   Il ______________ chez moi après le dîner.
5. (voyager, arriver) Simon et toi, vous ______________ en train.

   Vous ______________ hier soir.
6. (étudier, devenir) Alice et Anne ______________ l'informatique.

   Elles ______________ programmeuses.

Test 10. Verbes et expressions verbales. Complete the following sentences with the French equivalent of the English expression in italics. Be sure to use the appropriate construction.

1. Jacques *is getting fat.*	Jacques ____________________ .
2. Danièle *is waiting for* the bus.	Danièle ____________________ le bus.
3. Georges *is cleaning* his room.	Georges ____________________ sa chambre.
4. Sylvie *is visiting* a friend.	Sylvie ____________________ une amie.
5. Philippe *is doing* the dishes.	Philippe ____________________ la vaisselle.
6. Henri *is going shopping.*	Henri ____________________ .
7. Philippe *is cooking* this morning.	Philippe ____________________ ce matin.
8. Catherine *goes out* with her friends.	Catherine ________________ avec ses amis.
9. Albert *is wearing* a new jacket.	Albert ________________ une nouvelle veste.
10. Alain *is setting* the table.	Alain ____________________ la table.
11. Claudine *orders* ice cream.	Claudine __________________ de la glace.
12. The waiter *brings* the menu.	Le serveur ____________________ le menu.
13. René *is having lunch* with Paul.	Renée ____________________ avec Paul.
14. Mme Dupont *is renting* a car.	Mme Dupont ________________ une voiture.
15. Albert *meets* his friends in a café.	Albert ______________ ses amis dans un café.
16. Cécile *forgets* the date of the exam.	Cécile ________________ la date de l'examen.
17. Brigitte *looks for* her books.	Brigitte ____________________ ses livres.
18. Jean-François *finds* the books.	Jean-François ________________ les livres.

NOM ______________________ DATE ______________________

PARTIE C. VOCABULAIRE

Test 11. Qu'est-ce que c'est? Identify the following objects by writing the appropriate noun and the corresponding indefinite article: **un, une,** or **des.**

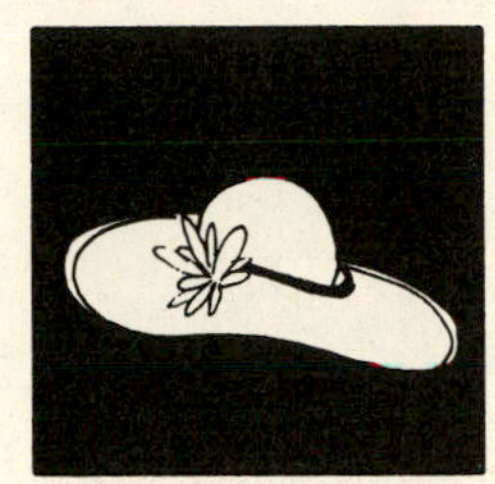

1. ______________________

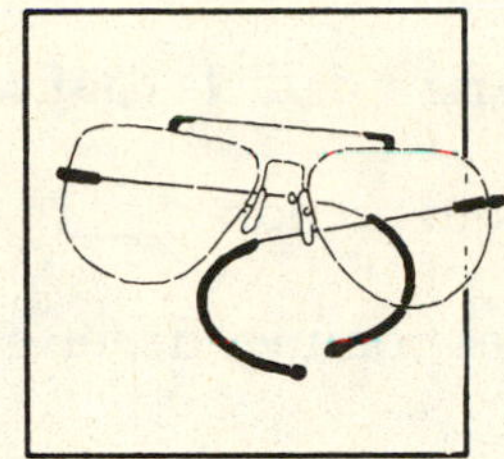

2. ______________________

3. ______________________

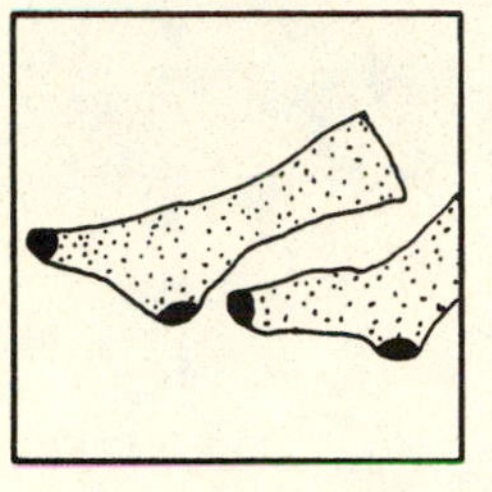

4. ______________________

5. ______________________

6. ______________________

7. ______________________

8. ______________________

9. ______________________

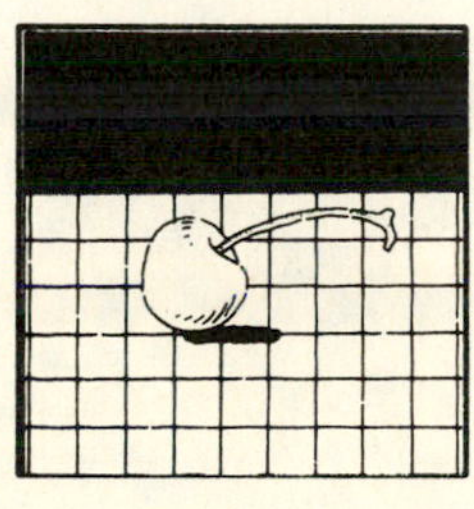

10. ______________________

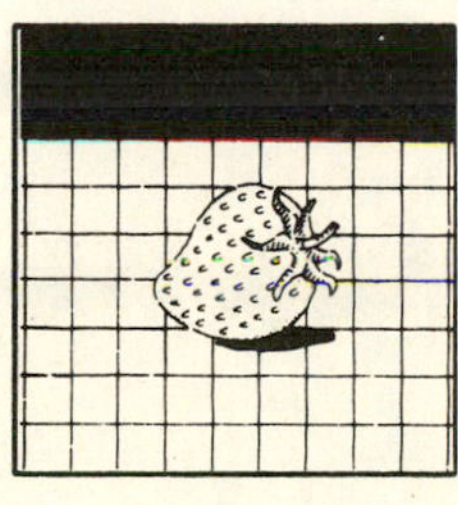

11. ______________________

12. ______________________

Test 12. Logique! Among the four options, select the one that completes the sentence logically. Circle the corresponding letter.

1. Francine est végétarienne. Elle ne mange pas de ____.

   a. pain b. poulet c. pamplemousse d. petits pois

2. Est-ce que tu vas mettre ____ sur ton pain?

   a. une pomme b. des frites c. du riz d. de la confiture

3. Quels légumes vas-tu prendre? Vas-tu prendre ____?

   a. des fraises b. des oranges c. des pommes de terre d. du gâteau

4. J'adore nager. C'est pourquoi je passe souvent les vacances ____.

   a. à la mer b. à la montagne c. avec mes valises d. en voyage

5. As-tu fait ____ de Pierre? C'est mon cousin.

   a. attention b. le ménage c. les valises d. la connaissance

6. Prends ton imperméable! Il va ____.

   a. pleuvoir b. grossir c. tomber d. faire beau

7. À quelle heure prenez-vous ____?

   a. la salle à manger b. le petit déjeuner c. la salle de séjour d. de saucisson

8. Roland prépare le repas dans ____.

   a. la cuisine b. le salon c. la fenêtre d. la chambre

9. Dans le salon il y a des ____ modernes.

   a. boissons b. meubles c. cantines d. déjeuners

10. L'année ____, nous sommes allés au Mexique.

    a. dernière b. prochaine c. première d. future

11. Sortez ____ cette porte.

    a. entre b. dans c. pour d. par

12. En général, il fait ____ en Floride.

    a. faim b. sommeil c. chaud d. froid

NOM ______________________ DATE ______________________

UNITÉ 7. À L'UNIVERSITÉ

Leçon 19. La course aux diplômes

1. Oui ou on? Read about the following people and say what they do or do not do. Fill in the blanks with the appropriate affirmative or negative forms of **suivre.** Use the present tense in items 1 to 6 and the passé composé in items 7 and 8. *[Section A, p. 277]*

Présent

1. Vous maigrissez. Vous ______________________ un régime, n'est-ce pas?
2. Nous étudions le français. Nous ______________________ le cours d'espagnol.
3. Jacqueline est très élégante. Elle ______________________ la mode *(fashion).*
4. Paul et André sont des enfants modèles. Ils ______________________ les mauvais exemples.
5. Je déteste les sports. Je ______________________ les matchs de football à la télé.
6. Tu veux être médecin. Tu ______________________ des cours de biologie.

Passé composé

7. Vous n'avez pas compris. Vous ______________________ l'explication du professeur.
8. Ces filles sont interprètes. Elles ______________________ des cours d'espagnol et d'allemand.

2. Désirs et possibilités. Say what the following people *want* to do by completing the first sentence in each pair with the appropriate form of the present tense of **vouloir.** Then say whether or not they *can* do other things by completing the second sentence with the appropriate affirmative or negative form of the present tense of **pouvoir.** Be logical! *[Section B, p. 278]*

❖ Vous *voulez* obtenir votre diplôme, n'est-ce pas?
Alors, vous *ne pouvez pas* rater tous vos examens.

1. Je ______________________ finir mes devoirs.

   Je ______________________ aller au cinéma avec vous.

2. Ces étudiants ______________________ aller à Versailles?

   Très bien! Ils ______________________ prendre le bus ou le train?

3. Marc ______________________ gagner de l'argent cet été.

   Il ______________________ partir en vacances avec ses copains.

4. Tu ________________________ apprendre le français.

Tu ________________________ suivre les cours de l'Alliance française.

5. Vous ________________________ aller dans ce restaurant végétarien?

D'accord, mais vous ________________________ commander de poulet.

6. Nous ________________________ voyager en France.

Nous ________________________ prendre le train ou louer une voiture.

3. Pour réussir à l'examen. The following students want to do well on the final exam. Say what they should do and what they should not do. Complete the sentences with the appropriate affirmative or negative forms of the present tense of the verb **devoir.** *[Section C, p. 280]*

❖ Vous ***ne devez pas*** être absents.

1. Tu ________________________ apprendre tes leçons.
2. Je ________________________ dormir en classe.
3. Nous ________________________ faire nos devoirs.
4. Vous ________________________ arriver à l'heure *(on time)* pour l'examen.
5. On ________________________ venir en classe.
6. Ces étudiants ________________________ faire des progrès.

4. Non! Read what the following people are doing. Tell them *not* to do these things, using the expression **il ne faut pas.** *[Section D, p. 282]*

❖ Tu fumes en classe. ***Il ne faut pas fumer en classe.***

1. Vous avez peur. ____
2. Tu es impatient. ____
3. Alain perd son temps. ____
4. Jacques et Paul grossissent. ____
5. Janine rate ses examens. ____

cessez de fumer grâce au plan de 5 jours

ligue vie et santé

NOM ______________________________ DATE ____________________

5. Qu'est-ce qu'il faut faire? Say what one should or should not do to achieve the following objectives. Use the constructions **il faut** and **il ne faut pas** plus an expression of your choice. *[Section D, p. 282]*

❖ Pour faire des progrès en français, ***il faut étudier. Il ne faut pas perdre son temps.***

1. Pour maigrir, ____

   ____

2. Pour avoir une profession intéressante, ______________________

   ____

3. Pour être populaire, ______________________________________

   ____

4. Pour être utile dans la société d'aujourd'hui, ____________________

   ____

6. Une classe de français très difficile. Complete the following description of a French class with an appropriate indefinite expression from the box. *[Vocabulaire, p. 284]*

tous les	**toutes les**	**tout le monde**	**chaque**	**un autre**	**plusieurs**	**de nombreux**

❖ Nous avons classe ***tous les*** jours à dix heures.

1. Dans la classe, il n'y a pas d'exception: ____________ doit parler français.
2. ____________ étudiant doit apporter son cahier.
3. Le professeur est très exigeant *(demanding)*. Il donne *(gives)* ____________ examens!
4. Nous allons avoir un examen lundi et ____________ examen jeudi prochain.
5. Nous devons écrire *(write)* ____________ compositions par semaine.
6. Heureusement *(Fortunately)*, ____________ classes ne sont pas comme ça *(like that)*.

COMMUNICATION

Your friend Denise asks you about university life and your future plans. Answer her.

1. Combien de cours est-ce que tu suis? Est-ce que ces cours sont difficiles?

2. Combien d'heures de préparation est-ce que tu dois faire pour chaque cours de français?

3. Qu'est-ce que tu dois faire ce soir avant et après le dîner?

4. Qu'est-ce que tu dois faire ce week-end?

5. Qu'est-ce que tu dois faire pour être reçu(e) à tes examens?

6. Qu'est-ce que tu peux faire avec ton diplôme?

7. Qu'est-ce que tu veux faire après l'université?

8. Est-ce que tu veux enseigner? Pourquoi ou pourquoi pas?

NOM ______________________ DATE ______________________

Leçon 20. Pas de panique!

1. Les spectacles. Say what the following people are seeing today or saw yesterday. Complete the sentences with the appropriate forms of **voir** in the present tense (items 1 to 6) and the passé composé (items 7 and 8). *[Section A, p. 289]*

Présent

1. Nous ______________ un film américain.
2. Janine et Paul ______________ une comédie.
3. Vous ______________ un film de science-fiction.
4. Je ______________ un western.
5. Tu ______________ un opéra.
6. Mon oncle ______________ une exposition *(exhibit)*.

Passé composé

7. Hier, Henri ______________ un très bon film.
8. Hier, nous ______________ un documentaire.

2. L'intrus *(The intruder)*. In each sentence the underlined direct object pronoun may refer to three of the four items, **a, b, c,** and **d.** The one to which it cannot refer is the intruder. Circle it! *[Section C, p. 291]*

❖ Je le reconnais sur cette photo.

a. Philippe b. ton cousin 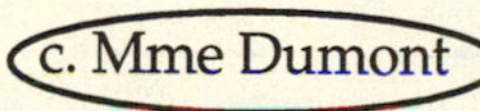 c. Mme Dumont d. le frère de Jacqueline

1. Oui, je la connais bien.

   a. Anne-Marie b. cette université c. ta cousine d. Henri

2. Non, nous ne les connaissons pas.

   a. tes amis b. cet étudiant c. vos frères d. Paul et Jean

3. Quand est-ce que vous le visitez?

   a. le musée b. ma région c. ce village d. le musée d'Orsay

4. Quand est-ce que tu les fais?

   a. tes devoirs b. les courses c. la vaisselle d. les valises

5. Nous la louons.

   a. votre maison b. cet appartement c. l'auto de Jacqueline d. la chambre de Pierre

3. Questions personnelles. Answer the following questions in complete sentences. Use a direct object pronoun in your answer. Your replies may be affirmative or negative. *[Sections B, C, pp. 290, 291]*

1. Connaissez-vous le (la) président(e) de votre université? ______
2. Connaissez-vous les parents de votre meilleur(e) ami(e)? ______
3. Est-ce que vos parents connaissent vos professeurs? ______
4. Étudiez-vous les maths? ______
5. Regardez-vous souvent la télé? ______
6. À la télé, regardez-vous les programmes de sport? ______
7. Chez vous, aidez-vous vos parents? ______
8. Achetez-vous le journal chaque jour *(every day)*? ______
9. Nettoyez-vous souvent votre chambre? ______

4. Relations personnelles. Describe your relationships with the people below, using some of the verbs in the box in affirmative or negative sentences. Use direct object pronouns. *[Section C, p. 291]*

aider **aimer** **respecter** **admirer** **comprendre** **écouter** **inviter** **trouver** **connaître**

1. votre meilleur ami ______
2. votre meilleure amie ______
3. votre mère ______
4. votre père ______
5. vos camarades de classe ______
6. le président ______
7. vos voisins ______

5. Oui ou non? Read how certain people feel or act toward others. On the basis of this information, make affirmative or negative sentences. Use direct object pronouns. *[Section C, p. 291]*

❖ Paul déteste Charles. (trouver sympathique)

Il ne le trouve pas sympathique.

1. Marc aime Caroline. (trouver intéressante)

______

2. Nous invitons souvent nos voisins. (connaître bien)

______

3. Paul est égoïste avec ses amis. (aider)

___

4. Les étudiants admirent le professeur. (écouter)

___

5. Jean-Louis pense souvent à Catherine. (oublier)

___

6. Je n'ai pas de sympathie pour les gens snobs. (comprendre)

___

6. Ce soir. Do you intend to do the following things tonight? Answer in the affirmative or the negative. Use object pronouns. *[Section D, p. 296]*

❖ Allez-vous inviter votre meilleur ami? ***Oui, je vais l'inviter. (Non, je ne vais pas l'inviter.)***

1. Allez-vous inviter votre meilleure amie? ___
2. Allez-vous acheter le journal? ___
3. Allez-vous regarder la télévision? ___
4. Voulez-vous écouter vos disques? ___
5. Devez-vous faire vos devoirs? ___
6. Devez-vous nettoyer votre chambre? ___

7. Le cancre *(The poor student).* Last night Jean-Louis did everything except study. Indicate this as you answer the following questions in the affirmative or in the negative in the passé composé.

❖ Jean-Louis a préparé ses cours? ***Non, il ne les a pas préparés.***

1. Jean-Louis a invité sa copine? ___
2. Il a fini ses devoirs? ___
3. Il a écouté ses cassettes? ___
4. Il a appris sa leçon d'anglais? ___
5. Il a mis la télé? ___
6. Il a étudié la grammaire? ___

COMMUNICATION

Caroline wants to know more about your relationships with different people. Answer her questions.

1. Qui est ton (ta) camarade de chambre? Est-ce que tu l'aides avec ses devoirs? Quelles choses est-ce que tu fais pour lui (elle)?

2. Est-ce que tu as de bonnes relations avec tes professeurs? Est-ce que tu les respectes? En général, comment les trouves-tu?

3. Est-ce que tu as des voisins sympathiques? Est-ce que tu les vois souvent? Est-ce que tu les invites chez toi? À quelle occasion?

4. À l'université, qui est ton (ta) meilleur(e) ami(e)? Depuis combien de temps est-ce que tu le (la) connais? Où et quand est-ce que tu l'as rencontré(e)?

5. Où habitent tes cousins? Est-ce que tu les vois souvent? Quand est-ce que tu les as vus pour la dernière fois *(time)*? Quand est-ce que tu vas les voir?

NOM ______________________ DATE ______________________

Leçon 21. Un contestataire

1. À la bibliothèque. The following students are at the library. Those on the left write while those on the right read. Express this by completing the sentences below with the appropriate forms of the verbs **écrire** and **lire** in the present tense (items 1 to 4) and the passé composé (item 5). *[Section A, p. 302]*

	écrire	lire
❖	Paul ***écrit*** à sa copine.	Denise ***lit*** le journal.
1.	J' __________ une lettre.	Ces étudiants __________ un roman.
2.	Nous __________ dans nos cahiers.	Je __________ un e-mail.
3.	À qui __________-vous?	Qu'est-ce que nous __________?
4.	Mes amis __________ à leurs copains.	Ces filles __________ *l'Express.*
5.	Hier, tu __________ à ton oncle.	Hier, vous __________ *le Figaro.*

2. Des excuses. Nobody wants to study today. Give each person's excuse. Use the construction **dire que,** as in the model. *[Sections A, B, pp. 302, 304]*

❖ Paul / être fatigué

Paul dit qu'il est fatigué.

1. Je / être malade *(sick)*

   ____

2. nous / avoir une entrevue professionnelle

   ____

3. vous / devoir aller chez le dentiste

   ____

4. Henri / devoir aider ses parents

   ____

5. mes amis / aller chez le médecin

   ____

6. tu / avoir la grippe *(flu)*

   ____

3. Rapports personnels. Say whether or not you do certain things for the people below. Use the expressions in parentheses and the appropriate indirect object pronouns. Your sentences may be affirmative or negative. *[Section C, p. 305]*

❖ votre meilleur ami (téléphoner) — ***Oui, je lui téléphone.***

ou: ***Non, je ne lui téléphone pas.***

1. votre meilleure amie (téléphoner souvent)

   ____

2. votre mère (demander des conseils)

   ____

3. vos parents (dire toujours la vérité)

   ____

4. votre camarade de chambre (parler de vos problèmes)

   ____

5. vos copains (écrire pendant les vacances)

   ____

4. Bons et mauvais rapports. Describe the relationships between the following people. Complete the sentences below with the appropriate direct object **(le, la, l', les)** or indirect object **(lui, leur)** pronouns. *[Section C, p. 305]*

❖ Voici Paul. Je *le* déteste. Je ne *lui* parle jamais.

1. Voici Sylvie. Paul __________ connaît bien. Il __________ téléphone souvent.
2. Voici Brigitte. Marc __________ écrit souvent. Il __________ envoie des poèmes.
3. Voici Jean-Claude. Pierre __________ rend visite. Il __________ rend ses magazines.
4. Voici Nathalie et Monique. Nous allons __________ écrire par courrier électronique.

   Nous allons __________ demander si elles veulent aller au cinéma ce week-end.
5. Voici Philippe et François. Je __________ téléphone parce que je veux __________ dire quelque chose.
6. Voici mes amis. Je __________ aime bien, mais je ne __________ comprends pas toujours.

NOM ______________________________________ DATE ___________________________

5. Merci! Read what the following people need or want to do. Say what their friends are doing for them. Use the verb in parentheses and the appropriate object pronoun. Use the present tense in sentences 1 to 4 and the passé composé in sentences 5 to 8. *[Section D, p. 308]*

❖ J'ai faim. Jacqueline *m'invite* au restaurant. (inviter)

❖ Nous avons parlé à Jacques. Il *nous a dit* la vérité. (dire)

Présent

1. Nous avons besoin d'argent. Nos amis __________________ 100 francs. (prêter)
2. Vous ne comprenez pas la question. Le professeur __________________. (aider)
3. Je ne connais pas cette ville. Mes amis __________________ la ville. (montrer)
4. Tu es seul ce week-end. Nous __________________. (rendre visite)

Passé composé

5. J'ai célébré mon anniversaire. Mes parents __________________ au restaurant. (inviter)
6. Tu as organisé une surprise-partie. Je __________________ mes disques. (prêter)
7. Nous avons écrit à Denise. Elle __________________. (répondre)
8. Anne a le courrier électronique. Je __________________ un e-mail hier. (envoyer)

6. Au bureau de tourisme. You are in charge of a tourist office in France. Your assistant asks you if he should do certain things. Answer him in the affirmative or in the negative using the appropriate object pronouns. *[Section E, p. 310]*

Votre assistant	Vous
❖ J'aide ce touriste?	Oui, *aidez-le!*
❖ Je parle à cette personne?	Non, *ne lui parlez pas!*
1. J'aide cette étudiante?	Oui, ______________________________
2. Je téléphone à M. Dupont?	Non, ______________________________
3. Je prête ce guide?	Non, ______________________________
4. Je réponds à ces personnes?	Oui, ______________________________
5. J'écris à ce client japonais?	Oui, ______________________________
6. J'envoie cet e-mail?	Non, ______________________________

7. Oui et non. You (and your friends) are in the situations described below. Ask a French friend to do certain things for you and to not do others. Study the model and be logical! *[Section E, p. 310]*

❖ Je veux t'écrire. (donner / ton adresse? ton numéro de téléphone?)
Donne-moi ton adresse. Ne me donne pas ton numéro de téléphone.

1. J'ai envie de dormir ce soir. (téléphoner / après dix heures? demain matin?)

2. Nous sommes végétariens. (servir / de la viande? des légumes?)

3. Je ne suis pas chez moi ce week-end. (rendre visite / lundi? samedi?)

4. Nous avons besoin d'argent. (donner / des conseils? 200 francs?)

COMMUNICATION

Isabelle wants to know more about your relationships with other people. Answer her.

1. Quand est l'anniversaire de ton (ta) meilleur(e) ami(e)? Qu'est-ce que tu vas lui donner? Qu'est-ce que tu lui as donné l'année dernière? Qu'est-ce qu'il (elle) t'a donné pour ton anniversaire?

2. En général, est-ce que tu prêtes tes affaires *(things)* à tes copains? Qu'est-ce que tu leur prêtes et qu'est-ce que tu ne leur prêtes pas? Et eux, qu'est-ce qu'ils te prêtent?

3. Quand tu voyages, est-ce que tu écris à tes parents? Qu'est-ce que tu leur envoies? Est-ce que tu leur achètes des cadeaux? Qu'est-ce que tu leur as acheté récemment *(recently)*?

NOM ______________________________ DATE ______________________

UNITÉ 8. HIER ET AUJOURD'HUI

Leçon 22. La vie urbaine: pour ou contre?

1. Leurs talents. Lisez la description des personnes suivantes. Ensuite décrivez leurs talents ou leur manque *(lack)* de talent. Pour cela, utilisez la construction **savoir** + infinitif dans des phrases affirmatives ou négatives. Soyez logique! *[Section A, p. 332]*

❖ Charles chante mal. ***Il ne sait pas chanter.***

1. Hélène danse bien. ______________________________
2. Nous parlons français. ______________________________
3. Je ne joue pas au bridge. ______________________________
4. Tu nages très mal. ______________________________
5. Mes amis jouent du piano. ______________________________
6. Vous faites bien la cuisine. ______________________________

2. Dans notre quartier. Complétez les phrases suivantes avec la forme appropriée de **connaître** ou de **savoir** au présent. *[Sections A, B, pp. 332, 333]*

1. Je ______________ mes voisins, mais je ne ______________ pas leurs parents.
2. Est-ce que tu ______________ ce restaurant? Est-ce que tu ______________ si la cuisine est bonne?
3. Nous ______________ M. Dupont, mais nous ne ______________ pas où il travaille.
4. Vous ______________ où est le cinéma, mais est-ce que vous ______________ à quelle heure est le film?
5. Mes amis ______________ Isabelle Dubois, mais ils ne ______________ pas l'immeuble où elle habite.

3. Opinions personnelles. Donnez votre opinion sur les personnes et les choses suivantes selon le modèle. *[Section C, p. 335]*

❖ New York / une ville / être très propre

New York est une ville qui (n')est (pas) très propre.

1. Boston et San Francisco / des villes / être très agréables

   ____

2. les Américains / des gens / être idéalistes

   ____

3. le président / un homme / avoir beaucoup d'idées

   ____

4. les professeurs / des gens / gagner bien leur vie

   ____

5. les Renault / des voitures / consommer *(to consume)* beaucoup d'essence *(gas)*

   ____

4. Oui ou non? Répondez affirmativement ou négativement aux questions suivantes. Vous pouvez utiliser un adverbe dans vos réponses. *[Section D, p. 337]*

❖ Vous aimez Chicago? ***Oui,*** c'est une ville ***que j'aime beaucoup.***

ou: ***Non,*** c'est une ville ***que je n'aime pas beaucoup.***

1. Vous connaissez Saint Louis? ______, c'est une ville ______________________
2. Vous admirez le président? ______, c'est un homme ______________________
3. Vous respectez les écologistes? ______, ce sont des personnes ______________________
4. Vous lisez *Time* magazine? ______, c'est un magazine ______________________
5. Vous parlez français? ______, c'est une langue ______________________
6. Vous invitez vos voisins? ______, ce sont des gens ______________________

5. *Qui* ou *que*? Complétez les phrases avec le pronom relatif approprié. *[Sections C, D, pp. 335, 337]*

❖ Voici un disque...
qui est extraordinaire.
que j'aime beaucoup.

1. Qui est le garçon...
   ______ a téléphoné?
   ______ tu attends?
   ______ t'a prêté sa voiture?
   ______ passe dans la rue?
   ______ tu invites chez toi?

2. Invitez-vous les gens...
   ______ sont amusants?
   ______ vont à l'université avec vous?
   ______ vous trouvez sympathiques?
   ______ vous invitent?
   ______ vous n'aimez pas?

3. Où est le journal...
   ______ j'ai acheté?
   ______ tu as lu?
   ______ parle de l'accident?
   ______ montre des photos extraordinaires?
   ______ vous avez trouvé sur la table?

4. Voilà des disques...
   ______ viennent de France.
   ______ j'écoute souvent.
   ______ mes parents détestent.
   ______ coûtent dix francs.
   ______ sont extraordinaires.

6. À Paris. Les personnes suivantes sont à Paris. Dites ce qu'elles font en complétant les phrases avec **qui** ou **que (qu')**. *[Sections C, D, pp. 335, 337]*

1. Nous déjeunons dans un restaurant ______ sert des spécialités vietnamiennes. Les touristes dînent dans un restaurant ______ le Guide Michelin recommande.
2. Mlle Martin habite dans un appartement ______ a une belle vue *(view)* sur Notre-Dame. Mes cousins habitent dans un studio ______ ils louent pour 2.000 francs par mois.
3. Nous travaillons dans un quartier ______ est très commerçant *(commercial)*. M. Moreau travaille dans une usine ______ est située dans la banlieue.
4. Ces étudiants vont à un cours ______ ils suivent depuis septembre. Je suis le cours d'un professeur ______ je trouve très intéressant.

7. C'est évident! *(It's obvious!)* Lisez la description des personnes suivantes. Ensuite, faites des phrases en utilisant les verbes entre parenthèses et l'expression négative **(ne ... rien** ou **ne ... personne)** qui convient. *[Section E, p. 339]*

❖ Janine n'a pas faim. (manger) *Elle ne mange rien.*

1. Je n'ai pas soif. (boire) ______________________
2. Ce week-end, nous devons étudier. (inviter) ______________________
3. Paul est très timide. (parler à) ______________________
4. Tu fais des économies. (acheter) ______________________
5. Sylvie est une nouvelle étudiante. (connaître) ______________________
6. Philippe a une excellente mémoire. (oublier) ______________________
7. Ces étudiants sont très égoïstes. (aider) ______________________

8. **Non!** Le week-end dernier, les personnes suivantes n'ont rien fait de spécial. Exprimez cela dans des phrases négatives en utilisant le passé composé des verbes entre parenthèses. *[Section E, p. 339]*

❖ (lire) Paulette ***n'a rien lu.***
❖ (sortir avec) André ***n'est sorti avec personne.***

1. (faire) Nous ____________________
2. (rencontrer) Vous ____________________
3. (apprendre) Je ____________________
4. (inviter) Tu ____________________
5. (téléphoner) Gisèle ____________________
6. (faire la connaissance de) Pierre ____________________

COMMUNICATION

Élisabeth, une amie française, demande votre opinion sur certains sujets. Répondez-lui en utilisant, si possible, des phrases avec **qui** et **que**.

❖ Est-ce que tu connais San Francisco? Que penses-tu de cette ville?
Je ne connais pas San Francisco.
C'est une ville que je n'ai jamais visitée, mais que j'aimerais beaucoup visiter.
C'est une ville qui a beaucoup de charme.

1. Est-ce que tu connais La Nouvelle-Orléans? Que penses-tu de cette ville?

____
____
____

2. Est-ce que tu lis *People* magazine? Que penses-tu de ce magazine?

____
____
____

3. Est-ce que tu aimes les films de Steven Spielberg? Que penses-tu de ses films?

____
____
____

4. Est-ce que tu écoutes souvent Madonna? Que penses-tu de cette chanteuse?

____
____
____

NOM ______________________ DATE ______________

Leçon 23. La télévision: un bien ou un mal?

1. La bonne vie *(The good life).* Informez-vous sur les personnes suivantes et dites comment elles vivent. Utilisez l'expression **vivre bien** dans des phrases affirmatives ou négatives au présent (phrases 1 à 4) et au passé composé (phrases 5 et 6). *[Section A, p. 345]*

Présent

1. Mme Richard est millionnaire. Elle ______________
2. Nous habitons dans une chambre d'étudiant minuscule. Nous ______________
3. Tu manges trop et tu ne fais pas d'exercice. Tu ______________
4. J'ai un très bon salaire. Je ______________

Passé composé

5. Mes grands-parents ont gagné un million à la loterie. Ils ______________
6. M. Moreau a trop travaillé et il n'a pas gagné d'argent. Il ______________

2. Non! Informez-vous sur les personnes suivantes. Complétez les phrases en utilisant le présent des verbes entre parenthèses et une des expressions suivantes. *[Section B, p. 346]*

ne ... jamais	**ne ... plus**	**ne ... pas encore**

❖ Maurice est végétarien.
(manger) Il *ne mange jamais* de viande.

1. Ce bébé *(baby)* a dix mois.
   (parler) Il ______________.
2. Mme Rémi est retraitée *(retired).*
   (travailler) Elle ______________.
3. Vous êtes très égoïstes.
   (aider) Vous ______________ vos amis.
4. Nous avons déménagé *(moved).*
   (habiter) Nous ______________ ici.
5. Je ne peux pas voter.
   (avoir) Je ______________ dix-huit ans.

3. C'est faux! Dites que les personnes suivantes n'ont jamais fait les choses dont *(of which)* elles sont accusées. Utilisez le passé composé des expressions entre parenthèses. *[Section B, p. 346]*

❖ (dire des mensonges) ***Je n'ai jamais dit de mensonges!***

1. (prendre le caméscope de Mélanie) Paul ______________________________
2. (partir sans payer) Nous ______________________________
3. (sortir avec la fiancée de Georges) Henri ______________________________
4. (écrire cette lettre d'insulte) Vous ______________________________

4. Les jobs. Quand ils étaient à l'université, certains étudiants avaient un job et travaillaient. D'autres ne travaillaient pas. Expliquez cela. *[Section C, p. 348]*

❖ Jacques (non) ***Il n'avait pas de job. Il ne travaillait pas.***

❖ Marie (oui) ***Elle avait un job. Elle travaillait*** dans une pharmacie.

1. Paul et Louis (oui) ______________________________ dans un garage.
2. Joëlle (oui) ______________________________ dans un restaurant.
3. Nous (oui) ______________________________ dans un café.
4. Vous (non) ______________________________
5. Je (non) ______________________________
6. Tu (non) ______________________________

5. Hier à midi. Dites où les personnes suivantes étaient hier à midi. Pour cela, mettez l'imparfait du verbe **être** dans le premier blanc. Dites aussi ce que faisaient ces personnes. Pour cela, mettez l'imparfait du verbe entre parenthèses dans le second blanc. *[Section C, p. 348]*

❖ Anne et Paul ___*étaient*___ à la bibliothèque. Ils ___*étudiaient*___. (étudier)

1. Monique ____________ dans un magasin. Elle ____________ une robe. (choisir)
2. Tu ____________ à la poste. Tu ____________ une lettre. (envoyer)
3. J'____________ au café. J'____________ un ami. (attendre)
4. Mes cousins ____________ chez moi. Ils me ____________ visite. (rendre)
5. Nous ____________ au restaurant. Nous ____________. (déjeuner)
6. Henri ____________ au lit. Il ____________ son petit déjeuner. (finir)

NOM ______________________________ DATE ______________________

6. En 1900. Voici certaines caractéristiques de la période actuelle. Dites si, oui ou non, ces caractéristiques existaient en 1900. Utilisez l'imparfait. *[Section C, p. 348]*

Maintenant	En 1900
❖ Les gens ont des voitures.	***Les gens n'avaient pas de voitures.***
1. La pollution est un problème sérieux.	______________________
2. Les femmes peuvent voter.	______________________
3. On va au cinéma.	______________________
4. Les gens ne travaillent pas le samedi.	______________________
5. On voyage en avion.	______________________
6. Les gens regardent la télévision.	______________________
7. Les appartements ont l'air conditionné.	______________________

7. Une fois n'est pas coutume. *(Once does not make a habit.)* Dites ce que faisaient habituellement les personnes suivantes pendant les vacances et ce qu'elles ont fait un jour particulier. Utilisez les verbes entre parenthèses. *[Section D, p. 350]*

❖ (dîner) D'habitude, Christine ***dînait*** chez elle.

Un soir, ***elle a dîné*** au restaurant.

1. (jouer) Le matin, nous ______________________ au tennis.

   Un matin, ______________________ au volley.

2. (téléphoner) Le lundi, Paul ______________________ à ses parents.

   Un lundi, ______________________ à un ami.

3. (dormir) Généralement, je ______________________ jusqu'à *(until)* huit heures.

   Une fois, ______________________ jusqu'à midi.

4. (aller) Le samedi, tu ______________________ dans une discothèque.

   Un samedi, ______________________ au cinéma.

5. (retrouver) Habituellement, vous ______________________ vos amis à la plage.

   Plusieurs fois, ______________________ vos amis au café.

6. (sortir) En général, Jacqueline ______________________ avec Pierre.

   Une ou deux fois, ______________________ avec Philippe.

7. (faire) Le week-end, nous ______________________ du camping.

   Un week-end, ______________________ un voyage en Italie.

8. À Paris. Des amis parlent de leur séjour à Paris. Complétez les phrases suivantes avec le passé composé ou l'imparfait des verbes entre parenthèses. *[Section D, p. 350]*

1. (suivre) Tous les matins, nous ________________________ des cours à l'Alliance française.
2. (déjeuner) Généralement, je ______________________ dans un petit café au Quartier latin.
3. (dîner) Pour son anniversaire, Nathalie ________________________ chez «Taillevent».
4. (rencontrer) Un jour, Pierre ________________________ un ami d'université dans la rue.
5. (aller) Le samedi soir, vous ________________________ au cinéma.
6. (prendre) D'habitude, je ________________________ mon petit déjeuner chez moi.
7. (faire) Un samedi après-midi, Caroline ________________________ une promenade à Versailles.
8. (communiquer) Chaque soir, je ________________________ avec ma famille par courrier électronique.

COMMUNICATION

Alain vous pose des questions sur votre vie lorsque *(when)* vous étiez à l'école secondaire. Répondez-lui.

1. Où habitais-tu? ____

2. À quelle école allais-tu? Qu'est-ce que tu étudiais?

   ____

   ____

3. Regardais-tu souvent la télé? Quel était ton programme favori?

   ____

   ____

4. Quels magazines lisais-tu? ____

   ____

5. Qui était ton (ta) meilleur(e) ami(e)? Qu'est-ce que vous faisiez ensemble?

   ____

   ____

6. Sortais-tu le week-end? Où allais-tu avec tes copains? Qu'est-ce que vous faisiez?

   ____

   ____

7. Qu'est-ce que tu faisais pendant les vacances? ________________________________

   ____

NOM ______________________________ DATE ______________________

Leçon 24. Un cambriolage

1. La soucoupe volante *(The flying saucer).* Imaginez qu'une soucoupe volante a atterri *(landed)* hier dans votre quartier. Dites ce que chacun faisait au moment de l'atterrissage *(landing).* Utilisez l'imparfait. *[Section B, p. 362]*

❖ (faire une promenade) Paul ***faisait une promenade.***

1. (étudier) Jacques ______________________
2. (dormir) Nous ______________________
3. (lire le journal) Vous ______________________
4. (jouer aux cartes) Tu ______________________
5. (dîner) Mes amis ______________________
6. (finir une lettre) Je ______________________
7. (rendre visite à un ami) Nous ______________________
8. (faire la cuisine) Louise ______________________
9. (attendre votre frère) Vous ______________________

2. Pourquoi? Expliquez pourquoi les personnes suivantes ont fait certaines choses. Utilisez l'imparfait et le passé composé selon le modèle. *[Sections A, C, pp. 359, 365]*

❖ Jacques / aller au restaurant / avoir faim

Jacques est allé au restaurant parce qu'il avait faim.

1. nous / aller au café / avoir soif

   ____
2. vous / mettre un manteau / avoir froid

   ____
3. Jacqueline / rester chez elle / être malade

   ____
4. mes cousins / aller en Espagne / vouloir apprendre l'espagnol

   ____
5. ma sœur / vendre sa voiture / avoir besoin d'argent

   ____
6. tu / prendre de l'aspirine / avoir une migraine terrible

   ____

3. Un événement. Complétez les phrases suivantes avec l'imparfait ou le passé composé des verbes entre parenthèses. *[Sections A, C, pp. 359, 365]*

1. (être) C'____________________ le week-end dernier.
2. (être) Il ____________________ deux heures de l'après-midi.
3. (faire) Il ____________________ beau.
4. (avoir) Je n'____________________ rien à faire.
5. (sortir) Je ____________________ de chez moi.
6. (faire) Je (J') ____________________ une promenade sur les Champs-Élysées.
7. (passer) Comme je ____________________ près de l'arc de Triomphe,

   (remarquer / regarder) je (j') _________________ des gens qui _________________ en l'air.
8. (regarder) Moi, je (j') ____________________ aussi.
9. (voir / faire) Je (J') ____________________ un jeune homme qui ____________________

   l'escalade *(scaling)* de l'arc de Triomphe.
10. (porter) Il ____________________ un grand drapeau *(flag)* blanc.
11. (arriver / arrêter) La police ____________________ et elle ____________________ le jeune homme.
12. (demander / faire) Un journaliste ____________________ au jeune homme ce qu'il *(what he)* ____________________ .
13. (répondre / vouloir) Le jeune homme ____________________ qu'il

    ____________________ protester contre le développement des armes nucléaires.

4. Le premier jour à l'université. Décrivez votre premier jour à l'université. Pour cela, répondez aux questions suivantes. *[Sections A–C, pp. 359–365]*

1. Quel jour était-ce? ____
2. Quel temps faisait-il? ____
3. Quel âge aviez-vous? ____
4. Est-ce que vos parents étaient avec vous? ______________________________
5. Est-ce que vous étiez un peu nerveux (nerveuse)? __________________________
6. Qui avez-vous rencontré? ______________________________________
7. À qui est-ce que vous avez parlé? __________________________________
8. Qu'est-ce que vous avez fait l'après-midi? _____________________________
9. Qu'est-ce que vous avez fait le soir? ________________________________

NOM ______________________________ DATE ______________________

5. C'est arrivé hier. Complétez les phrases suivantes avec l'imparfait ou le passé composé des verbes entre parenthèses. *[Section C, p. 365]*

❖ (passer / faire) Mon copain Pierre *est passé* chez moi pendant que je *faisais* les courses.

1. (être / entrer) Pendant qu'ils ________________ au cinéma, un cambrioleur ________________ chez les Dupont.
2. (voir / aller) Nous ________________ des étudiants qui ________________ à une manifestation *(demonstration).*
3. (aller / arrêter) Cet automobiliste ________________ à 150 kilomètres à l'heure quand la police l'________________.
4. (téléphoner / déjeuner) Ton cousin ________________ pendant que tu ________________ au restaurant.
5. (travailler / dormir) Personne n'a entendu le téléphone: mon frère ________________ dans le jardin et moi, je ________________.
6. (étudier / sortir) Jacqueline ________________ pendant deux heures et ensuite, elle ________________ avec une copine.

6. Et avant? Lisez ce que les personnes suivantes ont fait. Dites ce qu'elles avaient fait avant. Utilisez le plus-que-parfait du verbe en italique. *[Section D, p. 368]*

❖ Cet après-midi nous *avons visité* le musée d'Orsay.
Hier, nous *avions visité* le Centre Pompidou.

1. Ce matin, tu *as rencontré* Joséphine.
Hier, tu ____________________ sa cousine.
2. En 1992, nous *sommes allés* au Mexique.
En 1991, nous ____________________ en Argentine.
3. Ce semestre-ci, j'*ai étudié* l'espagnol.
C'était facile parce que le semestre d'avant j'____________________ le français.
4. Dimanche, Sophie *est sortie* avec son copain.
Samedi, elle ____________________ avec sa camarade de chambre.
5. Cette année, les étudiants *ont suivi* un cours d'histoire.
L'année d'avant, ils ____________________ un cours de philosophie.
6. L'été passé, Colette et Marie *ont visité* le pont du Gard.
Elles n'____________ pas ____________ ce lieu auparavant *(before).*

COMMUNICATION

Hier vous avez été témoin d'un cambriolage. La police vous pose des questions.

1. Quelle heure était-il?

____

2. Quel temps faisait-il?

____

3. Comment est-ce que le cambrioleur est sorti de la maison? Par la porte ou par la fenêtre?

____

4. Quels vêtements portait-il?

____

5. À qui a-t-il passé le sac *(bag)?*

____

6. Pouvez-vous décrire cette personne?

____

7. Comment les cambrioleurs sont-ils partis?

____

8. Avez-vous remarqué d'autres choses?

____

NOM ______________________ DATE ______________________

UNITÉ 9. IMAGES DE LA VIE

Leçon 25. Vive les loisirs!

1. Dans la course *(In the running).* Informez-vous sur les personnes suivantes et dites si oui ou non elles courent. Faites des phrases affirmatives ou négatives en utilisant le verbe **courir** au présent (phrases 1 à 4), à l'imparfait (phrases 5 et 6) et au passé composé (phrases 7 et 8). *[Section A, p. 382]*

Présent

1. Vous faites du jogging. Vous ______________________
2. Aujourd'hui, je suis malade. Je ______________________
3. Gisèle et Sophie font un marathon. Elles ______________________
4. Tu n'as pas d'énergie. Tu ______________________

Imparfait

5. Quand ma sœur était à l'université, elle faisait beaucoup de sport. Elle ______________________
6. Nous détestions le sport. Nous ______________________

Passé composé

7. M. Martin a voulu attraper *(to catch)* le bus. Il ______________________
8. Vous êtes arrivé(e) très en retard *(late)* en classe. Vous ______________________

2. Oui ou non? Répondez au questionnaire suivant en utilisant le pronom **y** dans des phrases affirmatives ou négatives. *[Section B, p. 383]*

❖ Allez-vous souvent au cinéma? *Oui, j'y vais souvent.*
ou: *Non, je n'y vais pas souvent.*

1. Allez-vous souvent chez vos amis? ______________________
2. Dînez-vous souvent à la cafétéria de l'université? ______________________
3. Habitez-vous sur le campus? ______________________
4. Passez-vous vos week-ends chez vos parents? ______________________
5. Jouez-vous souvent au tennis? ______________________
6. Avez-vous déjeuné au restaurant samedi soir? ______________________
7. Êtes-vous allé(e) en France? ______________________
8. Allez-vous aller au Canada cet été? ______________________

3. Des conseils. Voici certaines situations. Dites à un(e) ami(e) comment réagir *(to react).* Pour cela, faites des phrases affirmatives ou négatives en utilisant l'impératif des verbes entre parenthèses et le pronom qui convient **(y, lui ou leur).** *[Section B, p. 383]*

❖ Cette remarque est absurde. (répondre) ***N'y réponds pas!***

❖ Jacques est à l'hôpital. (rendre visite) ***Rends-lui visite!***

1. Ce film est extraordinaire. (aller) ______________________

2. Cette conférence *(lecture)* est stupide. (assister) ______________________

3. Ton frère célèbre son anniversaire. (écrire) ______________________

4. Tes amis dorment. (téléphoner) ______________________

5. Cette question est importante. (répondre) ______________________

6. Tes amis attendent ta réponse. (répondre) ______________________

4. Les loisirs. Complétez les dialogues en utilisant les illustrations. Notez que le verbe est au passé composé dans les dialogues 3 et 4. *[Section C, p. 384]*

❖ —Est-ce que Paul ***fait du jogging?***

—Non, ***il n'en fait pas*** souvent.

Présent

1.

Est-ce que Catherine ______________________?

Oui, elle ______________________ tous les jours.

2.

Où est-ce que vous ______________________?

Nous ______________________ sur le lac d'Annecy.

NOM ______________________ DATE ______________________

Passé composé

3. Est-ce que vous ______________ l'été dernier?

Non, nous ______________.

4. Est-ce que tes copains ______________ pendant les vacances?

Oui, ils ______________ plusieurs fois.

5. Au régime. Les personnes suivantes suivent un régime très strict pour maigrir. Répondez affirmativement ou négativement aux questions suivantes en utilisant le pronom **en.** Soyez logique! *[Section C, p. 384]*

❖ M. Richard mange du pain? *Non, il n'en mange pas.*

1. Ces étudiants font du sport? ______________
2. Catherine boit de la bière? ______________
3. Paul et André mangent des fruits? ______________
4. Antoine a fait du jogging? ______________
5. Mme Serraut a commandé des pâtes? ______________
6. Anne a mis du sucre dans son café? ______________

6. Les statistiques. Un employé du Bureau National des Statistiques vous pose les questions suivantes. Utilisez le pronom **en** dans vos réponses. *[Section D, p. 388]*

1. Combien de frères avez-vous? ______________
2. Combien de sœurs avez-vous? ______________
3. Combien de voitures ont vos parents? ______________
4. Combien de téléviseurs avez-vous chez vous? ______________
5. Avez-vous une minichaîne? ______________
6. Avez-vous un appareil-photo? ______________

7. En quelles quantités? Répondez aux questions suivantes affirmativement ou négativement. Utilisez le pronom **en** et une expression de quantité comme **beaucoup, assez, trop.** *[Section D, p. 388]*

1. Mangez-vous de la viande? ______________
2. Avez-vous des loisirs? ______________
3. Faites-vous du volley? ______________
4. Faites-vous des progrès en français? ______________
5. Gagnez-vous de l'argent en été? ______________

COMMUNICATION

Stéphanie vous pose des questions sur vos loisirs. Répondez-lui.

1. Est-ce que tu fais du jogging régulièrement *(regularly)?* Combien de kilomètres est-ce que tu cours par semaine?

2. As-tu un vélo? Est-ce que tu l'utilises souvent? En été, est-ce que tu fais souvent des promenades à bicyclette? Où vas-tu?

3. Quels sports pratiques-tu en été? Est-ce que tu as déjà fait du roller? Où est-ce que tu en as fait?

4. Aimes-tu la musique? Est-ce que tu as une chaîne stéréo? As-tu beaucoup de compact disques? Combien de disques ou de cassettes as-tu? Où est-ce que tu les achètes?

5. Est-ce que tu vas souvent au cinéma? Avec qui est-ce que tu y es allé(e) récemment *(recently)?*

NOM ______________________ DATE ______________________

Leçon 26. Pauvre Michel!

1. L'anatomie. Dites avec quelle partie du corps on fait les choses suivantes. *[Section A, p. 395]*

❖ regarder *On regarde avec les yeux.*

1. écouter ______________________
2. parler ______________________
3. jouer de la guitare ______________________
4. jouer au basket ______________________
5. jouer au football ______________________
6. sentir les odeurs ______________________
7. courir ______________________
8. mâcher *(to chew)* du chewing-gum ______________________

2. Le repos *(Rest).* Lisez ce que font les personnes suivantes le week-end. D'après vous, est-ce que ces personnes se reposent ou non? Exprimez votre opinion en utilisant le verbe réfléchi **se reposer** dans des phrases affirmatives ou négatives. *[Section B, p. 398]*

1. Nous travaillons. ______________________
2. Vous regardez la télé. ______________________
3. Je fais une promenade à la campagne. ______________________
4. Mlle Arnaud va au bureau. ______________________
5. Tu dors. ______________________
6. Ces étudiants nettoient leur appartement. ______________________
7. Paul et Denise écoutent de la musique. ______________________
8. Claudine répare sa voiture. ______________________
9. Je prends un bain chaud. ______________________

3. Les activités de la journée. Dites ce que font les personnes suivantes en utilisant les verbes pronominaux suggérés par les illustrations. (Si vous avez besoin d'aide dans le choix de ces verbes, consultez votre livre à la page 400.) *[Section B, p. 398]*

1. Tu ______________________________

2. M. Dupont ______________________________

3. Nous ______________________________

4. Je ______________________________

5. Éric et Joëlle ______________________________ dans la rue.

6. Je ______________________________

7. Vous ______________________________

8. André ______________________________

NOM ________________________________ DATE ________________________

4. Quel pronom? Lisez les phrases suivantes et complétez-les avec le pronom réfléchi ou le pronom complément d'objet entre parenthèses. *[Section B, p. 398]*

❖ (se, la) M. Richard a une nouvelle voiture. Il *la* lave souvent.

❖ (s', lui) Alice aime la musique. Son cousin *lui* achète des disques pour son anniversaire.

1. (se, le) Henri aime la marche à pied. Il ______ promène souvent.
2. (se, le) Paul a un camarade de chambre qui dort trop. Il doit ____ réveiller tous les matins.
3. (me, le) Mon chien *(dog)* a besoin d'exercice. Je ______ promène après le dîner.
4. (s', l') Michelle adore la lecture *(reading)*. Elle ______ achète souvent des romans policiers.
5. (se, la) Guy est secrètement amoureux *(in love)* d'Odile. Il _____ regarde souvent en classe.
6. (te, le) Voici le pain. Peux-tu ______ couper?

5. Quand? Les personnes suivantes ne font pas certaines choses. Dites quand elles vont les faire. *[Section C, p. 402]*

❖ Henri ne se couche pas. *Il va se coucher* à onze heures.

1. Tu ne te rases pas. ______________________________ avant le petit déjeuner.
2. Nous ne nous promenons pas. ______________________________ ce soir.
3. Mlle Mathieu ne se repose pas. ______________________________ ce week-end.
4. Vous ne vous lavez pas les mains. ______________________________ avant le dîner.
5. Je ne me brosse pas les dents. ______________________________ après le déjeuner.
6. Les étudiants ne se lèvent pas. ______________________________ à midi.

6. Activités. Dites ce que les personnes suivantes font ou ont fait. Pour cela, utilisez les verbes suivants au présent dans les phrases 1 à 4 et au passé composé dans les phrases 5 à 8. Soyez logique dans votre choix de verbes! *[Section D, p. 404]*

découvrir offrir ouvrir souffrir

Présent

1. Quand je vais chez le dentiste, je ____________________ toujours un peu!
2. Tu ____________________ du chocolat à tes amis.
3. Les étudiants ____________________ leurs livres à la page 125.
4. Le professeur ____________________ des erreurs dans les devoirs de ses étudiants.

Passé composé

5. Hier, nous ________________________ la fenêtre parce que nous avions chaud.

6. Philippe ________________________ un livre à Martine pour son anniversaire.

7. Mme Masson ________________________ quand son mari est mort.

8. Ces médecins ________________________ un nouveau vaccin.

COMMUNICATION

Stéphanie, une amie française, vous pose des questions sur vos habitudes personnelles. Répondez à ses questions.

1. À quelle heure est-ce que tu te lèves les jours de classe? À quelle heure est-ce que tu te lèves le dimanche?

   ____

   ____

2. À quelle heure est-ce que tu te couches quand tu as un examen? À quelle heure est-ce que tu te couches le samedi soir?

   ____

   ____

3. Avec quelle marque *(brand)* de savon est-ce que tu te laves? Préfères-tu prendre une douche ou un bain?

   ____

   ____

4. Est-ce que tu aimes la nature? Est-ce que tu aimes te promener dans la campagne? Est-ce que tu te promènes souvent en ville? Où vas-tu?

   ____

   ____

   ____

5. Est-ce que tu as parfois mal à la tête quand tu étudies trop? Qu'est-ce que tu fais dans ce cas *(case)?*

   ____

   ____

6. Est-ce que tu te reposes un peu pendant la journée? Quand? Qu'est-ce que tu fais? Est-ce que tu vas te reposer cet été? Qu'est-ce que tu vas faire?

   ____

   ____

NOM ______________________________ DATE ______________________

Leçon 27. Un rendez-vous

1. Activités. Informez-vous sur les personnes suivantes et complétez les phrases avec la forme qui convient d'un des verbes suivants. Soyez logique dans votre choix de verbe! *[Section A, p. 408]*

s'amuser **s'appeler** **s'arrêter** **s'asseoir** **se dépêcher** **s'excuser** **s'intéresser** **se mettre en colère** **s'occuper** **se préparer** **se souvenir** **se tromper**

❖ Paul lit un livre sur le bouddhisme. Il *s'intéresse* à la philosophie asiatique.

1. Nous étudions beaucoup. Nous ______________________ pour l'examen.
2. J'ai une excellente mémoire. Je ______________________ de tout.
3. Vous êtes poli(e). Vous ______________________ quand vous avez tort.
4. M. Simon ne veut pas rater *(to miss)* son bus. Il ______________________.
5. Nous avons très soif. Nous ______________________ dans un café.
6. Mme Bernard est ingénieur *(engineer)*. Elle ______________________ de la construction d'une nouvelle machine.
7. Vous êtes la fille de M. Rousset. Vous ______________________ Janine Rousset, n'est-ce pas?
8. Ces étudiants ne sont pas sérieux. Ils ______________________ toujours en classe.
9. Mon petit frère collectionne les timbres *(stamps)*. Il ______________________ à la philatélie.
10. M. Robichaud est absolument furieux. Il ______________________ quand son fils ne lui dit pas la vérité.
11. Nous sommes fatigués. Nous ______________________ sur le sofa.
12. Janine a fait une erreur dans le problème de maths. C'est curieux parce qu'en général,

    elle ne ______________________ jamais!

2. Expression personnelle. Parlez de vous-même. Pour cela, utilisez les verbes suivants dans des phrases affirmatives ou négatives de votre choix. *[Section A, p. 408]*

❖ (s'intéresser à) *Je m'intéresse à la musique. Je ne m'intéresse pas aux sports.*

1. (s'intéresser à) ______________________________

2. (se souvenir de) ______________________________

3. (s'occuper de) ______________________________

4. (s'entendre bien avec) ______________________________

5. (se disputer avec) ______________________________

3. Encouragements. Imaginez que vous avez un ami très impatient. Encouragez cet ami à changer d'attitude. Utilisez l'impératif à la forme affirmative ou négative. Suivez les modèles. *[Section B, p. 411]*

Le problème de votre ami:	**Vous l'encouragez:**
❖ Il ne se repose pas.	*Repose-toi!*
❖ Il s'énerve.	*Ne t'énerve pas!*
1. Il ne s'amuse pas.	______________
2. Il s'impatiente.	______________
3. Il se préoccupe inutilement *(without cause).*	______________
4. Il se met en colère.	______________
5. Il ne s'entend pas avec ses parents.	______________
6. Il se dispute avec ses amis.	______________

4. Des conseils. Analysez les situations suivantes et dites aux personnes suivantes de faire ou de ne pas faire les choses entre parenthèses. *[Section B, p. 411]*

❖ Tu es malade. (se lever) *Ne te lève pas!*
❖ Vous êtes fatigués. (s'asseoir) *Asseyez-vous!*

1. Vous êtes fatigués. (se reposer) ______________________________
2. Nous avons tort. (s'excuser) ______________________________
3. Tu as un examen important. (s'énerver) ______________________________
4. Vous devez finir vos devoirs. (s'amuser) ______________________________
5. Nous ne sommes pas prêts. (se dépêcher) ______________________________
6. Vous avez sommeil. (se coucher) ______________________________

NOM ______________________________ DATE ______________________________

5. L'amitié? Notre attitude envers *(toward)* certaines personnes dépend des sentiments que nous avons pour elles. Exprimez cela en complétant les phrases suivantes avec les verbes entre parenthèses dans des phrases affirmatives ou négatives. Soyez logique! *[Section C, p. 413]*

❖ Jacques et Caroline sont fiancés.
(s'aimer) Ils ***s'aiment.***

1. Paul et moi, nous sommes d'excellents amis.

   (s'entendre) Nous ______________________ bien.

   (se disputer) Nous ______________________.

2. Jacqueline et toi, vous n'êtes jamais d'accord!

   (se comprendre) Vous ______________________.

   (se parler) Vous ______________________.

3. Béatrice et Roland sont de bons voisins.

   (se connaître) Ils ______________________ bien.

   (s'inviter) Ils ______________________ souvent.

6. Samedi. Dites ce que les personnes suivantes ont fait samedi. Utilisez le passé composé. *[Section D, p. 414]*

❖ Catherine a dormi.
(se reposer) ***Elle s'est reposée*** .

1. Tu es allée à une fête.

   (s'amuser) ____.

2. Vous êtes allés à la campagne.

   (se promener) ____.

3. Mes copines ont pris le train à sept heures du matin.

   (se lever) ____ tôt *(early)*.

4. Ces étudiants ont dansé toute la nuit.

   (se coucher) ____ tard *(late)*.

5. Élisabeth a eu un problème avec sa sœur.

   (se disputer) ____ avec elle.

6. Je suis resté(e) à la bibliothèque.

   (se préparer) ______________________________________ pour l'examen de lundi.

7. Gisèle et Denise sont allées à un bal masqué *(costume party)*.

   (s'habiller) ______________________________________ d'une manière très originale.

8. Mes cousins n'ont rien fait.

   (se reposer) ____.

7. Pauvre Juliette! Juliette n'a pas eu de chance hier. Dites ce qu'elle a fait et ce qu'elle n'a pas fait. Utilisez les verbes entre parenthèses dans des phrases affirmatives ou négatives. Soyez logique! *[Section D, p. 414]*

❖ (se disputer) Juliette ***s'est disputée*** avec sa camarade de chambre.

❖ (se souvenir) Elle ***ne s'est pas souvenue*** d'un rendez-vous.

1. (se lever) Elle n'a pas entendu son réveil *(alarm clock)*, et elle ______________________ à l'heure *(on time)*.
2. (se dépêcher) Elle ______________________ et elle a raté *(missed)* son bus.
3. (se tromper) Elle ______________________ dans l'examen de biologie.
4. (s'impatienter) Elle a attendu ses copines qui ne sont pas venues et elle ______________________.
5. (s'amuser) Elle est sortie avec un garçon stupide et elle ______________________.
6. (se coucher) Finalement elle est rentrée chez elle et elle ______________________ parce qu'elle avait mal à la tête.

COMMUNICATION

Janine vous pose des questions sur votre manière de vivre *(way of life)*. Répondez à ses questions.

1. Est-ce que tu t'entends bien avec tes frères et sœurs? Est-ce que tu te disputes parfois avec eux? Quand est-ce que tu t'es disputé(e) avec eux pour la dernière fois? Pour quelle raison *(cause)*?

____

____

____

2. En général, est-ce que tu es patient(e) ou impatient(e)? Quelle était la dernière fois que tu t'es impatienté(e)? Pourquoi?

____

____

____

3. À quelle heure est-ce que tu t'es levé(e) ce matin? Qu'est-ce que tu as fait ensuite?

____

____

4. Quand est-ce que tu es sorti(e) avec tes copains? Où est-ce que vous vous êtes retrouvés? Qu'est-ce que vous avez fait ensuite? Est-ce que vous vous êtes amusés?

____

____

____

NOM ______________________ DATE ______________________

Révision 3: Leçons 19–27

By completing this series of short tests, you will be able to check your progress in French. Correct your work using the Answer Key at the back of the *Cahier d'activités.* If you make any mistakes on these tests, you may want to review the lesson sections indicated in brackets.

PARTIE A. STRUCTURES

Test 1. Les pronom compléments d'objet direct. Rewrite the following sentences, replacing the underlined expression with the appropriate direct object pronoun. *[20–C, D, E]*

❖ Jacques regarde le menu. *Jacques le regarde.*

1. Philippe regarde Cécile. ______________________
2. Nous invitons Christine et Robert. ______________________
3. J'aide ma cousine. ______________________
4. Nous écoutons nos disques. ______________________
5. François regarde l'amie de Paul. ______________________
6. Je ne veux pas cette cassette. ______________________
7. Je ne connais pas vos cousins. ______________________
8. Invite Sylvie. ______________________
9. N'invite pas Thomas et Jacques. ______________________
10. J'ai écouté tes disques. ______________________
11. Paul n'a pas aidé sa sœur. ______________________
12. Nous allons regarder la télé. ______________________

Test 2. Quel pronom? Complete the answers to the questions below by filling in the blanks with one of the following pronouns. *[20–C; 21–C; 25–B, C]*

le	**la**	**les**	**lui**	**leur**	**en**	**y**

1. Tu connais ce restaurant?
   Oui, je ________ connais bien.
2. Faites-vous de l'espagnol?
   Oui, nous ________ faisons.
3. Tu as parlé à Florence?
   Oui, je ________ ai parlé.
4. Vous pensez à ce problème?
   Oui, nous ________ pensons.
5. Roland boit du jus d'orange?
   Oui, il ________ boit.
6. Tu mets ta nouvelle veste?
   Oui, je ________ mets.
7. Tu regardes les photos de Jacqueline?
   Oui, je ________ regarde.
8. Tu téléphones aux cousins de Christophe?
   Oui, je ________ téléphone.
9. Vous dînez souvent dans cette cafétéria?
   Oui, nous ________ dînons souvent.
10. Vous avez besoin de ce livre?
    Oui, nous ________ avons besoin.

Test 3. ***Qui*** **ou** ***que?*** Complete the following sentences with **qui** or **que.** *[22–C, D]*

1. J'ai un ami ________ parle russe.
2. Michel a une moto ________ marche bien.
3. Qui est la fille ________ tu regardes?
4. Le livre ________ j'ai acheté n'est pas très intéressant.
5. Les disques ________ tu écoutes sont des disques ________ viennent de France.
6. Les étudiants ________ je vais inviter sont des étudiants ________ tu connais.

Test 4. Les constructions négatives. Answer the following questions in the negative. *[22–E; 23–B]*

1. Tu as entendu quelque chose? ________________________________
2. Quelqu'un a téléphoné? ________________________________
3. Tu habites encore à Paris? ________________________________
4. Paul est déjà parti? ________________________________
5. Quelque chose est arrivé? ________________________________
6. Tu as fait quelque chose ce week-end? ________________________________

NOM ______________________________ DATE ______________________

PARTIE B. VERBES

Test 5. Le présent des verbes irréguliers. Complete the sentences below with the appropriate present-tense forms of the verbs in the box. Be logical. *[19–A, B, C; 20–A, B; 21–A; 25–A; 26–D]*

connaître	**courir**	**devoir**	**dire**	**écrire**
lire	**ouvrir**	**pouvoir**	**suivre**	**voir**

1. Nous ______________ ton cousin. Il habite à Montréal, n'est-ce pas?
2. Je ______________ un cours de français à l'Université de Tours.
3. À qui ______________-vous cette lettre?
4. Anne et Christine ne ______________ pas voyager à l'étranger. Elles n'ont pas de passeport.
5. Est-ce que vous ______________ la vérité?
6. Quel journal est-ce que tes parents ______________?
7. François ______________ la fenêtre.
8. Je ne peux pas venir ce soir, je ______________ rester chez moi.
9. Janine ______________ dix kilomètres tous les jours.
10. Nous ______________ un bon film à la télé.

Test 6. Le passé composé des verbes irréguliers. Complete the sentences below with the passé composé of the verbs in parentheses. *[19–A, B, C; 20–A, B; 21–A; 22–A; 23–A; 25–A; 26–D]*

1. (devoir) À la douane *(customs)* nous ________________ montrer nos passeports.
2. (vivre) Michel ________________ un an au Japon.
3. (pouvoir) Est-ce que tu ________________ réparer ton vélo?
4. (ouvrir) Qui ________________ cette lettre?
5. (voir) Hier, j'________________ le nouveau film de Depardieu.
6. (lire) Est-ce que vous ________________ le journal ce matin?
7. (savoir) Comment est-ce que tu ________________ cela?
8. (courir) Hier après-midi, François ________________ plus de vingt kilomètres.
9. (connaître) Quand est-ce que tu ________________ mon cousin?
10. (vouloir) Pourquoi est-ce que tu ________________ partir?

Test 7. La forme de l'imparfait. Complete the following sentences with the appropriate imperfect forms of the verbs in parentheses. *[23–C]*

1. (habiter) J'________________ avec mes parents. Nous ________________ dans un grand appartement.
2. (finir) Vous ________________ votre travail à cinq heures. Mon frère ________________ à six heures.
3. (rendre) Tu ________________ visite à tes parents. Mes amis ________________ visite à leur oncle.
4. (avoir) J'________________ un vélomoteur. Nous ________________ une moto.
5. (faire) Nous ________________ du sport. Mes cousines ________________ du ski.
6. (être) Vous ________________ timide. Moi, je n'________________ pas patient avec vous.
7. (apprendre) J'________________ l'anglais. Mon frère ________________ l'espagnol.
8. (boire) Mes amis ________________ de la bière. Qu'est-ce que tu ________________?
9. (voir) Le samedi, je ________________ mes grands-parents. Le dimanche, Caroline ________________ ses cousins.
10. (lire) Tu ________________ des romans policiers. Vous ________________ des livres d'aventure.

Test 8. L'emploi de l'imparfait. Complete the following sentences with the appropriate imperfect or passé composé forms of the verbs in parentheses. *[23–C, D; 24–A, B, C]*

1. (visiter) Paul ________________ Québec en 1990.
2. (parler) Quand Sylvie était à Paris, elle ________________ très bien français.
3. (parler) Hier, Thomas ________________ au professeur de français.
4. (jouer) Marc est fatigué parce qu'il ________________ au football pendant deux heures.
5. (jouer) Maintenant je ne joue pas très bien au tennis, mais avant, je ________________ très bien.
6. (entrer, jouer) Quand le professeur ________________, les élèves ________________ aux cartes.
7. (être, rencontrer) Hier, quand j'________________ au café, je (j') ________________ une amie américaine.
8. (prendre, jouer) Cet après-midi, nous ________________ des photos des jeunes Français qui ________________ au football dans la rue.
9. (être, arriver) Il ________________ deux heures quand Pierre ________________.
10. (aller, faire) Albert ________________ à la plage parce qu'il ________________ beau.
11. (être, avoir) Hier, la visibilité ________________ très mauvaise et mon frère ________________ un accident.
12. (rester, avoir) Dimanche, Paul ________________ chez lui parce qu'il ________________ mal aux dents.

NOM ______________________________ DATE ______________________

Test 9. La forme des verbes réfléchis. Fill in the first blank with the appropriate present-tense form of the reflexive verb in parentheses. Fill in the second blank with the passé composé. Make the sentences affirmative or negative as indicated. *[26–B; 27–D]*

	Aujourd'hui	**Hier**
1.	(se laver)	
	Oui, je ______________.	Oui, je ______________ aussi.
2.	(se raser)	
	Non, Marc ______________.	Oui, il ______________.
3.	(se lever)	
	Non, vous ______________ tôt.	Oui, vous ______________ tôt.
4.	(se lever)	
	Oui, Anne ______________ tard.	Non, elle ______________ tard.
5.	(se promener)	
	Oui, nous ______________.	Non, nous ______________.
6.	(s'amuser)	
	Oui, Anne et Lucie ______________.	Non, elles ______________.
7.	(s'arrêter)	
	Oui, ces étudiants ______________ au café.	Non, ils ______________ à la bibliothèque.

Test 10. Quelques verbes pronominaux (présent, infinitif, impératif). Fill in the blanks with the appropriate verbs. *[26–B, C; 27–B]*

1.	Paul *wakes up* at seven.	Paul ______________ à sept heures.
2.	Thérèse *gets up* at eight.	Thérèse ______________ à huit heures.
3.	Philippe *goes to bed* late.	Philippe ______________ tard.
4.	We *are getting dressed.*	Nous ______________.
5.	My father *is shaving.*	Mon père ______________.
6.	I want *to rest.*	Je veux ______________.
7.	You can't *remember* that story.	Tu ne peux pas ______________ de cette histoire.
8.	We like *to go for walks.*	Nous aimons ______________.
9.	Pierre, *get up!*	Pierre, ______________!
10.	Marc et André, *don't get impatient!*	Marcel et André, ______________!
11.	Jacques, *don't stop* at the café.	Jacques, ______________ au café.
12.	*Let's hurry!*	______________!

PARTIE C. VOCABULAIRE

Test 11. Logique! Circle the letter of the option that completes the sentence logically.

1. M. Duroc suit un ____ parce qu'il veut maigrir.
   a. plat b. cours c. devoir d. régime
2. Après six heures du soir, il n'est pas nécessaire de payer le parking parce qu'il est ____.
   a. seul b. cher c. gratuit d. bon marché
3. Les Lagarde habitent un immeuble moderne dans ____.
   a. l'usine b. la banlieue c. le bâtiment d. la circulation
4. Ce soir, nous allons regarder ____ à la télévision.
   a. un feuilleton b. un cinéma c. une chaîne d. une scène
5. Écoutez! Est-ce que vous entendez ____? Qu'est-ce que c'est?
   a. cette bande dessinée b. ce roman c. la vérité d. ce bruit
6. Vraiment, je ne comprends pas ce que tu ____.
   a. rends b. prêtes c. peux d. veux dire
7. La police a posé des questions à un témoin qui a assisté ____.
   a. au cambriolage b. à l'émission c. au mensonge d. au roman policier
8. En hiver, quand il fait très froid, on peut faire ____.
   a. de la voile b. du patinage c. de la planche à voile d. de la natation
9. J'ai mal ____ parce que j'ai couru!
   a. au cou b. à la gorge c. à la figure d. aux jambes
10. Denise est restée chez elle parce qu'elle a un très mauvais ____.
    a. dos b. rhume c. peigne d. pied
11. Excusez-moi. Je me suis ____.
    a. arrêté d. trompé c. préoccupé d. préparé
12. Brosse-toi les dents avec ____.
    a. du savon b. un peigne c. les doigts d. du dentifrice

Test 12. Le mot exact. Fill in the blanks with the noun that logically completes the sentence.

1. M. Simonet va suivre un ____________________ parce qu'il veut maigrir.
2. J'ai réussi à l'examen et le professeur m'a donné une bonne ____________________.
3. À l'université, Christine étudie le ____________________ parce qu'elle veut être avocate.
4. Qui est l'____________________ qui a écrit ce roman?
5. Pierre est honnête. Il dit toujours la ____________________.
6. La ____________________ a annoncé du beau temps pour le week-end.
7. Cet immeuble n'est pas récent. Il a été construit *(built)* au dix-neuvième ______________.
8. Mon sport préféré est la ____________________! J'adore nager.
9. Michel a un ____________ avec Suzanne. Il va la retrouver au café des Arts à une heure.
10. J'ai une migraine. Je prends de l'aspirine parce que j'ai mal à la ____________________.

NOM ______________________ DATE ______________

UNITÉ 10. PERSPECTIVES D'AVENIR

Leçon 28. Le grand amour

1. La personnalité. Informez-vous sur les personnes suivantes. Utilisez ces renseignements pour les décrire. Utilisez le verbe **être** et la forme correcte d'un des adjectifs suivants. *[Section A, p. 437]*

actif **amoureux** **conservateur** **créateur** **ennuyeux** **étranger** **inquiet** **libéral** **loyal** **paresseux** **ponctuel** **sportif** **travailleur**

❖ Josiane et Marguerite font du jogging tous les jours. *Elles sont sportives.*

1. Janine est toujours à l'heure. ______________________
2. Isabelle pense toujours à Gérard. ______________________
3. Ces hommes politiques sont pour le progrès et le changement.

   ____
4. Ces filles ne préparent pas leurs examens.

   ____
5. La secrétaire de Mlle Maubert travaille beaucoup.

   ____
6. Mes amis sont très dévoués *(devoted)*.

   ____
7. Ces étudiantes habitent en France, mais elles ne sont pas françaises.

   ____
8. Vraiment, Thérèse n'est pas drôle. ______________________
9. Cette jeune artiste a une imagination extraordinaire.

   ____
10. Cette personne est extrêmement traditionnelle.

    ____
11. Michèle se préoccupe de tout. ______________________
12. Ces garçons sont extrêmement dynamiques.

    ____

2. Questions. Complétez les questions avec la forme correcte des adjectifs entre parenthèses. *[Section A, p. 437]*

❖ (paresseux) Est-ce que cette étudiante est *paresseuse* ?

1. (roux) Qui est la fille ____________________?
2. (jaloux) Pourquoi est-ce que Francine est ____________________?
3. (gentil) Est-ce que la sœur de Pierre est ____________________?
4. (favori) Quelle est ta recette *(recipe)* ____________________?
5. (gros) As-tu une ____________________ voiture?
6. (long) Est-ce que Jacqueline va mettre une robe ____________________?
7. (fou) Qui a eu cette idée *(idea)* ____________________?

3. Commentaires personnels. Complétez les phrases suivantes avec au moins deux adjectifs du Vocabulaire à la page 438 *[Section A, p. 437]*

1. Je suis ____________________
2. J'ai une amie ____________________
3. J'ai des amis ____________________
4. J'ai des professeurs ____________________
5. Aujourd'hui, les hommes sont ____________________
6. Aujourd'hui, les femmes sont ____________________
7. Je respecte les personnes ____________________
8. Je n'aime pas les gens ____________________

4. Des conseils. Donnez aux personnes suivantes certains conseils. Pour cela, utilisez l'impératif et un adverbe en **-ment** dérivé de l'adjectif souligné. *[Section B, p. 440]*

❖ Paul n'est pas sérieux. (travailler) ***Travaille sérieusement!***

1. Henri n'est pas consciencieux. (étudier) ____________________
2. Sylvie n'est pas calme. (parler) ____________________
3. Philippe et Guy ne sont pas discrets. (parler) ____________________
4. Albert n'est pas patient. (attendre) ____________________
5. Louise n'est pas prudente. (jouer) ____________________
6. Antoine n'est pas élégant. (s'habiller) ____________________
7. Thomas n'est pas franc. (parler) ____________________

NOM ______________________ DATE ______________________

5. L'interview. Un représentant d'Air France va interviewer les étudiants suivants. Dites dans quel ordre chacun va être interviewé. *[Section C, p. 443]*

❖ Monique (3e) *Monique est la troisième.*

1. Jacques (1er) ______________
2. Sylvie (2e) ______________
3. Henri (7e) ______________
4. Brigitte (8e) ______________
5. Paul (10e) ______________
6. Suzanne (12e) ______________
7. Hélène (15e) ______________
8. Marylène (20e) ______________
9. Roger (21e) ______________
10. Marc (22e) ______________

6. Des personnalités. Informez-vous sur les personnes suivantes et dites ce qu'elles font. Pour cela, utilisez les verbes entre parenthèses dans une construction employant l'infinitif. Notez que vos phrases peuvent être affirmatives ou négatives. Soyez logique! *[Section D, p. 444]*

❖ Vous êtes généreux. (hésiter / aider vos amis) *Vous n'hésitez pas à aider vos amis.*

1. Ces employés sont ponctuels. (commencer / travailler à neuf heures)

   ____

2. Caroline est sportive. (apprendre / faire du ski nautique)

   ____

3. Je suis travailleur. (s'arrêter / étudier)

   ____

4. Tu n'es pas ambitieux. (chercher / avoir des responsabilités)

   ____

5. Vous êtes consciencieux. (oublier / faire vos devoirs)

   ____

6. Ces étudiants sont paresseux. (essayer / faire des progrès)

   ____

7. Cette artiste est créatrice. (cesser / avoir des idées originales)

   ____

8. Nous sommes irrésolus *(indecisive).* (hésiter / prendre des décisions)

   ____

COMMUNICATION

Olivier va vous parler de lui-même. Il va aussi vous poser des questions. Répondez à ses questions.

1. Je suis assez sportif. Et toi? En ce moment, j'apprends à faire de la voile. Et toi, quels sports apprends-tu en ce moment? Quand as-tu appris à nager? à faire du ski?

2. En général, je suis un étudiant travailleur mais pas toujours. Et toi? Quelles sont les choses que tu oublies de faire? Quelles sont les choses que tu refuses de faire? Est-ce que tu regrettes d'être à l'université? Pourquoi ou pourquoi pas?

3. J'ai pris de bonnes résolutions récemment. Par exemple, j'ai décidé de faire du jogging tous les jours. J'ai aussi cessé de fumer. Est-ce qu'il y a des choses que tu as décidé de faire? Quoi? Est-ce qu'il y a des choses que tu t'es arrêté(e) de faire? Quoi?

4. Qu'est-ce que tu as décidé de faire cet été? Et après l'université? Est-ce que tu vas continuer à étudier le français l'année prochaine? Quelles choses vas-tu continuer à faire?

NOM ______________________________ DATE ______________________

Leçon 29. Dans dix ans

1. Sur les Champs-Élysées. Les personnes suivantes se promènent sur les Champs-Élysées. Dites qui elles aperçoivent ou qui elles ont aperçu. Utilisez le verbe **apercevoir** au présent (phrases 1 à 4) et au passé composé (phrases 5 et 6). *[Section A, p. 451]*

Présent

1. Nous ______________________ un ami d'université.
2. J'______________________ mon patron *(boss).*
3. André ______________________ le copain de sa sœur.
4. Mes amis ______________________ des touristes américains.

Passé composé

5. Hier, j'______________________ mon professeur d'histoire.
6. La semaine dernière, nous ______________________ un acteur célèbre *(famous).*

2. Vouloir, c'est pouvoir! *(Where there's a will, there's a way!)* Dites que les personnes suivantes réaliseront leurs projets. Utilisez le futur des verbes soulignés. *[Section B, p. 452]*

❖ Paul veut <u>habiter</u> à Paris. ***Il habitera à Paris.***

1. Michel veut <u>gagner</u> beaucoup d'argent. ______________________
2. Marc veut <u>se marier.</u> ______________________
3. Nous voulons <u>voyager.</u> ______________________
4. Je veux <u>réussir</u> dans mes études. ______________________
5. Ces étudiants veulent <u>choisir</u> une profession intéressante. ______________________

   ____
6. Sophie veut <u>apprendre</u> le russe. ______________________
7. Mes cousins veulent <u>maigrir.</u> ______________________
8. Je veux <u>écrire</u> un roman. ______________________
9. Vous voulez <u>vivre</u> à Paris. ______________________
10. Tu veux t'<u>amuser.</u> ______________________
11. Marc veut <u>partir</u> pour Tahiti. ______________________

3. Cet été. Dites ce que les étudiants vont faire cet été en complétant la première phrase avec le futur du premier verbe entre parenthèses. Puis, soyez logique et complétez la deuxième phrase avec la forme affirmative ou négative du futur du deuxième verbe entre parenthèses. *[Section B, p. 452]*

❖ (voyager / rester) Jean *voyagera*. Il *ne restera pas* chez lui.

1. (travailler / se reposer) Nous ________________. Nous ________________________.
2. (étudier / apprendre) Tu ________________ à l'Alliance française. Tu ________________________ l'espagnol.
3. (rester / partir) Vous ________________ chez vous. Vous ________________________ en vacances.
4. (passer / connaître) Je ______________ un mois en France. Je ____________________ des Français.
5. (suivre / grossir) Ces garçons ______________ un régime. Ils ____________________.
6. (acheter / se promener) Sylvie ______________ un vélo. Elle ____________________ dans la campagne.

4. Des projets. Décrivez les projets des personnes suivantes. Utilisez le futur des verbes suggérés. *[Section C, p. 456]*

aller avoir être faire

❖ Tu *seras* le président de ta compagnie. Tu *auras* beaucoup de responsabilités.

1. Nous ______________ un voyage en Asie. Nous ______________ au Tibet.
2. Christine ______________ millionnaire. Elle ______________ une Rolls Royce.
3. Mes copains ______________ beaucoup de vacances. Ils ______________ de la planche à voile tous les jours.
4. Je ______________ acteur de cinéma. J'______________ beaucoup d'admiratrices.
5. Vous ______________ à Monte Carlo. Vous ______________ fortune!

5. Quand? Dites quand vous ferez les choses suivantes. Utilisez le futur. *[Section C, p. 456]*

❖ aller en vacances ***J'irai en vacances en juin (dans deux mois, après les examens...).***

1. aller à la bibliothèque ____
2. faire les courses ____
3. avoir un examen ____
4. voir mes parents ____
5. obtenir mon diplôme ____
6. savoir piloter un avion ____
7. recevoir une lettre ____
8. courir dans une course *(race)* ____

NOM ______________________ DATE ______________________

6. Plus tard! (*Later!*) Pour le moment, les personnes suivantes ne font pas certaines choses. Dites quand elles feront ces choses. Utilisez le futur. *[Section C, p. 456]*

❖ Thomas ne va pas à la plage. ***Il ira à la plage*** dimanche.

1. Tu ne viens pas chez moi. ______________________ à trois heures.
2. Sylvie ne voit pas ses amis. ______________________ ce week-end.
3. Émilie n'envoie pas cette lettre. ______________________ demain.
4. Les étudiants ne doivent pas étudier. ______________________ pour l'examen.
5. Charles ne veut pas se reposer. ______________________ après le dîner.
6. Je ne peux pas t'aider. ______________________ dans deux heures.
7. Albert ne sait pas nager. ______________________ s'il prend des leçons.

7. Si... Dites ce que chaque personne fera dans les circonstances suivantes. Utilisez le futur et votre imagination! *[Section D, p. 460]*

❖ Si nous allons en France, ***nous visiterons Paris.***

1. Si Guillaume a une voiture, ______________________
2. Si Marie-Laure n'a pas son diplôme, ______________________
3. Si Raoul n'a rien à faire ce soir, ______________________
4. Si Claire et Élisabeth ont le temps, ______________________
5. Si François et Alain gagnent à la loterie, ______________________
6. Si Jean a de l'argent, ______________________

8. Conséquences. Certaines actions provoquent certaines conséquences. Expliquez cela selon le modèle. *[Section E, p. 461]*

❖ (réussir / étudier plus) ***Charles réussira quand il étudiera plus.***

1. (gagner de l'argent / travailler)

   Je ______________________

2. (maigrir / faire de l'exercice)

   Vous ______________________

3. (chercher du travail / avoir son diplôme)

   Catherine ______________________

4. (envoyer cette lettre / aller à la poste)

   Tu ______________________

5. (envoyer un télégramme / savoir la date de notre départ)

   Nous ____

6. (avoir des responsabilités / être la présidente de sa compagnie)

   Thérèse ____

COMMUNICATION

Jean-François vous pose des questions sur vos projets. Répondez-lui.

1. Qu'est-ce que tu feras ce week-end s'il fait beau? Où iras-tu? Et qu'est-ce que tu feras s'il pleut?

   ____

   ____

   ____

2. Qu'est-ce que tu feras quand tu auras ton diplôme? Et si tu n'as pas ton diplôme?

   ____

   ____

   ____

3. Qu'est-ce que tu feras avec ton argent quand tu auras un travail? Est-ce que tu t'achèteras une nouvelle voiture?

   ____

   ____

   ____

4. Quand est-ce que tu te marieras? Combien d'enfants auras-tu?

   ____

   ____

5. Qu'est-ce que tu feras dans dix ans? Où habiteras-tu? Est-ce que tu gagneras beaucoup d'argent? Comment est-ce que tu le dépenseras?

   ____

   ____

   ____

6. Qu'est-ce que tu feras quand tu seras à la retraite *(retired)*? Qu'est-ce que tu ne feras pas?

   ____

   ____

   ____

NOM ______________________________ DATE ____________________

Leçon 30. Si j'avais de l'argent...

1. Les vacances. Dites si oui ou non vous feriez les choses suivantes si c'étaient les vacances. Utilisez le conditionnel. *[Section A, p. 468]*

❖ travailler? *Oui, je travaillerais.*
ou: *Non, je ne travaillerais pas.*

1. étudier? ______________________________
2. lire des livres français? ______________________________
3. jouer au tennis? ______________________________
4. sortir souvent? ______________________________
5. dormir beaucoup? ______________________________
6. aller à la piscine? ______________________________
7. faire des promenades? ______________________________
8. être de mauvaise humeur? ______________________________
9. avoir beaucoup de rendez-vous? ______________________________
10. voir vos cousins? ______________________________
11. envoyer des lettres à vos amis? ______________________________
12. courir tous les jours? ______________________________

2. Avec plus d'argent. Tout le monde a une idée de ce qu'on peut faire avec plus d'argent. Dites ce que feraient les personnes suivantes. Utilisez le conditionnel. *[Section A, p. 468]*

❖ nous / faire un voyage en Grèce.
Nous ferions un voyage en Grèce.

1. Jacques / aller en Italie pendant les vacances

   ____

2. Anne et Nicole / être généreuses avec leurs amies

   ____

3. je / faire des économies

   ____

4. tu / vouloir voyager souvent

   ____

5. Alain / avoir un appartement à Paris

____

6. vous / envoyer de l'argent à vos parents

____

7. mes parents / pouvoir s'acheter une nouvelle voiture

____

8. nous / voir toutes les merveilles *(marvels)* du monde

____

9. Antoine / devenir un mécène *(patron of the arts)*

____

10. M. Richard / devoir payer plus d'impôts *(taxes)*

____

3. Commentaires personnels. Complétez les phrases avec une expression personnelle. *[Sections A, B, C, pp. 468, 470, 472]*

1. Si je n'allais pas à l'université, ______________________________
2. Si j'avais beaucoup de loisirs, ______________________________
3. Si je voulais être riche, ______________________________
4. Si mes amis et moi passions les vacances en Suisse, nous ______________________________
5. Si le professeur était malade, ______________________________
6. Si mes parents étaient millionnaires, ______________________________

4. Si... Les personnes suivantes ne font pas certaines choses. Expliquez ce qu'elles feraient si leur situation changeait. *[Sections A, B, C, pp. 468, 470, 472]*

❖ Tu n'as pas d'argent. Tu ne voyages pas.
Si tu avais de l'argent, tu voyagerais.

1. Paul n'a pas de voiture. Il ne va pas à la plage.

____

2. Nous ne sommes pas en vacances. Nous ne nous reposons pas.

____

3. Je ne travaille pas. Je ne gagne pas d'argent.

____

NOM ____________________ DATE ____________________

4. Sylvie ne se repose pas. Elle n'est pas en bonne santé.

____

5. Vous ne travaillez pas. Vous ne réussissez pas.

____

6. Jacques ne suit pas de régime. Il ne maigrit pas.

____

5. Annonces. Les personnes suivantes ont fait certaines annonces. Décrivez ces annonces selon le modèle. *[Section B, p. 470]*

❖ Paul / dire / passer cet après-midi
Paul a dit qu'il passerait cet après-midi.

1. mes cousins / téléphoner / venir demain

____

2. je / dire / répondre à ta lettre

____

3. Jacques et Émilie / annoncer / se marier en juin

____

4. Antoine / écrire / aller en Suisse pendant les vacances

____

6. Conditions. Complétez les phrases suivantes avec la forme et le temps approprié (présent, imparfait, futur, conditionnel) du verbe entre parenthèses. *[Section C, p. 472]*

1. (rester) Si je ____________________ chez moi cet été, je chercherai du travail.
2. (gagner) Qu'est-ce que tu ferais si tu ____________________ à la loterie?
3. (louer) Si nous allons en France, nous ____________________ une voiture.
4. (étudier) J'____________________ plus sérieusement si j'étais toi!
5. (faire) Si vous ____________________ attention, vous ne feriez pas d'erreur.
6. (aller) Nous ____________________ à la plage, s'il faisait beau!
7. (avoir) Si François ____________________ son appareil-photo, il prendra des photos.
8. (être) Si vous ____________________ plus généreux, vous aideriez vos amis!

7. Activités. Dites ce que font les personnes suivantes en complétant les phrases avec le présent d'un des verbes suggérés. *[Section D, p. 473]*

conduire	**construire**	**détruire**	**produire**	**traduire**

1. Cécile et Carmen sont interprètes aux Nations Unies. Elles ____________________ le discours *(speech)* du délégué mexicain.
2. Tu as décidé d'habiter en France. Tu ____________________ une maison en Normandie.
3. Mon oncle est vigneron *(wine grower).* Il ____________________ un excellent vin.
4. Vous êtes millionnaire. Vous ____________________ une Rolls Royce.
5. Ces enfants sont polis. Ils se ____________________ bien.
6. Je nettoie mon bureau. Je ____________________ toute les vieilles lettres.

COMMUNICATION

Hélène vous demande ce que vous feriez et ne feriez pas dans certaines circonstances. Répondez à ses questions.

1. Que ferais-tu si tu avais beaucoup d'argent?

   ____

   ____

2. Que ferais-tu si tu gagnais un voyage pour faire le tour du monde (*to go around the world)?*

   ____

   ____

3. Que ferais-tu si tu n'étais pas étudiant(e)?

   ____

   ____

4. Que ferais-tu si tu étais un(e) acteur (actrice) célèbre *(famous)?*

   ____

   ____

5. Que ferais-tu si tu pouvais changer le monde?

   ____

   ____

6. Que ferais-tu si tu n'avais plus que six mois à vivre?

   ____

   ____

NOM ______________________________ DATE ______________________

UNITÉ 11. LE MONDE ACTUEL

Leçon 31. Conversation avec un Québécois

1. Obligations personnelles? Dites si oui ou non vous devez faire les choses suivantes. Commencez vos phrases avec **il faut que** ou **il ne faut pas que.** *[Section A, p. 486]*

❖ vendre mon livre de français — ***Il faut que je vende mon livre de français.***
ou: ***Il ne faut pas que je vende mon livre de français.***

1. étudier ce soir ______________________________
2. travailler pendant les vacances ______________________________
3. maigrir ______________________________
4. réussir à l'examen de français ______________________________
5. perdre mon temps ______________________________
6. rendre visite à mes cousins cet été ______________________________
7. réfléchir à l'avenir ______________________________
8. m'impatienter ______________________________
9. me reposer ______________________________

2. Les bons conseils. Donnez des conseils aux personnes suivantes. Commencez vos phrases avec **il faut** ou **il ne faut pas** et le subjonctif du verbe entre parenthèses. *[Section A, p. 486]*

❖ (grossir) ***Il ne faut pas*** que vous ***grossissiez.***

1. (finir) ______________ que tu ______________ tes cours.
2. (dormir) ______________ que les étudiants ______________ en classe.
3. (écrire) ______________ que Paul ______________ à sa cousine pour son anniversaire.
4. (dire) ______________ que nous ______________ la vérité.
5. (partir) ______________ que les employés ______________ avant cinq heures.
6. (lire) ______________ que tu ______________ les lettres de ton camarade de chambre.
7. (conduire) ______________ que je ______________ prudemment *(carefully).*
8. (offrir) ______________ que nous ______________ un cadeau au professeur pour son anniversaire.

3. Les conseils. Donnez des conseils aux personnes suivantes. Pour cela, complétez les phrases avec le subjonctif des verbes entre parenthèses. (Attention: au subjonctif, ces verbes ont deux radicaux *[stems]!*) *[Sections B, C, pp. 488, 491]*

1. (boire) Il est bon que vous ____________________ du jus d'orange.

   Il est bon que ces athlètes ____________________ de l'eau minérale.

2. (obtenir) Il est important que j'____________________ un «A» en français.

   Il est nécessaire que nous ____________________ notre diplôme.

3. (apprendre) Il est essentiel que vous ____________________ à conduire.

   Il est utile que ces étudiants ____________________ à programmer.

4. (voir) Il est normal que tu ____________________ tes parents avant de partir.

   Il est préférable que nous ____________________ nos professeurs avant l'examen.

4. Oui ou non? Lisez ce que les personnes suivantes veulent faire. Dites ensuite si oui ou non elles doivent faire ces choses. Étudiez le modèle. *[Sections B, C, pp. 488, 491]*

❖ Tu organises une fête chez toi. (nécessaire / nettoyer ta chambre)

Il (n')est (pas) nécessaire que tu nettoies ta chambre.

1. Nous avons la grippe. (bon / boire du thé chaud)

   ____

2. Vous voulez réussir à l'examen. (indispensable / obtenir un «A»)

   ____

3. Jacqueline a mal à la tête. (nécessaire / voir un médecin)

   ____

4. Les Canadiens francophones veulent maintenir leur identité. (essentiel / maintenir leurs traditions)

   ____

NOM ______________________________ DATE ____________________

5. L'interview. Imaginez qu'une compagnie française recrute du personnel pour sa succursale *(branch)* aux États-Unis. Le chef du personnel va passer sur votre campus pour interviewer des étudiants. Dites que chacun doit avoir certains documents sur lui. Utilisez le subjonctif d'**avoir.** Dites aussi si oui ou non l'étudiant(e) doit faire certaines choses ou prendre certaines précautions. Utilisez le subjonctif d'**être** dans une phrase affirmative ou négative. *[Section D, p. 493]*

❖ Michèle (une carte d'identité / en retard)
Il faut que Michèle ait une carte d'identité. Il ne faut pas qu'elle soit en retard.

1. Paul (une photo / à l'heure) ______________________________

   ____

2. Marc et Robert (leurs diplômes / arrogants) ______________________________

   ____

3. nous (les résultats des examens / polis avec l'interviewer) ______________________________

   ____

4. vous (vos notes / timides) ______________________________

   ____

5. tu (une lettre de recommandation / nerveux [nerveuse]) ______________________________

   ____

6. je (mon curriculum vitae / sûr[e] de moi) ______________________________

   ____

6. Non! Un(e) camarade vous demande s'il (si elle) peut faire certaines choses. Répondez-lui négativement selon le modèle. *[Section E, p. 494]*

❖ Est-ce que je peux lire ton journal?
Non, je ne veux pas que tu lises mon journal.

1. Est-ce que je peux prendre ton auto?

   ____

2. Est-ce que je peux voir tes photos?

   ____

3. Est-ce que je peux venir chez toi après le dîner?

   ____

4. Est-ce que je peux boire cette bière?

   ____

7. Des souhaits. Décrivez ce que les personnes suivantes souhaitent pour les autres personnes. *[Section E, p. 494]*

❖ Le professeur / vouloir (nous / être à l'heure)
Le professeur veut que nous soyons à l'heure.

1. mes parents / souhaiter (je / avoir un bon travail)

____

2. je / préférer (vous / venir chez moi jeudi soir)

____

3. Mme Dupont / permettre (son fils / prendre la voiture)

____

4. Charles / désirer (ses copains / sortir avec lui dimanche)

____

COMMUNICATION

Danièle vous pose des questions sur ce que vous devez faire. Répondez à chacune de ses questions en faisant deux phrases.

❖ Qu'est-ce que tu dois faire ce week-end?

Il faut que je nettoie ma chambre.
Il faut aussi que je rende visite à mes grands-parents.

1. Qu'est-ce que tu dois faire ce soir?

____

____

2. Qu'est-ce que tu dois faire avant la fin du mois?

____

____

3. Qu'est-ce que tu dois faire avant les vacances?

____

____

4. Qu'est-ce que tu dois faire pour obtenir ton diplôme?

____

____

5. Qu'est-ce que tu dois faire pour trouver du travail?

____

____

NOM ______________________________ DATE ____________________

Leçon 32. Français ou Européens?

1. Des convictions. Expliquez les convictions des personnes suivantes. Utilisez le verbe **croire** aux mêmes temps (présent, imparfait, futur, passé composé) que le verbe souligné. *[Section A, p. 502]*

❖ Je *croirai* Jacques quand il dira la vérité.

1. Nous ____________ Véronique parce qu'elle est sincère.
2. Est-ce que le juge ____________ les témoins quand ils ont décrit l'accident?
3. Je ____________ toujours ce que mon professeur dit.
4. Tu ____________ au Père Noël *(Santa Claus)* quand tu étais enfant?
5. Est-ce que tes amis ____________ tout ce qu'ils lisent dans le journal?
6. Vous ____________ Monique quand vous parlerez à sa sœur.
7. Florence ____________ son copain quand il lui a raconté cette histoire *(story)* extraordinaire.

2. Oui ou non? Est-ce que les choses suivantes sont importantes pour vous? Exprimez votre opinion en utilisant l'adjectif entre parenthèses dans des phrases affirmatives ou négatives. *[Section B, p. 503]*

❖ faire du sport (bon) — ***Il est bon que je fasse du sport.***
(Il n'est pas bon que je fasse du sport.)

1. faire des progrès en français (nécessaire)

   ____

2. aller à l'université (utile)

   ____

3. pouvoir gagner beaucoup d'argent (indispensable)

   ____

4. savoir jouer au tennis (essentiel)

   ____

5. vouloir être indépendant(e) (normal)

   ____

3. Votre opinion. Exprimez votre opinion sur les sujets suivants. Pour cela, commencez vos phrases avec **je crois que** ou **je ne crois pas que.** Utilisez l'indicatif ou le subjonctif des verbes soulignés. *[Sections B, C, pp. 503, 504]*

❖ L'économie américaine est en danger? *Oui, je crois qu'elle est en danger.*
ou: *Non, je ne crois pas qu'elle soit en danger.*

1. La France est une grande puissance *(power)?*

   ____

2. Les Américains sont très patriotes?

   ____

3. Le président sait ce qu'il fait?

   ____

4. Les Martiens veulent conquérir le monde?

   ____

5. On va vers une dépression économique?

   ____

6. On peut arrêter (*stop*) le progrès?

   ____

4. Réactions. Chacun des événements suivants provoque une double réaction: chez les personnes qui sont directement concernées par cet événement et chez d'autres personnes. Décrivez cette double réaction selon le modèle. *[Section D, p. 506]*

❖ Pierre réussit à ses examens.
Pierre est fier ***de réussir à ses examens.***
Ses parents sont fiers ***qu'il réussisse à ses examens.***

1. Jacqueline va passer l'été au Canada. Elle est heureuse ______________________________

   Son frère est heureux ______________________________

2. Henri part en vacances. Il est content ______________________________

   Ses amis sont désolés ______________________________

3. Marc a un accident. Il est furieux ______________________________

   Ses parents sont furieux ______________________________

4. Je pars. Je suis triste ______________________________

   Mes amies sont tristes ______________________________

5. Tu fais des progrès en français. Tu es heureux ______________________________

   Ton professeur est heureux ______________________________

6. Philippe est malade. Il a peur ______________________________

   Sa mère a peur ______________________________

NOM ______________________ DATE ______________

5. Pourquoi? Les personnes suivantes font certaines choses pour aider d'autres personnes. Expliquez cela en utilisant **pour que** + subjonctif selon le modèle. *[Section E, p. 508]*

❖ (tu vas à la plage)
Je te prête ma bicyclette ***pour que tu ailles à la plage.***

1. (je vais en ville)

   Ma mère me prête sa voiture ______________________

2. (vous achetez ce livre)

   Je vous donne cinquante francs ______________________

3. (leurs enfants vont à l'université)

   Mes parents travaillent ______________________

4. (tu fais la connaissance de mon copain allemand)

   Je t'invite ______________________

5. (vous rencontrez mes amis)

   Je vous invite ______________________

6. (il fait une promenade)

   Tu prêtes ta voiture à Charles ______________________

7. (ils ont des nouvelles)

   Sylvie écrit à ses parents ______________________

6. La correspondance. Les personnes suivantes écrivent à d'autres personnes pour certaines raisons. Expliquez cela en utilisant les conjonctions suggérées et l'indicatif ou le subjonctif. *[Section E, p. 508]*

❖ Christine / à Paul / pour que / il / lui envoyer l'adresse de son frère
Christine écrit à Paul pour qu'il lui envoie l'adresse de son frère.

1. nous / au professeur / pour que / il / nous écrire des lettres de recommandation

   ____

2. je / à mes cousins / avant que / ils / partir en vacances

   ____

3. tu / à ta cousine / parce que / elle / venir de se marier

   ____

4. vous /à vos amis / pendant que / ils / être à Paris

   ____

5. M. Martin / à sa fille / depuis que / elle / être étudiante à Paris

   ____

6. Janine / à ses cousines / pour que / elles / venir chez elle pendant les vacances

   ____

7. Les attitudes. Complétez les phrases suivantes avec l'indicatif ou le subjonctif des verbes entre parenthèses. *[Section F, p. 510]*

1. (aller) Philippe ne sait pas que tu ____________________ en Europe cet été.
2. (venir) J'aimerais que vous ____________________ chez moi ce soir.
3. (faire) Le professeur déplore que nous ne ____________________ pas de progrès.
4. (être) Je m'impatiente parce que mes amis ne ____________________ pas à l'heure.
5. (connaître) Jean-Michel est très heureux depuis qu'il ____________________ Jeannette.
6. (pouvoir) Nous sommes contents que vous ____________________ passer les vacances avec nous.
7. (vouloir) Je doute que Marc ____________________ te prêter son auto.
8. (dire) Henri est sûr que vous ne ____________________ pas la vérité.
9. (partir) Je téléphonerai avant que tu ____________________ en Angleterre.
10. (savoir) Il faut absolument que vous ____________________ pourquoi je ne suis pas d'accord avec vous!

COMMUNICATION

Exprimez vos opinions et vos attitudes sur les sujets suivants. Utilisez des expressions comme **je pense, je doute, je suis content(e), j'aimerais, je souhaite,** etc.

❖ votre cours de français

En général, je suis content(e) de suivre ce cours. Je pense que le professeur est compétent. Je déplore parfois que les examens soient difficiles.

1. votre vie à l'université

____

____

2. vos relations avec vos amis

____

____

3. votre avenir

____

____

4. la politique internationale des États-Unis

____

____

NOM ______________________________ DATE ______________________

Leçon 33. La nouvelle technologie

1. Des relations personnelles. Décrivez les relations entre les personnes suivantes et les personnes entre parenthèses. Pour cela, complétez les phrases avec les pronoms compléments d'objet direct ou indirect qui conviennent. *[Section A, p. 516]*

❖ (sa cousine) Alain *lui* téléphone parfois, mais il ne *l'* invite jamais.

1. (mes voisins) Je ne _______ invite pas parce que je ne _______ connais pas très bien.
2. (ton copain) Nous _______ avons vu hier. Nous _______ avons donné notre numéro de téléphone.
3. (Nathalie) Je _______ ai demandé si elle voulait dîner avec moi quand je _______ ai rencontrée ce matin.
4. (les étudiants) Le professeur _______ aide. Il _______ explique la grammaire.
5. (moi) Tu _______ écoutes, mais est-ce que tu _______ comprends?
6. (toi) Je _______ trouve sympathique. Je vais _______ inviter à ma fête d'anniversaire.

2. Des services. Informez-vous sur les personnes suivantes. Dites à un(e) ami(e) français(e) de faire ou de ne pas faire les choses entre parenthèses. Pour cela, utilisez l'impératif dans des phrases affirmatives ou négatives et un pronom complément. Soyez logique! *[Section A, p. 516]*

❖ Caroline dort. (téléphoner) ***Ne lui téléphone pas!***

❖ Henri veut dîner avec toi. (inviter) ***Invite-le!***

1. Jacques a besoin d'argent. (prêter) ______________________ 100 francs!
2. Sylvie et Brigitte sont perplexes. (donner) ______________________ des conseils.
3. Thomas n'est pas chez lui. (rendre visite) ______________________
4. Ces gens ne disent pas la vérité. (écouter) ______________________
5. Nathalie ne va pas venir. (attendre) ______________________
6. Je ne comprends pas ce logiciel. (aider) ______________________
7. Nous avons besoin de compliments. (critiquer) ______________________
8. Je suis végétarien. (donner) ______________________ de viande.

3. **Bonnes vacances!** C'est bientôt les vacances. Lisez ce que font les personnes suivantes. Refaites les phrases en utilisant deux pronoms compléments pour remplacer les mots soulignés. *[Section B, p. 518]*

❖ Je donne son adresse à mes amis. ***Je la leur donne.***

1. Jacques donne son adresse à Catherine.

____

2. Tu envoies un fax à tes amis.

____

3. Francine donne son numéro de téléphone à Roger.

____

4. Nous rendons les livres à la bibliothécaire *(librarian).*

____

5. Marc vend sa machine à écrire à son camarade de chambre.

____

6. Le professeur rend l'examen aux étudiants.

____

7. Vous envoyez vos bagages *(luggage)* à vos parents.

____

8. Jean-Pierre explique ses projets de vacances à ses amis.

____

4. **Votre meilleur(e) ami(e).** Dites si oui ou non votre meilleur(e) ami(e) fait les choses suivantes pour vous. *[Section B, p. 518]*

❖ prêter ses CD? ***Oui, il (elle) me les prête.***

ou: ***Non, il (elle) ne me les prête pas.***

1. prêter sa voiture? ____
2. prêter son VTT? ____
3. donner des conseils? ____
4. dire toujours la vérité? ____
5. demander votre opinion? ____
6. raconter sa vie? ____
7. montrer ses photos? ____

NOM ______________________________ DATE ____________________

5. S'il te plaît! Imaginez qu'un ami vous parle des choses qu'il a. Demandez-les-lui, en utilisant les verbes entre parenthèses. *[Section C, p. 520]*

❖ J'ai une nouvelle moto. (prêter) ***Prête-la-moi, s'il te plaît!***

1. J'ai un vélomoteur. (prêter) ______________________
2. J'ai un logiciel intéressant. (montrer) ______________________
3. J'ai des belles photos. (montrer) ______________________
4. J'ai un vieux vélo. (donner) ______________________
5. J'ai des cassettes de musique pop. (vendre) ______________________
6. J'ai une guitare. (vendre) ______________________

6. Qu'est-ce qu'il doit faire? Robert vous demande s'il doit faire certaines choses. Répondez-lui affirmativement en utilisant deux pronoms compléments. *[Section C, p. 520]*

❖ Je prête mon vélo à Paul? Oui, ***prête-le-lui.***

❖ J'explique la leçon aux étudiants? Oui, ***explique-la-leur.***

1. Je montre mes photos à Denise? Oui, ______________________
2. Je rends ce livre au professeur? Oui, ______________________
3. Je dis la vérité à mes parents? Oui, ______________________
4. Je vends mon ordinateur à Luc? Oui, ______________________
5. Je prête ma voiture aux voisins? Oui, ______________________

7. Oui ou non? Répondez aux questions suivantes affirmativement ou négativement. Utilisez **en** et un pronom dans vos réponses. *[Section D, p. 521]*

❖ Mme Boutron est vice-présidente d'une banque. Elle prête de l'argent à ses clients?
Oui, elle leur en prête.

1. M. Nadou est pharmacien. Il vend de l'aspirine à ses clients?

   ____

2. Le professeur est strict. Il donne de bonnes notes à ce mauvais étudiant?

   ____

3. Sylvie est végétarienne. Elle sert de la viande à ses amis?

   ____

4. Ce médecin est compétent. Il nous a donné de bons conseils?

   ____

5. Tes parents sont généreux. Ils t'ont envoyé de l'argent?

   ____

COMMUNICATION

Nicole va vous poser des questions sur vos relations avec d'autres personnes. Répondez à ses questions.

1. As-tu un(e) camarade de chambre sympathique? Quelles choses fais-tu pour lui (elle)? Qu'est-ce qu'il (elle) fait pour toi?

____

____

____

2. Est-ce que tu connais bien tes voisins? Qu'est-ce que tu fais pour eux? Qu'est-ce que tu ne fais pas?

____

____

____

3. En général, est-ce que tu prêtes tes affaires *(things)* à tes copains? Est-ce qu'ils te rendent ces choses en bon état *(condition)?* Qu'est-ce que tu ferais si ce n'était pas le cas?

____

____

____

4. Si tu avais une voiture de sport, est-ce que tu la prêterais à tes copains? Si oui, à quelles conditions? Si non, pourquoi pas?

____

____

____

5. Est-ce que tu demandes parfois de l'argent à tes parents? Quand est-ce que tu leur en as demandé? Pourquoi faire?

____

____

____

NOM ______________________________ DATE ______________________

Révision 4: Leçons 28–33

By completing this series of short tests, you will be able to check your progress in French. Correct your work using the Answer Key at the back of the *Cahier d'activités.* If you make any mistakes on these tests, you may want to review the lesson sections indicated in brackets.

PARTIE A. STRUCTURES

Test 1. Adjectifs irréguliers. Complete the following sentences with the appropriate forms of the adjectives in parentheses. *[28–A]*

1. (franc) Cette personne est ________________.
2. (gentil) Mes nièces sont ________________.
3. (fou) Cette idée est absolument ________________.
4. (ponctuel) La secrétaire est ________________.
5. (sérieux) Ces étudiants sont ________________.
6. (paresseux) Janine et Thérèse sont ________________.

Test 2. L'emploi de l'infinitif après les verbes, les adjectifs et les noms. Complete the following sentences with **à** or **de,** if necessary. *[25–D]*

1. Nous apprenons ____ faire du ski.
2. Charles hésite ____ répondre.
3. Paul a oublié ____ téléphoner à Claire.
4. Albert espère ____ sortir ce week-end.
5. Martin s'est arrêté ____ fumer.
6. Henri rêve ____ faire un voyage cet été.
7. Mon cousin commence ____ étudier le russe.
8. Thomas refuse ____ travailler ce week-end.
9. Est-ce que tu as décidé ____ venir avec nous?
10. Nous avons réussi ____ trouver du travail.
11. Nous devons ____ partir avant midi.
12. Vous avez demandé à Jacqueline ____ nous contacter?
13. J'essaie ____ faire de l'exercice tous les jours.

Test 3. Les pronoms compléments d'objet direct et indirect. Complete the following sentences with the appropriate direct- or indirect-object pronouns replacing the person in parentheses. *[33–A]*

1. (Christine) Paul ________ connaît, mais il ne ________ parle pas souvent.
2. (mon cousin) Je ________ téléphone. Je ________ invite à dîner.
3. (mes amies) Je ________ trouve sympathiques. Je ________ rends souvent visite.
4. (Pierre et Jacques) Henri ________ aide. Il ________ prête ses notes.
5. (moi) Mes parents ________ aident, mais ils ne ________ prêtent pas toujours leur voiture.
6. (Sylvie et moi) Est-ce que tu ________ invites? Est-ce que tu ________ montres tes photos?

Test 4. L'ordre des pronoms compléments. Rewrite the following sentences, replacing the underlined words with two object pronouns. Be sure to use the correct pronoun sequence. *[33–B, C, D]*

1. Je prête mes disques à Marc. ________________________________
2. Paul vend sa guitare à Béatrice. ________________________________
3. Jacqueline donne les magazines à ses cousines. ________________________________
4. Anne dit la vérité à ses parents. ________________________________
5. Charles me prête sa bicyclette. ________________________________
6. Montre ton nouveau logiciel à Richard! ________________________________
7. Prête ta voiture à ses amis. ________________________________
8. Donnez-moi ce livre. ________________________________
9. J'invite mes amis au café. ________________________________
10. Nous donnons du chocolat aux enfants. ________________________________
11. Nous t'amenons à la bibliothèque. ________________________________
12. Je vous montre des photos. ________________________________

NOM ______________________________ DATE ______________________

PARTIE B. VERBES

Test 5. Les formes du futur. Complete the following sentences with the appropriate future forms of the verbs in parentheses. *[29–B, C]*

1. (habiter) L'année prochaine, j'__________________ avec mon frère.

   Nous __________________ dans un appartement.

2. (réussir) Tu __________________, mais tes amis ne __________________ pas.

3. (vendre) Charles __________________ son livre de maths.

   Est-ce que vous __________________ vos livres aussi?

4. (sortir) Je __________________ avec Denise. Nous __________________ ce soir.

5. (être) Vous __________________ riches et moi je __________________ heureux.

6. (avoir) Mon frère __________________ son diplôme en juin.

   Quand __________________-vous votre diplôme?

7. (faire) Je __________________ les exercices de grammaire demain.

   Et toi, quand est-ce que tu les __________________?

8. (aller) Nous __________________ en France cet été.

   Mes parents __________________ à Québec.

9. (venir) Tu __________________ à 4 heures.

   À quelle heure est-ce que tes amis __________________?

10. (recevoir) Je __________________ mon passeport en juin.

    Et vous, quand est-ce que vous __________________ votre passeport?

11. (pouvoir) Est-ce que vos amis __________________ sortir ce soir?

    Moi, je ne __________________ pas.

12. (courir) Ce week-end mes amis __________________ une distance de dix kilomètres.

    Est-ce que tu __________________ avec eux?

Test 6. Le conditionnel. Complete the following sentences with the appropriate conditional forms of the verbs in parentheses. *[30–A]*

1. (acheter) Avec mille dollars, j'_______________ une moto. Mon frère _______________ un téléviseur et une chaîne stéréo. Et vous, qu'est-ce que vous _______________?
2. (réussir) Avec plus de patience, nous _______________ à l'examen. Toi aussi, tu _______________ et tes amis _______________ aussi.
3. (être) Avec plus de chance, mon père _______________ millionnaire.
4. (aller) Avec plus d'argent, nous _______________ en France.
5. (avoir) Avec plus d'ambition, tu _______________ plus de responsabilités.
6. (faire) À ta place, je _______________ mes devoirs!
7. (pouvoir) Est-ce que vous _______________ venir à six heures?
8. (vouloir) Nous _______________ voir vos photos.

Test 7. L'emploi des temps avec *quand* et *si*. Read the sentences below carefully and determine whether the missing verbs should be in the present, the future, the conditional, or the imperfect. Fill in the blanks with one of the following: **travaille, travaillera, travaillerait, travaillait.** [29–D, E; 30–C]

1. Quand Paul _______________, il habitera à New York.
2. Si Suzanne _______________ cet été, elle ne voyagera pas avec ses parents.
3. Si Philippe _______________, il serait plus heureux!
4. Si Antoinette n'était pas étudiante, elle _______________ dans un magasin de disques.
5. Quand Alain _______________, il gagne beaucoup d'argent.
6. Si Robert avait besoin d'argent, il _______________ plus!
7. Si Thérèse _______________ pour cette compagnie, elle aurait beaucoup de responsabilités.
8. Si Albert ne _______________ pas cet été, il ira au Canada avec moi.
9. Jacqueline voyagera beaucoup quand elle _______________ pour cette firme internationale.
10. Irène gagnerait plus d'argent si elle _______________ à Paris.

NOM ________________________________ DATE ______________________

Test 8. Le subjonctif des verbes réguliers. Complete the following sentences with the appropriate subjunctive forms of the verbs in parentheses. *[31–A]*

1. (étudier, réussir) Le professeur veut que les étudiants ______________ et qu'ils ______________ à l'examen.
2. (manger, maigrir) Le médecin veut que mon père ______________ moins et qu'il ______________.
3. (finir, choisir) Mes parents veulent que je ______________ mes études et que je ______________ une profession intéressante.
4. (trouver, réussir) Je souhaite que vous ______________ du travail et que vous ______________ dans la vie.
5. (téléphoner, rendre) Mes grands-parents souhaitent que nous leur ______________ et que nous leur ______________ visite pendant les vacances.
6. (vendre, acheter) Ma mère veut que mon frère ______________ sa moto et qu'il ______________ une voiture.
7. (répondre, oublier) Je souhaite que mes amis ______________ à mes lettres et qu'ils n'______________ pas de me téléphoner.
8. (finir, jouer) Je souhaite que tu ______________ ton travail et que tu ______________ au tennis avec moi.

Test 9. Le subjonctif: formation régulière, verbes à deux radicaux. Fill in the blanks with the appropriate subjunctive forms of the verbs in parentheses. Although these verbs are irregular in the present indicative, their subjunctive is formed according to the regular pattern. *[31–B]*

1. (apprendre) Il est utile que tu ______________ le français et que tes amis ______________ l'espagnol.
2. (venir) Je souhaite que vous ______________ avec nous au cinéma. Je souhaite que vos amis ______________ aussi.
3. (boire) Le médecin ne veut pas que nous ______________ de la bière. Il ne veut pas que je ______________ de l'alcool.
4. (voir) Il faut que je ______________ le professeur. Il faut que vous le ______________ aussi.
5. (recevoir) Il faut que ces étudiants ______________ une bonne note en espagnol. Il faut que vous ______________ une bonne note en français.

Test 10. Des subjonctifs irréguliers. Fill in the blanks with the appropriate subjunctive forms of the verbs in parentheses. *[31–D; 32–B]*

1. (être) Il faut que je ______________ à l'aéroport à trois heures. Il faut que vous ______________ là aussi.
2. (avoir) Il faut que nous ______________ une bonne note à l'examen. Il faut que j'______________ un «A».
3. (aller) Le professeur souhaite que j'______________ en France avec mes amis. Il souhaite que nous ______________ à Paris.
4. (faire) Il faut que je ______________ des progrès. Il faut que vous ______________ attention!
5. (pouvoir) Je regrette que tu ne ______________ pas venir, mais je suis content que tes amis ______________ jouer au tennis avec moi.
6. (savoir) Il est utile que vous ______________ programmer. Il est bon que je ______________ utiliser cet ordinateur.
7. (vouloir) Je doute que François ______________ me prêter sa moto. Je doute que vous ______________ sortir avec nous.

Test 11. Indicatif ou subjonctif? Complete the sentences below with **est** *(indicative)* or **soit** *(subjunctive)*, as appropriate. *[31–C, E; 32–C, D, E, F]*

1. Je pense que Philippe ________ assez généreux.
2. Crois-tu qu'il ________ intelligent?
3. Isabelle doute qu'il ________ très dynamique.
4. Il faut que Thomas ________ chez le médecin à une heure.
5. Les parents d'Henri veulent que leur fils ________ architecte.
6. Je sais que Sylvie ________ la cousine de Pierre.
7. Paul est québécois. Il est normal qu'il ________ bon en français.
8. Catherine est ma meilleure amie. Je suis contente qu'elle ________ à la fête avec moi.
9. Paul parle très bien le français depuis qu'il ________ à Paris.
10. J'ai prêté ma voiture à Julien pour qu'il ________ à l'heure à son rendez-vous.
11. Janine est restée chez elle parce qu'elle ________ malade.
12. M. Dumas prête de l'argent à son fils jusqu'à ce qu'il ________ financièrement indépendant.

NOM ______________________________ DATE ______________________

Test 12. Des verbes irréguliers. Complete the following sentences with the French verbs that correspond to the English verbs in italics. Be sure to use the appropriate tense: présent or passé composé. *[29–A; 30–D; 32–A]*

1.	We don't *believe* you.	Nous ne te ______________ pas.
2.	I *believed* what you said.	J'______________ ce que tu as dit.
3.	I *drive* a French car.	Je ______________ une voiture française.
4.	When *did* you *drive* your friends to the airport?	Quand est-ce que tu ______________ tes amis à l'aéroport?
5.	They *receive* letters from their friends every day.	Ils ______________ des lettres de leurs amis tous les jours.
6.	When *did* you *receive* this telegram?	Quand est-ce que tu ______________ ce télégramme?

PARTIE C. VOCABULAIRE

Test 13. Logique! Select the option that completes the sentence logically. Circle the corresponding letter.

1. Je n'ai pas aimé ce film. Il était vraiment ____.

   a. génial b. doux c. ennuyeux d. net

2. Les employés de cette entreprise ont cinq semaines de ____ par an.

   a. congé b. départ c. fin d. fête

3. Vous devrez montrer votre passeport quand vous serez ____.

   a. en affaires b. informaticien c. fatigués d. à la douane

4. Il est important que tout le monde travaille pour ____.

   a. l'esprit b. la jeunesse c. la paix d. la langue

5. À quelle ____ roule cette voiture?

   a. chance b. avenir c. vie d. vitesse

6. Elle m'a dit que je pourrais partir en vacances. C'est ma ____.

   a. fonctionnaire b. cadre c. patronne d. infirmière

7. Bernard est au courant des problèmes ____. Il ne lit jamais de livres anciens!

   a. historiques b. internationaux c. personnels d. actuels

8. À la suite d'une longue guerre, les adversaires ont signé ____.

   a. un traité b. une loi c. une paix d. une frontière

LAB MANUAL

Jean-Paul Valette
Rebecca M. Valette

NOM ______________________________ DATE ______________________

UNITÉ 1. Bonjour, les Français!

Leçon 1. Bonjour!

Introduction

PRÉSENTATION

1. **Lecture.** Open your textbook to page 2. Follow the text as you listen to it. *Écoutez!*

2. **Pratique orale**

STRUCTURE ET VOCABULAIRE

Vocabulaire: Salutations

3. **Prononciation.** Open your textbook to page 6.

4. **Situation: Salutations**

❖ Philippe — ***Salut, Philippe!***

❖ Annie — ***Bonjour, Annie.***

PHONÉTIQUE

5. **Introduction à la phonétique française.** Open your textbook to page 8.

6. **Consonnes et voyelles** *(Consonants and vowels)*

❖ A. Marie
❖ B. Monique

	A	B	1	2	3	4	5	6	7	8
vowel sound	√									
consonant sound		√								

DIALOGUE

7. Bonjour!

❖ A. —*Bonjour!*
—*Bonjour!*

❖ B. —*À bientôt!*
—*À tout à l'heure.*

A. 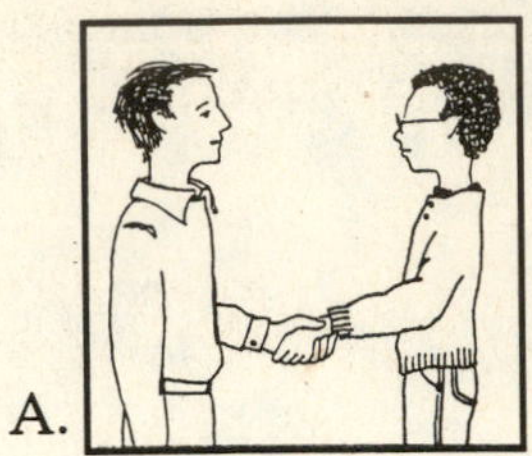

B. 

1. 

2. 

3. 

4. 

5. 

NOM ______________________________ DATE ______________________

DICTÉE

8. Salut!

—__________________! ____________________?

—_______, ______________________.

—Jean-Paul, ____________________________ Clara.

—_____________________.

—_____________________. ____________________!

NOM ______________________________ DATE ______________________

Leçon 2. Comment vas-tu?

PRÉSENTATION

1. **Lecture.** Open your textbook to page 10. Follow the text as you listen to it. *Écoutez!*

2. **Pratique orale**

PHONÉTIQUE

3. **Les lettre muettes.** Open your textbook to page 17.

STRUCTURE ET VOCABULAIRE

A. Formalisme et niveaux de langue *(Formality and Levels of Language)*

4. ***Vous* ou *tu*?**

❖ Ça va? *(informal)*

	❖	1	2	3	4	5	6	7	8
formal									
informal	√								

Vocabulaire: Salutations

5. **Prononciation.** Open your textbook to page 14.

6. **Situation: Bonjour!**

❖ Paul — ***Bonjour, Paul.***

❖ Mme Bissette — ***Bonjour, Madame.***

7. **Situation: Au revoir**

❖ Roger — ***Au revoir, Roger.***

1. Nathalie
2. Louise
3. Robert
4. Nicolas
5. Bernard
6. Marthe
7. Édith
8. Marc

B. Les marques orthographiques

8. Les marques orthographiques. Open your textbook to page 18.

9. Orthographe *(Spelling)*

1. hotel
2. garcon
3. foret
4. Leon
5. Joel
6. Michele
7. Melanie
8. Daniele
9. Francoise
10. Valerie

C. L'alphabet français

10. Prononciation

A B C D E F G H I J K L M N O P Q R S T U V W X Y Z

ABC DEF GHI JKL MNO PQR STU VWX YZ

11. Géographie

1. _ _ _ _ _
2. _ _ _ _ _
3. _ _ _ _ _ _ _ _
4. _ _ _ _ _ _ _ _ _
5. _ _ _ _ _ _ _
6. _ _ _ _ _ _ _ _ _ _ _

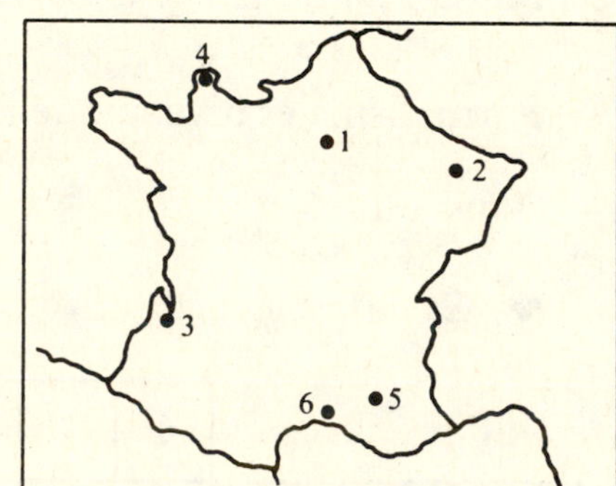

DIALOGUE

12. Ça va?

A.

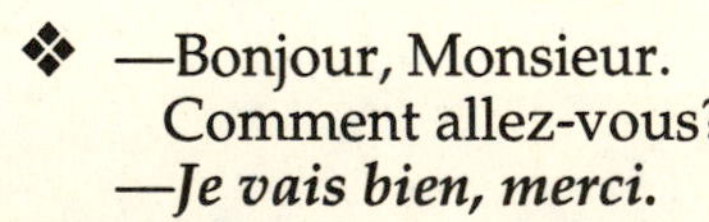

❖ —Bonjour, Monsieur.
Comment allez-vous?
—Je vais bien, merci.

B.

❖ —Bonjour, Michèle.
Ça va?
—Non, ça va mal.

1.

2.

3.

4.

5.

NOM ______________________________ DATE ______________________

DICTÉE

13. Salutations

—______________________________.

—______________________________.

—______________________________?

—______________________________. ____________________?

—____.

NOM ______________________ DATE ______________________

Leçon 3. Qui est-ce?

PRÉSENTATION

1. **Lecture.** Open your textbook to page 20. Follow the text as you listen to it. *Écoutez!*

2. **Compréhension du texte**

	1	2	3	4	5
vrai					
faux					

STRUCTURE ET VOCABULAIRE

A. Le genre des noms et des adjectifs

Vocabulaire: Quelques adjectifs de nationalité

3. **Qui est-ce?**

❖ A. —Qui est-ce? Une copine algérienne? ***—Oui, c'est une copine algérienne.***

❖ B. —Qui est-ce? Un copain anglais? ***—Oui, c'est un copain anglais.***

4. **Mes amis** *(My friends)*

❖ A. Voici un ami vietnamien. ***Et voilà aussi une amie vietnamienne.***

❖ B. Voici une amie suisse. ***Et voilà aussi un ami suisse.***

5. **Étudiants internationaux**

	1	2	3	4	5	6	7
Male							
Female							
Impossible to tell							

B. Les mots apparentés

6. Identifications

____________________ ____________________ ____________________

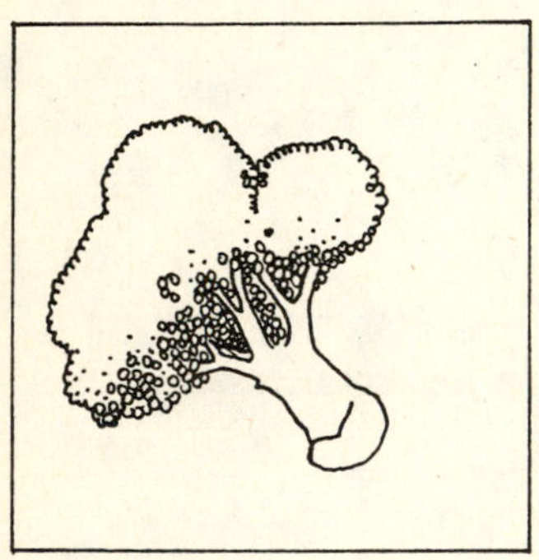

____________________ ____________________ ____________________

7. Orthographe

1. J'adore le ____________________.
2. Zineb téléphone à sa *(her)* ____________________ ____________________.
3. Maurice déteste ____________________.
4. Le ____________________ est mon *(my)* ____________________ préféré.
5. Marc prend un peu de *(a little)* ____________________ dans son *(his)*

   ____________________.
6. Le ____________________ aime la ____________________.

NOM ______________________ DATE ______________________

Vocabulaire: Préférences

8. En ville

❖ Mélanie

Mélanie adore la librairie.

1. Joëlle

2. Ourida

3. Alain

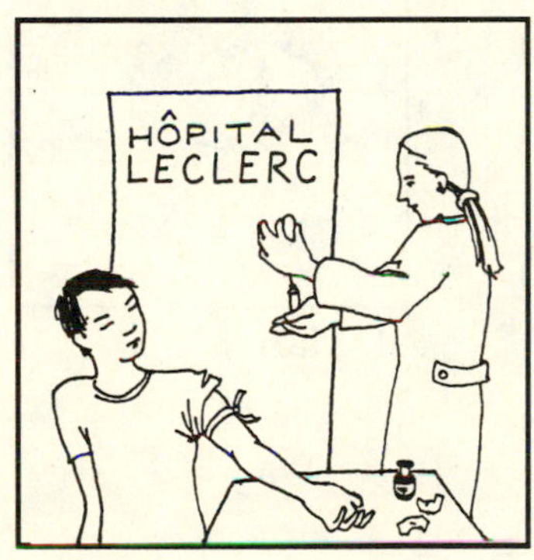

4. Tran

5. Hamid

6. Nicole

PHONÉTIQUE

9. Intonation (I). Open your textbook to page 30. Repeat after the speaker.

10. Situation: À Paris. Open your textbook to page 31, Activité 6. You are working as a tour guide in Paris. Point out the places listed in Activité 6 to the tourists in your group.

❖ l'hôtel Napoléon *Voilà l'hôtel Napoléon.*

DIALOGUE

11. Qui est-ce?

Michèle

❖ PHILIPPE: Qui est-ce?
VOUS: *C'est Michèle. Bonjour, Michèle.*

1. Dominique

2. Daniel

3. Sylvie

4. Marc

DICTÉE

12. Bonjour!

—______________________ Annie ________ Nicole. __________________________ Pascal,

____________________________________.

—____________________________________.

—____________________________________.

—____________________________________?

—____________________________________.

—____________________________________. __________________________.

NOM ______________________ DATE ______________________

Vivre en France 1. Pendant le cours

1. Contextes

1. a. The instructor notices that a student is about to make an error.

   b. Students want the instructor to pay attention to them.

2. a. The instructor wants a student to answer a question.

   b. The instructor wants the class to repeat a new expression.

3. a. The instructor wants a student to answer a question.

   b. The instructor wants a student to ask a question.

4. a. It's time to stop reading.

   b. It's time to read out loud from the text.

5. a. A student tells the instructor that she's speaking very fast.

   b. The instructor is happy with the student's response.

6. a. The instructor tells students to exchange papers.

   b. It's time to do some writing.

7. a. A student asks a favor of another student.

   b. The instructor asks a favor of the entire class.

8. a. The student doesn't understand the question.

   b. The student understands the question, but prefers to not answer.

9. a. A student needs to buy the text.

   b. A student asks how to express an English word in French.

10. a. The instructor tells the student that he's finally caught on.

    b. The instructor tells the student that he's guessed wrong.

2. En France

Cours à 9 heures

	Le professeur	Les étudiants	Personne *(No one)*
1. poser des questions	________	________	________
2. répéter des phrases *(sentences)*	________	________	________
3. donner *(give)* des instructions	________	________	________
4. corriger *(correct)*	________	________	________
5. réciter de la poésie	________	________	________
6. lire *(read)* dans le livre	________	________	________
7. communiquer	________	________	________
8. regarder des illustrations	________	________	________
9. aller *(go)* au musée	________	________	________
10. répondre aux questions	________	________	________
11. chanter des chansons *(songs)*	________	________	________
12. dire *(tell)* leurs préférences	________	________	________

On the basis of what you've observed in this class, are you interested in joining it?

Give some reasons why or why not. ____

____

____

NOM ______________________________ DATE ______________________

UNITÉ 2. Qui parle français?

Leçon 4. Au Canada

PRÉSENTATION

1. **Lecture.** Open your textbook to page 36. Follow the text as you listen to it.

2. **Compréhension du texte**

	1	2	3	4	5
vrai					
faux					

PHONÉTIQUE

3. **La liaison: pronom sujet + verbe**

As you recall, in French, a pronoun subject and its verb are always linked together and pronounced like one long word.

Répétez: **nous dînons** **vous jouez** **je visite**

When a subject pronoun ending on a silent "s" is followed by a verb beginning with a vowel sound, **liaison** occurs. This means that the "s" (representing the sound [z]) is pronounced as if it were the *first* sound of the verb. Note that **liaison** only occurs after the plural subject pronouns.

Répétez: **nous aimons** **vous arrivez** **ils écoutent** **elles étudient**
Vous habitez à Paris.
Nous invitons Philippe.

STRUCTURE ET VOCABULAIRE

A. Le présent des verbes en *-er* et les pronoms sujets

4. **Prononciation.** Open your textbook to page 43.

5. **Prononciation.** Open your textbook to page 44.

6. Pratique

❖ Marcel **habite** à Paris.
❖ Vous **aimez** Philippe.
❖ **Je** joue au tennis.

7. Identification de structures

	1	2	3	4	5	6	7	8
une personne								
un groupe								
impossible à dire								

B. La négation

8. Conversation: Pas moi *(Not me)*

❖ MICHÈLE: Sylvie travaille à Québec.
VOUS: ***Je ne travaille pas à Québec.***

9. Conversation: Contradictions

❖ PHILIPPE: Marie parle anglais.
VOUS: ***Ah non! Elle ne parle pas anglais.***

C. Les nombres de 0 à 12

10. Compréhension

0 1 2 4 5 6 7 8 9 10 11 12

11. Pratique

❖ 2 9 4
deux, neuf, quatre

A. 3 5 7 C. 2 9 11 E. 10 2 12

B. 8 0 1 D. 4 12 6 F. 7 8 11

12. Prononciation. Open your textbook to page 49.

Vocabulaire: L'heure

13. Prononciation. Open your book to page 50.

14. Conversation: L'heure

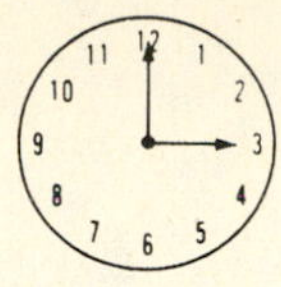

❖ MONIQUE: Quelle heure est-il?
VOUS: ***Il est trois heures.***

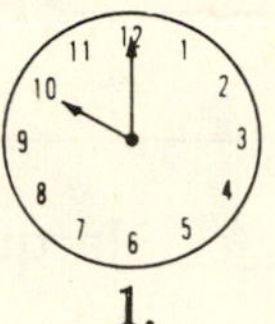
1.

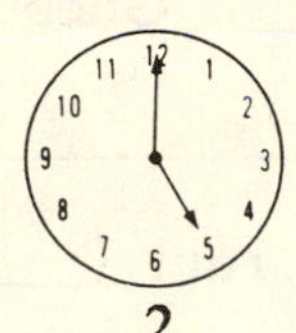
2.

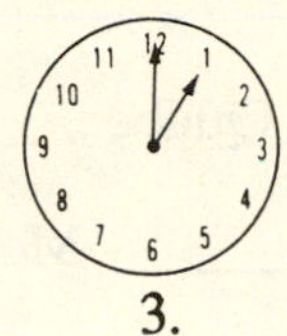
3.

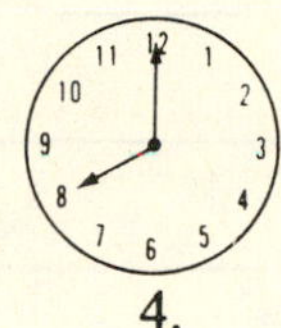
4.

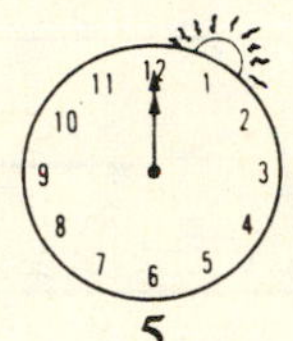
5.

DIALOGUE

15. Qu'est-ce que tu fais?

❖ PHILIPPE: Qu'est-ce que tu fais à deux heures?
VOUS: ***À deux heures, j'étudie.***

1.

2.

3.

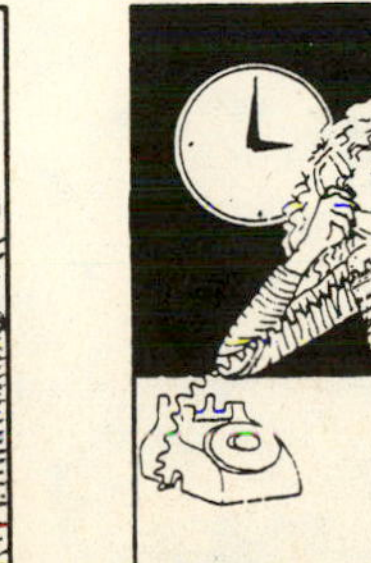
4.

5.

DICTÉE

16. Au Canada

______________________________ Paris? ________________ Québec ________ Paul

______ Jacques. ______________________ Québec, ______________________________

Québec. __________________________________ Montréal. Paul ____________ Jacques

____ l'Université Laval.

NOM ______________________ DATE ______________________

Leçon 5. À Dakar

PRÉSENTATION

1. Lecture. Open your textbook to page 52. Follow the text as you listen to it.

2. Compréhension du texte

	1	2	3	4	5	6	7	8
vrai								
faux								

PHONÉTIQUE

3. Intonation: Questions à réponse affirmative ou négative

In French, as in English, the voice rises at the end of a yes/no question.

Comparez: **Est-ce que tu travailles?**

Are you working?

Répétez: **Est-ce que vous voyagez?**
Est-ce que tu joues au tennis?
Est-ce que Marie nage bien?

In conversational French, questions can be formed without **est-ce que** simply by using a rising intonation.

Répétez: **Vous voyagez?**
Tu joues au tennis?
Marie nage bien?

Again in conversational French, if a yes answer is expected, questions can be formed by adding the tag **n'est-ce pas?** at the end of the sentence. Here the intonation falls on the main part of the sentence, and rises only on the **n'est-ce pas?**

Répétez: **Vous voyagez, n'est-ce pas?**
Tu joues au tennis, n'est-ce pas?
Marie nage bien, n'est-ce pas?

STRUCTURE ET VOCABULAIRE

Vocabulaire: Activités

4. **Prononciation.** Open your textbook to page 56.

5. **Situation: Clarifications**

❖ bien
Marie et Richard dansent.
Marie et Richard dansent bien.

1. mal
2. souvent
3. beaucoup
4. maintenant
5. toujours
6. aussi
7. assez bien
8. très souvent

A. Le verbe être

6. **Prononciation.** Open your textbook to page 57.

7. **Pratique**

❖ **Lamine** est à Paris.
❖ **Lamine** n'est pas en classe.

B. La construction infinitive

8. **Narration: C'est vrai!**

❖ Georges n'aime pas nager.
Georges déteste nager.

C. Questions à réponse affirmative ou négative

9. **Situation: Répétition**

❖ LAMINE: Vous aimez voyager?
VOUS: ***Est-ce que vous aimez voyager?***

10. **Conversation: Souvent?**

❖ LAMINE: Alain travaille.
VOUS: ***Est-ce qu'il travaille souvent?***

NOM ______________________ DATE ______________________

D. Les nombres de 13 à 99

11. Compréhension: Les nombres

13	14	15	16	17	18	19	20	
21	22	29	30	40	50	60		
61	62	69	70	71	72	73		
79	80	81	82	89	90	91	92	99

12. Compréhension: Les adresses

1. Paul: _____ , rue de la Pompe
2. Véronique: _____ , rue Daru
3. Élisabeth: _____ , avenue Daumesnil
4. Marc: _____ , boulevard des Italiens
5. Philippe: _____ , rue Sedaine
6. Jean-Claude: _____ , rue de la Boétie
7. Sylvie: _____ , rue de Sèvres
8. Robert: _____ , avenue Foch

Vocabulaire: Les divisions de l'heure

13. Prononciation. Open your textbook to page 64.

14. Compréhension: La montre de Claire *(Claire's watch)*

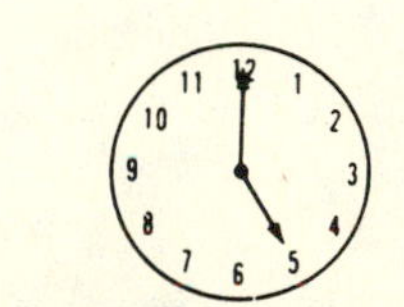

❖ Il est six heures.

	❖	1	2	3	4	5	6	7	8
oui									
non	×								

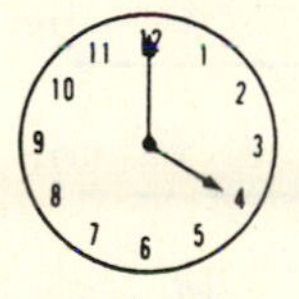
1.

2.

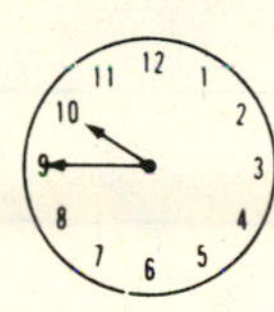
3.

4.

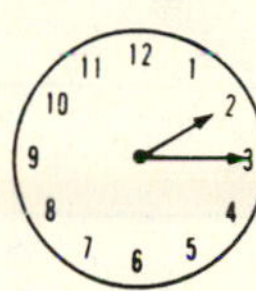
5.

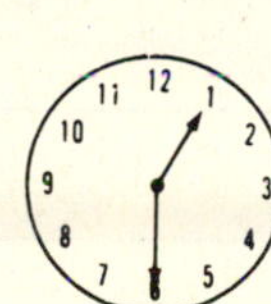
6.

7.

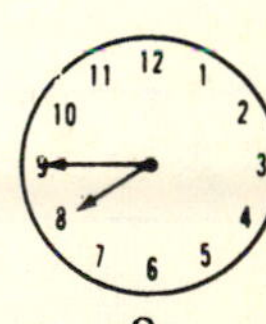
8.

15. Conversation: Quelle heure est-il?

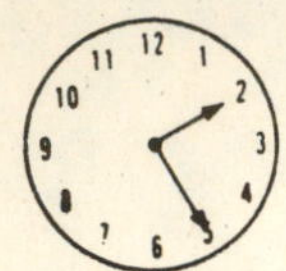

❖ PHILIPPE: Quelle heure est-il?
VOUS: *Il est deux heures vingt-cinq.*

1.

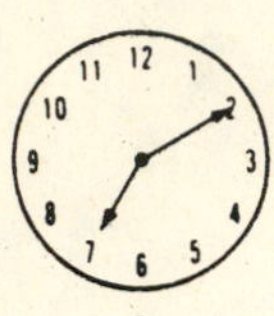
2.

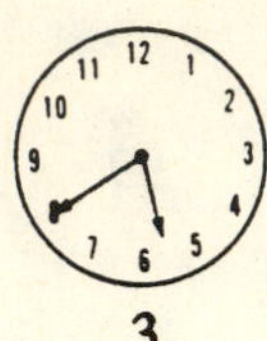
3.

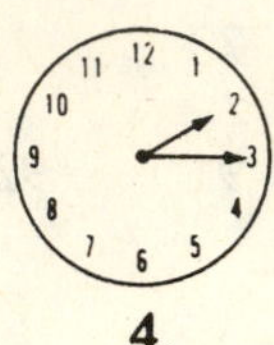
4.

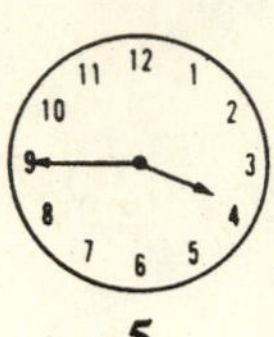
5.

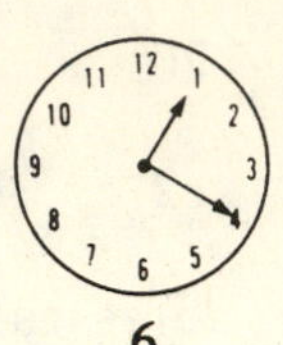
6.

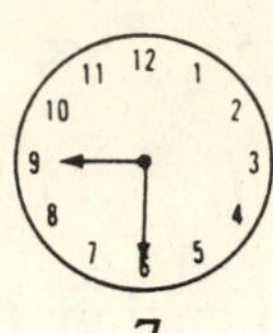
7.

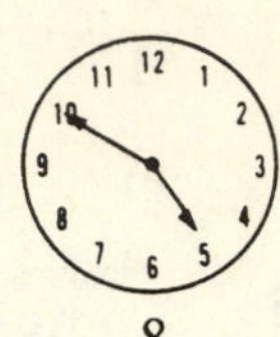
8.

DIALOGUE

16. Préférences et obligations

❖ Oui, je dois...
—Tu étudies?
—*Oui, je dois étudier.*

1. Oui, j'aime...
2. Oui, je peux...
3. Oui, je dois...
4. Oui, je voudrais...
5. Oui, je veux...
6. Non, je n'aime pas...
7. Non, je ne veux pas...
8. Non, je ne peux pas...
9. Non, je ne dois pas...

DICTÉE

17. Les voyages

____________________. ____________________________________.

____________________ Québec. ____________________ Montréal.

____?

____?

NOM ______________________________ DATE ______________________

Leçon 6. À Bruxelles, à l'Alliance française

PRÉSENTATION

1. **Lecture.** Open your textbook to page 68. Follow the text as you listen to it.

2. **Compréhension du texte**

	1	2	3	4	5
oui					
non					

PHONÉTIQUE

3. **Intonation: Questions d'information**

The intonation of information questions is different in French and English.

Comparez: **Qu'est-ce que tu regardes?**

What are you looking at?

In French information questions, the question words begin on a high pitch. Then the intonation drops, to rise slightly on the last syllable.

Répétez: **Qui joue au tennis?**
Comment allez-vous?
Quand est-ce que tu étudies?
Où est Philippe?

STRUCTURE ET VOCABULAIRE

A. Le pronom on

4. **Prononciation.** Open your textbook to page 72.

5. **Situation: Où est-ce qu'on parle français?**

❖ Paris? *Oui, on parle français à Paris.*

❖ San Francisco? *Non, on ne parle pas français à San Francisco.*

B. Questions d'information

6. **Prononciation.** Open your textbook to page 73.

7. **Pratique**

❖ **Où** est-ce que vous travaillez?
❖ **Quand** est-ce que tu rentres?
❖ **À quelle heure** est-ce qu'il téléphone?

8. **Situation: Questions**

❖ Pierre travaille. Pour qui?
Pour qui est-ce que Pierre travaille?

9. **Conversation: Comment?**

❖ JEAN-MICHEL: Jacqueline habite à Paris.
VOUS: ***Où est-ce qu'elle habite?***

C. Les pronoms accentués

10. **Situation: Avec insistance**

❖ Georges arrive à midi.
Lui, il arrive à midi.

11. **Conversation: Pourquoi?**

❖ PAUL: Je joue au tennis avec Charles.
VOUS: ***Pourquoi est-ce que tu joues avec lui?***

D. La date

12. **Prononciation.** Open your textbook to page 78.

13. **Situation: Demain**

❖ Aujourd'hui, c'est mardi.
Demain, c'est mercredi.

NOM ________________________________ DATE ________________________

14. Compréhension orale: Quelle est la date?

❖ J'arrive à Zurich le douze avril. *le 12 avril*

1. ______________________ 5. ______________________
2. ______________________ 6. ______________________
3. ______________________ 7. ______________________
4. ______________________ 8. ______________________

DIALOGUE

15. Questions

❖ CLAIRE: Où est-ce que tu habites?
VOUS: *J'habite à Paris.*

1.

2.

3.

4.

5.

DICTÉE

16. Le tennis

____?

______________ Paul ____ Philippe, ______________?

____?

____?

______________, ______________!

NOM ____________________ DATE ____________________

Vivre en France 2. L'identité

1. La bonne réponse

1. a. Je suis photographe.

   b. Oui, ça va.

   c. J'aime danser.

2. a. Oui, je suis marié.

   b. Non, je ne suis pas marié.

   c. Non, je n'habite pas à Marseille.

3. a. Le 15 janvier.

   b. À Montréal.

   c. Je ne suis pas d'accord.

4. a. Ce n'est pas moi.

   b. Je suis d'accord avec toi.

   c. Allô! C'est André Lucas.

5. a. Oui, elle parle français.

   b. Non, elle n'aime pas parler anglais.

   c. Oui, un instant. Ne quittez pas, s'il vous plaît.

6. a. À bientôt.

   b. Je suis né le 18 septembre.

   c. J'arrive à Paris le 8 octobre.

7. a. Oui, bien sûr. À lundi.

   b. Oui, je dois étudier lundi.

   c. Non, je n'aime pas travailler.

8. a. Bonjour, Thérèse, comment allez-vous?

   b. Qui est à l'appareil?

   c. Au revoir, à mardi!

2. **En France**

INSTITUT DE LANGUES MODERNES

Bulletin d'inscription

Nom : ______________________________

Prénom : ______________________________

Nationalité : ______________________________

Lieu de naissance : ______________________________

Adresse : ______________________________ Paris

Numéro de téléphone : ______________________________

Signature : ______________________________

NOM ______________________________ DATE ______________________

UNITÉ 3. Images de la vie

Leçon 7. La vie est belle!

PRÉSENTATION

1. Lecture. *Ouvrez votre livre à la page 86.* Open your textbook to page 86. *Écoutez!*

2. Compréhension du texte

	1	2	3	4	5	6
vrai						
faux						

PHONÉTIQUE

3. Les voyelles [ɛ̃] and [y]

The vowels [ɛ̃] and [y] are important to learn because they distinguish the articles **un** and **une.**

(a) *La voyelle* [ɛ̃]. The vowel [ɛ̃] is a nasal vowel. It can be spelled **un, in,** or **ain.** As you practice it, be sure *not* to pronounce an "n."

Répétez: **un un un**
cinq quinze vingt copain invite matin
Ils invitent quinze copains.
Il est cinq heures vingt du matin.

(b) *La voyelle* [y]. The vowel [y] does not exist in English. To pronounce [y], round your lips as you say [i].

Écoutez: [i] [y] [i] [y] [i] [y]

Répétez: **tu bien sûr salut calculatrice étudier utiliser**
Bien sûr, tu étudies.
Lucie utilise une calculatrice.
Tu as une voiture.

STRUCTURE ET VOCABULAIRE

A. Le verbe avoir

4. **Prononciation.** *Ouvrez votre livre à la page 88.* The verb **avoir** is irregular.

5. **Pratique**

❖ J'ai une mobylette.
❖ Est-ce que **Philippe** a une guitare?

B. Le genre des noms; l'article indéfini **un, une**

6. **Identification de structures**

	1	2	3	4	5	6	7	8
un homme								
une femme								

Vocabulaire: Les gens

7. **Prononciation.** *Ouvrez votre livre à la page 90.* Repeat the nouns after the speaker.

8. **Pratique**

❖ Je travaille avec **un garçon.**
❖ Philippe téléphone à **un ami.**
❖ Alice parle à **une dame.**

9. **Compréhension: Qui est-ce?**

❖ Voici une amie canadienne. *une amie*

1. ______________________ 4. ______________________
2. ______________________ 5. ______________________
3. ______________________ 6. ______________________

Vocabulaire: Les objets

10. **Prononciation.** *Ouvrez votre livre à la page 91.* Repeat the nouns after the speaker.

NOM ______________________________ DATE ______________________

11. Pratique

❖ Nous avons une **radio.**
❖ Avez-vous un **vélo?**
❖ Monique a une **auto.**

C. Le pluriel des noms; l'article indéfini **des**

12. Situation: Au grand magasin *(At the department store)*

❖ *—Est-ce que vous avez des cassettes?*

1. 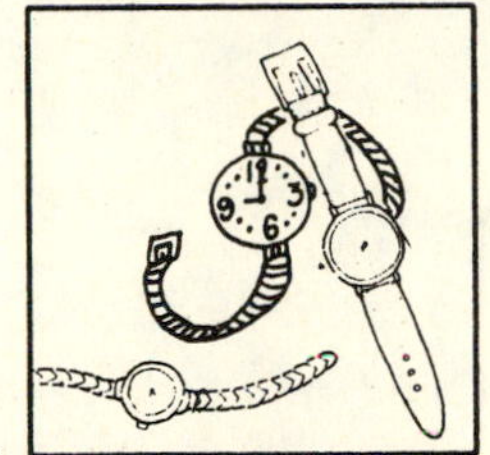
2. 
3. 

4. 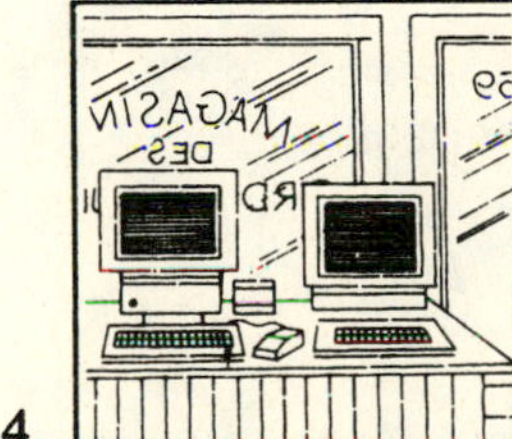
5. 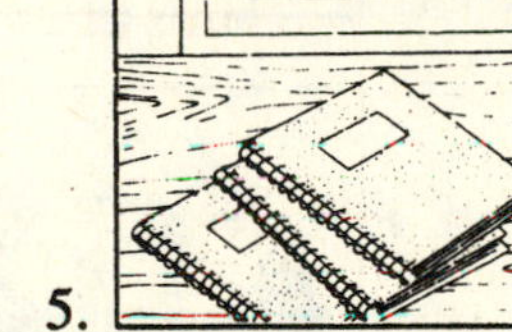
6. 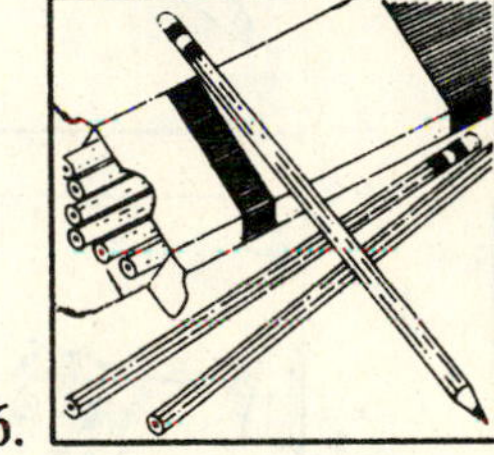

D. L'article indéfini dans les phrases négatives

13. Conversation: Caroline

❖ MONIQUE: Est-ce que Caroline a une voiture?
VOUS: ***Non, elle n'a pas de voiture.***

14. Situation: Possessions

❖ A. oui
Est-ce que Paul a des cassettes? ***Oui, il a des cassettes.***
❖ B. non
Est-ce que Sylvie et Marie ont une moto? ***Non, elles n'ont pas de moto.***

1. non 2. non 3. oui 4. oui 5. oui 6. non

E. L'expression il y a

15. Situation: L'appartement de Michel

❖ téléviseur (oui) — *Oui, il y a un téléviseur.*

❖ ordinateur (non) — *Non, il n'y a pas d'ordinateur.*

DIALOGUE

16. Questions

❖ CAROLINE: Qu'est-ce que c'est?

VOUS: *C'est un téléviseur.*

1. 

2. 

3. 

4. 

5.

6. 

DICTÉE

17. Jacqueline

__________ Jacqueline. ____________________. ____________________,

____________________________________. ________, ____________________,

________________________. __________, ______________________________

________________________?

NOM ______________________________ DATE ______________________

Leçon 8. Dans la rue

PRÉSENTATION

1. **Lecture.** Ouvrez votre livre à la page 100. Écoutez!

2. **Compréhension du texte**

	1	2	3	4	5	6	7	8
vrai								
faux								

PHONÉTIQUE

3. **Les voyelles [ə], [a], [e]**

The vowels [ə], [a], and [e] are important to learn because they distinguish the articles **le, la,** and **les.**

(a) The vowel [ə] is called a "mute e."

Écoutez: [ə] [ə] [ə]

Répétez: **le je ne que de ce**
au revoir demie regarder premier petit demain
Denise regarde le petit vélo.

(b) The letter "a" in French represents the sound [a].

Répétez: **a la ami cassette caméra camarade Canada**
Alice a la cassette de Madame Laval.

(c) The vowel sound [e] is different from its English counterpart because there is no glide in French.

Comparez: les LAY des DAY

Répétez: **et les des dîner premier marié réservé**
Vous voulez inviter des étudiants?
Les garçons utilisent le vélo et la moto.

STRUCTURE ET VOCABULAIRE

A. L'article défini **le, la, les**

4. Identification de structures

	1	2	3	4	5	6	7	8	9	10
un homme										
une femme										
des personnes										

5. Narration: Une étudiante sérieuse

❖ Il y a un garçon.
Monique ne regarde pas le garçon.

B. La forme des adjectifs de description

Vocabulaire: La description

6. Prononciation. *Ouvrez votre livre à la page 106.* Listen to the pronunciation of the masculine and feminine adjectives of description. Repeat each sentence as you hear it.

7. Description: Les jumeaux *(Twins)*

❖ Georges est brun. Et Sylvie?
Elle est brune aussi.

❖ Sophie est française. Et Paul?
Il est français aussi.

C. La place des adjectifs

8. Situation: Descriptions

❖ Voici un garçon. Il est intelligent. ***Voici un garçon intelligent.***
❖ Voilà une voiture. Elle est petite. ***Voilà une petite voiture.***

9. Pratique

❖ Thomas est un étudiant. (américain) ***Thomas est un étudiant américain.***
❖ Nous avons une auto. (japonais) ***Nous avons une auto japonaise.***
❖ Philippe et Pierre sont des amis. (bon) ***Philippe et Pierre sont de bons amis.***

NOM ______________________________ DATE ______________________

D. Il est ou c'est?

10. Conversation: Opinions

❖ —Le professeur est sympathique.
—Mais oui, c'est un professeur sympathique.

11. Narration: Explications

❖ J'ai un petit appareil-photo.
J'ai un appareil-photo. Il est petit.

DIALOGUE

12. Les amis

❖ STÉPHANIE: Tiens, Caroline est brune, n'est-ce pas?
VOUS: *Mais non, elle n'est pas brune. Elle est blonde.*

1.

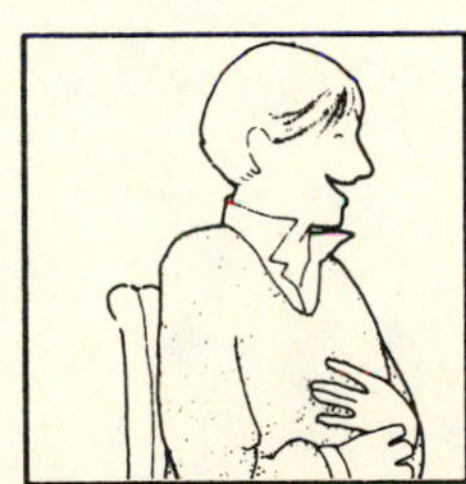
2.

3.

4.

5.

6.

DICTÉE

13. Suzanne

Suzanne ____. ________________________ Paris,

____. ____.

______________________________. ____.

__________, ____?

NOM ________________________ DATE ________________________

Leçon 9. Le temps libre

PRÉSENTATION

1. **Lecture.** Ouvrez votre livre à la page 112. Écoutez!

2. **Compréhension du texte**

1. ____________________ 4. ____________________

2. ____________________ 5. ____________________

3. ____________________

PHONÉTIQUE

3. **Les voyelles [o] et [ɔ]**

(a) *La voyelle* [o]. The vowel [o] is different from its English counterpart because there is no glide in French.

Comparez: au OH beau BOW

Répétez: **au vélo radio métro drôle à bientôt**
Margot va au château en vélo.
Léo reste à l'hôtel de Bordeaux.

(b) *La voyelle* [ɔ]. The vowel [ɔ] is somewhat similar to the "u" in the English word "up." However, the lips are more rounded in French.

Répétez: **école joli poli téléphone homme moderne**
Nicole téléphone à Monique.
Nous sommes d'accord avec Caroline.

STRUCTURE ET VOCABULAIRE

A. L'emploi de l'article défini dans le sens général

Vocabulaire: Les loisirs

4. **Prononciation.** *Ouvrez votre livre à la page 115.* Repeat the following nouns.

5. **Situation: Préférences**

❖ musique — ***J'aime la musique.***
❖ poker — ***Je n'aime pas le poker.***

B. Les contractions de l'article défini avec à et de

6. Situation: Nous parlons

❖ le professeur — *Nous parlons au professeur.*

❖ le professeur — *Nous parlons du professeur.*

7. Situation: Les loisirs

❖ le piano? — *Est-ce que tu joues du piano?*

❖ le football? — *Est-ce que tu joues au football?*

C. Le verbe **aller**; le futur proche avec **aller** + infinitif

8. Prononciation. *Ouvrez votre livre à la page 119.* The verb **aller** is the only irregular verb in **-er.** Repeat the verb forms and then repeat the sentences.

9. Pratique

❖ **Nous** allons à Paris.
❖ **Marie** ne va pas à Québec.
❖ **Vous** allez rester ici.

10. Identification de structures

	1	2	3	4	5	6	7	8
présent								
futur								

11. Conversation: Demain

❖ GEORGES: Tu joues au tennis aujourd'hui?
VOUS: ***Non, je vais jouer au tennis demain.***

Vocabulaire: Où et comment

12. Prononciation. *Ouvrez votre livre à la page 120.* Repeat the following nouns.

13. Compréhension orale

	1	2	3	4	5	6	7	8
logique								
illogique								

NOM ______________________________ DATE ______________________

D. La préposition chez

14. Situation: Qui travaille?

❖ Paul

Paul travaille chez lui.

E. Les questions avec inversion

15. Conversation: Pardon?

❖ ÉLISABETH: Nathalie arrive demain.
VOUS: *Quand arrive-t-elle?*

DIALOGUE

16. Où?

❖ GUY: Où est Philippe?
VOUS: ***Il est à la piscine.***

1.

2.

3.

4.

5.

6.

DICTÉE

17. Le temps libre

____?

______, ____ Jean-Michel.

____.

__________________________, ____

__________________________. ____?

NOM ______________________________ DATE ______________________

Vivre en France 3. En ville

1. La bonne réponse

1. a. Oui, c'est à droite.

   b. Non, ce n'est pas loin.

   c. Non, vous tournez à gauche.

2. a. Non, c'est tout près.

   b. Non, c'est au nord.

   c. Oui, c'est ça!

3. a. Non, il n'y a pas d'autobus.

   b. Il se trouve à côté de la pharmacie.

   c. L'autobus passe à dix heures et quart.

4. a. Il se trouve avenue des Acacias.

   b. Non, je ne parle pas anglais.

   c. Moi aussi, je vais là-bas.

5. a. Non, il n'y a pas de taxi.

   b. Mais oui, il y a des taxis ici.

   c. Vous devez traverser la rue Jacob et continuer tout droit.

6. a. C'est en face.

   b. C'est au sud.

   c. C'est à cent mètres.

7. a. Ce n'est pas ici.

   b. Allez là-bas en autobus.

   c. Oui, il y a un commissariat dans l'avenue de la Libération.

8. a. C'est un grand magasin.

   b. Non, je ne suis pas libraire.

   c. Oui, continuez tout droit. C'est à cent mètres à gauche.

2. En France

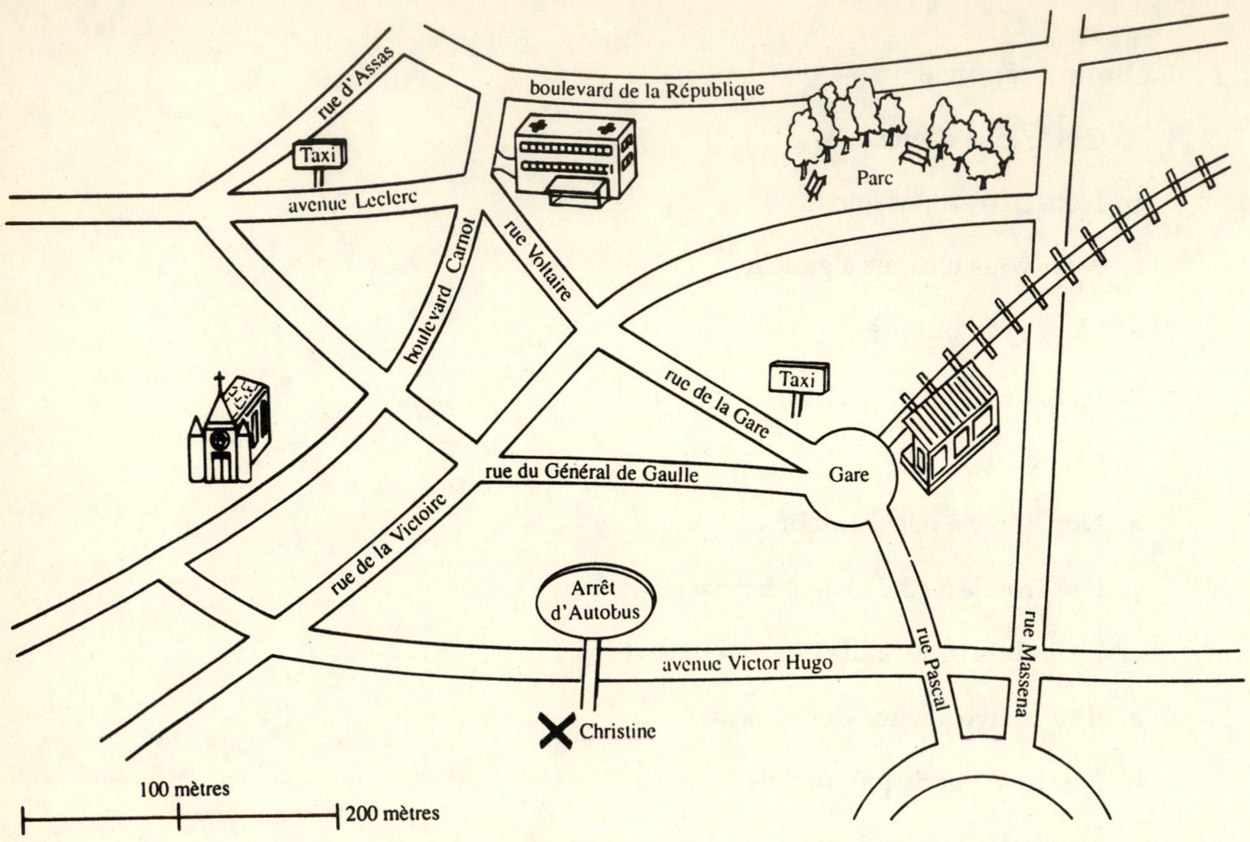
rue d'Assas
boulevard de la République
Taxi
avenue Leclerc
Parc
boulevard Carnot
rue Voltaire
rue de la Gare
Taxi
Gare
rue du Général de Gaulle
rue de la Victoire
Arrêt d'Autobus
avenue Victor Hugo
rue Pascal
rue Massena
Christine
100 mètres
200 mètres

NOM ______________________ DATE ______________________

UNITÉ 4. Problèmes d'argent

Leçon 10. Le budget de Martin

PRÉSENTATION

1. **Lecture.** Ouvrez votre livre à la page 132. Écoutez!

2. **Compréhension du texte**

	1	2	3	4	5	6
vrai						
faux						

PHONÉTIQUE

3. **La semi-voyelle [j]**

(a) *La combinaison* [j] + *voyelle.* The semi-vowel [j] is similar to the initial sound of the English word *yes.* The French counterpart, however, is shorter and more tense.

Comparez: piano PIANO

Répétez: **piano bien canadien hier premier**
juillet brillant payer nettoyer
Vous étudiez l'italien.
Nous payons le loyer le premier janvier.

(b) *La combinaison voyelle* + [j]. The combination vowel + [j] can occur at the end of a word. In this position the [j] is pronounced very distinctly.

Répétez: **travaille fille Marseille**
Les filles travaillent à Marseille.

STRUCTURE ET VOCABULAIRE

Vocabulaire: Les finances personnelles

4. Prononciation. Ouvrez votre livre à la page 133. Répétez les noms.

A. Les nombres de 100 à l'infini

5. Prononciation. Ouvrez votre livre à la page 134.

6. Compréhension orale

1.	100	1.000	8.000	5.	2.000	6.000	10.000
2.	100	120	210	6.	8.000	18.000	80.000
3.	300	1.300	3.000	7.	100	500	1.600
4.	50	150	1.500	8.	1.000	2.000	20.000

B. Le verbe **payer**

7. Prononciation. *Ouvrez votre livre à la page 136.* Listen to the forms of the verb **payer.** Then repeat the sentences.

8. Pratique

❖ **Nous** envoyons un télégramme.
❖ **Nous** nettoyons l'appartement.

C. L'expression **être à**

D. La possession avec **de**

9. Conversation: À qui est-ce?

❖ NADINE: La moto est à Pierre?
VOUS: ***Oui, c'est la moto de Pierre.***

E. Les adjectifs possessifs

10. Prononciation. *Ouvrez votre livre à la page 140.* Repeat after the speaker.

11. Conversation: Possessions

❖ DANIÈLE: C'est la voiture de Jacques?
VOUS: ***Oui, c'est sa voiture!***

NOM ______________________ DATE ______________________

12. Conversation: La famille

❖ non

M. JACOB: Est-ce que Jacqueline est votre sœur?

VOUS: *Non, ce n'est pas ma sœur.*

1. oui 2. oui 3. non 4. oui 5. oui 6. non 7. non

13. Conversation: La famille Dupont

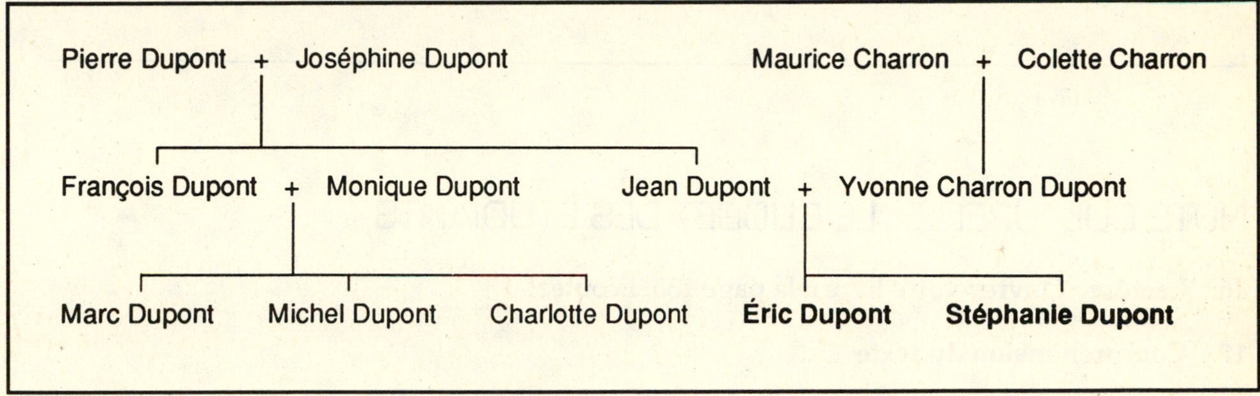

❖ MARTINE: Qui est Michel Dupont?

VOUS: *C'est leur cousin.*

❖ MARTINE: Qui sont Maurice et Colette Charron?

VOUS: *Ce sont leurs grands-parents.*

DIALOGUE

14. Le budget de Christine

❖ —Combien est-ce que Christine dépense pour le logement?

—Elle dépense deux mille francs.

Logement	2.000 Francs
Repas	500 Francs
Vêtements	600 Francs
Livres	230 Francs
Transports	220 Francs
Loisirs	200 Francs
	3.750 Francs

DICTÉE

15. Mes voisins

________________________________. ____________ Robert ________________.

__________________________. ____________ Alice ____________________.

______________________. ____.

NOTE CULTURELLE: LE BUDGET DES ÉTUDIANTS

16. Lecture. Ouvrez votre livre à la page 133. Écoutez!

17. Compréhension du texte

	1	2	3	4	5
vrai					
faux					

NOM ______________________________ DATE ______________________

Leçon 11. Un tee-shirt qui coûte cher

PRÉSENTATION

1. Lecture. Ouvrez votre livre à la page 144. Écoutez!

2. Compréhension du texte

	1	2	3	4	5	6
vrai						
faux						

PHONÉTIQUE

3. La lettre «e»

(a) The letter **é** and the verb endings **-er** and **-ez** represent the sound [e].

The letter "e" represents several sounds in French.

Répétez: **café école église aller dansez**
René va visiter l'université.

(b) The letters **è** and **ê** represent the sound [ɛ].

Répétez: **père mère frère fête être vêtements**
Mon père achète des vêtements.

(c) The letter **e** followed by a single consonant and a vowel represents the sound [ə].

Répétez: **chemise chemisier repas**
Denise aime la chemise de Renée.

In the middle of a word, the mute **e** is often dropped entirely.

Répétez: **samɇdi maintɇnant achɇter amɇner**
Nous amɇnons Cathɇrine à la fête samɇdi.

(d) The letter **e** followed by two consonants and a vowel represents the sound [ɛ].

Répétez: **veste lunettes verte cette merci**
Quelle veste est-ce qu'Annette va porter?

STRUCTURE ET VOCABULAIRE

Vocabulaire: Quelques vêtements

4. Prononciation. *Ouvrez votre livre à la page 146.* Repeat the items of clothing. Then repeat the names of the colors.

5. Pratique

❖ Je porte un **chemisier** jaune.
❖ Paul va porter un **costume** bleu.
❖ Marie a une jupe **marron.**

6. Compréhension orale

1. ______________________________
2. ______________________________
3. ______________________________
4. ______________________________
5. ______________________________
6. ______________________________
7. ______________________________
8. ______________________________
9. ______________________________

A. Les verbes **acheter** et **préférer**

7. Prononciation. Ouvrez votre livre à la page 148. Repeat the forms of the verbs.

8. Narration: Préférences

❖ Jean n'achète pas la veste rouge.
Il préfère la veste bleue.

B. L'adjectif interrogatif **quel**

9. Conversation: Caroline

❖ CAROLINE: J'achète des lunettes.
VOUS: ***Quelles lunettes achètes-tu?***

C. L'adjectif démonstratif **ce**

10. Conversation: Au grand magasin

❖ Raoul: Cette veste-ci est jolie.
Vous: ***Cette veste-là est jolie aussi.***

D. Le comparatif des adjectifs

NOM ______________________ DATE ______________________

11. Prononciation. Ouvrez votre livre à la page 152. Répétez les phrases.

12. Situation: Comparaisons

❖ Pierre est très grand. Jacques est grand.
Pierre est plus grand que Jacques.

❖ Ces chaussures-ci ne sont pas très confortables. Ces chaussures-là sont confortables.
Ces chaussures-ci sont moins confortables que ces chaussures-là.

DIALOGUE

13. En ville

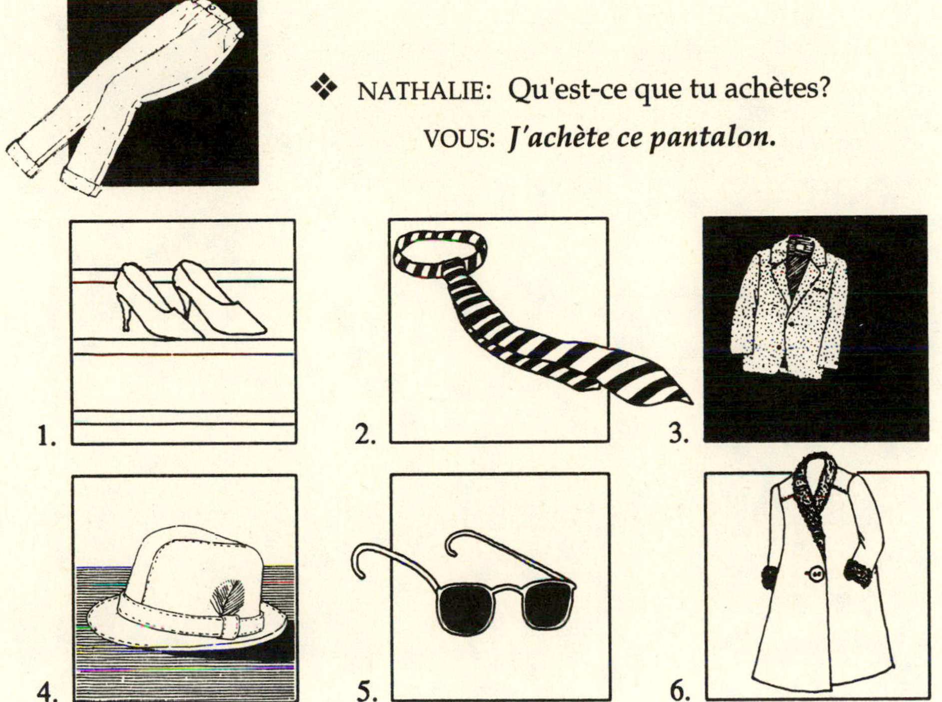

❖ NATHALIE: Qu'est-ce que tu achètes?
VOUS: ***J'achète ce pantalon.***

DICTÉE

14. Au magasin

______________________. ______________________.

______________________, ______________________.

____.

__________, ______________________?

NOTE CULTURELLE: LE SHOPPING

15. Lecture. Ouvrez votre livre à la page 145. Écoutez.

16. Compréhension du texte

	1	2	3	4	5	6
vrai						
faux						

NOM ______________________ DATE ______________________

Leçon 12. Le rêve et la réalité

PRÉSENTATION

1. **Lecture.** Ouvrez votre livre à la page 156. Écoutez!

2. **Compréhension du texte**

	1	2	3	4	5
vrai					
faux					

PHONÉTIQUE

3. **Liaison**

Many words in French end in a silent final consonant. In some instances, this consonant is pronounced with the next word when the next word begins with a vowel sound. The two words are then connected by **liaison.**

- Within a noun group, liaison is required between the words that introduce the noun.

Répétez:	**un appartement**	**un bon appartement**
	mon ami, ton école	**mon excellent ami**
	les enfants, mes amis,	**mes meilleurs amis**
	nos amis, vos amies	**nos chers amis**
	quelles étudiantes	**quels beaux enfants**
	aux étudiants	**aux nouveaux étudiants**

- Liaison is required between **plus, moins** + adjective.

Répétez: **plus amusant** **plus heureux** **plus optimiste**
moins intelligent **moins idéaliste** **moins énergique**

STRUCTURE ET VOCABULAIRE

A. Le verbe **faire**

4. **Prononciation.** *Ouvrez votre livre à la page 158.* The verb **faire** is irregular.

5. **Pratique**

❖ **Je** fais des projets.
❖ Qu'est-ce que **tu** fais ici?
❖ **Nous** ne faisons pas d'économies.

6. **Situation: Occupations**

❖ André / la vaisselle
André fait la vaisselle.

Vocabulaire: Le logement

7. **Prononciation.** *Ouvrez votre livre à la page 160.* Repeat the nouns after the speaker.

8. **Compréhension orale**

1. ______________________ 4. ______________________

2. ______________________ 5. ______________________

3. ______________________ 6. ______________________

Vocabulaire: Les prépositions de lieu

9. **Prononciation.** Ouvrez votre livre à la page 162. Répétez les prépositions et les phrases.

B. Les adjectifs **beau, nouveau, vieux**

10. **Prononciation.** Ouvrez votre livre à la page 164.

11. **Situation: Description**

❖ Paul a une voiture.
Paul a une belle voiture.

❖ J'ai une auto.
J'ai une nouvelle auto.

❖ Pierre porte une chemise.
Pierre porte une vieille chemise.

C. Le superlatif

12. Prononciation. Ouvrez votre livre à la page 165. Répétez les phrases.

13. Conversation: Ce sont les meilleurs!

❖ La classe MICHÈLE: C'est une fille intelligente, n'est-ce pas?
VOUS: ***Oui, c'est la fille la plus intelligente de la classe.***

1. la classe de français
2. la ville
3. la bibliothèque
4. le magasin
5. la région
6. la maison

D. Le temps

14. Prononciation. Ouvrez votre livre à la page 167.

DIALOGUE

15. Une question de temps

❖ MICHÈLE: Est-ce que tu vas nager?
VOUS: ***Non, je ne nage pas quand il fait mauvais.***

1.

2.

3.

4.

DICTÉE

16. Le week-end

______________________________________?

__________, __________________. ______________________,

____________________. __________, ____________

__________________. __________________, __________.

____.

NOTE CULTURELLE: LE LOGEMENT DES ÉTUDIANTS

17. Lecture. Ouvrez votre livre à la page 157. Écoutez!

18. Compréhension du texte

	1	2	3	4	5
vrai					
faux					

NOM ______________________ DATE ______________________

Vivre en France 4. La vie à Paris

1. La bonne réponse

1. a. Ça fait mille francs?

   b. Non, merci.

   c. J'ai besoin de bonnes chaussures de marche.

2. a. Quatre cent quatre-vingts francs.

   b. Dix francs.

   c. Je ne veux pas cette paire.

3. a. Montrez-moi cette cravate.

   b. Le trente-neuf seulement.

   c. Je préfère neuf billets de cent.

4. a. Une carte de crédit.

   b. Je vous dois cinquante francs.

   c. Cent cinquante francs, Madame.

5. a. Elles sont trop chères.

   b. Je peux payer avec un chèque?

   c. Où est la caisse?

6. a. Non, mais j'ai mon passeport.

   b. Voici mon carnet de chèques.

   c. J'ai plusieurs pièces de cinq francs.

7. a. Visa ou American Express.

   b. Non, je n'ai pas de carte de crédit.

   c. Allez à la Banque Nationale.

8. a. Certainement, voici dix dollars.

   b. Votre monnaie, Madame.

   c. Désolée, je n'ai pas de monnaie.

2. **En France**

Pour aller à la Bastille?

1. Fréquence des trains? ______________________________
2. Où prend-on les tickets? ______________________________
3. Carnet ou Carte Orange? ______________________________
4. Durée de validité de la Carte Orange? ______________________________
5. Quelle direction prendre? Mairie d'Issy ou Pont de Sèvres? ______________________________
6. Où changer? ______________________________
7. Correspondance? ______________________________
8. Où descendre? ______________________________

NOM ____________________ DATE ____________________

UNITÉ 5. Chez les Français

Leçon 13. Ma vision du bonheur

PRÉSENTATION

1. **Lecture.** Ouvrez votre livre à la page 176. Écoutez!

2. **Compréhension du texte**

	1	2	3	4	5	6	7	8
vrai								
faux								

PHONÉTIQUE

3. **Intonation: Les ordres**

In French, commands always begin on a high pitch. The voice then falls until the end of the sentence.

Écoutez: **Invite Philippe!**

Répétez: **Entrons!**
N'aie pas peur!
Va au café!
Ne sois pas timide!
Réponds au professeur!
Ne vendez pas vos livres!

STRUCTURE ET VOCABULAIRE

A. Expressions avec **avoir**

4. **Prononciation.** Ouvrez votre livre à la page 178. Répétez les expressions et les phrases.

5. **Situation: Quel âge ont-ils?**

❖ moi: 18 ans

Moi, j'ai dix-huit ans.

1. moi: 21 ans
2. toi: 16 ans
3. vous: 75 ans
4. mon grand-père: 80 ans
5. mon cousin: 30 ans
6. nous: 25 ans

6. **Situation: Logique**

❖ Béatrice achète une pizza.

Elle a faim.

B. Les verbes réguliers en -ir

7. **Prononciation.** Ouvrez votre livre à la page 181.

8. **Pratique**

❖ **Je** réussis à l'examen.
❖ Est-ce que **tu** grossis?
❖ **Tu** ne maigris pas.

9. **Situation: Au grand magasin**

❖ Paul regarde un livre.
Il choisit un livre.

C. Les verbes réguliers en -re

10. **Prononciation.** Ouvrez votre livre à la page 182.

11. **Pratique**

❖ **Je** réponds au professeur.
❖ **Je** n'entends pas la question.

12. **Compréhension: Les problèmes de l'existence**

	1	2	3	4	5	6	7	8
Oui, c'est un problème.								
Non, ce n'est pas un problème.								

NOM ______________________________ DATE ______________________________

D. L'impératif

13. Situation: S'il te plaît!

❖ jouer au tennis avec moi — *Joue au tennis avec moi, s'il te plaît!*
❖ perdre ton temps — *Ne perds pas ton temps!*
❖ aller au cinéma — *Allons au cinéma!*

DIALOGUE

14. Que font-ils?

❖ Janine est devant la poste.
JEAN-CLAUDE: Qu'est-ce qu'elle attend?
VOUS: *Elle attend le bus.*

1.

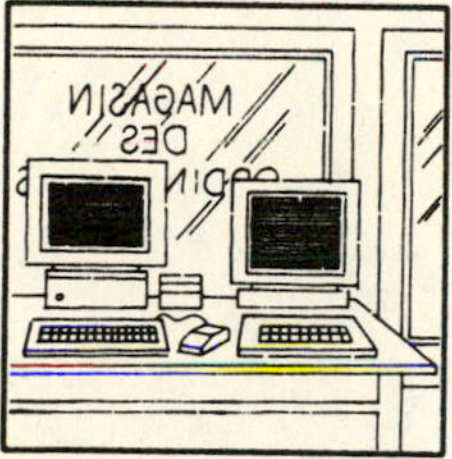

2.

3.

4.

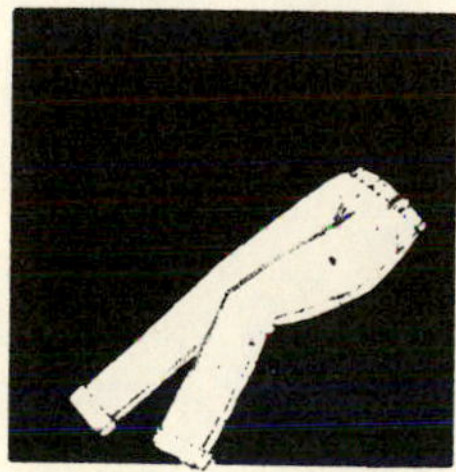
5.

DICTÉE

15. Sylvestre

____________ Sylvestre ________________. ________________________

en France. ______________________. ____________________________________.

____?

________________________________!

NOTE CULTURELLE: LES FRANÇAIS ET LE BONHEUR

16. Lecture. Ouvrez votre livre à la page 177. Écoutez!

17. Compréhension du texte

	1	2	3	4
vrai				
faux				

NOM ______________________________ DATE ______________________

Leçon 14. Un mois à Paris

PRÉSENTATION

1. **Lecture.** Ouvrez votre livre à la page 188. Écoutez!

2. **Compréhension du texte**

	1	2	3	4	5	6	7	8
vrai								
faux								

PHONÉTIQUE

3. **La voyelle nasale** [ɔ̃]

The nasal vowel [ɔ̃] is represented by the letters "on" and "om" when these letters occur at the end of a word or are followed by a consonant other than "n" or "m."

Contrast the nasal and non-nasal vowels in the following pairs of words.

Comparez: **Simon** — **Simone**
bon — **bonne**
Japon — **japonais**
son — **sommes**

Répétez: **on bon son maison salon pantalon oncle content**
Bonjour, Simon. Où sont Yvon et Léon?
Mon oncle Simon est très compétent.

STRUCTURE ET VOCABULAIRE

A. Le passé composé avec **avoir**

4. **Prononciation.** Ouvrez votre livre à la page 190. Répétez les phrases au passé composé.

5. **Pratique**

❖ Hier, j'ai dîné au restaurant.
❖ **Mon frère** a fini ce livre.
❖ J'ai attendu le bus.

6. **Identification de structures**

	1	2	3	4	5	6	7	8	9	10	11	12
présent												
passé composé												

7. **Situation: L'été dernier**

❖ voyager
L'été dernier, Caroline a voyagé.

8. **Narration: Hier aussi!**

❖ Aujourd'hui, Charles joue au tennis.
Hier aussi, il a joué au tennis.

B. Le passé composé dans les phrases négatives

9. **Narration: Bonnes résolutions**

❖ Ce matin, Éric va nettoyer sa chambre.
Hier soir, il n'a pas nettoyé sa chambre.

C. Les questions au passé composé

10. **Conversation: Pourquoi?**

❖ OLIVIER: Sophie a maigri.
VOUS: *Vraiment? Pourquoi a-t-elle maigri?*

Vocabulaire: Quand?

11. **Conversation: Avant**

❖ DENISE: Tu vas voyager l'été prochain?
VOUS: *Non, j'ai voyagé l'été dernier.*

NOM ______________________________ DATE ____________________

D. Les participes passés irréguliers

12. Prononciation. Ouvrez votre livre à la page 198.

13. Pratique

❖ J'ai eu un accident.
❖ **Alain** a été à Paris.
❖ **Jean-Paul** a fait une promenade.

14. Narration: Lundi

❖ Pierre a fait les courses.
Lundi ses sœurs ont fait les courses.

DIALOGUE

15. Le week-end dernier

❖ FLORENCE: As-tu dîné chez toi le week-end dernier?

VOUS: ***Non, je n'ai pas dîné chez moi. J'ai dîné au restaurant.***

1. 

2. 

3. 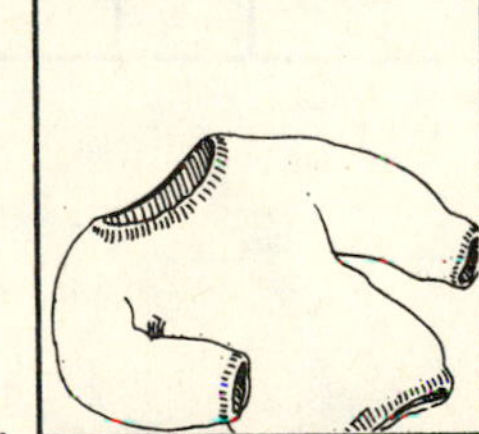

4. 

5. 

6. 

DICTÉE

16. Samedi dernier

____? _____, ____________________ Julien.

_______________, ______________________________. ______, ____________________

__________________________. ________, ____.

_____________, ____!

NOTE CULTURELLE: PARIS

17. Lecture. Ouvrez votre livre à la page 189. Écoutez!

18. Compréhension du texte

	1	2	3	4	5	6	7
vrai							
faux							

NOM ______________________________ DATE ______________________

Leçon 15. Séjour en France

PRÉSENTATION

1. Lecture. Ouvrez votre livre à la page 200. Écoutez!

2. Compréhension du texte

	1	2	3	4	5	6	7	8
vrai								
faux								

PHONÉTIQUE

3. La voyelle nasale [ɑ̃]

The nasal vowel [ɑ̃] is represented by the letters "an," "am," "en," or "em" when these letters occur at the end of a word or are followed by a consonant other than "n" or "m."

Contrast the nasal and non-nasal vowels in the following pairs of words.

Comparez: **an** — **année**
campagne — **camarade**
attends — **tennis**
printemps — **système**

Répétez: **an avant vacances lampe chambre**
en entrer vendre temps température
Les enfants passent les vacances à l'étranger.

STRUCTURE ET VOCABULAIRE

Vocabulaire: Vive les vacances!

4. Narration: Les vacances

❖ Jacqueline fait du ski.
Elle est en vacances.

A. Les verbes sortir, partir et dormir

5. **Prononciation.** Ouvrez votre livre à la page 203. Les verbes **sortir, partir** et **dormir** sont irréguliers.

6. **Pratique**

❖ **Michèle** sort demain soir.
❖ **Mes amis** ne partent pas.
❖ Est-ce que **vous** dormez bien?

B. Le passé composé avec être

7. **Prononciation.** Ouvrez votre livre à la page 205.

8. **Narration: Voyage en France**

❖ Philippe a visité Québec.
Il n'est pas allé en France.

9. **Identification de structures**

	1	2	3	4	5	6	7	8	9	10
présent										
passé composé										

10. **Compréhension orale**

❖ Hier, Jacqueline est sortie avec un ami canadien. ___*sortir*___

1. ____________________ 3. ____________________ 5. ____________________

2. ____________________ 4. ____________________ 6. ____________________

11. **Narration: Mata Hari**

❖ Mata Hari arrive à l'aéroport d'Orly.
Elle est arrivée à l'aéroport d'Orly.

C. La date et l'année

12. **Compréhension: Dates historiques**

❖ Les Parisiens ont pris la Bastille le 14 juillet 1789. *le 14 juillet 1789 / July 14, 1789*

1. ____________________ 4. ____________________ 6. ____________________

2. ____________________ 5. ____________________ 7. ____________________

3. ____________________

D. L'emploi du passé avec il y a

13. Narration: Il y a combien de temps?

❖ Jacques habite à Paris depuis trois mois.
Il est arrivé à Paris il y a trois mois.

E. La place de l'adverbe au passé composé

14. Conversation: Hier aussi

❖ ROBERT: Philippe joue bien au tennis.
VOUS: ***Hier aussi, il a bien joué au tennis.***

DIALOGUE

15. Voyage en France

❖ PIERRE: Quand es-tu arrivé(e) en France?
VOUS: ***Je suis arrivé(e) en France le 2 juillet.***

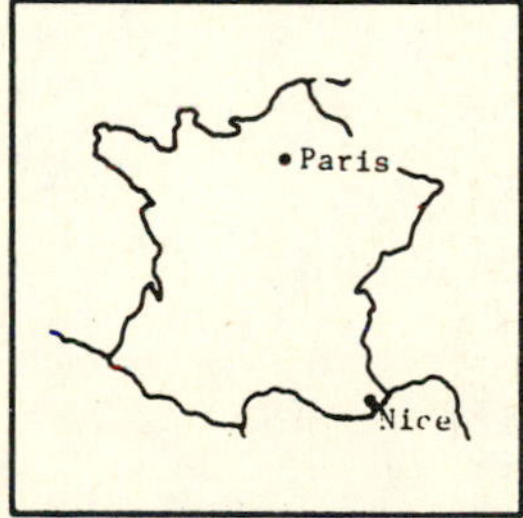

1.

2.

3.

4.

5.

6.

7.

DICTÉE

16. Au Canada

____________________, Georges ____ Sylvie.

__________________________ Paris ____________________. ______________________ Québec

____. ________, Georges ____________________

____.

NOTE CULTURELLE: LES ÉTUDIANTS ÉTRANGERS EN FRANCE

17. Lecture. Ouvrez votre livre à la page 201. Écoutez!

18. Compréhension du texte

	1	2	3	4
vrai				
faux				

NOM ______________________ DATE ______________________

Vivre en France 5. À l'hôtel

1. La bonne réponse

1. a. Parce que les lits sont confortables.
   b. Parce que j'aime la nature.
   c. Parce que c'est moins cher qu'à l'hôtel.
2. a. Nous avons réservé une chambre avec salle de bains.
   b. Nous sommes restés dans une pension.
   c. Nous sommes restés du premier au 10 juin.
3. a. Oui, c'est une chambre à un lit.
   b. Oui, j'ai une belle vue sur le parc.
   c. Oui, elle a l'air conditionné et la télé.
4. a. C'est 500 francs par jour.
   b. Je vais payer en espèces.
   c. Le service n'est pas inclus.
5. a. Non, nous n'acceptons pas les chèques de voyage.
   b. C'est la chambre 128.
   c. Non, je préfère utiliser ma carte de crédit.
6. a. Une semaine.
   b. Voici la clé.
   c. Dans une auberge de campagne.
7. a. À huit heures du matin.
   b. À midi et demi.
   c. Du 2 au 7 juillet.
8. a. Une chambre à la campagne.
   b. Une chambre avec salle de bains.
   c. La chambre 204.

2. **En France**

HÔTEL
DE LA PLAGE

Chambre nº: ______________________________

Nom du client: ______________________________

Nombre de personnes: ______________________________

Durée du séjour: ______________________________

Prix: ______________________________

NOM ______________________________ DATE ______________________

UNITÉ 6. Pourquoi la France?

Leçon 16. Pourquoi la France?

PRÉSENTATION

1. **Lecture.** Ouvrez votre livre à la page 228. Écoutez.

2. **Compréhension du texte**

❖ Il n'est pas étudiant. Il est photographe et il habite en Allemagne.

	❖	1	2	3	4	5	6	7	8	9	10
Per Eriksen											
Vanessa Bigelow											
Stefan Schmidt	✘										
Shigeko Hasegawa											
Peter de Jong											

PHONÉTIQUE

3. **Les lettres «gn»**

In French, the letters "gn" represent the sound [ɲ]. This sound is similar to the "ny" in *canyon*, but it is pronounced with more tension.

Répétez: **campagne montagne Espagne Allemagne espagnol**
Les montagnes en Allemagne sont magnifiques.
Agnès boit du champagne espagnol.

STRUCTURE ET VOCABULAIRE

A. Le verbe **venir**

4. **Prononciation.** Ouvrez votre livre à la page 230. Le verbe **venir** est irrégulier.

5. Pratique

❖ **Martine** vient de la piscine.
❖ **Marc** ne revient pas à midi.
❖ **Christine** est revenue avant-hier.

B. Le passé récent avec **venir de**

6. Identification de structures

	1	2	3	4	5	6	7	8	9	10
passé										
futur										

7. Narration: Pourquoi pas?

❖ Paul n'étudie pas.
Il vient d'étudier.

C. L'emploi de l'article défini avec les noms géographiques

Vocabulaire: Le monde

8. Prononciation. Ouvrez votre livre à la page 234.

9. Pratique

❖ français
la France

D. L'emploi des prépositions avec les villes et les pays

10. Narration: Nationalités

❖ Henri est français.
Il habite en France.

11. Narration: Origines

❖ Paul est français.
Il vient de France.

NOM ____________________ DATE ____________________

E. L'emploi du présent avec **depuis**

12. Conversation: Depuis quand?

❖ janvier
M. LECLERC: Depuis quand habitez-vous ici?
VOUS: ***J'habite ici depuis janvier.***

1. septembre
2. midi
3. sept heures
4. deux ans
5. un mois
6. cinq minutes

DIALOGUE

13. Quel pays?

❖ PIERRE: Où vas-tu passer l'été?
VOUS: ***Je vais passer l'été au Japon.***

❖ PIERRE: Quel pays veux-tu visiter?
VOUS: ***Je veux visiter la Grèce.***

1. Canada

2. Mexique

3. Brésil

4. Espagne

5. Irlande

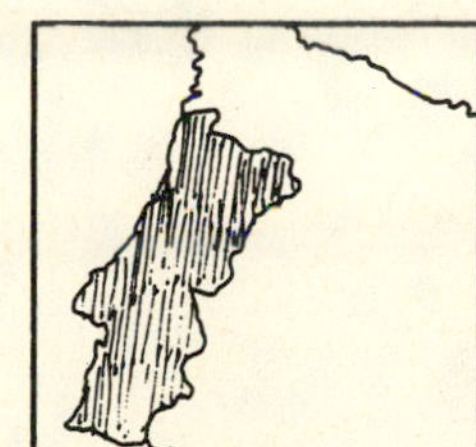

6. Portugal

DICTÉE

14. Catherine

____ Catherine.

____ Québec.

________________, ____________________________ Montréal.

____.

____.

NOTE CULTURELLE: LA FRANCE, UN PAYS TOURISTIQUE

15. Lecture. Ouvrez votre livre à la page 229. Écoutez!

16. Compréhension du texte

	1	2	3	4	5	6	7
vrai							
faux							

NOM ______________________ DATE ______________________

Leçon 17. Pour garder la ligne

PRÉSENTATION

1. **Lecture.** Ouvrez votre livre à la page 240. Écoutez!

2. **Compréhension du texte**

	1	2	3	4	5	6	7	8
André								
Yannick								

PHONÉTIQUE

3. **La lettre «h»**

In French, unlike English, the letter "h" is always silent.

(a) *Le «h» muet.* Most words that begin with "h" are treated as if they began with the vowel sound. Before a mute "h," elision and liaison are required.

Répétez: **l'homme** **un homme** **j'habite** **vous habitez** **l'heure**

En hiver, ces hommes partent à six heures.

(b) *Le «h» aspiré.* Some words that begin with "h" are treated as if they began with a consonant sound. These words are marked with an asterisk in the dictionary. Before an aspirate "h" there is never elision or liaison.

Répétez: **un hors-d'œuvre** **des haricots** **le hockey** **le huit**
Nous jouons au hockey le huit octobre.

STRUCTURE ET VOCABULAIRE

A. Le verbe **prendre**

4. **Prononciation.** Ouvrez votre livre à la page 242. Le verbe **prendre** est irrégulier.

5. **Pratique**

❖ **Marie** prend des pâtes.
❖ Apprenez-**vous** l'espagnol?
❖ **Je** n'ai pas compris la leçon.

B. L'article partitif

Vocabulaire: Au menu

6. **Prononciation.** Ouvrez votre livre à la page 245.

7. **Narration: À la cafétéria**

❖ François aime la salade.
Il va prendre de la salade.

C. L'article partitif dans les phrases négatives

8. **Situation: Au régime**

❖ le rosbif?
Il n'achète pas de rosbif.

D. Le verbe **boire**

9. **Prononciation.** Ouvrez votre livre à la page 248. Le verbe **boire** est irrégulier.

10. **Pratique**

❖ **Marc** ne boit pas de vin.
❖ **J'**ai bu du café.

Vocabulaire: Les boissons

11. **Prononciation.** Ouvrez votre livre à la page 248.

12. **Situation: Que boivent-ils?**

❖ la limonade?
Oui, ils boivent de la limonade.

13. **Compréhension**

1. ____________________ 4. ____________________ 7. ____________________
2. ____________________ 5. ____________________ 8. ____________________
3. ____________________ 6. ____________________ 9. ____________________

E. L'emploi idiomatique de **faire**

14. Conversation: Vos activités

❖ VINCENT: Tu aimes la photo?
VOUS: ***Oui, je fais de la photo.***

❖ VINCENT: Tu aimes le jogging?
VOUS: ***Non, je ne fais pas de jogging.***

DIALOGUE

15. Nourriture et boissons

❖ MARIE-NOËLLE: Qu'est-ce que tu bois?
VOUS: ***Je bois du café.***

1. 
2. 
3. 
4. 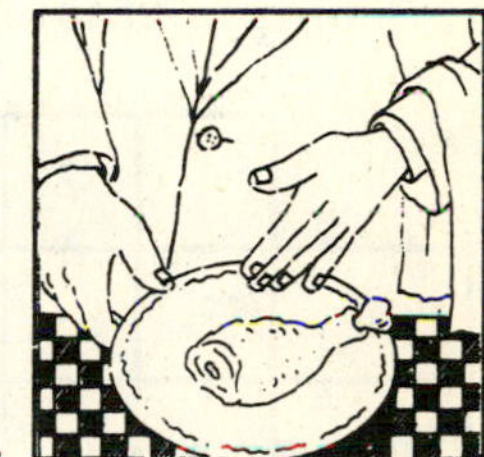
5. 
6. 
7. 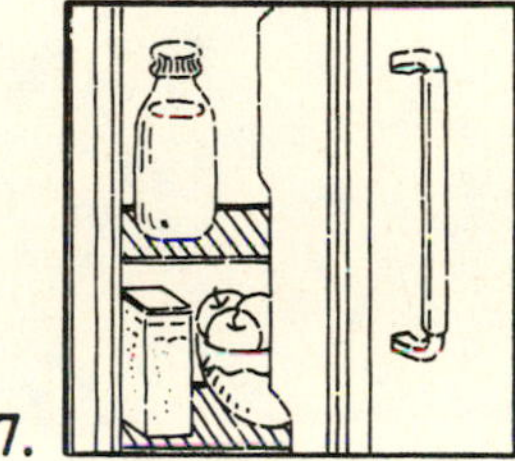
8. 
9. 
10. 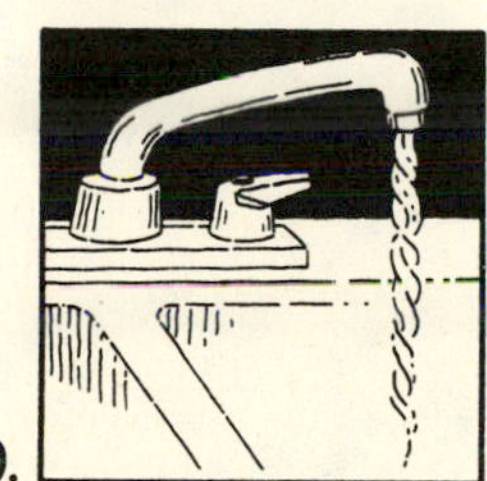

DICTÉE

16. Au restaurant

Guillaume et Suzanne ______________________. Guillaume ______________________.

____. ______________________________.

Suzanne ___________________________, _______________________________________

_______________________. ____

_______________________.

NOTE CULTURELLE: LA QUALITÉ DE LA VIE

17. Lecture. Ouvrez votre livre à la page 241. Écoutez!

18. Compréhension du texte

	1	2	3	4	5
vrai					
faux					

NOM ______________________ DATE ______________________

Leçon 18. Bon appétit!

PRÉSENTATION

1. **Lecture.** Ouvrez votre livre à la page 252. Écoutez!

2. **Compréhension du texte**

	1	2	3	4	5
vrai					
faux					

PHONÉTIQUE

3. **Les voyelles [ø] et [œ]**

The French vowels [ø] and [œ] have no counterparts in English.
(a) *La voyelle* [ø]. To pronounce the vowel [ø], round your lips tensely as you say the sound [e].

Répétez: **eux deux heureux Eugène serveuse il pleut**
Eugène n'est pas heureux quand il pleut.
Monsieur Lebleu dîne avec eux.

(b) *La voyelle* [œ]. To pronounce the vowel [œ], round your lips as you say the sound [ɛ].

Répétez: **sœur heure œuf beurre peur meuble**
Le professeur déjeune à une heure.
Ma sœur prend du beurre avec son œuf.

STRUCTURE ET VOCABULAIRE

Vocabulaire: Les repas

4. **Prononciation.** Ouvrez votre livre à la page 254.

5. Questions personnelles

	1	2	3	4	5	6	7	8
oui								
non								

A. Le verbe **mettre**

6. Prononciation. Ouvrez votre livre à la page 256. Le verbe **mettre,** *to put,* est irrégulier.

7. Pratique

❖ **Martine** met la table.
❖ Où est-ce que **tu** as mis la voiture?

B. L'emploi de l'article partitif, de l'article défini et de l'article indéfini

8. Conversation: Préférences

❖ PAUL: Aimes-tu le caviar?
VOUS: ***Oui, j'aime le caviar.***

❖ MICHÈLE: Manges-tu du caviar?
VOUS: ***Oui, je mange du caviar.***

Vocabulaire: Les fruits et les légumes

9. Prononciation. Ouvrez votre livre à la page 262.

10. Pratique

❖ **J'aime** les fruits.
❖ **J'aime** les fraises.

11. Compréhension: Au restaurant

Client 1: ______________________ Client 3: ______________________

Cliente 2: ______________________ Cliente 4: ______________________

NOM ______________________ DATE ______________

C. Expressions de quantité

12. Prononciation. Ouvrez votre livre à la page 262.

13. Conversation: D'autres quantités

❖ non, pas beaucoup

MARC: Est-ce que Paul a de l'argent?

VOUS: ***Non, il n'a pas beaucoup d'argent.***

1. oui, beaucoup
2. non, pas assez
3. oui, trop
4. non, pas beaucoup
5. oui, beaucoup

DIALOGUE

14. Nourriture et boissons

❖ —Qu'est-ce que tu as commandé?

—*J'ai commandé du poisson.*

1. 

2. 

3. 

4. 

5. 

6. 

7. 

8. 

DICTÉE

15. Au restaurant

____.

____.

François ______________________________________.

_____, ____.

NOTE CULTURELLE: LES REPAS FRANÇAIS

16. Lecture. Ouvrez votre livre à la page 253. Écoutez!

17. Compréhension du texte

	1	2	3	4	5
vrai					
faux					

NOM ______________________ DATE ______________________

Vivre en France 6. Au café

1. La bonne réponse

1. a. D'accord! Allons dans ce café.

   b. Moi aussi, j'ai soif.

   c. Bien sûr. Voulez-vous un croque-monsieur?

2. a. Bien sûr. Ça fait deux plus deux.

   b. Voilà! Ça fait 48 francs.

   c. Non, le service n'est pas compris *(included).*

3. a. Je vais prendre le lapin farci.

   b. J'aime les pommes frites.

   c. Non merci! Je suis végétarien.

4. a. Donnez-moi une crème caramel.

   b. Ça dépend. C'est combien?

   c. Pouvez-vous m'apporter une bière pression?

5. a. Voici le menu.

   b. Il y a des œufs mayonnaise.

   c. Il y a de la glace à la vanille.

6. a. Non, je ne veux pas de dessert.

   b. Oui, le serveur va apporter l'addition.

   c. Non, je vais prendre du jambon.

7. a. Bien sûr, j'adore la sole.

   b. Je préfère les légumes.

   c. Oui, donnez-moi de l'eau minérale, s'il vous plaît.

8. a. Oui, c'est cher.

   b. Non, il n'est pas ici.

   c. Attendez une seconde. Je vais préparer l'addition.

2. En France

RESTAURANT DES LILAS

Table n° 9

Hors-d'œuvre: ____________________

Plat principal: ____________________

Légumes: ____________________

Salade: ____________________

Fromage: ____________________

Dessert: ____________________

Boisson: ____________________

NOM ______________________ DATE ______________________

UNITÉ 7. À l'université

Leçon 19. La course aux diplômes

PRÉSENTATION

1. **Lecture.** Ouvrez votre livre à la page 272. Écoutez!

2. **Compréhension du texte**

	1	2	3	4
vrai				
faux				

PHONÉTIQUE

3. **Les semi-voyelles [w] et [ɥ]**

When the vowel sounds [w] and [y] are followed by another vowel in the same syllable, they are pronounced rapidly as semi-vowels.

(a) *La semi-voyelle* [w]. The semi-vowel [w] usually occurs together with the vowel [a]. In this combination, it is represented by the letters "oi."

Répétez: **moi voici toi vouloir devoir chinois soir**
Moi, je nettoie ma chambre ce soir.
Voilà la voiture de François.

The semi-vowel [w] also occurs in the combinations "oui" and "oin."

Répétez: **oui Louis Louise besoin moins**
Mais oui, Louise a besoin de Louis.

(b) *La semi-voyelle* [ɥ]. The semi-vowel [ɥ] usually occurs before the vowel [i]. It is similar to the vowel [y], but it is pronounced more rapidly and with greater tension. Keep your lips rounded and your tongue against the lower front teeth when pronouncing [ɥ].

Répétez: **lui huit suis nuit cuisine Suisse minuit**
Le huit juillet nous allons en Suisse.
Je suis chez lui.

STRUCTURE ET VOCABULAIRE

Vocabulaire: Les études

4. Prononciation. Ouvrez votre livre à la page 274.

5. Pratique

❖ **Marc** obtient de très bonnes notes.
❖ Anne et Marie **préparent** leur examen.

6. Compréhension orale

	1	2	3	4	5	6
logique						
illogique						

A. Le verbe suivre

7. Prononciation. Ouvrez votre livre à la page 277. Le verbe **suivre** est irrégulier.

8. Pratique

❖ **Tu** suis un régime.
❖ Quel cours suis-**tu?**

B. Les verbes **vouloir** et **pouvoir**

9. Prononciation. Ouvrez votre livre à la page 278. Les verbes **vouloir** et **pouvoir** sont irréguliers.

10. Narration: Mais non!

❖ Georges veut sortir.
Mais non, il ne peut pas sortir!

11. Narration: Ce soir

❖ Thérèse regarde la télé.
Elle ne veut pas sortir.

C. Le verbe **devoir**

12. Prononciation. Ouvrez votre livre à la page 280. Le verbe **devoir** est irrégulier.

13. Narration: Obligations

❖ Mon cousin travaille.
Il doit travailler.

14. Situation: Jean-Michel

❖ devoir
Jean-Michel est parti.
Il a dû partir.

❖ vouloir
Jean-Michel a voyagé.
Il a voulu voyager.

1. vouloir 2. pouvoir 3. devoir 4. pouvoir

D. L'expression impersonnelle **il faut**

15. Narration: Il faut

❖ Travaille! ***Il faut travailler!***

❖ Ne rate pas l'examen! ***Il ne faut pas rater l'examen!***

Vocabulaire: Expressions indéfinies de quantité

16. Prononciation. Ouvrez votre livre à la page 284.

17. Conversation: Que cherches-tu?

❖ JEANNE: Cherches-tu ce stylo?
VOUS: ***Non, je cherche un autre stylo.***

18. Jouons un rôle: La ville de Toulouse

❖ CHRISTINE: La ville est jolie, n'est-ce pas?
PIERRE: ***Oui, toute la ville est jolie.***

DIALOGUE

19. Activités

❖ FRANÇOISE: Qu'est-ce que tu veux faire ce soir?
VOUS: ***Je veux regarder la télé.***

1.

2.

3.

4.

5.

6.

DICTÉE

20. Ce soir

__________, ____.

______________________________, __________________________________.

__________, __________________________. __________________________.

______________________________, ______________________________________

______________________________.

NOTE CULTURELLE: LES EXAMENS ET LES DIPLÔMES FRANÇAIS

21. Lecture. Ouvrez votre livre à la page 273. Écoutez!

22. Compréhension du texte

	1	2	3	4	5	6
vrai						
faux						

NOM ____ DATE ____________________________

Leçon 20. Pas de panique!

PRÉSENTATION

1. **Lecture.** Ouvrez votre livre à la page 286. Écoutez!

2. **Compréhension du texte**

	1	2	3	4	5	6
vrai						
faux						

PHONÉTIQUE

3. **La consonne [l]**

- The French consonant [l] is a delicate or "light" L-sound.

  Écoutez: **il belle l'eau**

- The English consonant [l] is often much thicker or darker.

  Comparez: **il** EEL **l'eau** LOW

- In French, the consonant [l] is pronounced with the tip of the tongue touching the upper front teeth.

  Répétez: **elle il quel belle Paul lui leur utile facile**
  Il s'appelle Paul Laval.
  Lucille lui téléphone lundi.

STRUCTURE ET VOCABULAIRE

Vocabulaire: Les études supérieures

4. **Prononciation.** Ouvrez votre livre à la page 288.

5. Compréhension orale

	1	2	3	4	5	6	7	8
logique								
illogique								

A. Le verbe voir

6. Prononciation. Ouvrez votre livre à la page 289.

7. Pratique

❖ **Je** vois souvent mes parents.
❖ **Je** n'ai pas vu l'accident.

B. Le verbe **connaître**

8. Prononciation. Ouvrez votre livre à la page 290.

9. Pratique

❖ **Georges** connaît un bon restaurant.

C. Les pronoms le, la, les

10. Identification de structures

	1	2	3	4	5	6	7	8
Philippe								
Annie								
Jacques et Pierre								

11. Conversation: Moi aussi

❖ BÉATRICE: Je comprends mes parents.
VOUS: *Moi aussi, je les comprends.*

12. Conversation: Les garçons, non. Les filles, oui.

❖ JEAN-MICHEL: Tu connais Paul?
VOUS: *Non, je ne le connais pas.*

NOM ________________________________ DATE ________________________

Vocabulaire: Quelques verbes utilisés avec un complément d'objet direct

13. Prononciation. Ouvrez votre livre à la page 292.

D. Les pronoms **le, la, les** et l'infinitif

14. Conversation: Oui, bien sûr!

❖ NATHALIE: Vas-tu écouter le professeur?
VOUS: ***Oui, bien sûr, je vais l'écouter.***

E. Le passé composé: l'accord du participe passé

15. Conversation: Oui et non

❖ ÉRIC: Tu as invité Pierre?
VOUS: ***Oui, je l'ai invité.***

❖ ÉRIC: Tu as invité Marie?
VOUS: ***Non, je ne l'ai pas invitée.***

DIALOGUE

16. Où et quand?

❖ en Suisse
—Où as-tu acheté cette montre?
—Je l'ai achetée en Suisse.

1. dans la rue
2. dans la classe de français
3. au salon
4. au café
5. à huit heures
6. pendant les vacances
7. hier soir
8. à Montréal

DICTÉE

17. Monique et Henri

______________________ Monique? _______, ____.

____ Paris.

_____________________________________. _____________________________________ Henri.

________________________, ____.

____ l'Université de Grenoble.

NOTE CULTURELLE: LES ÉTUDES SUPÉRIEURES

18. Lecture. Ouvrez votre livre à la page 287. Écoutez!

19. Compréhension du texte

	1	2	3	4	5	6	7
vrai							
faux							

NOM ______________________________ DATE ______________________

Leçon 21. Un contestataire

PRÉSENTATION

1. Lecture. Ouvrez votre livre à la page 300. Écoutez!

2. Compréhension du texte

	1	2	3	4	5	6	7	8
vrai								
faux								

PHONÉTIQUE

3. La liaison: Le groupe verbal

As you recall, liaison is required between the subject pronoun and the verb. Liaison is also required between object pronouns and the verb.

Répétez: **Nous les envoyons.**
Vous nous écrivez.
Mes cousins nous invitent.
Nous voulons les obtenir.
Je vais vous aider.

STRUCTURE ET VOCABULAIRE

A. Les verbes **dire, lire, écrire**

4. Prononciation. Ouvrez votre livre à la page 302. Les verbes **dire, lire** et **écrire** sont irréguliers.

5. **Pratique**

❖ **Henri** dit des mensonges.
❖ **Marie** lit des bandes dessinées.
❖ **J'écris** un article.

B. La conjonction **que**

6. **Situation: Ils étudient trop!**

❖ Nous pensons
Nous pensons que nous étudions trop.

C. Les pronoms **lui, leur**

7. **Prononciation.** Ouvrez votre livre à la page 305.

8. **Identification de structures**

	1	2	3	4	5	6	7	8
Sylvie								
Marc et Éric								

Vocabulaire: Quelques verbes utilisés avec un complément d'objet indirect

9. **Prononciation.** Ouvrez votre livre à la page 306.

10. **Pratique**

❖ Est-ce que vous **parlez** à Jacqueline?
❖ Marc **demande** de l'argent à Nathalie.

11. **Conversation: Hier**

❖ MARTINE: Avez-vous téléphoné à vos parents?
VOUS: *Oui, je leur ai téléphoné.*

❖ MARTINE: Avez-vous téléphoné à votre cousine?
VOUS: *Non, je ne lui ai pas téléphoné.*

D. Les pronoms **me, te, nous, vous**

12. Jouons un rôle: Mais oui!

❖ THÉRÈSE: Tu me téléphones?
RICHARD: ***Mais oui, je te téléphone.***

❖ THÉRÈSE: Tu nous donnes cinq dollars?
THOMAS: ***Mais oui, je vous donne cinq dollars.***

E. La place des pronoms à l'impératif

13. Situation: S'il te plaît!

❖ téléphoner ce soir
Téléphone-moi ce soir!

14. Conversation: Fais-le toi-même!

❖ ALBERT: Invite Jacqueline!
VOUS: ***Invite-la toi-même!***

DIALOGUE

15. Qu'est-ce que tu fais?

❖ THOMAS: Qu'est-ce que tu écris à Jacqueline?
VOUS: ***Je lui écris une lettre.***

1. 

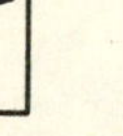

2. 

3. 

4. 

5. 

6. 

DICTÉE

16. J'ai besoin de mon livre

__________________ Christine, __________________? ______________________________

____________________________________. ____________________________________,

____. __________________________________.

____, s'il te plaît!

NOTE CULTURELLE: LES ÉTUDIANTS FRANÇAIS ET LA POLITIQUE

17. Lecture. Ouvrez votre livre à la page 301. Écoutez!

18. Compréhension du texte

	1	2	3	4	5	6
vrai						
faux						

NOM ______________________________ DATE ______________________________

Vivre en France 7. Le courrier

1. La bonne réponse

1. a. Il y a un livre.

   b. Il y a beaucoup de courrier.

   c. C'est à la poste restante.

2. a. Parce que les timbres sont bon marché.

   b. Je dois envoyer un télégramme.

   c. Je dois utiliser le code postal.

3. a. Je vais l'envoyer demain.

   b. J'ai besoin de deux timbres.

   c. Je voudrais l'envoyer en recommandé.

4. a. Non, il n'est pas encore parti.

   b. Oui, il est arrivé avec des copains.

   c. Oui! Tiens, ces cartes postales sont pour toi.

5. a. Parce que c'est près d'ici.

   b. J'attends une lettre de mon copain Pierre.

   c. J'ai besoin de timbres.

6. a. Je ne sais pas. Les tarifs postaux vont changer.

   b. Tiens, voilà un timbre par avion.

   c. Bien sûr, mais dis-moi, à qui est-ce que tu écris?

7. a. Parce que c'est moins cher que par avion.

   b. Oui, je vais envoyer un télégramme.

   c. J'ai l'intention d'écrire à ma cousine qui habite au Canada.

8. a. Mets-le ici à côté du nom de la ville.

   b. Ne l'envoie pas par la poste.

   c. Je ne sais pas. J'ai oublié.

2. **En France**

	valeur unitaire	quantité	total
TIMBRES			
	______	______	______
	______	______	______
	______	______	______
AÉROGRAMMES	______	______	______
total			

NOM ______________________________ DATE ______________________

UNITÉ 8. Hier et aujourd'hui

Leçon 22. La vie urbaine: Pour ou contre?

PRÉSENTATION

1. Lecture. Ouvrez votre livre à la page 328. Écoutez!

2. Compréhension du texte

	1	2	3	4	5	6	7	8	9	10	11	12
vrai												
faux												

PHONÉTIQUE

3. Les lettres «qu»

The letters "qu" almost always represent the sound [k].

Répétez: **qui Québec quand quartier politique physique**
Quand as-tu quitté Québec?
Monique a répondu à la question.
Dominique adore la musique classique.

STRUCTURE ET VOCABULAIRE

Vocabulaire: La ville

4. Prononciation. Ouvrez votre livre à la page 330.

5. Pratique

❖ Voici un beau **quartier.**
❖ Ce **quartier** est ancien.

A. Le verbe savoir

6. Prononciation. Ouvre votre livre à la page 332. Le verbe **savoir** est irrégulier.

7. Pratique

❖ **Marie** sait faire du ski.
❖ Sais-tu nager?

8. Situation: Le savoir

❖ Henri joue au tennis.
Il sait jouer au tennis.

B. Connaître vs. savoir

9. Situation: Bien sûr!

❖ le président de l'université
Bien sûr! Je connais le président de l'université.

C. Le pronom relatif **qui**

10. Situation: C'est vrai!

❖ New York est une ville intéressante.
C'est vrai! C'est une ville qui est intéressante.

D. Le pronom relatif **que**

11. Conversation: Oui, c'est ça!

❖ SYLVIANE: Tu achètes ce livre?
VOUS: *Oui, c'est le livre que j'achète.*

12. Situation: Comment s'appelle-t-elle?

❖ BERNARD: Une fille passe dans la rue.
VOUS: *Comment s'appelle la fille qui passe dans la rue?*

❖ BERNARD: Paul connaît une fille.
VOUS: *Comment s'appelle la fille que Paul connaît?*

NOM ______________________________ DATE ______________________

E. Les expressions **quelqu'un, quelque chose** et leurs contraires

13. Conversation: Non!

❖ FLORENCE: Vous invitez quelqu'un ce soir?
VOUS: ***Non, je n'invite personne.***

DIALOGUE

14. Où habites-tu?

1. ____ dans une ville. ____ à la campagne.
2. ____ dans le centre. ____ dans la banlieue.
3. ____ dans un immeuble. ____ dans une maison individuelle.
4. ____ (oui) ____ (non)
5. ____ (oui) ____ (non)
6. ____ (oui) ____ (non)
7. ____________________ habitants.

DICTÉE

15. Ma voisine

____

____________________. ____.

____

____________________. ____

____________________________________.

NOTE CULTURELLE: L'URBANISATION DE LA FRANCE

16. Lecture. Ouvrez votre livre à la page 329. Écoutez!

17. Compréhension du texte

	1	2	3	4	5	6
vrai						
faux						

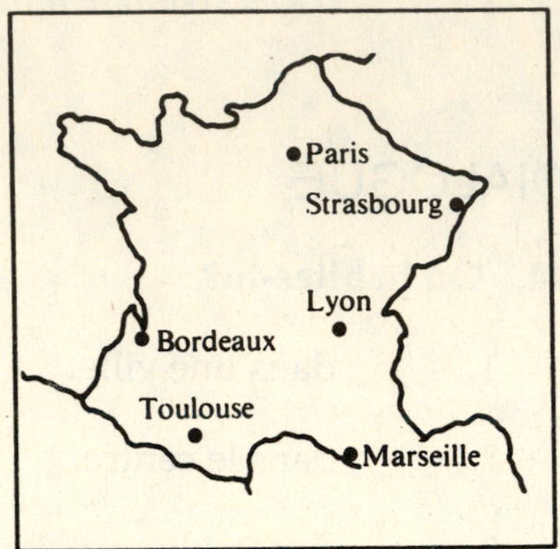

NOM ______________________________ DATE ______________________

Leçon 23. La télévision: Un bien ou un mal?

PRÉSENTATION

1. Lecture. Ouvrez votre livre à la page 342. Écoutez!

2. Compréhension du texte

	1	2	3	4	5	6
vrai						
faux						

PHONÉTIQUE

3. Les terminaisons *-tion* et *-sion*

Many French words end in **-tion** and **-sion.** These endings are usually pronounced [sjɔ̃] and [zjɔ̃]. The ending **-stion** as in **question** is pronounced [stjɔ̃]. In practicing these endings, pronounce the [j] rapidly with great tension. Avoid the "sh" [ʃ] or "zh" [ʒ] sounds that characterize the corresponding English endings.

Comparez: **station** STATION
mission MISSION
télévision TELEVISION

Répétez: **nation attention émission émotion exception**
télévision décision occasion
À la télévision, j'aime les émissions sportives.
Faites attention aux exceptions!

STRUCTURE ET VOCABULAIRE

Vocabulaire: La télévision

4. Situation: La télévision

❖ les informations?
Oui, il regarde les informations.

A. Le verbe vivre

5. Prononciation. Ouvrez votre livre à la page 345. Le verbe **vivre** est irrégulier.

6. Pratique

❖ **Nous** vivons aux États-Unis.

B. Quelques expressions négatives

7. Pratique

❖ **Brigitte** ne regarde jamais la télé.
❖ Monique ne **fume** plus.

8. Narration: Jamais!

❖ Paul déteste étudier.
Il n'étudie jamais.

C. L'imparfait

9. Prononciation. Ouvrez votre livre à la page 348. L'imparfait est un temps exprimant le passé.

10. Pratique

❖ **Je** regardais un dessin animé.
❖ **Je** n'étais pas en classe hier.
❖ Marc **finissait** le livre.

11. Narration: Avant!

❖ à Québec
Philippe habite à Paris.
Avant, il habitait à Québec.

1. à Marseille
2. l'italien
3. au football
4. en ville
5. les nouvelles
6. de la musique classique
7. les bandes dessinées
8. le samedi

D. L'imparfait et le passé composé: conditions habituelles et événements spécifiques

12. Identification de structures

	1	2	3	4	5	6	7	8
événement spécifique								
événement habituel								

Vocabulaire: Expressions de temps

13. Prononciation. Ouvrez votre livre à la page 352.

14. Jouons un rôle: Questions

❖ un an
YVES: Combien de temps as-tu habité à Québec?
GUY: ***J'ai habité un an à Québec.***

❖ à Paris
YVES: Et avant, où habitais-tu?
GUY: ***J'habitais à Paris.***

1. dans une pharmacie
2. dans un magasin de vêtements
3. avec Denise
4. avec Monique
5. deux fois
6. avec mes parents
7. dans la rue
8. au café

DIALOGUE

15. Pendant les vacances

❖ MARIE: Qu'est-ce que tu faisais le lundi soir?

VOUS: *Je suivais un cours de judo.*

	MATIN	APRÈS-MIDI	SOIR
LUNDI	*travailler au supermarché*		
MARDI			*sortir avec mes copains*
MERCREDI		*jouer au tennis*	
JEUDI		*déjeuner au restaurant*	
VENDREDI			*aller à la discothèque*
SAMEDI		*aller à la piscine*	
DIMANCHE	*dormir*	*regarder la télé*	

DICTÉE

16. Le fils des voisins

______________________________, ____.

____ Henri, ______________________________.

______________________________________. ____

______________________________________.

NOTE CULTURELLE: LA TÉLÉVISION EN FRANCE

17. Lecture. Ouvrez votre livre à la page 343. Écoutez!

18. Compréhension du texte

	1	2	3	4	5	6	7	8
vrai								
faux								

Leçon 24. Un cambriolage

PRÉSENTATION

1. **Lecture.** Ouvrez votre livre à la page 356. Écoutez!

2. **Compréhension du texte**

	1	2	3	4	5	6	7	8	9	10
vrai										
faux										

PHONÉTIQUE

3. **Les lettres «ai»**

At the end of a word, the letters "ai" represent the sound [e]. When followed by a silent final consonant, they also usually are prononced [e]. However, when followed by a pronounced consonant, they represent the sound [ɛ].

Comparez: j'ai — j'aime
français — française
fait — faire

Répétez: **j'ai le lait le fait anglais français**
j'aide semaine anniversaire fraise urbaine
Je n'ai pas pris de lait.
Tu m'aides la semaine prochaine?

NOTE: The letters "ain" and "aim" represent the nasal vowel [ɛ̃]

Répétez: **pain faim demain bain soudain**
Soudain Alain avait très faim.

STRUCTURE ET VOCABULAIRE

Vocabulaire: Événements

4. **Prononciation.** Ouvrez votre livre à la page 358.

A. Le passé composé et l'imparfait: événement spécifique et circonstances de l'événement

5. Identification de structures

	1	2	3	4	5	6	7	8	9	10	11	12	13	14
circonstance														
événement spécifique														

6. Jouons un rôle: Au commissariat de police

❖ dans la rue Carnot
L'INSPECTEUR: Où étiez-vous hier soir à huit heures?
ÉRIC: ***J'étais dans la rue Carnot.***

1. une promenade
2. mauvais
3. un homme assez grand
4. la Banque Nationale
5. un costume beige
6. un grand sac
7. appeler un taxi
8. jaune

B. L'imparfait et le passé composé: actions progressives et événements spécifiques

7. Narration: Hier

❖ Jacques dîne à six heures.
Hier, à six heures, il dînait.

8. Narration: La résidence

❖ Je fais mes devoirs.
Je faisais mes devoirs quand Robert est rentré.

C. L'imparfait et le passé composé dans la même phrase

9. Narration: Pourquoi pas?

❖ Nicole attend un ami.
Nicole n'est pas sortie parce qu'elle attendait un ami.

NOM ______________________________ DATE ______________________

10. Jouons un rôle: Pourquoi?

❖ J'ai faim.
OLIVIER: Pourquoi es-tu allée au restaurant?
NICOLE: ***Je suis allée au restaurant parce que j'avais faim.***

1. J'ai soif.
2. Je veux faire une promenade.
3. Je veux apprendre l'espagnol.
4. J'ai envie de lui parler.
5. J'ai l'intention d'étudier.

D. Le plus-que-parfait

11. Prononciation. Ouvrez votre livre à la page 368.

DIALOGUE

12. Alibis

chez lui

❖ —Où était M. Arnaud à dix heures?
—Il était chez lui. Il regardait la télé.

1. au bureau

2. dans sa chambre

3. au restaurant

4. à la bibliothèque

5. dans la rue

DICTÉE

13. Hier soir

________________, ____.

____ épouvantable. ________________

la visibilité____. ______________________,

____, ______________________________.

____ Jean-Claude. __________________________

______________________________________.

NOTE CULTURELLE: LES FRANÇAIS EN UNIFORME

14. Lecture. Ouvrez votre livre à la page 357. Écoutez!

15. Compréhension du texte

	1	2	3	4	5
vrai					
faux					

NOM ______________________________ DATE ______________________

Vivre en France 8. Les sorties

1. La bonne réponse

1. a. Le film *Indochine.*
   b. Je pense que c'est une pièce de Beckett.
   c. Non, je ne suis pas libre.
2. a. Je préfère les films de science fiction.
   b. On peut se retrouver devant le cinéma.
   c. On peut aller à la séance de vingt-deux heures.
3. a. Un excellent spectacle de variétés.
   b. Une exposition de peinture.
   c. Non, je n'ai pas eu le temps.
4. a. Oui, j'aimerais bien aller au concert.
   b. J'ai déjà assisté à cette conférence.
   c. Oh, tu sais, moi, je ne connais rien à l'art moderne.
5. a. Non, je dois étudier.
   b. Je veux bien.
   c. Je te remercie.
6. a. J'aimerais t'inviter demain soir.
   b. Je n'aime pas cette couleur.
   c. Volontiers, est-ce qu'il y a un café près d'ici?
7. a. C'est entendu!
   b. Je te remercie.
   c. Je suis désolé.
8. a. C'est d'accord!
   b. Oui, je vais aller à un concert avec mes copains.
   c. Tu es gentil, mais je ne suis pas d'accord.

2. **En France**

Rendez-vous

avec qui? ______________________________

quelle date? ___________________________

à quelle heure? ________________________

où? ___________________________________

nom du film? ___________________________

NOM ______________________ DATE ______________________

UNITÉ 9. Images de la vie

Leçon 25. Vive les loisirs!

PRÉSENTATION

1. **Lecture.** Ouvrez votre livre à la page 378. Écoutez!

2. **Compréhension du texte**

	1	2	3	4	5	6
vrai						
faux						

PHONÉTIQUE

3. **Les consonnes [ʒ] et [g]**

(a) *La consonne* [ʒ]. The consonant [ʒ] is similar to the sound represented by the letter "g" in the English word *mirage.* Do not pronounce a [d] before [ʒ], unless there is a "d" in the written form of the French word, as in **budget.**

Répétez: **je Jean âge argent régime logement gymnastique**
Quel âge a Gigi?
Jacques fait du patinage avec Roger.

(b) *La consonne* [g]. The French consonant [g] is produced with greater tension than the corresponding sound in English.

Répétez: **grand grippe guitare garçon glace langue**
Guy va garder la guitare de Margot.
Guillaume est un grand garçon.

STRUCTURE ET VOCABULAIRE

Vocabulaire: La santé, les sports et les loisirs

4. Prononciation. Ouvrez votre livre à la page 380.

5. Compréhension orale

	1	2	3	4	5	6	7	8
logique								
illogique								

A. Le verbe **courir**

6. Prononciation. Ouvrez votre livre à la page 382. Le verbe **courir** est irrégulier.

7. Pratique

❖ **Nous** courons tous les jours.
❖ **Tu** n'as pas couru très vite.

B. Le pronom **y**

8. Conversation: Où allez-vous?

❖ M. DURAND: Allez-vous souvent au cinéma?
VOUS: ***Oui, j'y vais souvent.***

❖ M. DURAND: Allez-vous souvent chez le dentiste?
VOUS: ***Non, je n'y vais pas souvent.***

9. Conversation: Que fait Bernard?

❖ CHARLOTTE: Est-ce que Bernard joue au tennis?
VOUS: ***Oui, il y joue.***

❖ CHARLOTTE: Est-ce qu'il téléphone à ses amis?
VOUS: ***Oui, il leur téléphone.***

C. Le pronom **en**

10. Conversation: Un végétarien!

❖ ANNE: Est-ce qu'il mange du rosbif?
VOUS: ***Non, il n'en mange pas.***

11. Conversation: Conseils

❖ MONIQUE: Est-ce que je dois faire de l'athlétisme?
VOUS: ***Oui, fais-en!***

D. Le pronom **en** avec les expressions de quantité

12. Conversation: Nous aussi!

❖ ALAIN: En France, nous avons beaucoup de travail.
VOUS: ***Nous aussi, nous en avons beaucoup.***

DIALOGUE

13. Activités

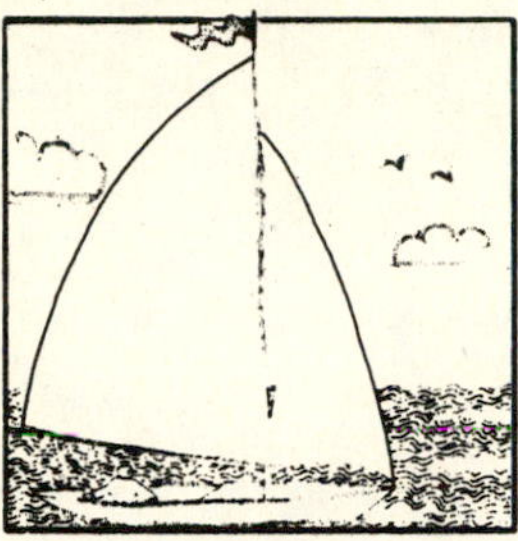

à Toulon

❖ ANNE: Qu'est-ce que Jacques fait en été?
VOUS: ***Il fait de la voile.***

ANNE: Ah bon, et où est-ce qu'il en fait?
VOUS: ***Il en fait à Toulon.***

1. en Suisse

2. à la Martinique

3. en Normandie

4. à Biarritz

5. au parc Monceau

DICTÉE

14. À la mer

_______________________________________? _______________________,

_______________________________________. _______________________________

_______________________________. _______________________________________.

_______________, ____.

_____________________________, ____.

NOTE CULTURELLE: LA CIVILISATION DES LOISIRS

15. Lecture. Ouvrez votre livre à la page 379. Écoutez!

16. Compréhension du texte

	1	2	3	4	5	6
vrai						
faux						

NOM ________________________ DATE ________________

Leçon 26. Pauvre Michel!

PRÉSENTATION

1. **Lecture.** Ouvrez votre livre à la page 392. Écoutez!

2. **Compréhension du texte**

	1	2	3	4	5	6	7	8
vrai								
faux								

PHONÉTIQUE

3. **La chute de la voyelle [ə]**

The mute "e" of the reflexive pronouns **me, te,** et **se** is dropped in rapid conversation when the preceding word ends in a vowel sound.

Répétez: **je me lève** — **je mé lève**
tu te rases — **tu té rases**
je me réveille — **je mé réveille**
tu te couches — **tu té couches**

When the preceding word ends in a consonant sound, the mute "e" is pronounced. Compare the following examples of rapid speech. In the first group of words in each pair, the reflexive pronoun is preceded by a consonant sound: the vowel [ə] is pronounced.

Comparez et répétez: **il se rase** — **Jean sé rase**
elle se réveille — **Marie sé réveille**
Paul se promène — **Guy sé promène**

STRUCTURE ET VOCABULAIRE

Vocabulaire: Quelques activités

4. **Prononciation.** Ouvrez votre livre à la page 394.

A. L'emploi de l'article défini avec les parties du corps

Vocabulaire: Les parties du corps

5. Prononciation. Ouvrez votre livre à la page 395.

6. Compréhension orale

1. ______________________
2. ______________________
3. ______________________
4. ______________________
5. ______________________
6. ______________________

B. Les verbes pronominaux: formation et sens réfléchi

7. Prononciation. Ouvrez votre livre à la page 398.

8. Pratique

❖ **Pierre** se regarde dans la glace.
❖ **Je** ne me coupe jamais.
❖ Est-ce que **Paul** s'achète des disques?

Vocabulaire: Quelques occupations de la journée

9. Prononciation. Ouvrez votre livre à la page 400.

10. Pratique

❖ Nous **nous reposons** maintenant.
❖ Tu ne **te rases** pas?

11. Jouons un rôle: Mme Charron est curieuse.

❖ à sept heures
MME CHARRON: À quelle heure est-ce que vous vous réveillez?
PHILIPPE: ***Je me réveille à sept heures.***

1. à sept heures et quart
2. dans la salle de bains
3. avec un rasoir électrique
4. dans ma chambre
5. en voiture
6. après le déjeuner
7. à onze heures et demie

C. L'infinitif des verbes pronominaux

12. Narration: Demain aussi

❖ Charles se promène.
Demain aussi, il va se promener.

D. Le verbe **ouvrir**

13. Prononciation. Ouvrez votre livre à la page 404.

DIALOGUE

14. Qu'est-ce que tu cherches?

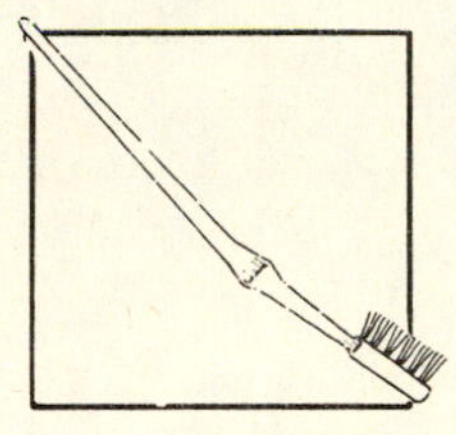

❖ VÉRONIQUE: Qu'est-ce que tu cherches?
VOUS: *Je cherche la brosse à dents.*
VÉRONIQUE: Ah bon? Pourquoi est-ce que tu en as besoin?
VOUS: *Je vais me brosser les dents.*

1. 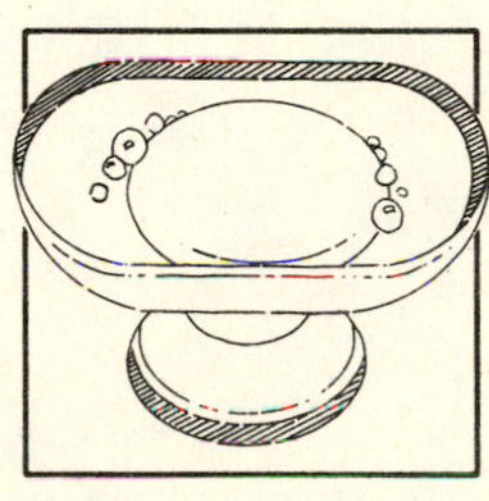
2. 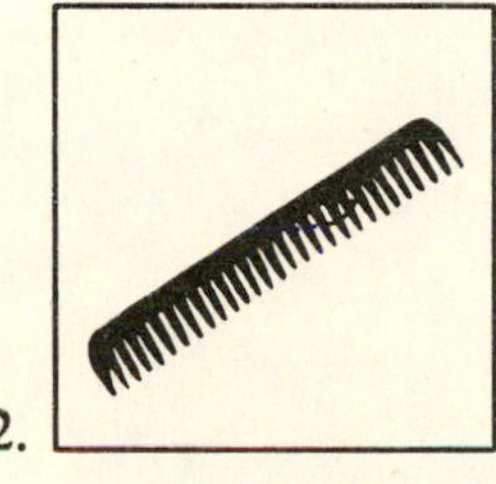
3. 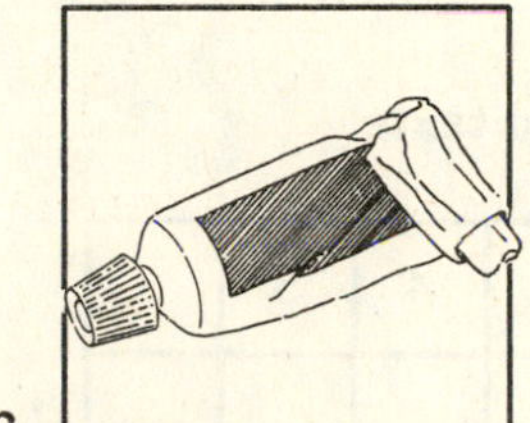
4. 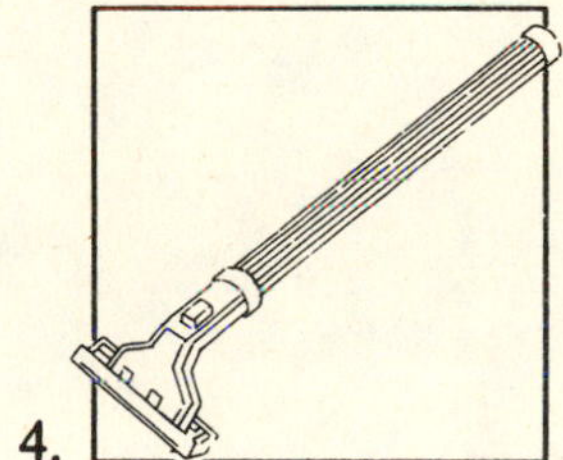
5. 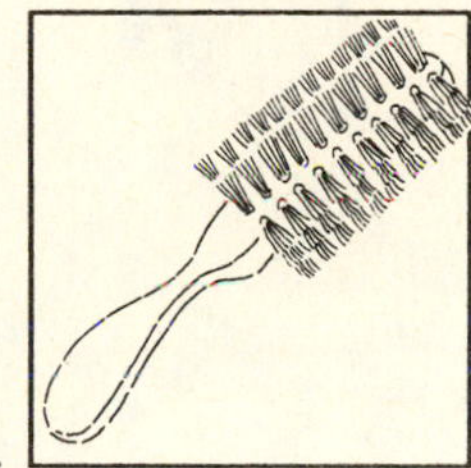

DICTÉE

15. Le dimanche

____?

______, ____.

____________, ____________, __________________________.

____________, _____________________________ Marie-Laure.

____.

______, ____?

NOTE CULTURELLE: LA VIE EN APPARTEMENT

16. Lecture. Ouvrez votre livre à la page 393. Écoutez!

17. Compréhension du texte

	1	2	3	4	5	6
vrai						
faux						

NOM ______________________________ DATE ______________________

Leçon 27. Un rendez-vous

PRÉSENTATION

1. **Lecture.** Ouvrez votre livre à la page 406. Écoutez!

2. **Compréhension du texte**

	1	2	3	4	5	6	7	8
vrai								
faux								

PHONÉTIQUE

3. **Les consonnes [p], [t] et [k]**

The French consonants [p], [t], and [k] are pronounced differently from their English counterparts. To understand this difference more clearly, perform the following experiment. Hold a piece of paper in front of your mouth as you say the English words "pot," "top," and "cot." The paper will move somewhat because you release a puff of air when you pronounce the initial English consonants "p," "t," and "k." Now try the same experiment with the English words "spot," "stop," and "Scot." The paper hardly moves because the consonants are pronounced without a puff of air when they follow an "s." In French the consonants [p], [t], and [k] in initial position are always pronounced *without* a puff of air.

Répétez: **pied peigne patinage parc problème**
tête temps trop tard tôt
cou corps cœur couper casser courir
Pierre est plus pessimiste que Paul.
Thomas a téléphoné trop tard.
Catherine a cassé la caméra de Kiki.

STRUCTURE ET VOCABULAIRE

Vocabulaire: Entre amis

4. **Prononciation.** Ouvrez votre livre à la page 408.

A. Les verbes pronominaux: sens idiomatique

5. Prononciation. Ouvrez votre livre à la page 408.

6. Pratique

❖ **Bernard** se souvient de ce restaurant.
❖ Nous **nous dépêchons.**

7. Compréhension orale

	1	2	3	4	5	6	7	8
logique								
illogique								

B. L'impératif des verbes pronominaux

8. Situation: S'il te plaît!

❖ se préparer pour le concert — ***Prépare-toi pour le concert!***
❖ s'impatienter — ***Ne t'impatiente pas!***

9. Situation: Les bons conseils

❖ Vos amis ne se dépêchent pas. — ***Dépêchez-vous!***
❖ Vos amis se disputent. — ***Ne vous disputez pas!***

C. Les verbes pronominaux: sens réciproque

10. Prononciation. Ouvrez votre livre à la page 413.

D. Le passé composé des verbes pronominaux

11. Prononciation. Ouvrez votre livre à la page 414. Le participe passé des verbes pronominaux est formé avec le verbe **être.**

12. Identification de structures

	1	2	3	4	5	6	7	8	9	10
présent										
passé										

13. Narration: Hier

❖ Nathalie se repose. *Hier aussi, elle s'est reposée.*

❖ Marie ne s'amuse pas. *Hier non plus, elle ne s'est pas amusée.*

14. Conversation: Samedi dernier

❖ ÉLISABETH: Est-ce que tu t'es levé(e) tôt?
VOUS: *Oui, je me suis levé(e) tôt.*

ÉLISABETH: Est-ce que tu t'es reposé(e)?
VOUS: *Non, je ne me suis pas reposé(e).*

DIALOGUE

15. Le week-end dernier

❖ à dix heures
—À quelle heure est-ce que tu t'es levé(e)?
—Je me suis levé(e) à dix heures.

1. à un copain
2. à deux heures
3. une promenade en ville
4. dans un café
5. à la terrasse
6. des glaces
7. au cinéma
8. un film d'Hitchcock
9. à sept heures

DICTÉE

16. Guy et Suzanne

______________, Guy _______________________. ____________________________________.

_______, ____________________________ Suzanne. ____________________________________

____. _______________________________,

____. Guy et Suzanne _______________________

______________________________. ______________________________? _______________.

NOTE CULTURELLE: OÙ ET COMMENT LES JEUNES FRANÇAIS SE RENCONTRENT-ILS?

17. Lecture. Ouvrez votre livre à la page 407. Écoutez!

18. Compréhension du texte

	1	2	3	4	5	6	7	8
vrai								
faux								

NOM ______________________ DATE ______________________

Vivre en France 9. Le sport et la santé

1. La bonne réponse

1. a. Non, je suis allé à la mer.
   b. Oui, je me suis bien bronzé.
   c. Non, mais j'ai pris un bon bain de soleil.
2. a. Je lève des poids.
   b. Je vais tous les soirs au Stade Municipal.
   c. Je fais de la planche à voile.
3. a. Oui, nous aimons faire du bateau.
   b. Non, nous détestons faire du camping.
   c. Oui, et nous avons fait plusieurs longues randonnées à pied.
4. a. Je faisais de l'aviron.
   b. Je me sens déprimé.
   c. Je me suis coupé au pied.
5. a. Oui, je fais du ski de fond.
   b. Écoute, j'aimerais bien ... mais je ne sais pas nager!
   c. Non, merci. Je n'ai pas envie de lever des poids.
6. a. Oui, je suis en bonne santé.
   b. Oui, je crois que j'ai la grippe.
   c. Oui, j'ai une douleur dans la jambe.
7. a. Oui, j'ai un rhume.
   b. Non, je n'ai pas de migraine.
   c. Oui, je crois que j'ai trop mangé.
8. a. Je suis tombé de vélo.
   b. Je me suis baigné.
   c. J'ai fait une promenade à cheval.

9. a. Je vais à la mer et je me bronze.
   b. Je ne fais jamais de deltaplane.
   c. Je mange modérément et je fais du jogging tous les jours.
10. a. Je me sens déprimé.
   b. J'ai couru pendant quinze kilomètres.
   c. Je me suis blessé au pied.
11. a. Oui, je suis allé à la mer.
   b. Oui, je fais de l'athlétisme.
   c. Hélas, non! Je me suis cassé la jambe le jour de mon arrivée.
12. a. Je me suis foulé le poignet.
   b. Je suis allé à la montagne.
   c. Je ne me suis pas assez entraîné.

2. En France

CLUB DE SPORT

★ ★ **LE GYMNAUTE** ★ ★

Questionnaire personnel

NOM et PRÉNOM				
SPORTS PRATIQUÉS	NIVEAU*			
	faible	assez bon	bon	excellent
ÉTAT DE SANTÉ				

*Niveau *(m)* = *level*

NOM ______________________ DATE ______________________

UNITÉ 10. Perspectives d'avenir

Leçon 28. Le grand amour

PRÉSENTATION

1. **Lecture.** Ouvrez votre livre à la page 434. Écoutez!

2. **Compréhension du texte**

	1	2	3	4	5	6	7	8
vrai								
faux								

PHONÉTIQUE

3. **Consonnes finales**

When the last syllable of a word or group of words in French ends in a consonant sound, that consonant is strongly released; that is, it is very distinctly pronounced. In English, on the other hand, final consonants are often not released, or they are pronounced with very little tension. As you practice the following words, release the final consonants very clearly.

Répétez: **robe douce stade actif longue gentille**
grec cruel dame personne préoccupe
chère rousse nette sportive heureuse

STRUCTURE ET VOCABULAIRE

Vocabulaire: L'amitié, l'amour et le mariage

4. **Prononciation.** Ouvrez votre livre à la page 436.

5. Compréhension orale

	1	2	3	4	5	6
d'accord						
pas d'accord						

A. Adjectifs irréguliers

6. Prononciation. Ouvrez votre livre à la page 437.

7. Identification de structures

	1	2	3	4	5	6	7	8	9	10
masculin										
féminin										

8. Conversation: Eux aussi!

❖ ALAIN: Alice est sérieuse. Et ses frères?
VOUS: ***Ils sont sérieux aussi.***

9. Situations: Est-ce que c'est vrai?

❖ Henri n'aime pas travailler. Il est paresseux.
C'est vrai! Il est paresseux.

❖ Louis déteste jouer au tennis. Il est très sportif.
C'est faux! Il n'est pas très sportif.

B. Les adverbes en **-ment**

10. Conversation: Comment?

❖ PAUL: Georges est sérieux. Comment étudie-t-il?
VOUS: ***Il étudie sérieusement.***

C. Les nombres ordinaux

11. Pratique

❖ cinq
cinquième

NOM ______________________ DATE ______________________

D. La construction verbe + infinitif

Vocabulaire: Verbes suivis de l'infinitif

12. Prononciation. Ouvrez votre livre à la page 445.

13. Pratique

❖ J'**apprends à** faire du ski.
❖ Tu **décides de** travailler.
❖ Claire **va** étudier.

14. Réactions personnelles

	1	2	3	4	5	6	7	8
moi aussi								
pas moi								

DIALOGUE

15. Concierge

❖ —Où habite Mlle Dupuis?
*—**Elle habite au cinquième étage** (floor).*

LOCATAIRE	ÉTAGE
Arnaud	12
Beaudoin	8
Charron	21
Dupuis	5
Eckenspieler	11
Fabre	9
Guignard	16
Henri	2
Lévy	10
Marceau	7
Pascal	1
Reboul	6
Velasquez	3

DICTÉE

16. Étienne et ses sœurs

______________ Étienne? ____.

____. Christine ______________

__________________, ____.

Catherine ____.

____.

NOTE CULTURELLE: LES FRANÇAIS ET LE MARIAGE

17. Lecture. Ouvrez votre livre à la page 439. Écoutez!

18. Compréhension du texte

	1	2	3	4	5
vrai					
faux					

NOM ______________________________ DATE ____________________

Leçon 29. Dans dix ans

PRÉSENTATION

1. **Lecture.** Ouvrez votre livre à la page 448. Écoutez!

2. **Compréhension du texte**

	1	2	3	4	5	6	7	8
Emmanuel								
Alice								
Martin								
Jonathan								

PHONÉTIQUE

3. **La consonne [r]**

The French letter "r" never represents the sound of the English "r." The French "r" is a soft sound pronounced at the back of the throat. To learn to pronounce the French [r], say "ah" and clear your throat at the same time: [a] + (forced [r]).

Répétez: **a-ra a-ra a-ra**

Now practice the following words and sentences using the French [r].

Répétez: **Paris Robert reçoit regrette**
j'irai je ferai je saurai je voudrai je recevrai
Roger devra rester à Rome.
René arrivera à Rouen mercredi.

STRUCTURE ET VOCABULAIRE

A. Le verbe recevoir

4. **Prononciation.** Ouvrez votre livre à la page 451.

5. **Pratique**

❖ Je reçois mon diplôme.
J'ai reçu mon diplôme.

B. Le futur: formation régulière

6. **Prononciation.** Ouvrez votre livre à la page 452.

7. **Pratique**

❖ **Je** dînerai à huit heures.
❖ **Je** réussirai à mon examen.
❖ **Je** ne répondrai jamais à cette lettre.

8. **Conversation: Les vacances**

❖ STÉPHANIE: Est-ce que tu vas travailler?
VOUS: *Oui, je travaillerai.*

❖ STÉPHANIE: Est-ce que tu vas écrire un roman?
VOUS: *Non, je n'écrirai pas de roman.*

C. Futurs irréguliers

9. **Prononciation.** Ouvrez votre livre à la page 456.

10. **Conversation: Le week-end**

❖ ROBERT: Est-ce que tu vas aller à la piscine?
VOUS: *Oui, j'irai à la piscine.*

❖ ROBERT: Est-ce que tu vas aller à la bibliothèque?
VOUS: *Non, je n'irai pas à la bibliothèque.*

11. **Narration: Demain**

❖ Jean-Paul ne fait pas les courses.
Il fera les courses demain.

Vocabulaire: Quelques professions

12. **Prononciation.** Ouvrez votre livre à la page 458.

NOM ______________________________ DATE ____________________

13. Compréhension orale

❖ Catherine: (infirmière) ou journaliste?

1. Pierre:	vendeur	ou	médecin?
2. Philippe:	ouvrier	ou	fonctionnaire?
3. Marie-Thérèse:	avocate	ou	ingénieur?
4. Antoine:	vendeur	ou	architecte?
5. Hélène:	patronne	ou	journaliste?
6. Albert:	employé	ou	médecin?
7. Henriette:	cadre	ou	fonctionnaire?
8. Thomas:	écrivain	ou	avocat?

D. La construction si + présent

14. Narration: À Paris

❖ Paul veut visiter le Louvre.

Si Paul va à Paris, il visitera le Louvre.

E. L'emploi des temps après **quand**

15. Narration: Quand?

❖ Marie doit avoir son passeport.

Quand Marie aura son passeport, elle ira à Paris.

DIALOGUE

16. D'accord!

❖ à deux heures

ANNE-MARIE: Va à la poste!

VOUS: ***D'accord, j'irai à la poste à deux heures.***

1. avant le dîner
2. après la classe
3. avant le week-end
4. pour le rendez-vous
5. pour la classe d'histoire
6. demain
7. dimanche soir
8. avant jeudi

DICTÉE

17. Voyage en Italie

______________________________, ______________________________

__________________ Charles. ______________________________.

______________________________, ______________________________.

____.

______________________________ télégramme ______________________________

__________________.

NOTE CULTURELLE: STABILITÉ ET MOBILITÉ

18. Lecture. Ouvrez votre livre à la page 449. Écoutez!

19. Compréhension du texte

	1	2	3	4	5	6
vrai						
faux						

NOM ______________________________ DATE ______________________

Leçon 30. Si j'avais de l'argent...

PRÉSENTATION

1. **Lecture.** Ouvrez votre livre à la page 464. Écoutez!

2. **Compréhension du texte**

	1	2	3	4	5	6	7	8
vrai								
faux								

PHONÉTIQUE

3. **Intonation à l'intérieur de la phrase**

Within a longer declarative French sentence, the voice rises at the end of each group of words. In English, on the contrary, the voice drops at the end of each group of words.

Comparez: Si j'avais le temps, j'apprendrais le chinois.

If I had the time, I would learn Chinese.

Répétez: **Si je pouvais conduire, je louerais une voiture.**
Si tu partais plus tôt, tu serais à l'heure.
Si nous avions de l'argent, nous irions en France.

STRUCTURE ET VOCABULAIRE

Vocabulaire: Projets de vacances

4. **Prononciation.** Ouvrez votre livre à la page 466.

A. Le conditionnel: formation

5. Prononciation. Ouvrez votre livre à la page 468.

6. Pratique

❖ **Henri** achèterait une voiture.
❖ **Bernard** ne fumerait plus.
❖ Où irais-**tu**?

7. Identification de structures

	1	2	3	4	5	6	7	8	9	10	11	12
certitude: futur												
hypothèse: conditionnel												

B. Le conditionnel: emploi

8. Situation: En France

❖ aller à Paris — ***Oui, j'irais à Paris.***
❖ aller dans les Alpes — ***Non, je n'irais pas dans les Alpes.***

9. Narration: Avec mille dollars

❖ Je voudrais aller en Espagne.
Avec mille dollars, j'irais en Espagne.

10. Narration: Qu'est-ce qu'il a dit?

❖ JEAN-PHILIPPE: Élisabeth écrira un roman.
VOUS: ***Il a dit qu'Élisabeth écrirait un roman.***

C. Résumé: l'emploi des temps après si

11. Narration: Si nous avions le temps...

❖ Tu voudrais écrire des poèmes.
Si tu avais le temps, tu écrirais des poèmes.

D. Le verbe **conduire**

12. Prononciation. Ouvrez votre livre à la page 473. Le verbe **conduire** est irrégulier.

NOM ______________________________ DATE ______________________

DIALOGUE

13. Conditions

❖ ROBERT: Qu'est-ce que tu achèterais si tu avais mille dollars?
VOUS: ***J'achèterais un ordinateur.***

1. 
2. 
3. 
4. 
5.
6. 

DICTÉE

14. Après l'université

____?

________________________________. ________________________________,

________________________________. ________________________________.

__________ Japon ________ Chine. ________________ France ________________.

NOTE CULTURELLE: VIVE LES VACANCES!

15. Lecture. Ouvrez votre livre à la page 465. Écoutez!

16. Compréhension du texte

	1	2	3	4	5	6
vrai						
faux						

NOM ______________________________ DATE ______________________

Vivre en France 10. En voyage

1. La bonne réponse

1. a. Il coûte 150 francs.

   b. Non, il est occupé.

   c. Oui, il est direct.

2. a. Il part dans dix minutes.

   b. Désolé, le guichet est fermé.

   c. Bien sûr, allez à la porte F.

3. a. Oui, il y a un aéroport très moderne à Genève.

   b. Non, l'avion de Genève part de la porte B.

   c. Je ne pense pas. On m'a dit que l'avion était direct.

4. a. Je ne sais pas. Je pense que les passagers ont déjà embarqué.

   b. Mais oui! Allez au comptoir d'Air Maroc.

   c. Ça dépend. Est-ce que vous avez beaucoup de bagages?

5. a. Je rentre le 18 juillet.

   b. Je vais à Tours en septembre.

   c. Non, donnez-moi un aller simple.

6. a. Non, il y a une correspondance à Saint-Pierre-des-Corps.

   b. Non, il y a une escale à Mont-de-Marsan.

   c. Non, il est occupé.

7. a. Non, il n'y a pas d'escale.

   b. Non, il a une demi-heure de retard.

   c. Non, il part dans une heure.

8. a. Allez sur le quai B.

   b. Allez au guichet 2.

   c. Il part du quai 18.

9. a. Les trains sont tous à l'heure.

   b. Il a dix minutes d'avance.

   c. Je ne sais pas. Vous pouvez demander au bureau de renseignements.

10. a. Oui, j'ai choisi mon siège.

   b. Non, je n'ai pas ma carte d'accès à bord.

   c. Non, je vais les garder avec moi.

2. En France

FICHE DE RÉSERVATION
NOM: ____________________
PRÉNOM: ____________________
COMPAGNIE AÉRIENNE: ____________________
VOL N°: ____________________
DESTINATION: ____________________
DATE DE DÉPART: ____________________
DATE DE RETOUR: ____________________
MODE DE PAIEMENT: ____________________

NOM ______________________ DATE ______________________

UNITÉ 11. Le monde actuel

Leçon 31. Conversation avec un Québécois

PRÉSENTATION

1. **Lecture.** Ouvrez votre livre à la page 482. Écoutez!

2. **Compréhension du texte**

	1	2	3	4	5	6	7
vrai							
faux							

PHONÉTIQUE

3. **Les lettres «in» et «im»**

The letters "in" and "im" represent the nasal vowel [ɛ̃] when followed by a consonant sound.

Contrastez:	**Non-nasal**	**Nasal**
	inutile	inviter
	imaginatif	impulsif
	immeuble	impatient

Répétez: **imperméable impulsif indiscret infirmier**
inquiet informatique ingénieur instant intéressant
Mme Imbert s'intéresse à l'informatique.

STRUCTURE ET VOCABULAIRE

Vocabulaire: Traditions

4. **Prononciation.** Ouvrez votre livre à la page 484.

A. La formation du subjonctif: verbes à un radical

5. **Prononciation.** Ouvrez votre livre à la page 486.

6. **Pratique**

❖ Il faut que **mes amis** réussissent.
❖ Il faut que **mes parents** répondent.
❖ Il faut que **tu** partes.

7. **Jouons un rôle: Le contraire**

❖ YVES: Philippe ne sort pas.
MARIE: ***Il faut qu'il sorte.***

B. La formation du subjonctif: verbes à deux radicaux

8. **Prononciation.** Ouvrez votre livre à la page 488.

9. **Conversation: Obligations scolaires**

❖ DENIS: Est-ce que vous achetez beaucoup de livres?
VOUS: ***Oui, il faut que j'achète beaucoup de livres.***

C. L'emploi du subjonctif après certaines expressions d'obligation et d'opinion

10. **Prononciation.** Ouvrez votre livre à la page 491.

D. Le subjonctif d'**être** et d'**avoir**

11. **Prononciation.** Ouvrez votre livre à la page 493. Les verbes **être** et **avoir** ont un subjonctif irrégulier.

12. **Pratique**

❖ Il est dommage que **je** sois en retard.
❖ Il est dommage que **vous** n'ayez pas d'argent.

E. L'emploi du subjonctif après les verbes de volonté

13. **Identification de structures**

	1	2	3	4	5	6	7	8
le sujet (infinitif)								
une personne différente (subjonctif)								

14. Jouons un rôle: Révolte!

❖ LA MÈRE: Je veux que tu mettes la table.
NICOLE: ***Je ne veux pas mettre la table.***

15. Conversation: Non!

❖ LE COUSIN: Est-ce que je peux fumer dans ta chambre?
VOUS: ***Non, je ne veux pas que tu fumes dans ma chambre.***

DIALOGUE

16. Désolé(e)!

❖ —Est-ce que tu veux sortir avec moi jeudi?
—Désolé(e), mais il faut que je passe à la bibliothèque.

CALENDRIER DE LA SEMAINE	
LUNDI	*conduire Michèle à l'aéroport*
MARDI	*nettoyer l'appartement*
MERCREDI	*suivre le cours de l'Alliance française*
JEUDI	*passer à la bibliothèque*
VENDREDI	*finir le devoir de maths*
SAMEDI	*dîner chez les Descroix*
DIMANCHE	*rendre visite à mes grands-parents*

DICTÉE

17. Les courses

_________________________________. _________________________________.

___________, ____.

_________________________________. _____, _________________________.

____________________. _____, _____________________________________.

NOTE CULTURELLE: LES CANADIENS D'EXPRESSION FRANÇAISE

18. Lecture. Ouvrez votre livre à la page 483. Écoutez!

19. Compréhension du texte

	1	2	3	4	5	6	7	8
vrai								
faux								

NOM ______________________________ DATE ______________________

Leçon 32. Français ou Européens?

PRÉSENTATION

1. **Lecture.** Ouvrez votre livre à la page 498. Écoutez!

2. **Compréhension du texte**

	1	2	3	4	5	6	7	8	9	10
vrai										
faux										

PHONÉTIQUE

3. **Les lettres «s», «c» et «ç»**

(a) *La lettre* «s». Between two vowels, the letter "s" represents the sound [z].

Écoutez: rose musique

In other positions, the letter "s" represents the sound [s].

Écoutez: souvent reste

Répétez: **hasard entreprise réaliser chose épouser**
santé esprit impossible conserver sûr
Isabelle est sûre de réussir dans son entreprise.

(b) *La lettre* «c». Before the letters "e," "i," and "y," the letter "c" represents the sound [s].

Écoutez: certain citoyen cyclone exercice

Before the letters "a," "o," and "u," before a consonant, and in final position, the letter "c" represents the sound [k].

Écoutez: cadre cœur curieux crème avec

Répétez: **nécessaire médecin bicyclette douce**
avocat congé chacun croire parc
Caroline et Cécile se rencontrent au cinéma.

(c) *La letter* «ç». The letter "ç" *(c cedilla)* always represents the sound [s]. It occurs only before "a," "o," and "u."

Répétez: **ça français garçon commençons reçu**
François est reçu à son examen de français.

STRUCTURE ET VOCABULAIRE

Vocabulaire: La politique internationale

4. **Prononciation.** Ouvrez votre livre à la page 501.

A. Le verbe **croire**

5. **Prononciation.** Ouvrez votre livre à la page 502. Le verbe **croire** est irrégulier.

6. **Pratique**

❖ **Marthe** ne croit pas au progrès.

B. Subjonctifs irréguliers

7. **Prononciation.** Ouvrez votre livre à la page 503. Les verbes **faire, vouloir, pouvoir, savoir, aller** et **vouloir** ont un subjonctif irrégulier.

8. **Pratique**

❖ Maman veut que **je** fasse les courses.
❖ Il est dommage que **tu** ne puisses pas venir.
❖ Il vaut mieux que **je** sache la vérité.
❖ Il est normal que **tu** veuilles être médecin.
❖ Il faut qu'**Éric** aille en Espagne.

C. L'emploi du subjonctif après les expressions de doute

9. **Identification de structures**

	1	2	3	4	5	6	7	8	9	10
Je sais... (indicatif)										
Je doute... (subjonctif)										

10. **Conversation: J'en doute!**

❖ GEORGES: Le français est difficile.
VOUS: ***Je doute que le français soit difficile.***

11. Situation: Opinions

❖ Jacques est sûr... *Jacques est sûr que le français est utile.*
❖ Vous doutez... *Vous doutez que le français soit utile.*

D. L'emploi du subjonctif après les expressions d'émotion

12. Prononciation. Ouvrez votre livre à la page 506.

13. Pratique

❖ **Je regrette** que tu ne puisses pas venir.
❖ **Je suis heureuse** que tu reçoives ton diplôme.

14. Narration: Réactions

❖ Paul est content. Marie va en France.
Paul est content que Marie aille en France.

E. L'emploi du subjonctif après certaines conjonctions

15. Prononciation. Ouvrez votre livre à la page 508.

16. Pratique

❖ **Je** resterai ici jusqu'à ce que Marc vienne.
❖ Marc part pour que **je** puisse être seul.

17. Conversation: Au téléphone

❖ NICOLE: Nathalie va partir en voyage.
VOUS: *Je téléphonerai à Nathalie avant qu'elle parte en voyage.*

F. Résumé: Les principaux emplois du subjonctif

18. Compréhension orale

	1	2	3	4	5	6	7	8	9	10	11	12
indicatif												
subjonctif												

DIALOGUE

19. Réactions

❖ JEAN-LOUIS: Je vais gagner à la loterie.
VOUS: *Je doute que tu gagnes à la loterie.*

1. 
2. 
3. 
4. 
5. 
6. 

DICTÉE

20. Visite à Genève

____,

____.

____

____.

NOTE CULTURELLE: L'EUROPE UNIE

21. Lecture. Ouvrez votre livre à la page 500. Écoutez!

22. Compréhension du texte

	1	2	3	4	5	6	7	8
vrai								
faux								

NOM ______________________ DATE ______________________

Leçon 33. La nouvelle technologie

PRÉSENTATION

1. Lecture. Ouvrez votre livre à la page 512. Écoutez!

2. Compréhension du texte

	1	2	3	4	5	6	7	8
vrai								
faux								

PHONÉTIQUE

3. Syllabation

Speakers of French tend to make every syllable end on a vowel sound. In liaison, therefore, the liaison consonant is pronounced as if it were the first sound of the following word. When two consonant sounds come together in a word, there is a tendency to end the first syllable on the vowel sound and begin the next syllable with two consonant sounds. Practice French syllabication by pronouncing the following words and sentences according to the divisions indicated.

Répétez: **i•l es•t im•po•rtant**

le•s É•tat•s-U•nis

ju•squ'à -ce qu'i•l a•rrive

à l'heu•re a•ctuelle

i•l a•rri•ve dan•s u•n in•stant

STRUCTURE ET VOCABULAIRE

Vocabulaire: La technologie

4. Prononciation. Ouvrez votre livre à la page 515.

A. Révision: Les pronoms compléments d'objet direct et indirect

5. Conversation: Curiosité

❖ MME GASSE: Vous regardez souvent la télévision?
VOUS: ***Oui, je la regarde souvent.***

B. L'ordre des pronoms compléments

6. Prononciation. Ouvrez votre livre à la page 518.

7. Conversation: La photo

❖ oui
MIREILLE: Est-ce qu'Anne donne sa photo à son ami Paul?
VOUS: ***Oui, elle la lui donne.***

1. oui
2. oui
3. non
4. non

8. Conversation: La chambre de Philippe

❖ oui
MIREILLE: Est-ce que Philippe montre à Alice son nouveau livre?
VOUS: ***Oui, il le lui montre.***

1. oui
2. oui
3. non
4. non

9. Conversation: Les prêts *(Loans)*

❖ JULIEN: Marc a ta guitare.
VOUS: ***Je sais. Je la lui ai prêtée.***

10. Jouons un rôle: Oui ou non

❖ MICHEL: Est-ce que tu me prêtes ta voiture?
GEORGES: ***Oui, je te la prête.***

❖ ALAIN et CHARLES: Est-ce que tu nous prêtes ta voiture?
GEORGES: ***Non, je ne vous la prête pas.***

C. L'ordre des pronoms à la forme affirmative de l'impératif

11. Situation: S'il te plaît!

❖ Prête-moi ta guitare!
Prête-la-moi, s'il te plaît!

NOM ____ DATE ____________________________

D. L'ordre des pronoms avec y et en

12. Narration: Pierre

- ❖ Pierre donne des conseils à son frère. — ***Oui, il lui en donne.***
- ❖ Pierre ne prête jamais d'argent à sa sœur. — ***Non, il ne lui en prête jamais.***
- ❖ Pierre nous amène au cinéma. — ***Oui, il nous y amène.***

DIALOGUE

13. Mes copains et moi

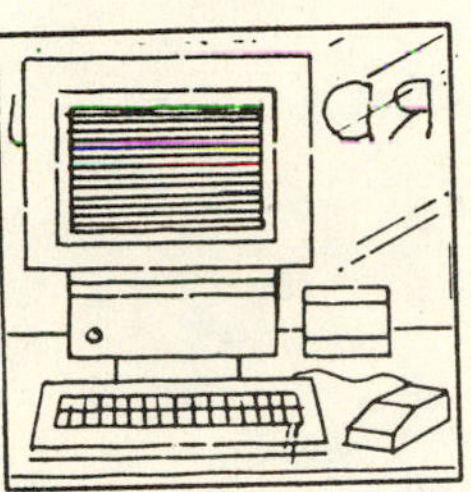

pour une semaine

❖ EMMANUEL: Qu'est-ce que tu as prêté à Jacques?
VOUS: ***Je lui ai prêté mon ordinateur.***
EMMANUEL: Pour combien de temps est-ce que tu le lui as prêté?
VOUS: ***Je le lui ai prêté pour une semaine.***

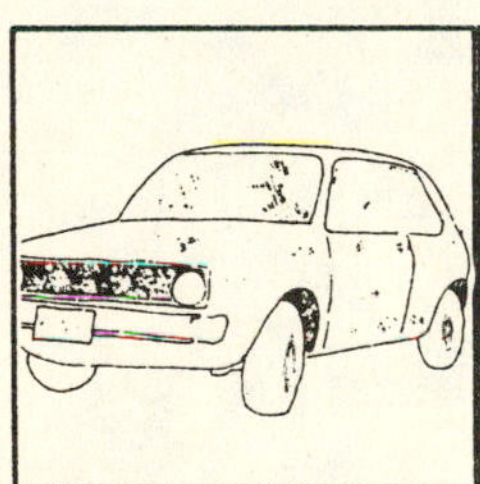

pour le week-end

pour 500 francs

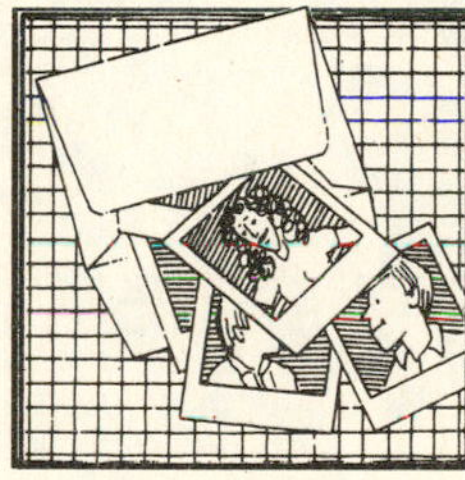

hier soir

pour sa fête

DICTÉE

14. Mon vélo

______________________________. ______________________________ Thomas.

________________________. ____,

____.

NOTE CULTURELLE: LES FRANÇAIS ET LA TECHNOLOGIE

15. Lecture. Ouvrez votre livre à la page 514. Écoutez!

16. Compréhension du texte

	1	2	3	4	5	6
vrai						
faux						

Vivre en France 11. L'achat des vêtements

1. La bonne réponse

1. a. C'est vrai, elle est très chic.

   b. Je l'ai trouvée trop longue.

   c. Je l'ai achetée dans une boutique de soldes rue de Sèvres.

2. a. Non, elle est en laine!

   b. Non, elle n'est pas en caoutchouc.

   c. Oui, c'est du velours.

3. a. Je cherche des boucles d'oreille.

   b. Je cherche des mocassins.

   c. Ces chaussures sont trop étroites.

4. a. Je chausse du trente-huit.

   b. Il ne me va pas. Il est trop long.

   c. Je n'ai pas de pointure.

5. a. Je préfère le foulard en soie.

   b. Je ne sais pas. Quelle est ta taille?

   c. J'aime la veste, mais je n'aime pas le pantalon.

6. a. Oui, bien sûr. Voici un mouchoir.

   b. Non, je n'ai pas besoin d'argent.

   c. Désolé, mais je n'ai pas mon portefeuille sur moi.

7. a. Je vais mettre mon blouson de cuir.

   b. Je vais porter ma nouvelle ceinture.

   c. Je ne sais pas. Peux-tu me prendre les mesures?

8. a. Non, il n'est pas en soie.

   b. Non, il est trop serré.

   c. Oui, il va mettre son écharpe.

9. a. Oui, elle a acheté une bague en or.

b. Non, ce n'est pas sa pointure.

c. Non, elle a acheté une Toyota d'occasion.

10. a. Elle portait une ceinture blanche.

b. Elle porte un trente-sept.

c. Elle est allée au marché aux puces.

2. En France

Au Grand Bazar **BUREAU DES RÉCLAMATIONS** Déclaration de perte	
	Description
Vêtements	
Chaussures	
Autres objets	

Pas de Problème!
VIDEO WORKBOOK

Rick Altman

INTRODUCTION

Welcome to ***Pas de problème!***—a new kind of video that encourages you to understand and solve problems regularly encountered in French-speaking cultures. The ***Pas de problème!*** video and workbook were created to work together as a single unit.

Each of the twelve modules of the ***Pas de problème!*** video has three parts: the **Main Narrative,** the **Gros plan,** and the **Problème!** When each module opens, the number and title appear on the screen and the narrator gives a brief description **(Mise en scène)** of the setting and circumstances of the module. Then the **Main Narrative** begins. In this section, the characters encounter and resolve problems commonly encountered by people in Paris or the French provinces. When directions in the Video Workbook say to watch the first part of the video only, this refers to the **Main Narrative.** You will know the **Main Narrative** is over when the **Gros plan** begins, signaled by the appearance of a small title flag at the bottom of the screen. Through a montage of scenes, the **Gros plan** offers a close-up of some aspect of the module theme. Next comes the **Problème!,** where the characters encounter a problem for which they have not found a solution (but which can eventually be solved with the help of workbook activities).

The ***Pas de Problème!*** workbook will help you learn to use your French to solve everyday problems. For each of the video sections **(Main Narrative, Gros plan, Problème!)** you will find a sequence of activities that will familiarize you with life in a French-speaking country and give you a chance to practice French in a real-world situation. **Préparation** activities introduce you to the theme and help you practice the vocabulary and structures necessary to work with the video. These should be done before viewing. The **Visionnement** activities should be done while watching the video (in class or in the language lab), with the sound on or off as indicated by the following symbols:

IMAGE, NO SOUND

SOUND AND IMAGE TOGETHER

PAUSE

You may pause or replay the video as often as necessary to complete the activities. The **Application** activities are designed to expand on the vocabulary, structures, and cultural concerns covered in the module, and to reinforce issues you have covered in your textbook. At the end of each module is a **Supplément** section, providing further opportunities for exploration of the topics covered in the module. Many of the activities are meant to be done with a partner, as indicated by the following symbol:

Pas de problème! has been carefully designed to create an atmosphere very much like the one you might find if you took a trip to France. The situations and locations are real; the problems are the same ones that students regularly encounter abroad. The documents you will work with in the WORKBOOK are authentic. And, of course, the language used is a language you would hear in France. Don't worry if you don't understand every word—you are not supposed to! Life isn't a grammar book with vocabulary arranged in alphabetical order; neither is this video. Instead of concentrating on comprehending every word, use your knowledge of life and video to predict what the characters are probably doing and saying. This is the kind of skill you will need for survival in a French-speaking country; it is also the kind of skill that will help you ultimately, with the help of the workbook's carefully targeted activities, to understand both what is being communicated in the video and how you yourself can achieve maximum communication.

Enjoy watching the video and doing the activities in the workbook. Take full advantage of this exposure to the culture and the language of the French-speaking world. ***Amusez-vous bien!***

R.A.

NOM ______________________________ DATE ______________________

MODULE I AU TENNIS

MISE EN SCÈNE

Jean-François est québécois; il est à Paris depuis *(since)* quelques jours seulement. Cet après-midi *(This afternoon)* il joue au tennis avec son ami René. Il passe chez lui *(He drops by his apartment)* pour chercher *(pick up)* ses affaires de tennis. Il retrouve René au tennis du bois de Vincennes.

PRÉPARATION

A. L'agenda de Jean-François. Here is Jean-François's schedule for the day. Read this schedule and answer the following questions accordingly.

9 h	petit déjeuner *(breakfast)* avec Claude
10 h	Louvre, visite de la Pyramide
12 h 30	chez Madeleine, déjeuner *(lunch)* avec M. Rigal
14 h	bibliothèque de la Sorbonne, devoir de maths
15 h 15	la maison, affaires de tennis
16 h	bois de Vincennes, tennis avec René
19 h 30	dîner
21 h	café, travail jusqu'à *(until)* 23 heures

1. Est-ce que Jean-François joue au tennis à deux heures?

   ____

2. Jean-François visite-t-il le Louvre à dix heures du matin?

   ____

3. Est-ce que Jean-François prend *(eat)* le petit déjeuner à neuf heures du soir?

   ____

4. Où est Jean-François à deux heures et quart?

   ____

5. À quelle heure Jean-François rentre-t-il à la maison?

   ____

6. Est-ce que Jean-François dîne à midi et demi?

   ____

7. À quelle heure Jean-François travaille-t-il au café?

   ____

8. Est-ce que Jean-François dîne avec M. Rigal?

   ____

B. Présentations et salutations. Introduce three of the following people to a classmate. Your classmate should greet each person appropriately. Then switch roles while your classmate introduces the other three to you. Follow the models.

❖ my neighbor *(mon voisin)* M. Antoine
VOUS: ***Je te présente mon voisin, M. Antoine.***
VOTRE PARTENAIRE: ***Bonjour, Monsieur.***

my brother *(mon frère)* Luc
VOUS: ***Je te présente mon frère, Luc.***
VOTRE PARTENAIRE: ***Salut!***

1. my friend *(mon ami)* Jacques
2. my sister *(ma sœur)* Anne
3. my neighbor *(ma voisine)* Mme Labelle
4. my teacher *(mon professeur)* . . .
5. my classmate *(mon [ma] camarade de classe)* . . .
6. my cousin *(mon cousin)* Vincent

C. C'est qui? Circle the subject of each underlined verb in the following sentences.

1. —Où est-il? Que cherche-t-il?
   —Il passe chez lui pour chercher ses affaires de tennis.
2. —On joue jusqu'à quelle heure?
   —Nous rentrons à midi.
3. —Vous travaillez à l'université?
   —Oui, ce soir nous étudions à la bibliothèque.
4. —Marc, je te présente ma cousine.
   —Je suis enchanté, Nathalie.
5. —Est-ce qu'Isabelle est libre?
   —Je ne pense pas.

VISIONNEMENT

D. Qu'est-ce qui se passe? *(What's going on?)* Often the image provides extremely useful clues for understanding the dialogue. First read the following questions. Then watch the segment without the sound and circle the best response to each question.

1. Qui prend *(takes)* le métro?
   a. Marie-Christine
   b. Alissa
   c. Yves
   d. Jean-François
2. Où est-ce que Jean-François retrouve son ami René?
   a. dans le métro
   b. chez lui
   c. au tennis
   d. au cinéma
3. Qui sert *(serves)* le premier?
   a. Jean-François
   b. René
4. À votre avis *(In your opinion)*, qui est la jeune fille?
   a. une amie de Jean-François
   b. la cousine de Jean-François
   c. la mère *(mother)* de René
   d. la cousine de René

5. À votre avis, qu'est-ce que René dit *(say)* à la fille?
   a. Je te présente Jean-François.
   b. Mon ami joue très bien.
   c. Je travaille à l'université ce soir.
   d. Je suis très fatigué.

6. À votre avis, que dit la fille à la fin *(end)?*
   a. Pas du tout!
   b. Je suis malade *(sick)!*
   c. Formidable!
   d. Sûrement pas!

E. Où sont-ils? Que font-ils? Watch the segment again, this time with the sound on. Circle the correct response for each question.

1. Où est Jean-François au début *(at the beginning)?*
   a. devant Notre-Dame de Paris
   b. au Centre Pompidou
   c. à la place de la Concorde
   d. au bois de Vincennes

2. Où est-ce que Jean-François retrouve son ami René?
   a. au bois de Boulogne
   b. à la Tour Eiffel
   c. au bois de Vincennes
   d. à la pyramide du Louvre

3. Jusqu'à quelle heure René et Jean-François jouent-ils?
   a. deux heures
   b. trois heures
   c. quatre heures
   d. cinq heures

4. Qui travaille à l'université ce soir?
   a. René
   b. Jean-François

5. Qui va au cinéma ce soir?
   a. René
   b. Jean-François

6. Jean-François est
   a. français.
   b. parisien.
   c. canadien.
   d. suisse.

7. Qui est-ce que Jean-François regarde souvent?
   a. Nathalie
   b. son cousin
   c. René
   d. Marie-Christine

8. Qui est Marie-Christine?
   a. l'amie de Jean-François
   b. l'amie de René
   c. la cousine de Jean-François
   d. la cousine de René

9. Qui est l'amie de Marie-Christine?
   a. Nathalie
   b. Jean-François
   c. René
   d. Renée

10. Qu'est-ce que Jean-François fait *(is doing)* ce soir?
    a. Il travaille à l'université.
    b. Il joue au tennis.
    c. Il va au cinéma.
    d. Il reste chez lui.

GROS PLAN LES SPORTS

PRÉPARATION

F. En quelle saison? Look at the following list of sports that are popular in France. Which sports are played in winter *(en hiver)*, in spring *(au printemps)*, in summer *(en été)*, in fall *(en automne)?* Fill in the chart by checking the appropriate season(s) for each sport.

	HIVER	PRINTEMPS	ÉTÉ	AUTOMNE
le tennis				
la voile				
le hockey sur glace				
l'équitation				
le saut à ski				
le vélo				
la natation				
le ski alpin				
le kayak				
le football				

G. Un centre sportif au Québec. Read this ad for a Sports Center in Québec and circle the best response for each of the following questions. More than one correct answer may be possible.

1. Où est la Rivière Rouge?
   a. au Canada
   b. à une heure de Montréal
   c. à une heure d'Ottawa
   d. au Québec
2. Quels sports est-ce qu'on peut pratiquer sur la Rivière Rouge?
   a. l'équitation c. le rafting
   b. le football d. le kayak
3. Qu'est-ce qu'une journée de rafting inclut?
   a. une présentation vidéo
   b. l'équipement
   c. les services d'un guide
   d. le voyage en car *(bus)*
4. Pour vingt dollars peut-on passer une journée au meilleur centre d'aventures au Québec?
   a. oui b. non
5. Pour soixante-neuf dollars est-il possible de faire du rafting sur la Rivière Rouge?
   a. oui b. non
6. Est-il possible de déjeuner au meilleur centre d'aventures au Québec?
   a. oui b. non

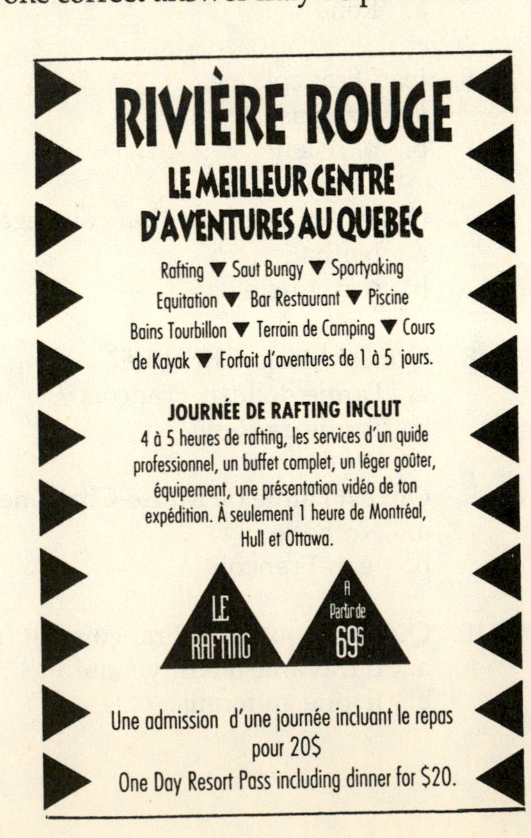

NOM ______________________________ DATE ____________________

VISIONNEMENT

H. Que voyez-vous? Review the list of sports in Activity F, then view the segment without the sound and check off the names of sports from the following list that you see in the **Gros plan.**

____	l'équitation	____	le judo
____	le tennis	____	le baseball
____	le golf	____	la pétanque*
____	le ski alpin	____	le jogging
____	le vélo	____	le tennis de table
____	le kayak	____	la voile
____	le football américain	____	le football
____	le rugby	____	le basketball

**Pétanque*, or *boules*, is a popular French game (especially in the south of France) played by two teams of two to four players who compete by trying to throw their hard metal balls *(boules)* as close as possible to a small wooden ball *(cochonnet)* tossed at random some 15–30 feet away.

I. Les Français et le sport. View the segment again, this time with the sound on. Check off the words you hear in the left column.

____	les rivières	____	____	l'air	____
____	le ski	____	____	descendre	____
____	le vélo	____	____	un bon effort	____
____	la mer	____	____	la terre	____
____	le tennis	____	____	le football	____
____	la pétanque	____	____	la montagne	____
____	l'équitation	____	____	la forêt	____
____	monter	____	____	courir	____
____	les lacs	____	____	une bonne fatigue	____
____	les sports	____			

J. Un peu d'ordre. Now listen again and, in the right column of Activity I, number the words and expressions you checked off according to the order in which you heard them.

PROBLÈME!   AU CINÉMA

PRÉPARATION

K. Que faire? With a partner play the roles of two friends who will be spending a Saturday together. One likes sports, the other prefers quieter activities. Use the vocabulary provided.

faire du jogging	**nager**	**danser**	**étudier**
écouter la radio	**skier**	**jouer au tennis**	**travailler**
chanter	**manger une pizza**	**patiner**	**regarder la télévision**

❖ VOUS: ***Désires-tu faire du jogging?***
VOTRE PARTENAIRE: ***Moi, je préfère regarder la télé.***
VOUS: ***Mais, aimes-tu danser?***
VOTRE PARTENAIRE: ***Non, je préfère...***

L. Pas possible! With a partner, play the roles of a ticket agent and a client. Each time the client requests a ticket for a specific time and date, the agent says that it's not available. Choose from the following list of activities displayed in the agent's window.

❖ CLIENT(E): ***Un billet pour* Carmen *le sept juin, s'il vous plaît!***
L'AGENT(E): ***Je regrette, mais* Carmen *finit le deux juin.***
CLIENT(E): ***Alors, un billet pour* Fantasia.**
L'AGENT(E): **...**

TICKETS

OPERAS:	**Manon Lescaut** (Opéra de la Bastille)	*du 10 au 19 mai*
	Carmen (Opéra Comique)	*jusqu'au 2 juin*
MUSIQUE:	**Johnny Hallyday** (Bercy)	*12 mai seulement*
	Charles Trenet (Châtelet)	*16 mai seulement*
	Orchestre de Paris (Champs-Elysées)	*aujourd'hui seulement*
VISITES:	**Bateau-mouche sur la Seine** (dîner possible)	*tous les jours*
	Folies-Bergère (interdit aux moins de 18 ans)	*tous les jours sauf lundi*
	Versailles la nuit	*le week-end seulement*
FILMS:	**Napoléon d'Abel Gance** (avec musique spéciale)	*en semaine*
	Un homme et une femme (nouvelle version)	*tous les jours à 20h et 22h30*
	Fantasia (en stéréo Dolby)	*tous les jours à 20h30*

VISIONNEMENT

M. Le corps parle. View the segment without the sound, paying close attention to the body language of Marie-Christine and Jean-François. Then answer the following questions.

1. How does Marie-Christine greet Jean-François?

____

2. What else do Marie-Christine and Jean-François do that Americans don't typically do?

____

NOM ______________________________ DATE ____________________

N. Au cinéma. Now watch the segment with the sound. Then answer the following questions.

1. Où est Jean-François? ______________________________
2. Où est Nathalie? ______________________________
3. Quelle sorte de films Jean-François aime-t-il? ______________________________
4. Pour quelle sorte de film Jean-François demande-t-il deux billets? ______________________________
5. Pourquoi y a-t-il un problème? ______________________________

APPLICATION

O. Qu'est-ce qu'on va faire? What would you do if you were in the same situation as Marie-Christine and Jean-François? Column A contains a list of the types of films you like and Column B lists the types of films your partner likes. Study these lists, then look at the film schedule that follows. Discuss the films now playing with your partner and decide on a film that you both will enjoy.

A	B
les films d'aventure	les comédies
le fantastique	les mélodrames
les films violents	les comédies musicales
les films policiers	les films classiques

❖ VOUS: *Désires-tu voir* La Belle et la Bête*?*

VOTRE PARTENAIRE: *Non, pas vraiment. Je n'aime pas beaucoup les films comme ça. Je préfère voir* L'Amant*. J'adore les mélodrames. D'accord?*

VOUS: *En réalité, je n'aime pas beaucoup les mélodrames. Je préfère voir un film d'aventure.*

VOTRE PARTENAIRE: *Peut-être un film classique qui est aussi un film d'aventure?* etc.

CINEMA

GAUMONT OPERA, 31 bd des Italiens, 2e arrondissement, métro Opéra, 40F **La Belle Histoire** (aventures), 19h, 21h20 **La Belle et la Bête** (fantastique classique) 18h30, 20h30, 22h30 **L'Amant** (mélodrame intime) 19h20, 21h40

CINE BEAUBOURG, 50 rue Rambuteau, 3e arrondissement, métro Rambuteau, 41 F **Une femme sous influence** (mélodrame), 20h, 22h **Tirez sur le pianiste** (policier classique), 19h30, 21h50 **Blanche Neige** (fantastique pour enfants), 18h, 19h40, 21h20

ACTION ECOLES, 23 rue des Écoles, 5e, métro Cluny-la Sorbonne, 38F **Festival James Bond** (aventures), 18h, 20h, 22h **Cérémonie secrète** (mélodrame), 18h30, 20h30, 22h30

ACTION RIVE GAUCHE, 5 rue des Écoles, 5e, métro Cardinal Lemoine, 38F **Chantons sous la pluie** (comédie musicale), 19h, 20h45, 22h30 **Indochine** (mélodrame/aventures), 19h30, 21h45 **La soupe au canard** (comédie), 18h40, 20h20, 22h

SUPPLÉMENT

P. Soirées parisiennes. Read the following excerpt from a letter written by Jean-François, then answer the questions that follow.

> Chère Gisèle,
>
> J'aime bien Paris. Il y a toujours beaucoup de choses à faire. Souvent je passe la soirée *(evening)* au café avec des amis. Nous jouons aux cartes, ou nous étudions, ou nous parlons politique, ou nous mangeons quelque chose. Quelquefois *(sometimes)* je vais à la bibliothèque ou au musée. De temps en temps, j'étudie un peu. Quand je suis fatigué ou malade *(sick)*, je regarde la télévision ou j'écoute la radio ou la stéréo. Quand j'ai de l'argent, je vais au cinéma avec Claude. Claude aime beaucoup les comédies musicales et les mélodrames. Moi j'aime beaucoup la science-fiction et les films d'aventure.
>
> Amitiés,
>
> Jean-François

1. Que fait Jean-François *(What does Jean-François do)* quand il est sans *(without)* argent?

   ____

2. Que fait-il quand il a de l'argent?

   ____

3. Que fait-il quand il est malade?

   ____

4. Quand il va au café, qu'est-ce qu'il fait?

   ____

5. Qu'est-ce qu'il fait avec Claude?

   ____

6. Quelle sorte de films est-ce qu'il aime?

   ____

NOM ______________________ DATE ______________________

MODULE II LE COUP DE FIL

MISE EN SCÈNE

Aujourd'hui Jean-François retrouve Marie-Christine pour faire des courses *(to do some shopping)* ensemble. Marie-Christine habite rive gauche *(on the Left Bank),* dans le 6ème arrondissement. C'est le quartier *(neighborhood)* des étudiants, des librairies, des cafés et des universités.

PRÉPARATION

A. La rive gauche. Read the following paragraph about the Left Bank of Paris. Then, complete the sentences that follow.

La rive gauche de Paris est un endroit *(place)* très vivant *(lively),* surtout dans son centre historique (les 5ème, 6ème et 7ème arrondissements *[districts]).* C'est d'abord le quartier des universités (avec la Sorbonne, la première université de Paris). Il y a donc beaucoup de librairies et il y a des étudiants partout *(everywhere).* On trouve aussi beaucoup de cafés rive gauche, et beaucoup de boutiques qui sont peut-être *(perhaps)* petites mais qui sont souvent très chics. Tout le monde *(Everybody)* connaît *(knows)* les églises de la rive gauche: Saint-Germain-des-Prés, Saint-Séverin, Saint-Sulpice. Mais la rive gauche est aussi le quartier du gouvernement. Dans le palais du Luxembourg siège *(meets)* une partie importante du gouvernement de la République, le Sénat.

1. La première université de Paris s'appelle ______________________.
2. Près *(Near)* des universités on trouve beaucoup de ______________________.
3. Les boutiques de la rive gauche sont souvent ______________________.
4. Le Sénat siège dans ______________________.
5. Le ______________ arrondissement est un arrondissement de la rive gauche.
6. La rive gauche se trouve au ______________ de la Seine (nord/sud).

B. Et votre université? Pourquoi votre université est-elle spéciale? Expliquez à un(e) ami(e) français(e) deux ou trois choses intéressantes à propos de *(about)* votre université ou de votre ville.

____

____

____

____

C. Le plan. Study this map of part of the Left Bank of Paris. Then answer the questions, using the expressions provided.

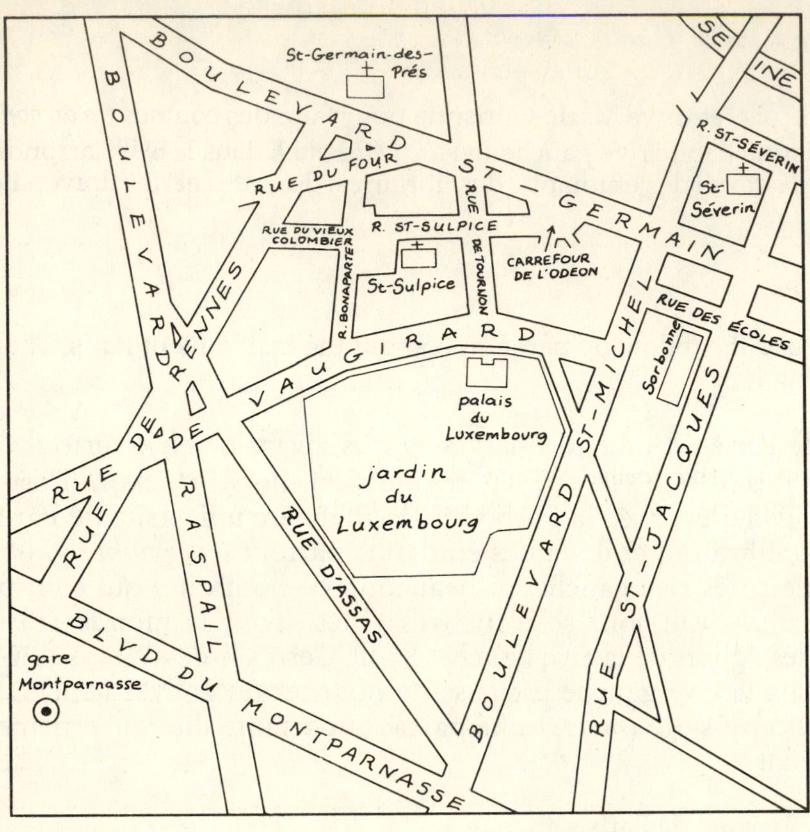

prends/prenez (la rue)	*(take)*	**à gauche**	*(left)*
tourne/tournez (dans la rue)	*(turn)*	**tout droit**	*(straight)*
traverse/traversez	*(cross)*	**à droite**	*(right)*

1. Vous êtes sur le boulevard Saint-Michel et une femme vous demande: «S'il vous plaît, où est Saint-Germain-des-Prés?» ____________________

____

2. Vous sortez *(You are leaving)* de la gare Montparnasse et un jeune homme demande: «L'église Saint-Sulpice, s'il vous plaît!» ____________________

____

3. Vous êtes dans la rue du Four, et quelqu'un vous demande le chemin pour *(way to)* la gare Montparnasse. Quelle est votre réponse? ____________________

____

4. Vous habitez la rue de Rennes, près du boulevard Montparnasse. Un autre étudiant qui étudie à la bibliothèque de la Sorbonne va vous rendre visite ce soir. Expliquez-lui le chemin pour aller chez vous. ____________________

____

5. Vous habitez près de Saint-Séverin, votre amie est à Saint-Sulpice. Elle téléphone et demande le chemin pour venir chez vous. Que dites-vous? ____________________

____

NOM ______________________ DATE ______________________

VISIONNEMENT

D. Que voyez-vous? Now view the Module II dialogue **"Le coup de fil"** without the sound. Make a list of the aspects you see that are typical of the Left Bank according to the description in Activity A.

Monuments	Autres choses
______________________	______________________
______________________	______________________
______________________	______________________
______________________	______________________

E. Les yeux travaillent. Often the image provides extremely useful clues for understanding the dialogue. Watch the segment without the sound and guess what is happening in the following situations. You may answer these questions in English.

1. What's written on the paper Jean-François is holding? ______________________
2. Where is he going? ______________________
3. What does he say to the woman in the street? ______________________
4. What does he say to the woman in the phone booth? ______________________
5. What does he ask the man next to the phone booth? ______________________
6. Whom does Jean-François call? ______________________
7. What does he ask? ______________________

F. Les mots-clés *(Key words).* Based on your answers to Activity E, what words do you expect to hear in this segment? Circle the words in the following list that you expect to hear.

comment	**autoroute**	**hors-d'œuvre**
porte d'entrée	**croissant**	**urgent**
allô	**fermée** *(closed)*	**grande**
code	**cher** *(expensive)*	**rue**
beaucoup	**rouge**	**numéro**

G. Les mots du dialogue. Now watch the segment with the sound and cross out the words in Activity F that you hear in the dialogue.

H. Le sens du dialogue. View the segment again with the sound. Did you guess right? This time answer the questions in French.

1. Qu'est-ce qui est écrit sur le papier de Jean-François? ______________________
____
2. Où va-t-il? ____
3. Que dit Jean-François à la dame dans la rue? ______________________
____
4. Que dit Jean-François à la dame dans la cabine téléphonique? ______________________
____
5. Que dit Jean-François au monsieur près de la cabine téléphonique? ______________________
____
6. À qui Jean-François téléphone-t-il? ______________________
7. Qu'est-ce qu'il demande? ______________________

I. Les réponses. During this segment Jean-François finds out about two things he needs. The lady in the street tells him about one, while the man near the phone booth tells him about the other. List the two items and describe what Jean-François needs each for.

1. ____
____
2. ____
____

J. Le chemin de Jean-François. Now view the dialogue one last time. Mark the route taken by Jean-François on this map.

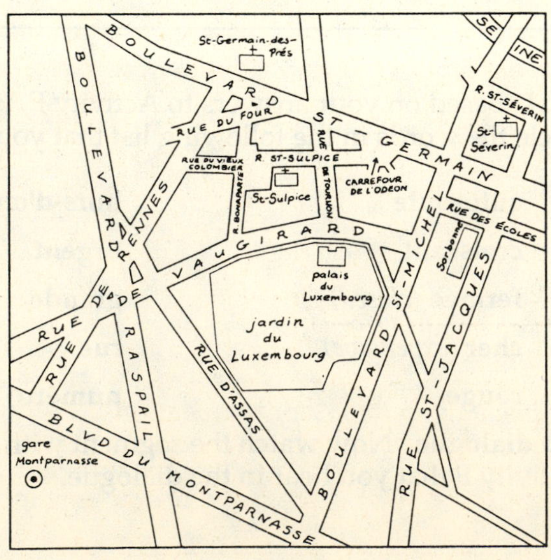

NOM ______________________ DATE ______________________

GROS PLAN LA TÉLÉCARTE

PRÉPARATION

K. Au téléphone. Imagine that you are an exchange student in France trying to place an overseas call. With a partner, play the roles of operator and student. Use expressions from the list provided.

Allô.	*Hello.*
Je voudrais téléphoner à...	*I want to call (a person) . . .*
Je voudrais appeler le...	*I want to call (a number) . . .*
Quel numéro demandez-vous?	*What number are you calling?*
Ne quittez pas!	*Don't hang up!*
Mettez votre carte dans la fente.	*Put your card in the slot.*
Composez le numéro.	*Dial the number.*
Il faut une autre carte.	*You need another card.*

VISIONNEMENT

L. Le bon ordre. View the segment without the sound. Then put the following activities in the order in which they appear. Circle the activity that doesn't take place during this segment. The first one has been done as a model.

____ raccrocher	____ patienter	____ enlever la carte
____ parler à l'opérateur	____ composer le numéro	____ introduire la carte
____ décrocher	__1__ entrer dans la cabine	

M. Comment téléphoner? Now view the segment with the sound and answer the following questions.

1. En général, qu'est-ce qui est nécessaire pour téléphoner dans les cabines «téléphoniques»?
____
2. Qu'est-ce qu'on peut acheter *(can buy)* dans tous les agences de France Télécom?
____
3. Qu'est-ce qu'on peut acheter dans tous les bureaux de tabac?
____
4. Quelle est la première chose qu'il faut faire *(necessary to do)* pour téléphoner?
____
5. Qu'est-ce qu'on apprend *(learns)* dans le message digital?
____
6. Qu'est-ce qu'il faut faire ensuite *(next)?*
____
7. Qu'est-ce qu'il faut faire à la fin de la communication?
____
8. Qu'est-ce qu'il faut employer pour entrer dans le nouveau monde des communications?
____

APPLICATIONS

N. L'écran digital. Here are sample instructions that might appear on the screen of a French telephone booth. Read each instruction, then circle the letter of the action that you should carry out.

INTRODUISEZ VOTRE CARTE

a. Achetez une autre carte.
b. Mettez votre télécarte dans la fente.
c. Tapez le nom de votre carte.
d. Il n'y a pas d'unités.

PATIENTEZ, SVP

a. Ne faites rien.
b. Votre carte n'est pas bonne.
c. Composez votre numéro.
d. Mettez votre télécarte dans la fente.

CRÉDIT : 19 UNITÉS, NUMÉROTEZ

a. Votre carte est bonne, attendez.
b. Votre communication coûte 19 francs.
c. Vous avez déjà demandé trop de crédit.
d. Votre carte est bonne, composez votre numéro.

CRÉDIT ÉPUISÉ, RACCROCHEZ SVP

a. Votre carte est bonne, attendez.
b. Votre carte est bonne, composez votre numéro.
c. Votre carte est mauvaise, attendez.
d. Votre carte est mauvaise, posez le téléphone.

NUMÉRO APPELÉ : 37522908

a. Appelez le numéro affiché.
b. Le numéro de ce téléphone est 37522908.
c. Le numéro 37522908 appelle cette cabine téléphonique.
d. Vous avez appelé le numéro affiché.

REPRENEZ VOTRE CARTE

a. La communication est terminée; la machine garde votre carte.
b. Achetez une autre carte.
c. Il faut une autre carte, celle-ci n'est plus bonne.
d. La communication est terminée; retirez votre carte.

O. Les instructions. Look carefully at the drawing of a French phone booth on the facing page. Then provide the following information.

1. 43 26 32 68 est le numéro de quoi?

____

2. Qui répond quand on compose le 18?

____

3. Quel numéro faut-il composer pour avoir les renseignements?

____

4. Quel est l'indicatif pour les États-Unis?

____

5. Quel numéro faut-il composer pour avoir les renseignements aux États-Unis?

____

6. Que faut-il faire si l'appareil est en panne?

____

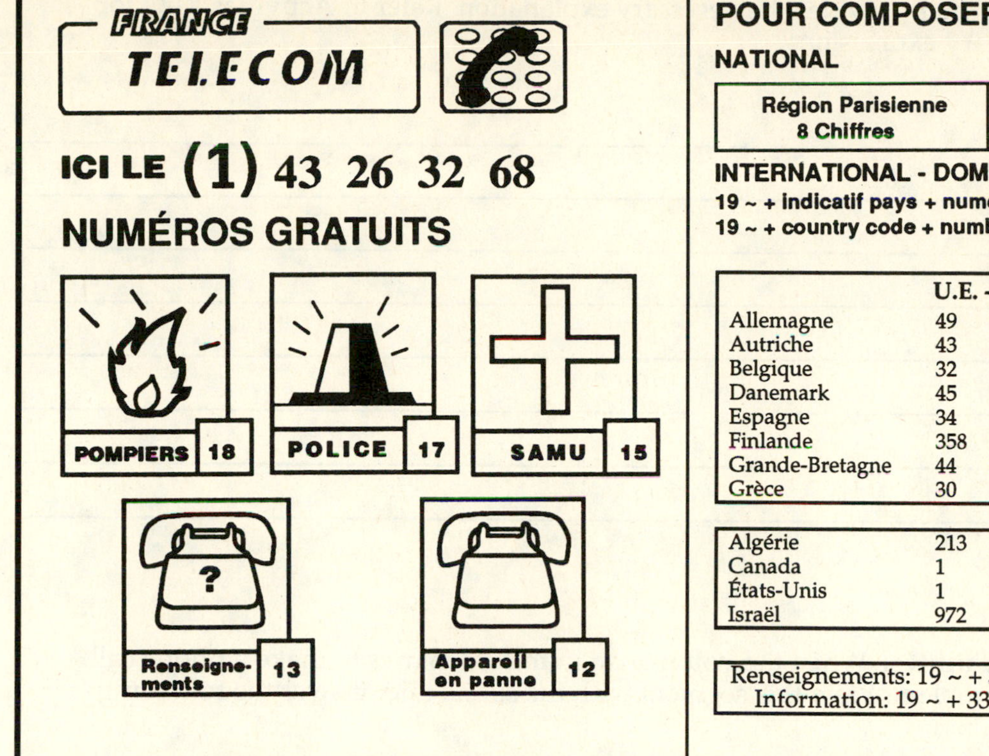

Pays	Indicatif	Pays	Indicatif
Allemagne	49	Irlande du Nord	44
Autriche	43	Irlande (Rép. d')	353
Belgique	32	Italie	39
Danemark	45	Luxembourg	352
Espagne	34	Pays-Bas	31
Finlande	358	Portugal	351
Grande-Bretagne	44	Suède	46
Grèce	30		

Pays	Indicatif	Pays	Indicatif
Algérie	213	Japon	81
Canada	1	Maroc	212
États-Unis	1	Suisse	41
Israël	972	Tunisie	216

Renseignements: 19 ~ + 33 + 22 + indicatif pays
Information: 19 ~ + 33 + 12 + country code

PROBLÈME!   PLUS D'UNITÉS

PRÉPARATION

P. Acheter une télécarte. In this segment, Jean-François has to go to a **(bureau de) tabac** *(tobacco shop)* to buy a **télécarte** in order to make a phone call. Imagine the conversation between Jean-François and the salesperson from whom he buys the **télécarte.** Don't forget that Jean-François doesn't know anything about **télécartes** (the price, the number of **unités** on the card, whether there are different kinds of cards, etc.). Add to the following conversation at least three more exchanges between Jean-François and the salesperson.

LE VENDEUR (LA VENDEUSE): ***Bonjour, Monsieur. Vous désirez?***
JEAN-FRANÇOIS: ***Je désire quelque chose pour téléphoner.***
LE VENDEUR (LA VENDEUSE): ***Qu'est-ce que vous désirez exactement?***

____

____

____

____

____

____

____

____

Q. Comment ça marche. You have bought a **télécarte.** Ask a partner how to use it. Your partner provides the necessary explanation. Refer to Activities K–O for the necessary expressions.

VISIONNEMENT

R. Plus d'unités. When the young man in the video tries to make a phone call, he has a problem. View this segment with the sound and answer the following questions.

1. Qu'est-ce que le jeune homme dans la vidéo veut faire *(wants to do)?*
2. Quel problème a-t-il?
3. Que peut-il faire *(What can he do)* maintenant s'il a une autre carte dans la poche (*his pocket)?*
4. Que peut-il faire maintenant s'il a de l'argent *(money)* dans son portefeuille *(wallet)?*
5. Que peut-il faire s'il n'a ni *(neither)* carte ni *(nor)* argent?

APPLICATION

S. Comment on téléphone avec la télécarte. On the next page, you will see a technical explanation of the electronic **puce** *(chip,* literally *flea,* because of its small size and shape) at the heart of the **télécarte** and French public telephones. First read the explanation. (Don't worry if you cannot understand every word.) Then answer the questions.

1. Combien de publiphones y a-t-il en France?
2. Quand on introduit la carte dans le publiphone, qu'est-ce qui se passe *(what happens)?*

NOM ______________________ DATE ______________________

3. Où se trouve la puce? ______________________
4. Qu'est-ce que le réseau de microfils *(microwire network)* et que contient-il? ______________________
5. Qu'est-ce qu'il y a à chaque carrefour *(intersection)* dans le réseau de microfils? ______________________
6. Qu'est-ce qui se passe aux fusibles *(fuses)* de la puce au fur et à mesure des communications *(with each phone call)*? ______________________

SUPPLÉMENT

T. Plus ça change, plus c'est la même chose. With a partner, imagine the conversations between a student in Paris during the time of the old black telephone and a local operator who shares his or her problems with callers. You may give the phone number in French style (437 = **quatre cent trente-sept)** or in Canadian style (437 = **quatre-trois-sept).** The operator will tell you about the problems of his or her daughter, his or her little boy, or his or her neighbor Rosalie. You, of course, will try to show interest in these problems. Here are the people you call. Follow the model.

❖ Votre sœur Françoise à New York (212/288-4237)

L'ÉTUDIANT(E): ***Allô. Je voudrais* (would like to) *téléphoner à ma sœur à New York, s'il vous plaît. Deux cent douze, deux cent quatre-vingt-huit, quarante-deux, trente-sept.***

LE (LA) STANDARDISTE: ***Ah oui, comment va votre sœur maintenant? Est-elle toujours malade?***

L'ÉTUDIANT(E): ***Heureusement, elle n'est plus malade.***

LE (LA) STANDARDISTE: ***C'est bien. Ma voisine Rosalie est malade depuis deux semaines. C'est difficile. J'ai préparé de la soupe pour son dîner.***

L'ÉTUDIANT(E): ***Ah bon!...***

1. Votre frère Victor à Chicago (312/376-8997)
2. Vos parents qui voyagent en France (33/1-42.69.17.26)
3. Votre amie Germaine qui habite près de chez vous (37.52.36.95)
4. Votre copain Bruno en Suisse (41/84.72.98.67)

U. Le dialogue écrit. When you have finished the oral interchange of the preceding activity, choose your best dialogue and write it out.

____

____

____

____

____

____

____

____

NOM ______________________________ DATE ______________________

MODULE III LE MÉTRO

MISE EN SCÈNE

Paris est une grande ville *(city)*, mais les transports en commun *(public transportation)* sont faciles *(easy)* à employer et pas chers. Aujourd'hui, Marie-Christine et Jean-François traversent *(cross)* la ville pour visiter un grand magasin *(department store)*.

PRÉPARATION

A. Le métro en France. Read the following paragraph and answer the questions.

Cinq villes françaises ont un chemin de fer *(railroad)* métropolitain, ou métro: Bordeaux, Lille, Lyon, Marseille et, bien sûr, Paris. Inauguré en 1900, le métro de Paris a aujourd'hui un réseau *(network)* long de plus de trois cents kilomètres. C'est le troisième métro du monde en longueur, après les métros de Londres et New York. Dans les 368 stations, il y a soixante kilomètres de quais *(platforms)*. Les stations les plus fréquentées sont les grandes gares *(railroad stations)*: Gare Saint-Lazare, Gare du Nord, Gare Montparnasse, Gare de l'Est, Gare de Lyon, Gare d'Austerlitz. En tout, six milliards *(billion)* de voyageurs par an, avec quatre cent millions de voyageurs supplémentaires sur le Réseau Express Régional *(Regional Express Network)*, ou RER, qui sert *(serves)* la banlieue *(suburbs)* parisienne. Depuis *(Since)* août 1991, il n'y a qu'une seule *(there's only one)* classe dans le métro, toute la journée. Mais attention, le RER garde encore les deux classes traditionnelles, première et seconde, sur la totalité de ses 358 kilomètres.

1. Paris n'a pas le seul métro en France. Combien d'autres villes françaises ont un métro?

   ____

2. Le métro de Paris a quel âge? ______________________________

3. Combien de métros sont plus longs que le métro parisien? ______________________

4. Combien y a-t-il de stations dans le métro de Paris? ______________________

5. Quelles sont les stations les plus fréquentées? ______________________

   ____

6. Combien de voyageurs y a-t-il chaque année sur le métro de Paris? ______________

   ____

7. Combien de voyageurs y a-t-il tous les ans sur le RER? ______________________

   ____

8. Est-ce que le métro a deux classes? Et le RER? ______________________

   ____

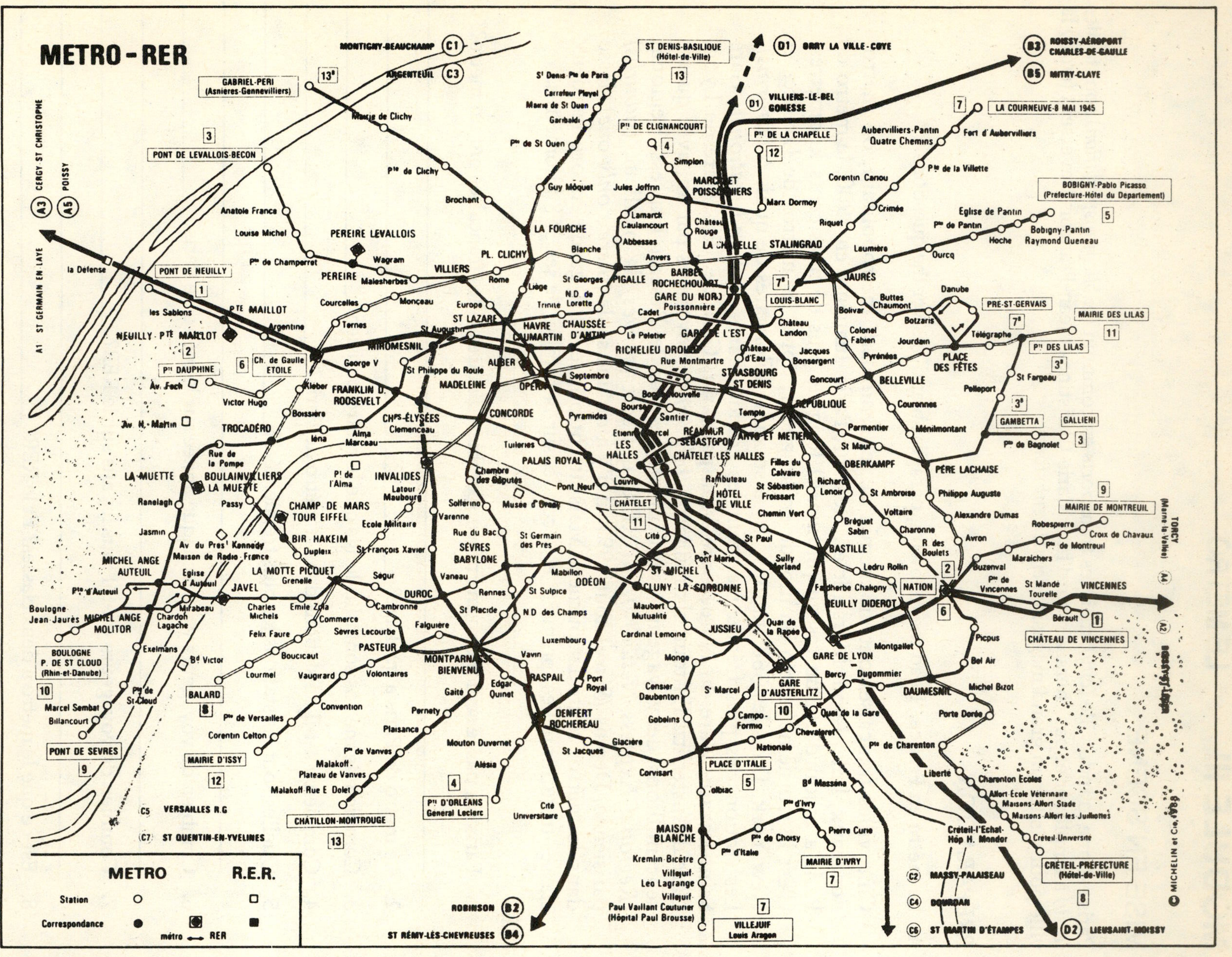
METRO - RER
METRO
R.E.R.
Station
Correspondance
métro ⟷ RER
MICHELIN et Cie 1989
NATION
CHÂTEAU DE VINCENNES
MAIRIE DES LILAS
MAIRIE DE MONTREUIL
PONT DE LEVALLOIS-BECON
PONT DE NEUILLY
PONT DE SEVRES
MAIRIE D'ISSY
CHATILLON-MONTROUGE
MAIRIE D'IVRY
CRÉTEIL-PREFECTURE (Hôtel-de-Ville)
GABRIEL-PERI (Asnières-Gennevilliers)
ST DENIS-BASILIQUE (Hôtel-de-Ville)
LA COURNEUVE-8 MAI 1945
BOBIGNY-Pablo Picasso (Prefecture-Hôtel du Departement)
BOULOGNE P. DE ST CLOUD (Rhin-et-Danube)
VILLEJUIF Louis Aragon
PLACE D'ITALIE
GARE D'AUSTERLITZ
GARE DE LYON
CHATELET
LES HALLES
OPERA
CONCORDE
INVALIDES
TROCADÉRO
MONTPARNASSE BIENVENUE
DENFERT ROCHEREAU
BASTILLE
RÉPUBLIQUE
STALINGRAD
PL. CLICHY
ST LAZARE
ST MICHEL
ODEON
A5 POISSY
A3 CERGY ST CHRISTOPHE
A1 ST GERMAIN EN LAYE
B2 ROBINSON
B4 ST RÉMY-LÈS-CHEVREUSES
B3 ROISSY-AÉROPORT CHARLES-DE-GAULLE
B5 MITRY-CLAYE
TORCY (Marne la Vallée)
C2 MASSY-PALAISEAU
C6 ST MARTIN D'ÉTAMPES
D2 LIEUSAINT-MOISSY
C5 VERSAILLES R.G
C7 ST QUENTIN-EN-YVELINES
C3 ARGENTEUIL
C1 MONTIGNY-BEAUCHAMP
D1 ORRY LA VILLE-COYE
D1 VILLIERS-LE-BEL GONESSE

NOM ________________________________ DATE ____________________________

B. Comment y aller? Look at the Paris métro map on the preceding page and decide whether the following statements are true **(Vrai)** or false **(Faux).** Circle the appropriate letter.

V F 1. Marie-Christine et Jean-François sont à la station Sèvres–Babylone. Pour aller à l'Opéra par métro, ils passent par la station Place de la Concorde et la station Gare Saint-Lazare.

V F 2. Si la ligne numéro huit (Balard–Créteil) est fermée, on peut prendre *(can take)* la direction Nation et on doit changer à la Bastille.

V F 3. Si la ligne numéro douze (Mairie d'Issy–Porte de la Chapelle) est fermée, on peut prendre la ligne numéro dix et changer à Odéon et à Réaumur-Sébastopol.

V F 4. Si, après leur visite à l'Opéra, Marie-Christine et Jean-François désirent aller au cinéma Action Rive Gauche (Métro Cardinal Lemoine), ils peuvent prendre la ligne numéro sept et changer à Place d'Italie.

V F 5. Si après le cinéma Marie-Christine et Jean-François désirent visiter l'arc de Triomphe (Métro Charles de Gaulle–Étoile), ils peuvent prendre la ligne numéro huit et changer à Place de la Concorde.

VISIONNEMENT

C. Qu'est-ce qu'il faut faire? Watch the segment with the sound on and answer the following questions.

1. Marie-Christine et Jean-François sont devant quelle station de métro?
   a. Opéra c. Saint-Sulpice
   b. Porte de la Chapelle d. Sèvres–Babylone
2. Selon *(According to)* Marie-Christine, quelle direction faut-il prendre pour aller aux Galeries Lafayette?
   a. Porte de la Chapelle c. Créteil
   b. Porte d'Orléans d. Porte de Clignancourt
3. Toujours selon Marie-Christine, quelle ligne de métro faut-il prendre?
   a. ligne deux c. ligne dix
   b. ligne douze d. ligne dix-huit
4. Selon Jean-François, où faut-il changer de ligne de métro?
   a. Opéra c. Madeleine
   b. Créteil d. Porte de Clignancourt
5. Toujours selon Jean-François, à quelle station faut-il descendre?
   a. Madeleine c. Créteil
   b. Opéra d. Porte d'Orléans
6. Que suggère le passant *(passerby)?*
   a. Il suggère de prendre l'autobus. c. Il suggère de prendre le batobus.
   b. Il suggère de prendre un taxi. d. Il suggère de prendre une autre ligne.
7. Que demande Marie-Christine?
   a. C'est quel autobus? c. Où se trouve l'entrée du métro?
   b. Où est le taxi? d. Où est l'arrêt?
8. Que demande Jean-François?
   a. Où est ma Carte Orange? c. Est-ce que je peux utiliser ma Carte Orange?
   b. Où est mon ticket? d. Où est-ce qu'on achète un ticket?

GROS PLAN LE TRANSPORT EN COMMUN

VISIONNEMENT

D. Que voyez-vous? Watch the **Gros plan** of Module III: **"Le transport en commun"** with the sound off. Check off any of the following modes of transportation that you see in the **Gros plan.** Then watch the beginning of the Module III dialogue **"Le métro"** and circle the names of all the modes of transportation that you see there.

____ la moto	____ la mobylette
____ le taxi	____ l'autobus
____ le bateau *(boat)*	____ la bicyclette
____ le métro	____ l'avion
____ la voiture	____ le funiculaire *(funicular railway)*
____ le camion *(truck)*	

E. Les moyens de transport. Watch the **Gros plan** again and complete the following sentences by drawing a line to match each mode of transportation to the appropriate description.

La voiture	est à Montmartre.
Le taxi	a un chauffeur qui s'arrête *(stops)* où on veut *(wants).*
L'autobus	ferme à une heure du matin.
Le funiculaire	porte le nom d'un chanteur et acteur français.
Le batobus	est difficile à conduire *(to drive)* à Paris parce qu'il y a beaucoup de circulation *(traffic).*
Le métro	est toujours vert.

POUR UN OU QUELQUES VOYAGES

LE TICKET

Vous pouvez acheter des tickets à l'unité ou par carnets de 10.

Ils sont valables pour un seul trajet :

Dans le **métro**, le tarif est indépendant du parcours à effectuer et un seul ticket permet la libre correspondance entre les lignes.

Pour le **RER**, le tarif dépend de la classe choisie (1re ou 2eme classe) et du trajet.

Cependant sur la section urbaine du RER (gares RER de Paris et gare de Gentilly), la tarification est indépendante du trajet et permet la libre correspondance entre les lignes de métro et du RER. Au-delà de cette section urbaine, le prix des tickets dépend du parcours.

Pour le **bus**, chaque ligne est divisée en plusieurs sections. Un ticket n'est valable que pour un trajet compris dans une ou deux sections. Pour 3 sections ou plus, il faut utiliser 2 tickets pour les bus de Paris (numéros de lignes inférieurs à 100 et Montmartrobus) et de 2 à 6 tickets pour les bus de banlieue (numéros de lignes supérieurs à 100), pour le bus PC, Balabus et Orlybus. Un tarif spécial est appliqué sur les Noctambus, lignes de bus de nuit dans Paris.

Pour le **funiculaire** de Montmartre, un ticket permet d'effectuer un aller simple (montée ou descente).

Pour Orlyval, entre Antony et l'aéroport d'Orly, une tarification spéciale est appliquée.

Tickets	2e classe	1re classe (1)
Ticket métro-autobus à l'unité	5,50 F	8,50 F
Carnets de 10 tickets • plein tarif	34,50 F	52,00 F
Tickets RER pour trajets Paris-Banlieue	jusqu'à	jusqu'à
• plein tarif	18,00 F	28,00 F
Orlybus	6 tickets ou 1 billet spécial à 21,00 F	
Noctambus • trajet simple : 3 tickets		
• 2 trajets consécutifs avec correspondance à Châtelet : 4 tickets		
Orlyval (+ RER via Antony) • trajet Orly <—> Paris : 55,00 F		
• autres trajets : de 46,00 F à 85,00 F		

(1) 1re classe uniquement sur le RER.

NOM ______________________ DATE ______________

APPLICATIONS

F. Le ticket. Read the information on the previous page about the Paris transportation system. You may not understand every word, but you should be able to find the answers to these questions.

1. Combien de tickets y a-t-il dans un carnet *(pack)?*

   ____

2. Combien coûte un carnet?

   ____

3. Combien de tickets faut-il *(are necessary)* pour prendre le métro?

   ____

4. Combien de tickets faut-il pour un trajet *(trip)* de cinq sections en autobus?

   ____

5. Combien de tickets faut-il pour monter *(go up)* à Montmartre par le funiculaire et pour redescendre *(come back down)?* ______________________

   ____

6. Si vous désirez prendre l'autobus pendant la nuit, combien de tickets faut-il?

   ____

G. Les endroits. Decide where each person is going based on what each is going to do. Then complete the sentences. Choose from the following list. Use the correct verb form of **aller** and don't forget to make contractions **(à + le = au, à + les = aux).**

la piscine	**la banque**	**la pharmacie**	**le centre commercial**
l'aéroport	**le cinéma**	**la boulangerie**	**la pâtisserie**

❖ J'aime manger les gâteaux. ***Je vais à la pâtisserie.***

1. Jean-François finit son séjour en France. Il retourne au Canada cet après-midi.

   ____

2. Marie-Christine veut acheter une nouvelle robe pour la boum.

   ____

3. Moustafa a mal à la tête *(headache).*

   ____

4. Nathalie a envie de nager.

   ____

5. Nous préférons regarder un film.

   ____

6. Tu désires acheter une baguette.

   ____

PROBLÈME!   LA CARTE ORANGE QUI NE MARCHE PAS

PRÉPARATION

H. La Carte Orange. Following is a description of how a monthly public transportation pass works in Paris. Answer the questions based on the passage.

POUR UNE SEMAINE OU POUR UN MOIS : LA CARTE ORANGE
(Coupon Jaune ou Coupon Orange)

La carte orange se compose d'une carte nominative (avec une photo) accompagnée:
• d'un **coupon jaune** hebdomadaire : valable du lundi au dimanche inclus,
• d'un **coupon orange** mensuel : valable du premier au dernier jour du mois,
sur l'ensemble des lignes de métro, bus, RER, trains SNCF Ile-de-France, bus APTR ou ADATRIF, sur le funiculaire de Montmartre et sur le Balabus, le Montmartrobus, les Noctambus, Orlybus, Orlyrail et Roissy dans la limite des zones choisies.

Carte Orange	Coupon jaune (hebdomadaire)		Coupon orange (mensuel)	
	2e cl.	1re cl.(1)	2e cl.	1re cl.(1)
Zones 1-2	54 F	81 F	190 F	285 F
Zones 1-2-3	71 F	115 F	247 F	399 F
Zones 1-2-3-4	98 F	169 F	342 F	589 F
Zones 1-2-3-4-5	119 F	211 F	416 F	737 F
Zones 1-2-3-4-5-6	123 F	219 F	429 F	763 F
Zones 1-2-3-4-5-6-7	137 F	247 F	481 F	867 F
Zones 1-2-3-4-5-6-7-8	153 F	279 F	534 F	973 F

Les coupons mensuels sont en vente à partir du 20 du mois pour le mois suivant.

Emploi de la Carte Orange

Dans le métro, on introduit le coupon de Carte Orange dans la machine de contrôle, comme un ticket de métro. Par contre *(on the other hand)* dans l'autobus il ne faut pas *(one must not)* introduire le coupon de Carte Orange dans la petite machine de contrôle qui sert *(is used)* pour les tickets parce que cela détruit *(destroys)* les informations conservées sur la bande magnétique du coupon; il suffit *(it's enough)* d'avoir toujours en sa possession une Carte Orange et un coupon valable. En cas de démagnétisation de votre coupon, adressez-vous au guichet *(ticket window)* d'une station de métro ou d'une gare. Il vous sera remis *(You will be given)* un nouveau coupon.

1. La Carte Orange est composée de deux parties. L'une est un coupon orange mensuel *(monthly)*. Quelle est l'autre partie? ______________________

2. Le coupon orange mensuel est valable de quel jour à quel jour?

   ____

3. Voici une liste de transports parisiens. Soulignez *(Underline)* les transports où on peut *(can)* employer une Carte Orange.

le métro	les taxis	le RER
l'autobus	le batobus	Orlybus
le funiculaire de Montmartre	les bateaux-mouches	les Noctambus

4. Combien coûte une Carte Orange en deuxième classe pour les zones un et deux (Paris et les environs immédiats)? ______________________

5. Combien coûte une Carte Orange pour les zones un à huit (toute la région parisienne, jusqu'à cinquante kilomètres de Paris)? ______________________

6. Quand les coupons mensuels sont-ils mis en vente *(put on sale)?*

   ____

7. Vous êtes dans une station de métro le 26 mars et vous voulez acheter un coupon mensuel de Carte Orange pour les zones un, deux, trois et quatre. Que dites-vous *(say)* pour acheter votre coupon? ______________________

   ____

8. Quelle est la réponse de l'employé(e) *(employee)?* ______________________

   ____

NOM ______________________________ DATE ____________________

VISIONNEMENT

I. Qu'est-ce qui se passe? Watch the **Problème** section with the sound on and answer the following questions.

1. Qui prend *(takes)* le métro? ______________________________
2. Qui prend l'autobus? ______________________________
3. Quel est le problème de Jean-François? ______________________________
   ____
4. Qu'est-ce que Marie-Christine demande à Jean-François? ______________________________
   ____
5. Qu'est-ce qui a causé le problème de Jean-François? ______________________________
   ____

APPLICATION

J. Problèmes/Solutions. Write a short dialogue with a classmate. (Refer to Activity H for the necessary vocabulary.) Imagine that you both put your **Cartes Oranges** in the bus machine and now they won't work in the métro. You'll need to address the following issues:

1. Où êtes-vous? ______________________________
2. Où allez-vous? ______________________________
3. Comment est-ce que vous y allez? ______________________________
   ____
4. Avez-vous de l'argent? (Combien d'argent faut-il? Combien d'argent avez-vous?)
   ____
5. Avez-vous des amis qui habitent dans le quartier?
   ____

SUPPLÉMENT

K. Suivez le guide. Imagine you are visiting Paris with a friend and you are staying at a hotel near the Arc de Triomphe. Study the list of well-known tourist sights and locate them on the métro map. Then give your partner directions to go to three different sights from the hotel. Can he or she find them by tracing the route on the map according to your directions? Begin at métro station Charles de Gaulle–Étoile and use the expressions from the model.

Code on map	Tourist sight	Métro stop
A.	Arc de Triomphe	Charles de Gaulle–Étoile
B.	Musée Rodin	Invalides
C.	Notre-Dame	Cité
D.	Centre Pompidou	Châtelet–Les Halles
E.	La Sorbonne	Cluny–La Sorbonne
F.	Opéra de la Bastille	Bastille
G.	Madeleine	Madeleine

❖ ***Trouve* (Find) *la station* Charles de Gaulle–Étoile.**
***Prends* (Take) *la direction* Château de Vincennes.**
(Remember: the direction of a métro line refers to the name of the stops on either end of the line. For example, line #1 can be taken in the direction of Pont de Neuilly or Château de Vincennes.)
***Change* (Get off) *à la station* Châtelet.**
***Prends la correspondance et prends la ligne numéro 4, direction* Porte d'Orléans.**
Descends à la station* Cité. *Quel monument vas-tu visiter?

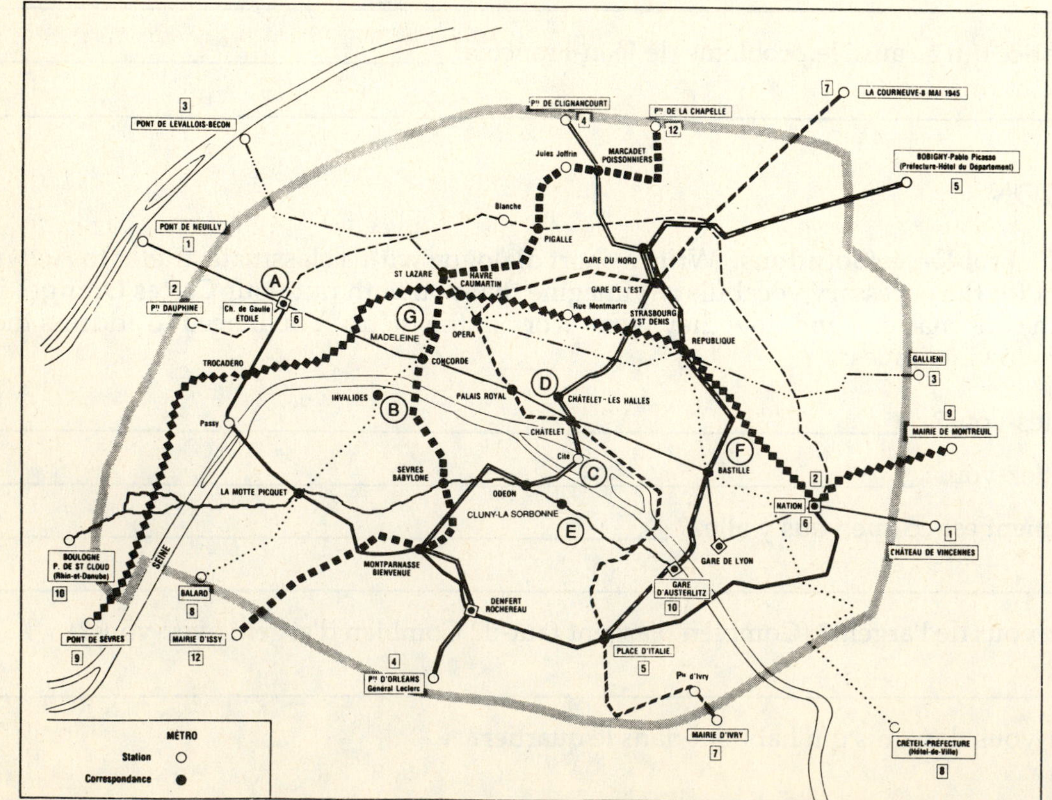

NOM ______________________________ DATE ______________________

MODULE IV LA BOULANGERIE

MISE EN SCÈNE

Ce matin, Jean-François et Marie-Christine doivent *(must)* retrouver des amis au café, mais Jean-François trouve que le petit déjeuner au café est trop cher. Pas de problème! Marie-Christine lui suggère d'acheter des croissants dans une boulangerie. Pendant *(During)* ce temps, elle fait du café.

PRÉPARATION

A. À la boulangerie. Here are some of the expressions you will need to understand the problem that Jean-François has run into today. Match each expression with its definition by writing the appropriate number in front of each definition.

1. la boulangerie
2. le boulanger
3. le four
4. le blé
5. la farine
6. le pain
7. les œufs
8. le croissant
9. le pain aux raisins
10. la pâtisserie

____ petite pâtisserie en forme de quart de lune *(moon)*

____ aliment *(food)* sucré cuit *(cooked)* au four et souvent mangé comme dessert

____ aliment ovale employé dans la pâtisserie

____ C'est lui qui fait le pain.

____ aliment fabriqué avec de la farine *(flour)* et cuit au four

____ On y *(there)* fait et vend le pain.

____ On y cuit le pain.

____ petit pain rond et plat, légèrement sucré, couvert de raisins secs

____ céréale utilisée dans la confection du pain

____ poudre faite avec une céréale (du blé *[wheat]*, par exemple) employée dans la confection du pain

B. Comment est-ce qu'on y va? Do this exercise with a partner. First, one of you asks the other for directions to get from your French class to each of the places mentioned. Work together to write the instructions down in the space provided. Use the vocabulary provided and follow the **Modèle.**

traverse	**ensuite** *(then)*	**à côté de**	**derrière**
tourne	**puis** *(then)*	**loin de**	**devant**
prends *(take)*		**près de**	**à droite**
continue	**la rue** *(street)*	**entre**	**à gauche**

❖ Votre maison

VOUS: *Comment est-ce qu'on va à votre maison?*

VOTRE PARTENAIRE: *Prends la rue du Lac à gauche et traverse le pont. Ensuite tourne à droite dans la première rue et c'est la maison verte à gauche.*

1. votre maison

2. votre restaurant préféré *(favorite)*

3. un supermarché

4. une banque

VISIONNEMENT

C. Regardez bien! View the first part of Module IV without the sound. Make a list of any object or building that you see for which you know the French word.

OBJETS	**BÂTIMENTS**

NOM ______________________________ DATE ______________________

D. Écoutez bien! Now view the first part of Module IV with the sound, then answer the questions.

1. Que cherche Jean-François?

____

2. Où a-t-il déjà cherché?

____

3. Qu'est-ce qu'il demande à l'artiste?

____

4. Que dessine *(draws)* l'artiste?

____

5. Quelle heure est-il quand Jean-François quitte l'artiste la première fois *(first time)?*

____

6. Quel jour de la semaine est-ce?

____

APPLICATION

E. Enfin une boulangerie ouverte! Complete the following paragraph by providing the passé composé of the verbs in parentheses. You must choose whether to use **avoir** or **être** as the auxiliary verb. Remember to make the past participle agree when appropriate. Make all other necessary changes (**Je → J'**, etc.).

Je ____________________ (aller) à Montmartre ce matin. Je ____________________ (chercher) une boulangerie ouverte partout. D'abord je ____________________ (monter) en haut de *(to the top of)* la rue des Abbesses, mais je ____________________ (ne pas trouver) de boulangerie. Je ____________________ (demander) à un artiste qui me ____________________ (indiquer) une autre boulangerie, mais encore une fois je le ____________________ (trouver) fermée. Ensuite je ____________________ (retourner) voir l'artiste, qui me ____________________ (donner) une autre indication. Je ____________________ (descendre) tout en bas de *(to the very bottom of)* la rue Lepic où je ____________________ (tomber) enfin sur une boulangerie ouverte. Je ____________________ (entrer) dans la boulangerie et je ____________________ (demander) deux croissants.

F. Le pain. Try to match each French expression with its English equivalent by writing the appropriate number in the blank provided. (The answers for Activities F and G are provided at the end of the module.)

1.	le pain bénit	____	(our) daily bread
2.	le pain complet	____	spice bread (gingerbread)
3.	le pain d'épices	____	cake of soap
4.	le pain de mie	____	sandwich bread
5.	le pain de campagne	____	toast
6.	le pain noir	____	country-style bread
7.	le pain rassis	____	roll
8.	le petit pain	____	consecrated bread (for Holy Communion)
9.	le pain perdu	____	French toast
10.	le pain quotidien	____	whole-grain bread
11.	le pain de savon	____	black bread (pumpernickel)
12.	le pain grillé	____	stale bread

G. Encore du pain. Now do the same thing with the following phrases using the word **pain.**

1.	avoir du pain sur la planche *(cutting board)*	____	to sell like hotcakes
2.	acheter pour une bouchée *(mouthful)* de pain	____	good-hearted
3.	bon comme du bon pain	____	to begin with the dessert
4.	gagner *(to earn)* son pain	____	as long as a month of Sundays
5.	manger son pain blanc le premier	____	to have no stomach for it
6.	retirer *(to pull out)* le pain de la bouche *(mouth)* de quelqu'un	____	to have your work cut out for you
7.	long comme un jour sans *(without)* pain	____	to bump someone off
8.	ne pas manger de ce pain-là	____	to buy for a mere song
9.	ôter *(take away)* le goût *(taste)* du pain à quelqu'un	____	to earn one's living
10.	se vendre comme des petits pains	____	to deprive someone of basic necessities

NOM ______________________________ DATE ______________________

GROS PLAN LA BOULANGERIE

PRÉPARATION

H. Seriez-vous un bon boulanger ou une bonne boulangère? Following is a synopsis of the bread-making process, but many of the important words are left out. Fill in the missing words, choosing from the list provided. Some words will be used more than once. You will not always use the article.

la tartine	*buttered bread*	**la pâte**	*dough*
la farine	*flour*	**le sandwich**	*sandwich*
le blé	*wheat*	**le four**	*oven*
l'eau *(f.)*	*water*	**la boulangerie**	*bakery*
le pain	*bread*	**le pain grillé**	*toast*

1. Au début, avec du bon ______________, on fait de la bonne ______________.
2. On livre *(delivers)* ______________ à la boulangerie.
3. Le boulanger mélange ______________ avec de ______________ et de la levure *(yeast).*
4. Le boulanger pétrit ce mélange, qui devient une ______________ épaisse *(thick).*
5. Quand il a pesé *(weighed)* la ______________ il la laisse lever *(rise).*
6. Quand la pâte a levé, il la met au ______________.
7. Quand la ______________ est cuite, on l'appelle du ______________.
8. Le ______________ est ensuite vendu dans une ______________.
9. Avec le ______________ on peut faire des ______________, des ______________ ou du ______________.

VISIONNEMENT

I. Est-ce vrai? View the **Gros plan** and decide if the following statements are true **(Vrai)** or false **(Faux).** Circle the appropriate letter.

V F 1. Le boulanger s'appelle Jacques.

V F 2. Il commence à préparer le pain à quatre heures.

V F 3. Il chauffe *(heats)* son four à l'électricité.

V F 4. Son four est en métal.

V F 5. Le boulanger prépare le pain à l'aide d'une machine électrique.

V F 6. Le pâtissier emploie un rouleau à main *(rolling pin)* pour étaler *(roll out)* sa pâte.

V F 7. Le boulanger pèse le pain à la main.

V F 8. Le pâtissier casse *(breaks)* les œufs à la main.

V F 9. Le boulanger travaille sur une vieille planche en bois *(old wooden breadboard).*

V F 10. Le boulanger fait aussi de la pâtisserie *(pastry).*

J. Avez-vous faim? At the end of this **Gros plan** you see a display of bakery goods. Complete the following list by filling in the missing prices. Then give a brief description of each item.

PRODUIT	PRIX	DESCRIPTION
croissant		
petit pain		
pain aux raisins		
pain au chocolat		
pain au lait		
chausson aux pommes		

APPLICATION

K. L'alimentation des Français. Look carefully at the following table, then answer the questions.

L'ALIMENTATION DES FRANÇAIS (en kilogrammes par personne par an)					
	Pain	**Graisses *(Fat)***	**Sucre**	**Viande *(Meat)***	**Pommes de terre *(Potatoes)***
1880	219	18	1	20	201
1910	182	22	5	35	189
1936	128	30	22	47	143
1970	81	35	20	84	96
1982	69	40	14	110	70

1. Les Français ont sans arrêt *(constantly)* augmenté *(increased)* leur consommation *(consumption)* de certains aliments. Lesquels? ______________________________
2. De quels aliments les Français ont-ils diminué *(decreased)* continuellement la consommation? ______________________________
3. De quel aliment est-ce que les Français ont commencé assez récemment à diminuer la consommation? ______________________________
4. En quelle année est-ce que la consommation de pain et la consommation de viande en France étaient *(were)* presque égales *(equal)*? ______________________________
5. Comment expliquez-vous ces changements dans la nourriture *(food)* des Français?

   ____
6. À votre avis, quelles sont les différences entre les statistiques d'alimentation pour la France et pour les États-Unis? ______________________________

NOM ______________________ DATE ______________________

PROBLÈME! IL N'Y A PAS DE CROISSANTS!

VISIONNEMENT

L. Les mots employés. Watch the **Problème** of Module IV with the sound on. Pay special attention to the characters' vocabulary choices. Then provide the following words used in the video.

1. un synonyme de «tout à fait» ______________________
2. un synonyme de «absolument» ______________________
3. le contraire de «les premières» ______________________
4. les ingrédients employés dans les croissants ______________________
5. le mot employé pour exprimer la qualité des croissants ______________________
6. un synonyme de «je regrette» ______________________

M. Des solutions. At the end of this **Problème,** Jean-François says: **"Oh non, qu'est-ce que je vais faire maintenant?"** Watch the **Problème** again, with the sound on. Then suggest four possible solutions to Jean-François's dilemma.

1. ______________________
2. ______________________
3. ______________________
4. ______________________

APPLICATIONS

N. À votre tour. Now formulate the sentences you would use to carry out each of the four suggestions you made in Activity M.

1. ______________________
2. ______________________
3. ______________________
4. ______________________

O. Que demandez-vous? In the accompanying drawing you can see many of the products typically sold in a French bakery. For each of the suggested situations, what would you say to the bakery clerk to order the items you need? Follow the **Modèle.**

❖ Vous habitez seul(e) *(alone)* et vous n'avez rien *(nothing)* à manger pour votre petit déjeuner *(breakfast)*.
VOUS: ***Un croissant, s'il vous plaît!***

1. Vous habitez seul(e) et vous n'avez rien à manger pour votre petit déjeuner.

   VOUS: ____

2. Vous habitez avec un(e) ami(e) et vous attendez deux ami(e)s pour le petit déjeuner.

   VOUS: ____

3. Vous devez *(are supposed to)* faire des sandwichs pour un(e) collègue et vous.

   VOUS: ____

4. Votre famille (père, mère, deux sœurs et un frère) a besoin de pain pour un souper *(supper)* en semaine.

   VOUS: ____

5. Votre famille (la même *[same]* que dans la question précédente) attend la visite de deux oncles et deux tantes pour un repas de fête, le dimanche à midi.

   VOUS: ____

6. Vous n'avez que *(only have)* cinq francs, mais vous avez faim.

   VOUS: ____

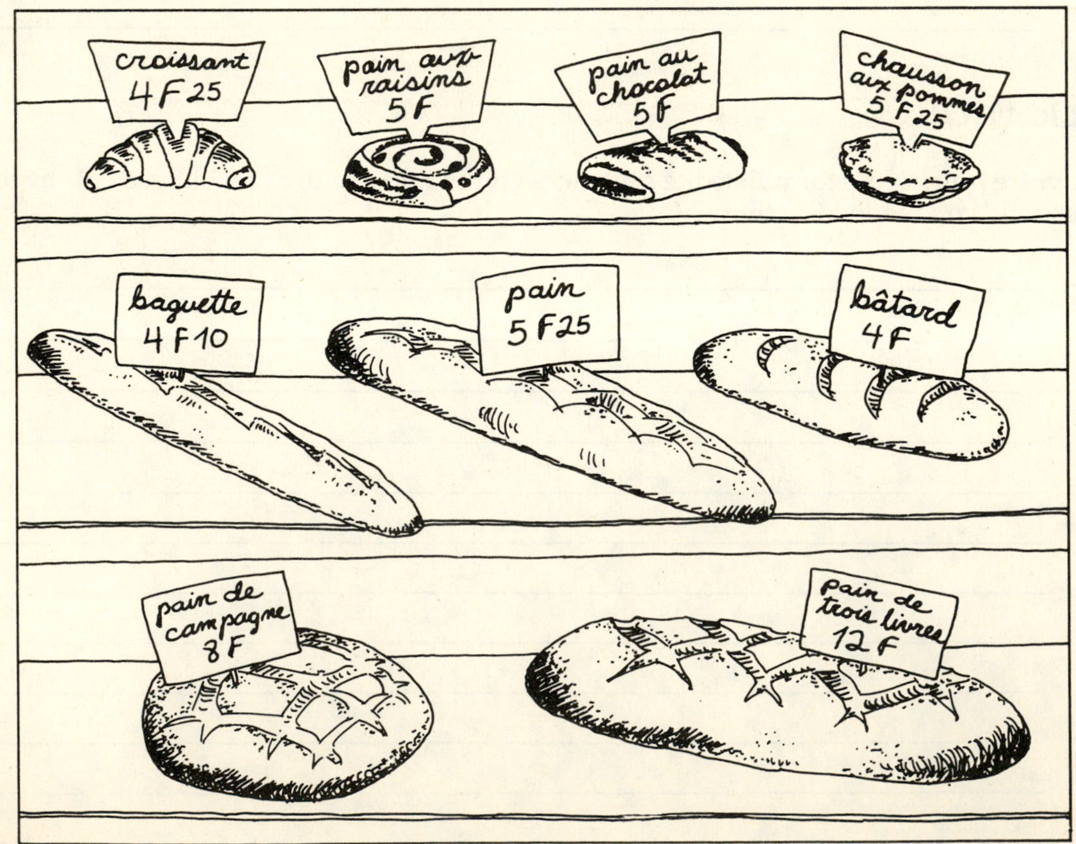

NOM ______________________________ DATE ______________________

SUPPLÉMENT

P. À la boulangerie. With a partner, play the roles of customer and clerk at a bakery. Act out each of the cases mentioned in Activity O to its logical conclusion. Follow the **Modèle.**

❖ VOUS: ***Un croissant, s'il vous plaît!***
VOTRE PARTENAIRE: ***Au beurre?***
VOUS: ***Ah oui, bien sûr.***
VOTRE PARTENAIRE: ***Ça fait quatre francs.***
VOUS: ***Voici cinq francs.***
VOTRE PARTENAIRE: ***Et voici votre monnaie* (change).**
VOUS: ***Merci beaucoup. Au revoir, Madame.***
VOTRE PARTENAIRE: ***Je vous en prie* (You're welcome). *Au revoir et bonne journée.***

La vente du pain

Answers to Activity F, p. 354: 10, 3, 11, 4, 12, 5, 8, 1, 9, 2, 6, 7
Answers to Activity G, p. 354: 10, 3, 5, 7, 8, 1, 9, 2, 4, 6

NOM ______________________ DATE ______________________

MODULE V AU CAFÉ

MISE EN SCÈNE

Pas loin de l'opéra de la Bastille, Bruno et Alissa attendent au café l'arrivée de leur amie Marie-Christine et de Jean-François, qu'ils ne connaissent pas encore *(don't know yet).*

PRÉPARATION

A. Quelques endroits francophones. Lisez soigneusement *(carefully)* les informations qui suivent au sujet de quatre endroits francophones de cultures différentes. Ensuite *(Then)* répondez aux questions.

	Réunion	**Sénégal**	**Québec**	**Maroc**
statut légal	DOM[1]	république indépendante	province canadienne	royaume indépendant
habitants	Réunionnais	Sénégalais	Québécois	Marocains
capitale	Saint-Denis	Dakar	Québec	Rabat
superficie	2.510 km^2	196.722 km^2	1.540.680 km^2	710.000 km^2
population	600.000	7.900.000	6.896.000	28.000.000
religion	catholique	musulmane	catholique	musulmane
industries	sucre, rhum, tourisme	huile d'arachide,[2] poissons en boîte[3]	pêche,[4] bois,[5] minéraux, hydroélectricité	poissons en boîte, textiles, agrumes[6]

1. Quel endroit est le plus grand? ______________________
2. Quel endroit a la population la plus nombreuse *(large)*? ______________________
3. Comment est-ce qu'on appelle les habitants de ces quatre endroits? ______________________
____
4. De quel pays les habitants de la Réunion sont-ils citoyens? ______________________
5. De quel pays les habitants du Québec sont-ils citoyens? ______________________
6. Est-ce que le Sénégal ou le Québec a plus d'habitants? ______________________
7. Où la pêche est-elle une industrie importante? ______________________
8. Où les fruits sont-ils un produit important? ______________________

Maintenant formulez deux autres questions au sujet de ces informations que vous allez poser à votre camarade de classe.

9. ______________________
10. ______________________

1. département d'outre-mer *(an overseas part of France)*; 2. peanut oil; 3. canned fish; 4. fishing; 5. wood; 6. citrus fruits

VISIONNEMENT

B. Comprenez-vous? Regardez la première partie du Module V sans le son et répondez aux questions suivantes. (Si vous voulez, vous pouvez répondre en anglais aux questions 3 et 6.)

1. Où se passe *(is happening)* cette scène?

   ____

2. À votre avis *(In your opinion)*, quels personnages se connaissent *(know each other)* déjà?

   Quels personnages ne se connaissent pas encore? ______________________________

   ____

3. Sur quoi est-ce que votre jugement est basé?

   ____

4. À votre avis, qu'est-ce que le garçon de café demande?

   ____

5. À votre avis, à quel moment de la journée cette scène se passe-t-elle?

   ____

6. Sur quoi est-ce que votre jugement est basé?

   ____

C. Qui le fait? Maintenant regardez la vidéo avec le son et identifiez les personnages (Marie-Christine, Jean-François, Alissa ou Bruno) qui font les actions suivantes. Mettez un «X» dans la colonne qui convient.

M-C	J-F	A	B	
___	___	___	___	1. Le personnage qui dit qu'il ne connaît pas beaucoup de Français.
___	___	___	___	2. Le personnage qui dit qu'il est sénégalais.
___	___	___	___	3. Le personnage qui dit que la France lui plaît.
___	___	___	___	4. Le personnage qui commande un café noir.
___	___	___	___	5. Le personnage qui commande un café crème.
___	___	___	___	6. Les deux personnages qui commandent un chocolat chaud.
___	___	___	___	7. Le personnage qui ne veut pas qu'un voyage coûte trop cher.
___	___	___	___	8. Le personnage qui suggère un voyage à Trouville.
___	___	___	___	9. Le personnage qui suggère un voyage en Bourgogne.
___	___	___	___	10. Le personnage qui suggère un voyage en Normandie.
___	___	___	___	11. Les personnages qui décident de rester à Paris.
___	___	___	___	12. Les personnages qui décident de partir en Normandie.

NOM ______________________________ DATE ____________________

APPLICATIONS

D. Quelque chose à boire? Posez les questions suivantes à votre partenaire. Il (Elle) doit répondre avec des phrases complètes. Ensuite changez de rôles et votre partenaire vous posera les mêmes questions. N'oubliez pas de faire les contractions nécessaires avec **de** et, au négatif, d'utiliser **pas de** ou **pas d'**.

1. Que bois-tu quand tu as très soif?
2. Chez toi, que boit-on avec un très bon dîner de poisson? et avec du rosbif?
3. Que bois-tu le matin?
4. Boit-on jamais *(ever)* de la bière chez toi? Préfères-tu boire de la bière américaine ou étrangère?
5. Préfères-tu boire du Coca ou de la limonade *(lemon-lime soda)?*

E. Au café. Faites cette activité avec un(e) partenaire. L'un joue le rôle d'un(e) touriste, l'autre joue le rôle d'un serveur (d'une serveuse) de café. Lisez d'abord la liste des consommations d'un café parisien. Ensuite jouez les situations suivantes. Suivez le modèle.

1. C'est l'après-midi et le (la) touriste désire boire du vin.
2. Le (La) touriste désire commander quelque chose pour son enfant.
3. Le (La) touriste commande une bière.
4. C'est le matin et le (la) touriste désire boire du café.

Café de la Bastille

café express 8,00F
café au lait 10,00F
chocolat chaud 10,00F
thé 9,00F
bière pression 9,00F
bière en bouteilles: française 12,00F
étrangère 16,00F
vin rouge 8,00F
vin blanc sec 8,00F
vin blanc doux 10,00F
Coca-cola 12,00F
Orangina 12,00F

Service (15%) compris

❖ C'est l'après-midi et le (la) touriste désire boire du vin.

SERVEUR: ***Que désirez-vous?***
TOURISTE: ***Je voudrais un verre de vin, s'il vous plaît.***
SERVEUR: ***Du vin rouge ou du vin blanc?***
TOURISTE: ***Du vin blanc.***
SERVEUR: ***Nous avons un vin blanc sec* (dry) *et un vin blanc doux qui est plus sucré* (sweet).**
TOURISTE: ***Je préfère le vin blanc doux, s'il vous plaît.***
SERVEUR: ***Voilà votre vin, Monsieur.***
TOURISTE: ***Ça fait combien?***
SERVEUR: ***C'est 10 F, Monsieur.***
TOURISTE: ***Voilà 20 F.***
SERVEUR: ***Et votre monnaie, 10 F.***
TOURISTE: ***Merci, Monsieur.***

GROS PLAN LE TEMPS LIBRE

PRÉPARATION

F. Divertissements. Étudiez cette liste d'activités et répondez aux questions.

	cinéma	musée	opéra	concert	château	cathédrale	mer	lac	montagne
Trouville	x			x			x		
Annecy	x	x		x	x	x		x	x
Vichy	x	x		x					
Aix-en-Provence	x	x		x		x			
Strasbourg	x	x	x	x		x			
Chinon	x	x		x	x				

1. De toutes ces activités, quelle est votre activité préférée?

   ____

2. Quelle activité préférez-vous parmi les activités offertes à Aix-en-Provence?

   ____

3. Si vous aimez l'opéra, où faut-il aller?

   ____

4. Où est-il possible de visiter un château?

   ____

5. Quelle ville offre la possibilité de faire de la voile *(to go sailing)* sur un lac *(lake)?*

   ____

6. Vous aimez les vieilles cathédrales, votre ami(e) préfère les vieux châteaux. Où pouvez-vous aller ensemble?

   ____

7. Si vous aimez la mer, quelle ville faut-il choisir *(choose)?*

   ____

8. Dans quelle ville désirez-vous passer des vacances? Pourquoi?

   ____

   ____

NOM ______________________________ DATE ______________________

VISIONNEMENT

G. Que voyez-vous? Regardez le **Gros plan** du Module V «Le temps libre» sans le son et indiquez avec un «X» dans la colonne de gauche les activités que vous voyez dans la vidéo.

_____ le château _____

_____ le cinéma _____

_____ les patins à roulettes *(roller skates)* _____

_____ le concert _____

_____ le parc d'attractions *(amusement park)* _____

_____ la mer *(sea)* _____

_____ le musée _____

_____ l'opéra _____

_____ le vélo _____

_____ la cathédrale _____

_____ le bateau _____

H. Mettez les mots dans l'ordre! Maintenant regardez encore une fois *(once more)* la vidéo. Dans la colonne de droite dans l'Activité G, mettez le numéro qui correspond à l'endroit de l'attraction dans la vidéo.

APPLICATIONS

I. Un week-end spécial. Imaginez que vous lisez la phrase suivante dans une brochure: «En fonction de *(Depending on)* vos préférences, vous pouvez passer un week-end de rêve en Normandie, en Bourgogne, en Alsace ou sur la Côte d'Azur.» Vous allez tout de suite dans une agence de voyage et l'agent vous pose les questions suivantes. Comment répondez-vous?

1. Où est-ce que vous voulez aller?

   ____

2. Quand voulez-vous partir?

   ____

3. Voulez-vous partir en train, en avion ou avec une voiture de location?

   ____

4. Quelle classe d'hôtel préférez-vous? un hôtel à une, deux, trois ou quatre étoiles *(stars)* ou une auberge de jeunesse *(youth hostel)*?

   ____

5. Désirez-vous une chambre qui donne sur la rue ou sur la cour *(courtyard)*?

   ____

6. Que préférez-vous, une baignoire *(bathtub)* ou une douche *(shower)*?

   ____

J. Les hôtels à Chartres. Avec un(e) ami(e), vous avez décidé de passer un week-end à Chartres. Il (Elle) vous a demandé de vous renseigner sur *(find out about)* les hôtels. Consultez cette liste d'hôtels et suivez les instructions.

		1 ÉTOILE		*2 ÉTOILES*		*3 ÉTOILES*	
		HÔTEL DE L'ÉCU CHARTRES	HÔTEL SAINT JEAN CHARTRES	HÔTEL DE LA POSTE CHARTRES	HÔTEL DES SPORTS CHARTRES	LE GRAND MONARQUE CHARTRES	NOVOTEL CHARTRES
1 PERS	SIMPLE	100 F	90 F / Tel	160 F/ TV+Tel	125 F /Tel	-	-
	SIMPLE - WC	-	-	160 F /TV+Tel	-	-	-
	DOUCHE	160 F	-	195 F /TV+Tel	135 F /Tel	-	-
	DOUCHE - WC	180 F	-	215 F /TV+Tel	150 F /Tel	312 F /TV+Tel	-
	CABINET TOILETTE	100 F	-	-	-	-	-
	BAIN	160 F	-	-	-	-	-
	BAIN - WC	180 F		260 F /TV+Tel	160 F /Tel	420/530 F TV+Tel	390 F TV+Tel
2 PERS	SIMPLE	110 F	100 F /Tel	160 F /TV+Tel	125 F /Tel	-	-
	SIMPLE - WC		-		-	-	-
	DOUCHE	160 F	130 F /Tel	200 F /TV+Tel	150 F /Tel	-	-
	DOUCHE - WC	180 F /TV	165 F /Tel	220 F /TV+Tel	175 F /Tel	355 F /TV+Tel	-
	CABINET TOILETTE	110 F	105 F /Tel	-	-	-	-
	BAIN	200 F /TV	130 F /Tel	-	-	-	-
	BAIN - WC	220 F /TV		270 F /TV+Tel	210 F / Tel	525/625 F TV + Tel	470 F TV+Tel
	PETIT DÉJEUNER	23 F	20 F	35,50 F	25 F	45 F	47 F

Décrivez à un(e) partenaire, qui joue le rôle de votre ami(e) au téléphone, les chambres et les prix des hôtels chartrains (à Chartres). Votre partenaire exprime ses préférences, mais vous n'êtes pas toujours d'accord. Décidez ensemble quel genre de chambre et d'hôtel vous préférez. Suivez le modèle.

❖ VOUS: ***Je suggère Le Grand Monarque.***
VOTRE PARTENAIRE: ***Combien coûtent les chambres?***
VOUS: ***Elles sont assez chères.***
VOTRE PARTENAIRE: ***Ah, non! Est-ce qu'il y a un hôtel moins cher?***
VOUS: ***Bien sûr, si tu veux. Il y a...***

PROBLÈME! LE TRAIN NE CIRCULE QUE LES DIMANCHES ET FÊTES

PRÉPARATION

K. L'horaire des trains. Voici une partie du tableau horaire *(schedule)* pour les trains allant *(that go)* de Paris au Mans. Étudiez cet horaire et répondez aux questions suivantes.

1. De quelle gare parisienne ces trains partent-ils? ____________________
2. Si on prend le train à Paris le dimanche à sept heures, à quelle heure arrive-t-on à Nogent-le-Rotrou? ____________________
3. Si on prend le train à Paris le lundi à sept heures, est-ce qu'on s'arrête *(stop)* à Bretoncelles? ____________________

4. Quelle est la durée *(length)* du trajet de Paris au Mans par TGV?

____

5. C'est dimanche et vous êtes à Condé-sur-Huisne. Quel est le premier train de la journée pour aller au Mans? ______________________

6. Un lundi matin vous êtes à Paris à neuf heures. Est-il possible d'arriver à La Loupe avant onze heures? Comment? ______________________

7. Jeudi matin. Vous arrivez à la gare Montparnasse à huit heures et demie. Vous êtes très pressé(e) *(in a hurry)* d'arriver au Mans. Quel train faut-il prendre?

____

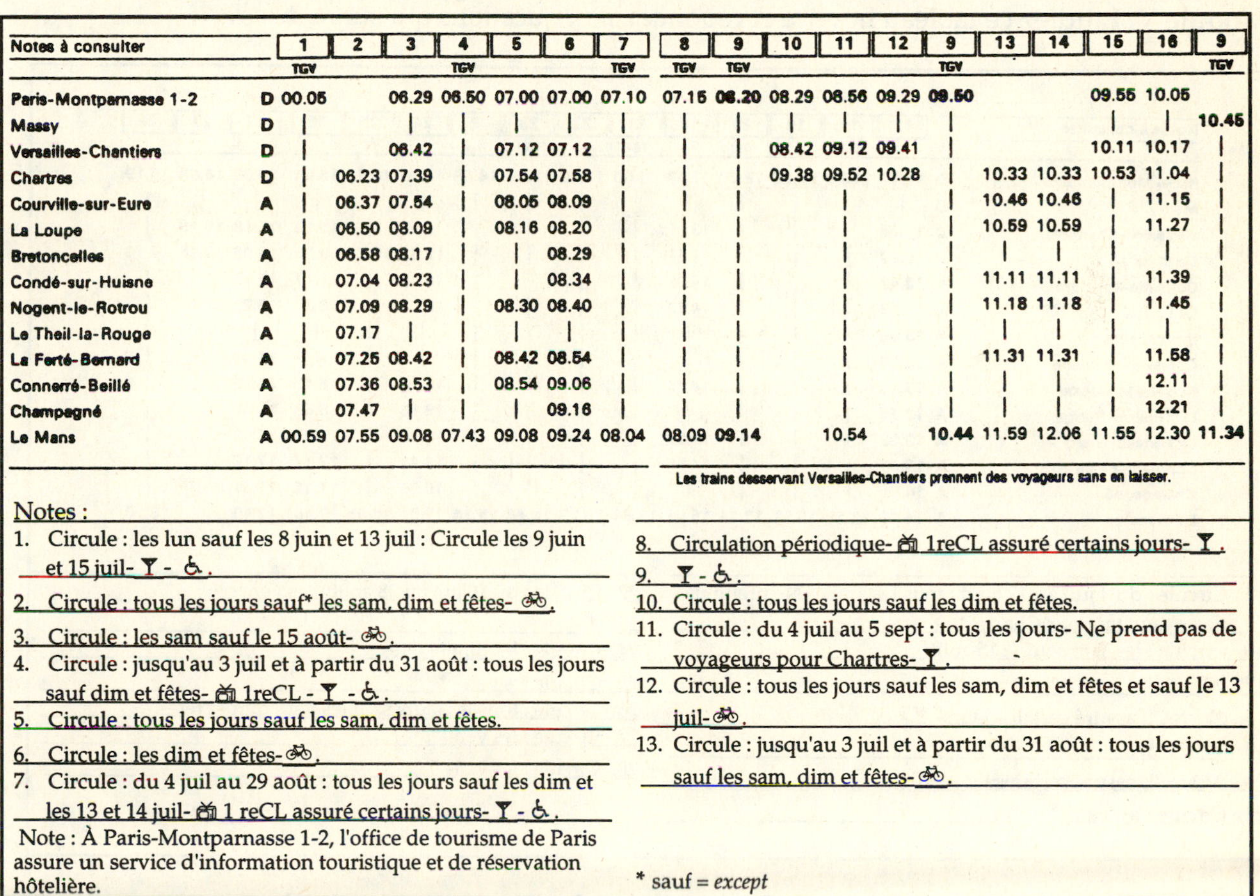

Notes à consulter		1	2	3	4	5	6	7	8	9	10	11	12	9	13	14	15	16	9
		TGV			TGV			TGV	TGV	TGV				TGV					TGV
Paris-Montparnasse 1-2	D	00.05		06.29	06.50	07.00	07.00	07.10	07.15	08.20	08.29	08.56	09.29	09.50			09.55	10.05	
Massy	D																		10.45
Versailles-Chantiers	D			06.42		07.12	07.12				08.42	09.12	09.41				10.11	10.17	
Chartres	D		06.23	07.39		07.54	07.58				09.38	09.52	10.28		10.33	10.33	10.53	11.04	
Courville-sur-Eure	A		06.37	07.54		08.05	08.09								10.46	10.46		11.15	
La Loupe	A		06.50	08.09		08.16	08.20								10.59	10.59		11.27	
Bretoncelles	A		06.58	08.17			08.29												
Condé-sur-Huisne	A		07.04	08.23			08.34								11.11	11.11		11.39	
Nogent-le-Rotrou	A		07.09	08.29		08.30	08.40								11.18	11.18		11.45	
Le Theil-la-Rouge	A		07.17																
La Ferté-Bernard	A		07.25	08.42		08.42	08.54								11.31	11.31		11.58	
Connerré-Beillé	A		07.36	08.53		08.54	09.06											12.11	
Champagné	A		07.47				09.16											12.21	
Le Mans	A	00.59	07.55	09.08	07.43	09.08	09.24	08.04	08.09	09.14		10.54		10.44	11.59	12.06	11.55	12.30	11.34

Les trains desservant Versailles-Chantiers prennent des voyageurs sans en laisser.

Notes :

1. Circule : les lun sauf les 8 juin et 13 juil : Circule les 9 juin et 15 juil- 🍸 - ♿.
2. Circule : tous les jours sauf* les sam, dim et fêtes- 🚲.
3. Circule : les sam sauf le 15 août- 🚲.
4. Circule : jusqu'au 3 juil et à partir du 31 août : tous les jours sauf dim et fêtes- 📺 1reCL - 🍸 - ♿.
5. Circule : tous les jours sauf les sam, dim et fêtes.
6. Circule : les dim et fêtes- 🚲.
7. Circule : du 4 juil au 29 août : tous les jours sauf les dim et les 13 et 14 juil- 📺 1 reCL assuré certains jours- 🍸 - ♿.
8. Circulation périodique- 📺 1reCL assuré certains jours- 🍸.
9. 🍸 - ♿.
10. Circule : tous les jours sauf les dim et fêtes.
11. Circule : du 4 juil au 5 sept : tous les jours- Ne prend pas de voyageurs pour Chartres- 🍸.
12. Circule : tous les jours sauf les sam, dim et fêtes et sauf le 13 juil- 🚲.
13. Circule : jusqu'au 3 juil et à partir du 31 août : tous les jours sauf les sam, dim et fêtes- 🚲.

Note : À Paris-Montparnasse 1-2, l'office de tourisme de Paris assure un service d'information touristique et de réservation hôtelière.

* sauf = *except*

VISIONNEMENT

L. Que devinez-vous? Regardez le **Problème** du Module V. Ensuite répondez aux questions suivantes.

1. Où sont Alissa et Bruno?
   a. au marché
   b. dans un train
   c. devant une gare
   d. dans le métro
2. Qu'est-ce qu'Alissa est partie faire?
   a. acheter des sandwichs
   b. acheter des billets
   c. demander l'heure
   d. téléphoner à son ami Noël

3. Selon Alissa, quel train faut-il prendre? À quelle heure?
   a. le train 3376
   b. le train 33176
   c. le train 3016
   d. le train 13617
4. Pourquoi Bruno n'est-il pas d'accord?
   a. Ce train ne circule que les dimanches et fêtes.
   b. Il est trop tard pour prendre ce train.
   c. Ce train n'a que la première classe.
   d. Bruno est trop fatigué.

APPLICATIONS

M. Le tableau horaire. Voici le tableau horaire que Bruno regarde dans le **Problème** du Module V. Étudiez ce tableau horaire et répondez aux questions qui suivent.

Notes à consulter		17	18	19	20	10	21	22	23	9	24	25	26	27	27	28
			TGV		TGV		TGV		TGV	TGV						
Paris-Montparnasse 1-2	D	11.14	11.25	11.28	12.20	12.59	13.00	13.40	13.50	14.20	14.30	15.02	15.05	15.05	16.03	16.19
Massy	D	|	|	|	|	|	|	|	|	|	|	|	|	|	|	|
Versailles-Chantiers	D	11.26	|	|	|	13.11	|	|	|	|	14.42	|	15.18	15.18	16.16	|
Chartres	D	12.27	|	|	|	13.51	|	|	|	|	15.32	15.54	16.06	16.06	17.16	17.10
Courville-sur-Eure	A	12.42	|	|	|	14.01	|	|	|	|	15.43	|	16.17	16.17		|
La Loupe	A	12.56	|	|	|	14.13	|	|	|	|	15.55	|	16.29	16.28		|
Bretoncelles	A	13.05	|	|	|	|	|	|	|	|	|	|	|	|		|
Condé-sur-Huisne	A	13.10	|	|	|	|	|	|	|	|	|	|	|	16.40		|
Nogent-le-Rotrou	A	13.16	|	|	|	14.26	|	|	|	|	16.10	|	16.43	16.46		|
Le Theil-la-Rouge	A	13.25	|	|	|	|	|	|	|	|	16.18	|	16.53	16.54		|
La Ferté-Bernard	A	13.32	|	|	|	14.39	|	|	|	|	16.26	|	17.02	17.02		|
Connerré-Beillé	A	13.47	|	|	|	14.51	|	|	|	|	16.41	|	17.17	17.17		|
Champagné	A	14.01	|	|	|	|	|	|	|	|	16.55	|	17.32	17.31		|
Le Mans	A	14.09	12.19	13.11	13.14	15.05	13.54	15.23	14.44	15.14	17.04	16.55	17.40	17.40		18.10

15. Circule : du 4 juil au 29 août : tous les jours - Ne prend pas de voyageurs pour Chartres- 🍸 - ♿.
16. Circule : les sam sauf le 15 août.
17. 🚲.
18. 🚗 1reCL assuré certains jours- 🍸 - ♿.
19. 🍸 🍴 - ♿.
20. 🚗 1reCL assuré certains jours- 🍸.
21. Circule : les ven- 🍸 - ♿.
22. Circule : du 10 juil au 28 août : les ven.
23. 🍸.
24. Circule : les dim et fêtes.
25. Circule les ven- 🍸 🍴.
26. Circule : tous les jours sauf les ven, dim et fêtes.
27. Circule : les ven.
28. Circule : les ven- 🍸.

1. C'est jeudi et Alissa veut prendre le train de deux heures et demie. Quel est le problème?

   ____

2. Quel autre train Alissa et Bruno peuvent-ils prendre cet après-midi pour aller à Nogent-le-Rotrou? ______________________________

3. Avec ce train, à quelle heure arrivent-ils à Nogent-le-Rotrou?

   ____

4. Expliquez à Bruno et Alissa ce qu'ils doivent faire.

   ____

5. Jouez le rôle d'Alissa. Que dites-vous pour acheter les billets?

   ____

NOM ______________________________ DATE ______________________

N. Un renseignement *(Piece of information)*, **s'il vous plaît.** Faites cette activité avec un(e) partenaire, qui joue le rôle d'un(e) employé(e). Demandez les informations suivantes à votre partenaire, qui consulte les tableaux horaires et vous donne les renseignements demandés. Vous êtes à Paris.

❖ Il est six heures vingt, lundi. Vous voulez le prochain train pour Nogent-le-Rotrou.
VOUS: ***À quelle heure le premier train pour Nogent-le-Rotrou part-il?***
VOTRE PARTENAIRE: ***Il part à sept heures.***

1. Jeudi après-midi. Vous voulez arriver au Mans demain avant onze heures.
2. Il est quatorze heures quarante, vendredi. Vous voulez arriver à Condé-sur-Huisne avant dix-huit heures.
3. Vous voulez savoir quand part le premier train de la journée, pour Nogent-le-Rotrou, samedi.

SUPPLÉMENT

O. La lettre. Alissa écrit une lettre à sa tante à la Réunion pour raconter sa journée—la discussion au café, les problèmes à la gare, et puis le voyage jusqu'à Nogent-le-Rotrou. À la page suivante, écrivez cette lettre pour elle. Utilisez le **passé composé** et les expressions utiles. Commencez par «Chère Tante» et finissez avec «Je t'embrasse». N'oubliez pas que vous jouez le rôle d'Alissa.

POUR RACONTER LA SÉQUENCE D'UNE HISTOIRE

d'abord *first*
puis *then*
ensuite *then*
après *afterward*
enfin *finally*

POUR PARLER DU PASSÉ

Je suis allée...
J'ai rencontré...
Nous avons parlé...
Nous avons bu... / J'ai bu...
Nous avons décidé de...
Nous sommes allé(e)s...
Nous avons eu...

Chère Tante,

Je t'embrasse,

NOM ______________________________ DATE ______________________

MODULE VI LE CHÂTEAU SAINT-JEAN

MISE EN SCÈNE

Bruno et Alissa ont finalement décidé de prendre le train de 15 h 05, qui passe par Chartres. En attendant, ils ont appelé *(called)* leur ami Noël. Noël a promis *(promised)* de venir les chercher à la gare et de les amener *(take)* au château Saint-Jean.

PRÉPARATION

A. Formules de politesse. Lisez le texte suivant, en faisant bien *(paying close)* attention aux différences entre les nombreuses façons de saluer *(greet)* quelqu'un. Ensuite décidez comment il faut saluer les personnes mentionnées.

> Comment est-ce qu'on salue les gens? En France il y a beaucoup de conventions à ce propos. Avec les gens qu'on ne connaît pas très bien (les gens à qui on dit «vous»), on se serre *(shakes)* la main et on emploie une formule de politesse comme «Bonjour, Monsieur Goudet, comment allez-vous?» ou «Bonsoir, Madame Maupoix, vous allez bien?». Avec les gens qu'on connaît bien (les gens à qui on dit «tu»), on emploie plutôt *(instead)* la bise *(kiss),* c'est-à-dire qu'on touche alternativement les deux joues *(cheeks)* de l'autre personne avec sa propre *(own)* joue (mais les hommes, même *[even]* quand ils se connaissent bien, se serrent souvent la main plutôt que de faire la bise).
>
> Combien de bises faut-il? Ça dépend où on est! À Paris la bise est double (c'est-à-dire, on touche d'abord la joue gauche et ensuite la joue droite, ou vice versa), mais en Bourgogne elle est triple (trois fois plutôt que deux); dans le Perche (et dans beaucoup d'autres régions agricoles) on fait la bise quatre fois. Il y a même des endroits où on fait la bise cinq fois!
>
> Quelle formule de politesse faut-il employer? En faisant la bise on emploie une formule plus familière. Chez les adultes on dit souvent: «Bonjour (Bonsoir) Roger, ça va bien (ou "comment vas-tu")?» ou encore, plus familièrement: «Bonjour Ludovic, ça va la petite famille (ou "ton œil ne te fait pas trop mal")?» Chez les jeunes, on a plutôt tendance à dire «Salut Ludo» (ou tout autre terme familier, comme «gars», «fiston» ou «pote»). Entre eux, les jeunes emploient même parfois des expressions populaires, comme «Salut Michel, ça boume?» (=«ça va bien?»). Notez qu'une formule comme «Bonjour» ou «Bonsoir» est rarement employée sans le titre Monsieur, Madame, Mademoiselle ou le nom de la personne à qui on parle.

Donnez la formule de politesse que vous allez employer pour saluer chacune des personnes suivantes. Écrivez (1) si vous serrez la main à la personne ou si vous faites la bise (et combien de bises vous faites) et (2) ce que vous dites à chaque personne.

1. Votre professeur

____

____

2. Le président de votre université

____

____

3. Votre copine *(friend)* Micheline

4. Un étudiant qu'un ami vient de vous présenter, qui s'appelle Georges Strasser

5. Votre voisine dans le Perche, Odile Odin

6. Le père de votre voisin parisien, Gérard Dorchêne

7. Une étudiante que vous connaissez depuis plus d'un an

8. Votre ami Jean-Loup, que vous connaissez depuis toujours

VISIONNEMENT

B. Descriptions. Regardez la première partie du Module VI sans le son et essayez de deviner *(guess)* quel adjectif de la liste ci-dessous *(below)* décrit chaque nom.

1. la ____ cheminée	a. belle
2. le ____ château	b. bonne
3. la construction ____	c. beaux
4. les ____ merles	d. beau
5. la ____ chaleur	e. solide
6. la vue ____	f. spectaculaire

C. Avez-vous bien deviné? Maintenant, regardez la vidéo encore une fois, mais cette fois avec le son, et corrigez votre travail dans l'Activité B.

NOM ______________________________ DATE ______________________________

D. Noms et adjectifs. Regardez toute la première partie du Module VI **«Le château Saint-Jean»** et indiquez le chiffre (1–12) qui correspond à l'ordre dans lequel vous entendez les mots suivants. Ensuite, regardez la vidéo une autre fois et fournissez les adjectifs qui modifient les noms. Certains noms n'ont pas d'adjectif.

____	les merles	____________	____	les soldats	____________
____	le chauffage	____________	____	le Moyen Âge	____________
____	la salle	____________	____	la cheminée	____________
____	le bois	____________	____	les remparts	____________
____	la chaleur	____________	____	les tours	____________
____	la vallée	____________	____	l'Huisne	____________

APPLICATIONS

E. Salutations. Regardez le début seulement *(only)* du Module VI, jusqu'au *(until the)* moment où la voiture de Noël quitte *(leaves)* la gare de Nogent-le-Rotrou. Notez bien la façon *(the way)* dont Alissa, Bruno et Noël se saluent. Après, choisissez un(e) partenaire et dites comment vous vous saluez quand vous jouez les rôles suivants. Changez souvent de partenaire pendant cette activité (et inventez des noms intéressants!). Suivez les formules dans le texte de l'Activité A.

FORMEL	**FAMILIER**
Bonjour/Bonsoir...	**Salut...**
Monsieur/Madame/ Mademoiselle	**Ça va?**
	Tu vas bien?
Comment allez-vous?	**Ça boume?**

1. deux ami(e)s qui se connaissent depuis toujours
2. deux étudiant(e)s qui ne se connaissent pas très bien, et qui vont jouer aux échecs pour la première fois
3. un(e) étudiant(e) et son professeur
4. un(e) étudiant(e) et la mère d'un(e) ami(e)
5. un(e) étudiant(e) et un(e) ami(e) de Bourgogne
6. un(e) étudiant(e) et un(e) garagiste

F. Le château Saint-Jean. Lisez le prospectus et répondez aux questions suivantes avec des phrases complètes.

1. Pendant quels siècles le château Saint-Jean a-t-il été construit?

   ____

2. Quelles sont les heures d'ouverture du château l'hiver? l'été?

   ____

   ____

3. Est-ce que le château Saint-Jean est fermé le dimanche? un autre jour de la semaine?

   ____

   ____

4. Combien coûte l'entrée pour une famille de deux adultes et trois enfants? ______________

   ____

   ____

5. Combien coûte l'entrée pour une classe de quinze enfants, une institutrice et une accompagnatrice? ______________

   ____

   ____

6. Quelle gare parisienne faut-il emprunter *(use)* pour aller à Nogent-le-Rotrou? ______________

   ____

   ____

7. Combien de temps dure le trajet *(trip)* en train? en voiture? ______________

   ____

   ____

8. Pour voir les châteaux de la Loire, quelle direction faut-il prendre, en quittant Nogent-le-Rotrou? ______________

   ____

   ____

Eure & Loir

NOGENT-LE-ROTROU

France - Centre - Val de Loire

Photo : Caroline Rose pour PAP

CHÂTEAU SAINT-JEAN

XIè – XIIIè – XVè siècles

Classé monument historique en 1950

Musée municipal : Histoire locale, Ethnographie, Beaux-Arts

- **HORAIRES :**
  - Du 1er mai au 31 octobre : de 10 h à 12 h et de 14 h à 18 h
  - Du 1er novembre au 30 avril : de 10 h à 12 h et de 14 h à 17 h
  - Fermeture hebdomadaire le mardi.
- **TARIFS :**
  - Adultes : 8,50 F, Enfants : 3,50 F
  - Tarifs réduits pour les groupes à partir de 12 personnes (4,50 F et 2,20 F)
- **ACCÈS :**
  SNCF : Paris-Montparnasse 1 h 30
  Route : RN 23 1 h 40 – A11 1 h 30 sortie Luigny

Parking autos et autocars sur le site

28400 Nogent-le-Rotrou – Tél. 37 52 18 02
ou Office de Tourisme – Tél. 37 52 16 22

ALENÇON
CHARTRES
PARIS
N23
D 955
BELLÊME
NOGENT-LE-ROTROU
LA FERTÉ-BERNARD
LUIGNY
BROU
A11
CHÂTEAUDUN
vers Châteaux de la Loire
REGION CENTRE
LE CŒUR-DE-FRANCE

NOM ______________________ DATE ______________________

G. Quelques renseignements. Lisez le texte suivant. Puis répondez aux questions.

> Dominant la ville la fière silhouette du Château Saint-Jean est un témoignage unique de l'architecture du Moyen Âge et du glorieux passé de Nogent-le-Rotrou. Le donjon rectangulaire de 30 mètres de haut surplombe de 60 mètres la vallée de l'Huisne. Sa construction commence dans les premières années du XIe siècle sous le règne de ROTROU I, premier seigneur de Nogent. C'est à GEOFFROY IV, premier Comte du Perche vers 1079, que l'on doit la fortification du donjon. Elle est suivie à la fin du XIIe siècle et au XIIIe siècle par la construction de l'enceinte circulaire : sept tours renforcent la défense de l'édifice.
>
> Parmi les nombreux sièges subis, celui de 1428, mené par le Comte de SALISBURY, fut particulièrement violent. L'incendie du donjon anéantit l'intérieur de la construction. C'est aux demoiselles d'ARMAGNAC, propriétaires au tout début du XVIe siècle, que l'on doit l'aspect actuel du Château Saint-Jean : un logis de deux étages fut construit au-dessus de la voûte d'entrée et les tours surélevées.
>
> De SULLY, qui devint propriétaire en 1624, date le charmant petit pavillon de style Louis XIII adossé au rempart Nord.
>
> Les salles du château, entièrement restaurées depuis les années 60, abritent un musée d'ethnographie et d'histoire locale (objets et témoignages de la vie rurale du Perche, de l'histoire du château et de la ville) et des expositions temporaires.

1. Quelle est la hauteur du donjon *(dungeon)?*

   ____

2. Quelle est sa forme *(shape)?*

   ____

3. Qui est Rotrou I?

   ____

   ____

4. Quand est-ce que le donjon a été fortifié?

   ____

5. Quand est-ce que le donjon a brûlé *(burned)?*

   ____

6. Vers (*Around)* quelle année est-ce que la famille d'Armagnac a entrepris *(undertook)* la restauration du château?

   ____

GROS PLAN LE CHÂTEAU

PRÉPARATION

H. Un peu de recherche. Voici une liste de châteaux français particulièrement connus *(well-known).* Avec l'aide d'une encyclopédie ou d'un dictionnaire encyclopédique, précisez si ces châteaux ont été construits au Moyen Âge (avant le 15ème siècle), à l'époque de la Renaissance (15ème et 16ème siècles), à l'époque classique (17ème et 18ème siècles) ou plus récemment—en France, tous les bâtiments qui ont été construits depuis la Révolution de 1789 sont considérés comme récents. Ensuite, avec l'aide d'un atlas ou d'une carte de France, situez les châteaux sur la carte ci-dessous. Remarquez que deux de ces châteaux se trouvent à Paris.

	ÉPOQUE			
Bâtiment	**Moyen Âge**	**Renaissance**	**Classique**	**Moderne**
le château d'Amboise				
le château d'Angers				
le château de Carcassonne				
le château de Chambord				
le château de Chinon				
le château de Fontainebleau				
le Louvre				
le palais du Luxembourg				
le château de Versailles				

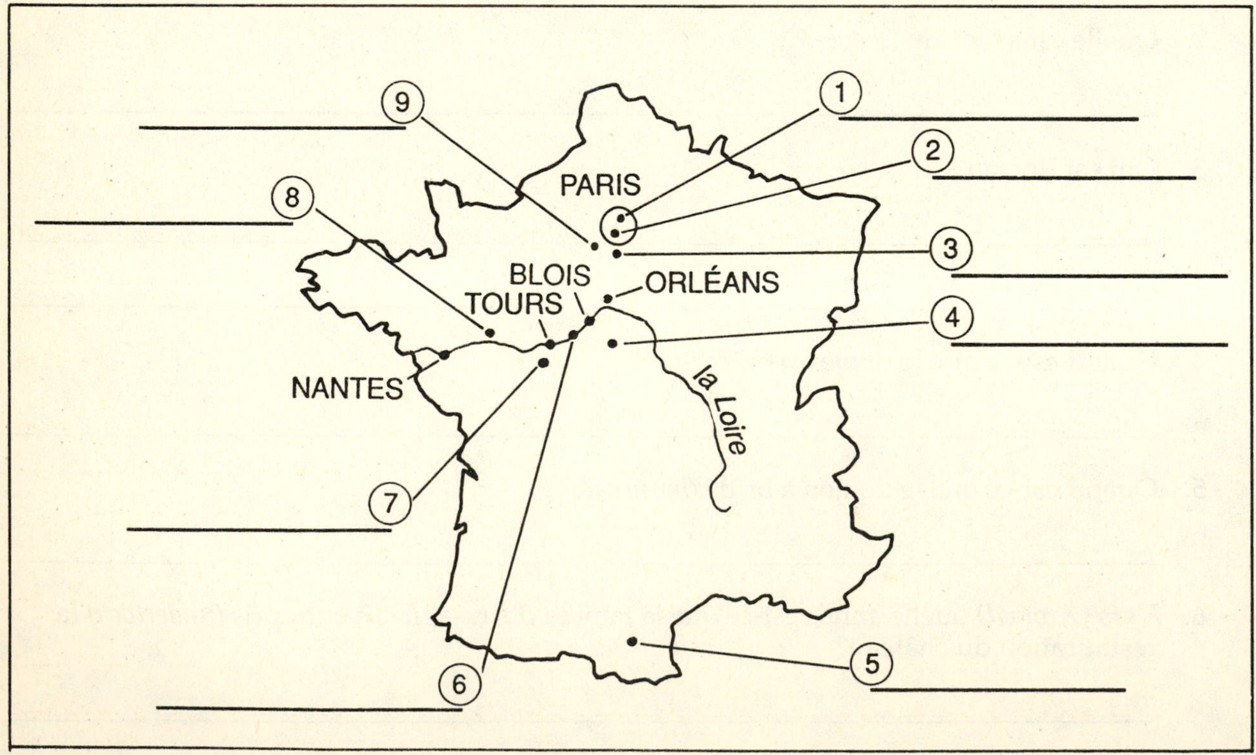

NOM ____________________ DATE ____________________

VISIONNEMENT

I. L'époque des châteaux. Regardez le **Gros plan** du Module VI **«Le château»** et notez l'époque de construction citée dans la vidéo.

Endroit	**Époque des châteaux**
En Alsace	
Le long de la Seine	
Dans le Midi	
Dans la région de Bordeaux	
Dans la vallée de la Loire	
Près de Paris	
À Nogent-le-Rotrou	

J. Châteaux de France. Regardez encore une fois le **Gros plan** du Module VI et faites particulièrement attention aux caractéristiques des châteaux. Ensuite, répondez aux questions suivantes.

1. Qu'est-ce que tous les châteaux ont en commun?
2. Qu'est-ce que beaucoup de châteaux du Moyen Âge ont en commun?
3. Qu'est-ce que les châteaux de la Renaissance et de l'époque classique ont en commun?
4. Décrivez le château Saint-Jean à Nogent-le-Rotrou.
5. Qui a fait construire le petit pavillon (la petite maison) contre les remparts du château Saint-Jean? ____________________
6. Quel genre ou style de château préférez-vous? Pourquoi?

PROBLÈME!   PLUS DE PELLICULE

PRÉPARATION

K. Formidable! Les Français ont une grande variété de mots pour dire qu'ils aiment beaucoup quelque chose, par exemple,

superbe, formidable, extraordinaire, exquis;

ou, sur un ton plus familier (surtout chez les jeunes),

chouette, sympa, extra, super.

Employez un de ces mots dans une phrase complète pour répondre à chacune des questions suivantes. Imaginez que vous êtes avec des amis au centre commercial. Ils demandent votre opinion sur les vêtements qu'ils essaient *(try on).*

❖ VOTRE AMI(E): ***Comment trouves-tu cette veste?***
VOUS: ***Elle est chouette!***

1. Comment tu trouves ce pull?

   VOUS: ______________________________

2. Que pensez-vous de cette chemise?

   VOUS: ______________________________

3. Tu aimes ces chaussures?

   VOUS: ______________________________

4. Comment est-ce que vous trouvez cette jupe?

   VOUS: ______________________________

5. Est-ce que cette cravate vous plaît?

   VOUS: ______________________________

VISIONNEMENT

L. Quelques détails. Regardez le **Problème** du Module VI et choisissez la meilleure réponse à chacune des questions suivantes.

1. Où se trouvent *(are located)* les personnages?
   a. dans le donjon
   b. dans une tour
   c. sur les remparts
   d. dans la salle des gardes
2. Quand Bruno appelle *(calls)* son ami Noël «gars», c'est quel niveau *(level)* de langue?
   a. littéraire
   b. familier
   c. sénégalais
   d. régional
3. Quand Alissa demande à Bruno de lui donner «l'appareil», qu'est-ce qu'elle veut?
   a. la caméra
   b. la pellicule *(roll of film)*
   c. le film
   d. l'appareil-photo

4. Alissa n'a plus de pellicule. Où est-ce qu'on met une pellicule?
   a. dans sa caméra
   b. dans son appareil-photo
   c. à l'entrée
   d. dans ses cheveux
5. Noël dit: «Ce n'est pas la peine!» Quel est le sens de cette expression?
   a. Ça me fait mal!
   b. Ça ne me cause pas de mal!
   c. Ne t'en fais pas *(Don't be upset)!*
   d. Ce n'est pas utile!
6. Alissa dit «zut». Pourquoi?
   a. Elle n'est pas contente.
   b. Elle est ravie *(delighted).*
   c. Elle n'a plus d'argent.
   d. Elle est heureuse.

APPLICATIONS

M. Le dimanche. Aujourd'hui vous visitez la capitale de votre état, mais vous n'avez plus de pellicule. Où pouvez-vous aller pour en acheter *(to buy some)?* Mentionnez plusieurs magasins différents parce que c'est dimanche et beaucoup de magasins sont fermés.

______________________ ______________________

______________________ ______________________

______________________ ______________________

N. Les magasins. Tracez une ligne entre les achats et le nom du magasin qui convient. Attention! N'essayez pas d'acheter des saucisses dans une pharmacie!

ACHATS	**MAGASINS**
une règle *(ruler)* et un cahier	une épicerie
des oranges et des pommes	une pharmacie
des cachets *(tablets)* d'aspirine	une librairie
du pâté et des côtelettes de porc	une papeterie
un camembert et un brie	une crémerie
le Guide Michelin de la Normandie	une charcuterie

O. Les achats. Faites cette activité avec un(e) partenaire. Jouez les rôles d'un(e) touriste et un(e) Français(e). Le (La) touriste demande où on peut acheter trois des choses mentionnées. Le (La) Français(e) répond. Ensuite, changez de rôles pour les trois autres choses.

❖ TOURISTE: ***Dis, où trouve-t-on de l'aspirine?***
FRANÇAIS(E): ***Dans une pharmacie, bien sûr!***

1. des escalopes de veau
2. un journal
3. un gâteau
4. du riz
5. un médicament
6. une lampe

SUPPLÉMENT

P. À la pharmacie. En France, beaucoup de gens demandent des conseils au pharmacien ou à la pharmacienne quand ils se sentent un peu mal. Avec un(e) partenaire, jouez les rôles d'un(e) malade et du pharmacien (de la pharmacienne). Voici quelques exemples de problèmes et de remèdes.

Problèmes

J'éternue *(I'm sneezing).*
J'ai mal au dos.
J'ai mal au pied.
J'ai mal au ventre.
J'ai 40 (degrés) de fièvre.

Remèdes

Buvez beaucoup de jus d'orange ou prenez de la vitamine C.
Prenez deux cachets d'aspirine.
Restez au lit.
Faites plus d'exercice.
Couvrez-vous.
Prenez du sirop anti-toux *(cough syrup).*
Allez voir un spécialiste.
Consultez votre médecin.
Prenez beaucoup de liquides.
Mangez moins.

❖ CLIENT(E): ***Je tousse beaucoup. Qu'est-ce que je dois faire?***
PHARMACIEN(NE): ***Ne parlez pas trop. Prenez du sirop anti-toux.***

NOM ______________________________ DATE ____________________

MODULE VII LA POSTE

MISE EN SCÈNE

Après leur visite au château Saint-Jean, Bruno et Alissa descendent en ville et vont chacun de son côté *(go their separate ways)*. Alissa part acheter une pellicule et Bruno va chercher des cartes postales.

PRÉPARATION

A. Vive la différence! Pour chacun des éléments suivants, dites quelles sont les différences entre Paris et une petite ville de province. Soyez aussi spécifique que possible.

1. les magasins

   À PARIS: ______________________________

   EN PROVINCE: ______________________________

2. les rues

   À PARIS: ______________________________

   EN PROVINCE: ______________________________

3. les divertissements *(entertainment)*

   À PARIS: ______________________________

   EN PROVINCE: ______________________________

4. le bruit

   À PARIS: ______________________________

   EN PROVINCE: ______________________________

5. la vie culturelle

   À PARIS: ______________________________

   EN PROVINCE: ______________________________

6. les amitiés *(friendships)*

   À PARIS: ______________________________

   EN PROVINCE: ______________________________

   Est-ce qu'il y a les mêmes différences aux États-Unis entre une grande ville et une petite ville? ______________________________

   ____

   Que préférez-vous? ______________________________

   ____

VISIONNEMENT

B. L'ambiance d'une petite ville. Regardez la vidéo **«La poste»** sans le son et faites une liste de toutes les activités, tous les monuments, tous les magasins que vous voyez. N'hésitez pas à arrêter *(stop)* la vidéo autant de fois que vous voulez pour bien voir l'arrière-plan *(background)* de l'image.

ACTIVITÉS	MONUMENTS	MAGASINS
________________	________________	________________
________________	________________	________________
________________	________________	________________
________________	________________	________________
________________	________________	________________
________________	________________	________________

C. Qu'entendez-vous? Maintenant regardez la vidéo **«La poste»** avec le son. Bruno demande plusieurs fois des indications *(directions)* pour trouver la poste. Quelles sont les réponses des différentes personnes?

1. Alissa: ____
2. Le jeune homme: ____
3. Le groupe de femmes: ____
4. Le couple: ____

APPLICATIONS

D. Comment y va-t-on? Faites cette activité avec un(e) partenaire. Une personne est un(e) touriste qui veut faire le tour des monuments de Nogent-le-Rotrou. L'autre personne joue le rôle des différents passants qui habitent Nogent-le-Rotrou. Le (La) touriste demande le chemin *(route)* entre les monuments. Chaque fois, le (la) passant(e) répond à l'aide du plan ci-contre.

❖ Du point de départ (le coin de la rue Saint-Hilaire et la rue Villette-Gâté) à la poste:

TOURISTE: ***Pouvez-vous m'indiquer le chemin de la poste, s'il vous plaît?***

PASSANT(E): ***Prenez la rue Saint-Hilaire et tournez à gauche dans la rue Tochon. Ensuite, prenez la première à gauche et la poste est à droite.***

1. De la poste à l'église Saint-Hilaire
2. De l'église Saint-Hilaire à l'Hôtel de Ville
3. De l'Hôtel de Ville au château Saint-Jean

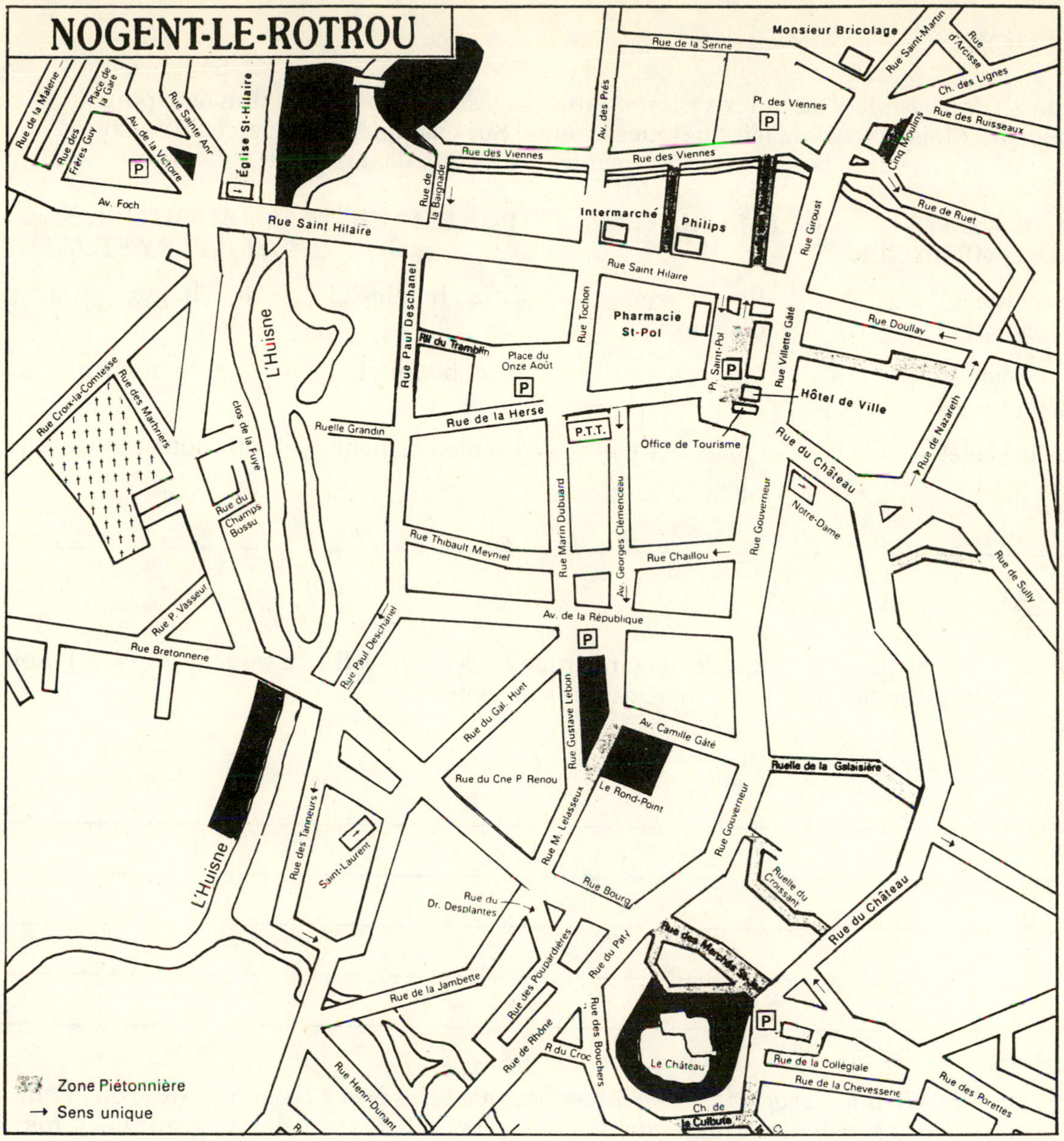

NOGENT-LE-ROTROU

Zone Piétonnière
→ Sens unique

E. En voiture. Cette fois-ci, le (la) touriste désire faire le tour de quelques magasins à Nogent-le-Rotrou, mais en voiture. Il (Elle) est avec Noël. Noël n'a pas envie de conduire *(drive)*; il a donc *(therefore)* passé le volant *(steering wheel)* au (à la) touriste. Le (La) touriste demande le chemin et Noël répond.

❖ du château Saint-Jean à la Pharmacie Saint-Pol

TOURISTE: ***Comment est-ce que je vais à la Pharmacie Saint-Pol?***

NOËL: ***Prends la rue du Château. Ensuite, tourne à gauche dans la rue de Sully, puis à droite dans la place Saint-Pol. La pharmacie se trouve à gauche.***

1. De la Pharmacie Saint-Pol à la poste
2. De la poste à Intermarché
3. De l'Intermarché à Monsieur Bricolage
4. De Monsieur Bricolage au magasin d'électroménager *(appliances)* Philips

GROS PLAN LA BOUTIQUE

PRÉPARATION

F. Les achats *(Purchases).* Vous allez visiter quatre magasins et vous avez une liste pour chaque magasin. Mais vous avez fait quelques erreurs! Sur chaque liste, encerclez l'achat *(the purchase)* qui n'est pas sur la bonne liste *(the right list)* et ajoutez-le où il faut.

MAGASIN D'ÉLECTROMÉNAGER	FLEURISTE	PHARMACIE	BIJOUTERIE *(JEWELRY STORE)*
une machine à laver *(washing machine)*	des cachets d'aspirine	de la vitamine C	une bague *(ring)*
un lave-vaisselle *(dishwasher)*	des roses	un bouquet	une montre
un bracelet	des marguerites *(daisies)*	des médicaments	un Monsieur Café
______________	______________	______________	______________

VISIONNEMENT

G. Les magasins. Regardez le **Gros plan** du Module VII **«La boutique»** sans le son et faites une liste de cinq magasins que vous voyez.

1. ______________________________
2. ______________________________
3. ______________________________
4. ______________________________
5. ______________________________

H. Les vitrines *(Shop windows).* Imaginez que vous êtes à Nogent-le-Rotrou et que vous devez acheter les articles mentionnés dans la liste suivante. Regardez le **Gros plan** du Module VII avec le son et tracez une ligne entre le nom du magasin que vous voyez et les achats mentionnés.

1. des lunettes	Monoprix
2. du savon, du shampooing	Pharmacie
3. des bijoux	Bijouterie
4. un journal	Boucherie Moderne
5. de la viande	Maison de la Presse
6. des vêtements	Gitem/Philips
7. des articles pour tous les jours	Maxi Pulls
8. de la porcelaine pour les jours de fête	L'Art de la Table
9. de l'électroménager	Optique

NOM ______________________________ DATE ____________________

APPLICATION

I. Les banques. À Nogent-le-Rotrou il y a plusieurs banques. Presque toutes ces banques ont des guichets automatiques *(automatic teller machines).* Lisez les informations suivantes sur les guichets automatiques de la Banque Nationale de Paris (BNP) et répondez aux questions.

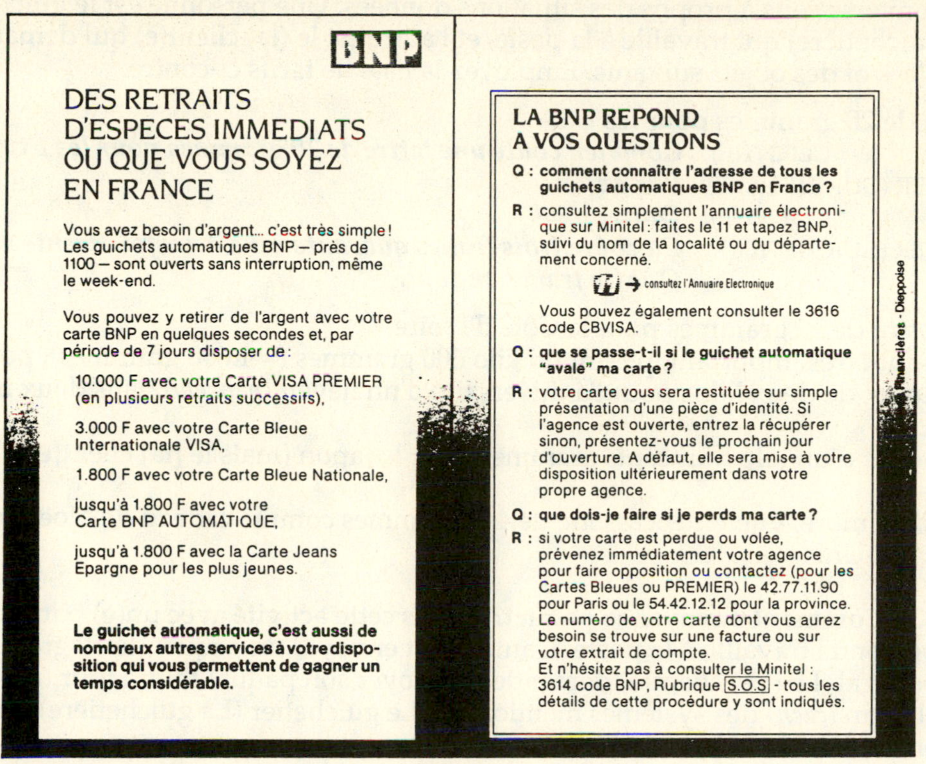

1. Combien de guichets automatiques la BNP offre-t-elle? ______________________

   ____

2. Avec une Carte Bleue Internationale VISA, combien de francs peut-on retirer par période de sept jours? ______________________

3. Qu'est-ce qu'il faut faire pour connaître l'adresse d'un guichet automatique? __________

   ____

4. Qu'est-ce qui se passe si le guichet automatique avale votre carte (c'est-à-dire si la machine ne vous rend pas votre carte)? ______________________

   ____

5. Si vous perdez votre carte, que faut-il faire si vous habitez Paris? Et si vous habitez la province? ______________________

   ____

6. Qu'est-ce qu'on peut trouver sur le Minitel: 3614 code BNP? ______________________

   ____

PROBLÈME! PAS ASSEZ D'ARGENT

PRÉPARATION

J. Ça fait combien? Faites cette activité avec un(e) partenaire. Inventez les conversations à propos des situations données. Une personne est le guichetier (la guichetière) qui travaille à la poste, et l'autre est le (la) client(e) qui demande le prix d'envoi des objets suivants. Employez la liste de tarifs ci-contre.

❖ une lettre de 20 grammes pour les USA

CLIENT(E): ***Combien coûte une lettre de 20 grammes pour les États-Unis?***
GUICHETIER (GUICHETIÈRE): ***Par avion?***
CLIENT(E): ***Oui.***
GUICHETIER (GUICHETIÈRE): ***Ça coûte trois francs quarante plue deux fois trente centimes. Quatre francs en tout.***

1. une lettre de 50 grammes pour la Côte d'Ivoire
2. un paquet très important, pesant un kilo 600 grammes (= 1.600 grammes), pour la Suisse
3. un paquet de deux kilos pour l'anniversaire d'un neveu *(nephew)* dans deux mois au Canada
4. un paquet d'un kilo huit cents grammes pour le Japon (mais le [la] client[e] n'a que cent francs)
5. le 10 décembre, une vidéocassette de 450 grammes comme cadeau de Noël pour sa mère aux États-Unis

K. Comment envoyer ce paquet? Faites cette activité avec un(e) partenaire. Une personne travaille à la poste. L'autre veut envoyer un paquet de 50 grammes au Sénégal. Le (La) client(e) demande d'envoyer son paquet tour à tour *(in turn)* par chacun *(each)* des systèmes mentionnés. Le guichetier (La guichetière) doit répondre en expliquant le prix de l'envoi.

❖ Envoi comme LETTRE mais sans surtaxe avion

CLIENT(E): ***Je voudrais envoyer ce paquet au Sénégal comme LETTRE, mais sans surtaxe avion, s'il vous plaît.***
GUICHETIER (GUICHETIÈRE): ***Ça fait six francs, s'il vous plaît.***

1. Envoi comme PETIT PAQUET
2. Envoi comme PETIT PAQUET avec service rapide
3. Envoi comme PETIT PAQUET en service économique

VISIONNEMENT

L. À la poste. Regardez le **Problème** du Module VII avec le son et répondez aux questions suivantes.

1. Qu'est-ce que Bruno veut envoyer?
   a. deux cartes postales et un colis *(package)*
   b. six cartes postales, un colis et une lettre
   c. deux lettres et un paquet
   d. trois cartes postales et un colis
2. Où est-ce qu'il veut les envoyer?
   a. à Saint-Étienne
   b. au Sénégal
   c. à Dakar
   d. à Paris
3. Ça coûte combien d'envoyer les cartes?
   a. sept francs
   b. cinq francs
   c. seize francs
   d. dix francs

NOM ______________________________ DATE ______________________

4. Combien pèse le paquet?
   a. neuf grammes
   b. neuf cents grammes
   c. neuf kilos
   d. neuf cents kilos
5. Combien coûte le paquet?
   a. soixante francs
   b. deux francs
   c. soixante-dix francs
   d. soixante-deux francs
6. Pourquoi est-ce que Bruno n'a pas l'air *(doesn't look)* content?
   a. Il est fatigué.
   b. Il a perdu son portefeuille.
   c. Il n'a pas assez d'argent.
   d. Il n'a pas d'argent.

POUR VOS ENVOIS A L'ETRANGER

Pour vos envois de correspondances

En service rapide

AEROGRAMME :
Lettre préaffranchie à tarif unique quel que soit le pays de destination. Tarif : **4,50 F.**

LETTRES :
Les lettres sont transportées par avion vers la majorité des pays.

Le tarif d'une lettre = tarif de base + surtaxe avion

TARIFS DE BASE : Mention LETTRE au-dessus de 20 g.

Poids / Pays	20 g	50 g	100 g	250 g	500 g	1 000 g	2 000 g
CEE, Autriche Liechtenstein Suisse	2,50 F	4,20 F	6,40 F	20,00 F	32,00 F	53,00 F	75,00 F
Pays d'Afrique francophone	3,40 F	6,00 F	9,00 F	20,00 F	28,00 F	38,00 F	54,00 F
Autres pays	3,40 F	6,40 F	11,00 F	20,00 F	32,00 F	53,00 F	75,00F

SURTAXES AVION : applicables dès le 1er gramme.

	par 10 g
Zone 1 CEE, Autriche, Liechtenstein, Suisse Autres pays d'Europe, Algérie, Maroc et Tunisie	0,00 F
Zone 2 Pays d'Afrique francophone, lettre jusqu'à 20 g pour les lettres de plus de 20 g Proche Orient, Canada, USA	0,00 F 0,30 F 0,30 F
Zone 3 Autres pays d'Amérique, d'Afrique et d'Asie	0,50 F
Zone 4 Océanie	0,70 F

Pour vos envois de colis

PETITS PAQUETS :

TARIFS DE BASE :

Poids jusqu'à	100 g	250 g	500 g	1 000 g	2 000 g	3 000 g
Tarifs	7,50 F	12,50 F	18,00 F	33,00 F	45,00 F	60,00 F

En service rapide

Le tarif d'un petit paquet en service rapide par avion = tarif de base + surtaxe avion

SURTAXES AVION : applicables dès le 1er gramme.

	par 10 g
Zone 1 CEE, Autriche, Liechtenstein, Suisse Autres pays d'Europe, Algérie, Maroc et Tunisie	0,00 F 0,10 F
Zone 2 Pays d'Afrique francophone Proche Orient, USA, Canada	0,30 F
Zone 3 Autres pays d'Amérique, d'Afrique et d'Asie	0,50 F
Zone 4 Océanie	0,70 F

En service économique

Le tarif d'un petit paquet par avion en service économique = tarif de base + surtaxe SAL
(SAL : transport par avion avec priorité d'embarquement réduite)

SURTAXES SAL* : applicables dès le 1er gramme.

	par 10 g
Zone 1 Europe	0,00 F
Zone 2 Pays d'Afrique francophone Proche Orient, USA, Canada	0,10 F
Zone 3 Autres pays d'Amérique, d'Afrique et d'Asie	0,30 F
Zone 4 Océanie	0,40 F

APPLICATION

M. Qu'est-ce qu'on peut faire? Avez-vous jamais *(ever)* eu le même problème que Bruno? Qu'est-ce qu'on peut faire dans ces circonstances? Faites une liste des solutions possibles.

1. ____________________

____

____

2. ____________________

____

____

3. ____________________

____

____

4. ____________________

____

____

SUPPLÉMENT

N. Trouvez-vous l'erreur? La guichetière dans le **Problème** du Module VII s'est trompée *(made a mistake).* Savez-vous quelle était son erreur? Regardez la vidéo et comparez le prix qu'elle donne avec les informations données dans la liste des prix. Expliquez l'erreur.

O. La Carte Bleue. Bruno a eu des difficultés à la poste, mais pas vous, parce que vous avez un compte à la BNP et une Carte Bleue Internationale VISA. Consultez cette brochure et complétez le dialogue qui suit. Vous devez demander à la guichetière le chemin de *(the route to)* la BNP. La guichetière doit vous indiquer le chemin de la BNP.

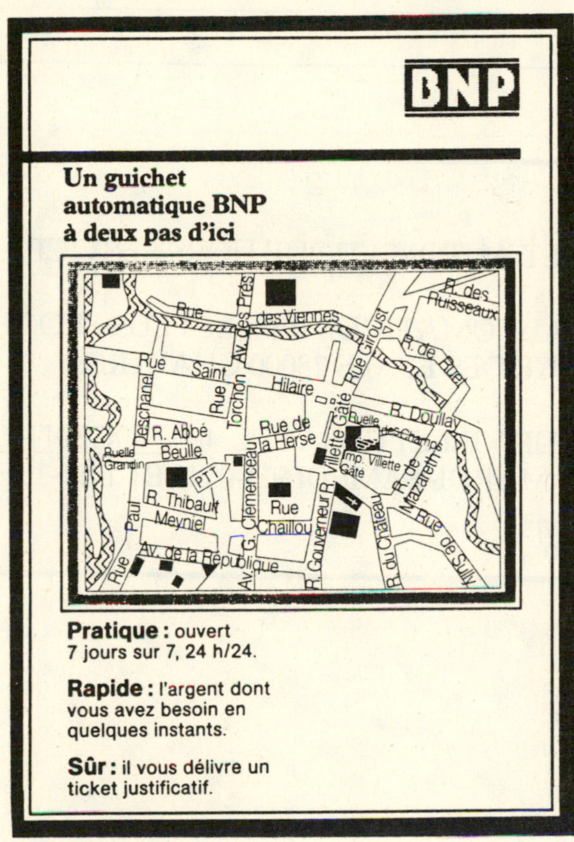

Vous: ____

____

Guichetière: ____

____

P. Au guichet automatique. Lisez le message (ci-dessous) au guichet automatique et répondez aux questions suivantes.

1. Si vous allez à la BNP de Nogent-le-Rotrou lundi, est-ce que la banque est ouverte? ____

   ____

2. Si le guichet automatique de Nogent-le-Rotrou est fermé, où pouvez-vous aller? ______

   ____

3. Est-ce que vous pouvez retirer de l'argent quand la BNP de Nogent-le-Rotrou est fermée? Comment? ____

   ____

GUICHET AUTOMATIQUE HORS-SERVICE.

GUICHET AUTOMATIQUE BNP LE PLUS PROCHE:
PLACE DES ÉPARS 28000 CHARTRES.

GUICHET BNP 13, RUE VILLETTE GÂTÉ 28400 NOGENT-LE-ROTROU
OUVERT MARDI–SAMEDI 9H–12H ET 14H-18H.

NOM ______________________ DATE ______________________

MODULE VIII EN PANNE

MISE EN SCÈNE

Après leurs achats *(purchases)* à Nogent-le-Rotrou, Alissa et Bruno retrouvent Noël, qui les conduit *(drives them)* chez lui, à travers *(through)* le beau paysage *(countryside)* percheron (du Perche), avec ses collines *(hills)*, ses champs *(fields)* et ses petites fermes *(farms)*.

PRÉPARATION

A. Un peu de géographie. Observez attentivement la carte ci-dessous et répondez aux questions qui suivent.

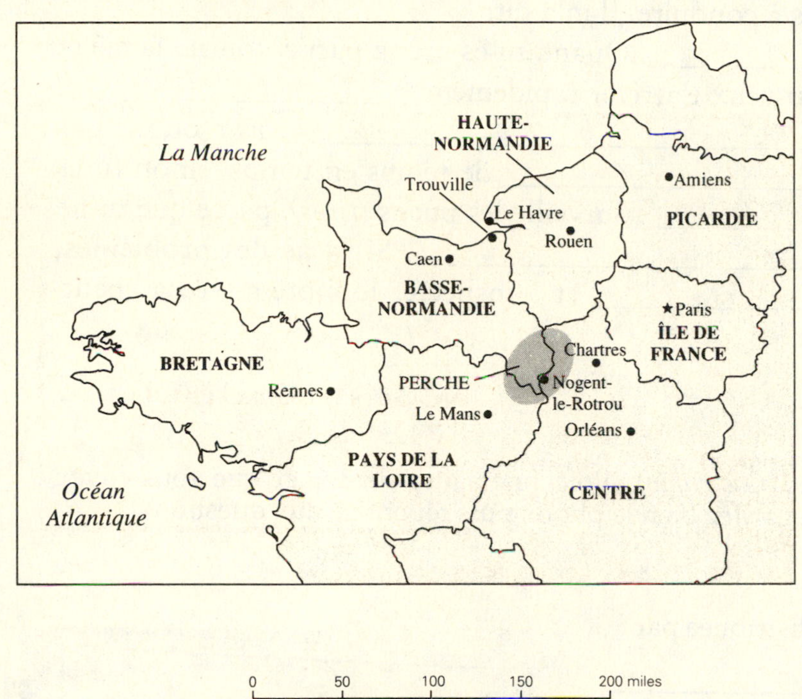

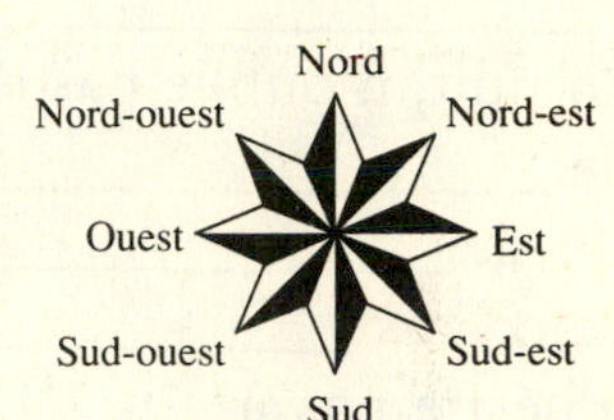

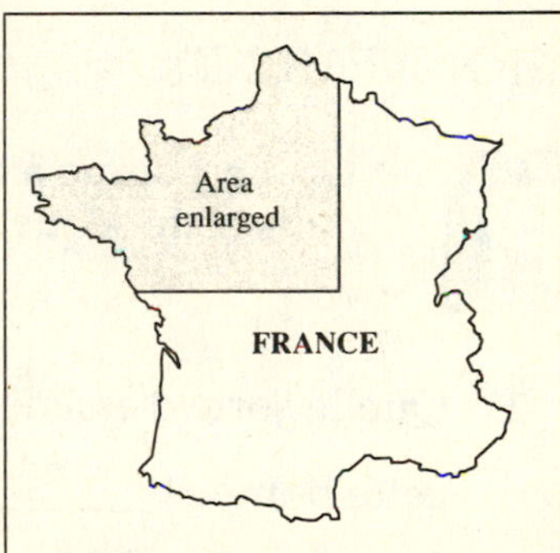

1. Dans quelle direction se trouve le Perche, par rapport à *(with respect to)* Paris? ______________________

2. À quelle distance? ______________________

3. Le Perche se trouve à cheval sur *(partially within)* quelles régions? ______________________

4. Nogent-le-Rotrou se trouve à mi-chemin *(halfway)* entre quelles villes? ______________________

5. Quelle ville se trouve entre le Perche et Paris? ______________________

6. Quelles sont les plus grandes villes de la Haute-Normandie? ______________________

B. Comment conduire? Voici quelques expressions très utiles pour les automobilistes. Complétez l'histoire de Jean-François en employant l'expression qui convient. N'oubliez pas de mettre le verbe à l'impératif quand c'est nécessaire.

allumer les phares	*to turn on the headlights*
tomber en panne	*to have a breakdown*
faire le plein	*to fill up the gas tank*
ouvrir le capot	*to open the hood*
crever	*to get a flat*
mettre la clé de contact	*to put the key in the ignition*
démarrer	*to start up*
donner un coup de freins	*to step on the brakes*

C'est mon père qui m'a appris à conduire. Il m'a dit: «Commence par ____________________. Quand tu es prêt à partir, tourne la clé et ____________________. Si tu veux t'arrêter rapidement, ____________________. La nuit, n'oublie pas d'____________________________________. Et n'oublie pas de ____ de temps en temps; sinon tu es sûr de ____________________________. Surveille les pneus *(tires)*, parce que tu ne veux pas ____. Si tu as des problèmes, n'hésite pas à ________________________ et à inspecter le moteur—tu as peut-être grillé le system électrique.»

VISIONNEMENT

P

C. La pompe à essence *(Gas pump)*. Voici une pause-sur-image que vous voyez dans cette séquence. Regardez bien la photo, puis répondez aux questions.

1. Quelle sorte d'essence est distribuée par cette pompe? ________________________

   ____

2. Quel est le prix de l'essence par litre?

   ____

3. Ça fait à peu près combien de dollars par litre? ($1.00 = environ *[approximately]* 5F.) ________________________

4. Ça fait à peu près combien de dollars pour un «gallon»? (Un «gallon» = 3,78 litres.)

   ____

5. Combien de litres ont été distribués au moment où cette photo a été prise *(taken)*?

   ____

6. Quel est le prix total à payer? ____

NOM ______________________ DATE ______________________

D. Que devinez-vous? Regardez la première partie du Module VIII **«En panne»** sans le son. Est-ce que vous pouvez deviner les actions et le dialogue de cette scène? Montrez que vous comprenez ce qui se passe *(is happening)* en répondant aux questions suivantes. N'oubliez pas que votre capacité de comprendre une langue étrangère *(foreign)* dépend souvent de votre capacité de comprendre **«à demi-mot»,** c'est-à-dire qu'il n'est pas toujours nécessaire de tout entendre pour comprendre.

1. À votre avis, quand la voiture traverse la campagne, que disent Bruno et Alissa? ______________________

2. À votre avis, quand la voiture s'arrête, qu'est-ce qui se passe? ______________________

   Que dit Alissa? ______________________

   Que dit Bruno? ______________________

   Que répond Noël? ______________________

3. À votre avis, quand la voiture arrive à la station-service, qu'est-ce qui se passe? ______________________

   Que dit Noël? ______________________

   Que dit le garagiste quelques instants après? ______________________

4. À votre avis, quand Noël sort *(takes out)* son porte-monnaie, qu'est-ce qui se passe? ______________________

   Que dit le garagiste? ______________________

   Que répond Noël? ______________________

5. Quand Noël et Alissa remontent dans *(get back in)* la voiture, qu'est-ce qui se passe à votre avis? ______________________

   Que dit Noël? ______________________

6. Quand Noël ressort *(gets back out)* de la voiture, qu'est-ce qui se passe à votre avis? ______________________

   Que dit Noël? ______________________

   Que répond le garagiste? ______________________

7. Quand le garagiste enlève *(lifts)* un fil brûlé *(burnt wire)* du moteur, qu'est-ce qui se passe à votre avis? ______________________

   Que dit le garagiste? ______________________

APPLICATIONS

E. Avez-vous bien deviné? Maintenant regardez **«En panne»** avec le son. Avec un(e) partenaire, évaluez vos réponses à l'Activité D.

F. Comprenez-vous la publicité? Voici un autocollant *(self-adhesive sticker)* qui fait la publicité de Shell Superplus Sans Plomb 98. Expliquez chacune *(each)* des expressions de cet autocollant. Donnez autant d'informations que vous pouvez.

1. SHELL ______________________________
____
2. SUPERPLUS ______________________________
____
3. SANS PLOMB *(lead)* ______________________________
____
4. 98 ______________________________
____
5. Je roule ______________________________
____
6. plus propre ______________________________
____

NOM ______________________________ DATE ____________________

GROS PLAN LA VOITURE

PRÉPARATION

G. Une mauvaise influence. Lisez le dialogue suivant entre un juge et une mère qui veut envoyer son fils de dix-huit ans en prison. Ensuite, répondez aux questions.

Le Juge: Comment, Madame, vous voulez voir votre fils en prison?

Madame Chevrolet: Oui, Monsieur le juge. Je vais vous expliquer. Jusqu'à l'âge de dix-sept ans, mon Bernard était un enfant modèle. Il débarrassait *(cleared)* la table, il faisait la vaisselle, il rangeait *(straightened)* ses affaires, il faisait son lit. Jamais il ne disait un mot de travers *(unpleasant)*. Il était toujours gentil avec sa maman. Et puis un jour il a eu dix-huit ans. Tous les jours il me disait: «Maman, paie-moi l'auto-école. Je veux passer mon permis *(license)*.»

Le Juge: Alors, évidemment, vous lui avez payé l'auto-école.

Madame Chevrolet: Bien sûr, Monsieur le juge. Vous pensez bien, un enfant si gentil! Mais l'auto-école ne lui a pas fait de bien. Le jour où il a passé son permis il m'a dit: «À tout à l'heure *(See you soon)*, maman.» Et il a pris les clés de ma deux-chevaux *(small Citroën car)* et il est parti. Je ne l'ai pas revu ce jour-là. Il est revenu le lendemain matin *(following morning)*, avec le visage changé. Maintenant il ne fait plus son lit, il ne range rien, il ne débarrasse rien, il ne fait même plus la vaisselle.

Le Juge: Et vous croyez *(believe)* que la solution est de le mettre en prison? Je vous suggère plutôt de vendre la deux-chevaux.

1. Quelle sorte d'enfant était Bernard avant de passer son permis de conduire? ____________
   ____
   ____
2. Qu'est-ce qu'il faisait toujours à cette époque-là? ____________________
   ____
   ____
3. Quand est-ce qu'il a commencé à changer? ____________________
   ____
4. Quelle sorte de voiture Mme Chevrolet avait-elle à l'époque? ____________________
   ____
5. À votre avis, pourquoi est-ce que Bernard a changé? ____________________
   ____
   ____
6. Qu'est-ce que le juge a suggéré pour résoudre *(solve)* le problème? ____________________
   ____
   ____

VISIONNEMENT

H. Le long de la route. D'abord, lisez les questions suivantes. Ensuite, regardez le **Gros plan** du Module VIII **«La voiture»** sans le son et répondez aux questions.

1. Pourquoi certains panneaux de signalisation routière *(road signs)* sont-ils bleus et d'autres blancs? (Pensez aux panneaux américains.) ______________________

   ____
2. Que fait l'homme debout *(standing up)* dans une station-service à côté d'une voiture blanche? ____
3. Qu'est-ce qui est arrivé *(happened)* à la voiture de sport rouge? ______________________

   ____
4. Comment s'appelle la petite voiture rouge et noire immatriculée *(with license plate number)* 5899RJ28? ____
5. À votre avis, dans quelle ville la voiture de sport rouge se trouve-t-elle? ______________

   ____
6. Dans quelle ville les dernières scènes de ce **Gros plan** se passent-elles *(take place)?* ______

   ____

I. Comparez! Maintenant regardez le **Gros plan** avec le son et écrivez une phrase qui compare les choses mentionnées. Employez les adjectifs entre parenthèses et suivez le modèle. N'oubliez pas de faire l'accord entre le sujet et l'adjectif.

❖ les voitures dans le petit village et sur l'autoroute (nombreux)
Les voitures sont moins nombreuses dans le petit village que sur l'autoroute.

1. la vitesse maximale sur l'autoroute et sur les routes nationales (élevé) ______________

   ____
2. le prix du super et de l'essence ordinaire (cher) ______________________

   ____
3. les personnes devant le concessionnaire Peugeot *(Peugeot dealer)* et le musée Renault (nombreux) ____
4. le prix de la petite voiture rouge et noire et la voiture de l'avenir (cher) ______________

   ____
5. la taille *(size)* d'un autobus et la taille d'une voiture (grand) ______________________

   ____

NOM ______________________________ DATE ______________________

PROBLÈME! LE SYSTÈME ÉLECTRIQUE GRILLÉ

PRÉPARATION

J. L'accident. Dans le rapport d'accident (ci-dessous) il manque *(are missing)* plusieurs mots ou expressions. En vous référant au diagramme, complétez les mots qui manquent.

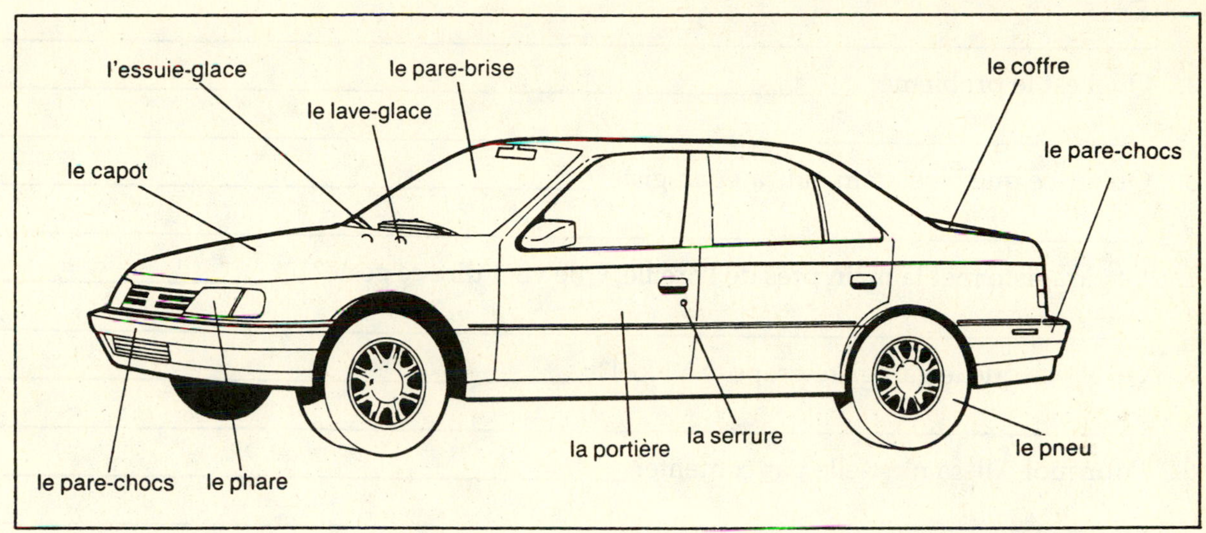

RAPPORT D'ACCIDENT n° 719 **DATE** ______________

VOITURE ACCIDENTÉE

Marque: Peugeot modèle: 309 GTI

année: 1992 couleur: noir

AVANT: Le plastique protecteur du ______________ gauche est cassé; le lave-glace ne marche plus parce que ______________ a été plié en deux; ______________ a été cassé en mille morceaux *(pieces)*.

CÔTÉ GAUCHE: ______________ avant ne ferme plus. La vitre de la ______________ arrière est cassée.

CÔTÉ DROIT: La clé ne rentre plus dans les deux ______________; les deux ______________ sont crevés *(flattened)*.

ARRIÈRE: ______________ arrière a été endommagé par le pare-chocs de la voiture qui suivait *(followed)*; les articles dans ______________ sont cassés.

NOM DE L'INSPECTEUR ______________

VISIONNEMENT

K. Pauvre Noël! Regardez le **Problème** du Module VIII avec le son et répondez aux questions suivantes.

1. Qui a découvert le problème de la voiture de Noël? ____
2. Quel est le problème? ____
3. Qu'est-ce que Noël demande au garagiste? ____
4. Le garagiste met la main près de l'oreille. Que veut dire ce geste? ____
5. Qu'est-ce que le garagiste propose à Noël? ____
6. Pourquoi Alissa n'est-elle pas contente? ____

APPLICATIONS

L. En panne *(Broken down)*. Imaginez que votre voiture est en panne. Votre garagiste ne peut la réparer que *(not until)* demain, en fin de journée, et pourtant vous devez être à Paris demain matin. Qu'est-ce que vous faites? Dressez ici une liste des solutions possibles.

1. ____
2. ____
3. ____
4. ____

M. Au téléphone. Avec un(e) partenaire, simulez le coup de fil entre Alissa et Yves, son ami parisien, qu'elle appelle pour lui expliquer la situation. Ensuite, expliquez à Yves ce que vous allez faire (en choisissant une des solutions de l'activité précédente).

Allô. C'est ... à l'appareil.
Je regrette, mais...
Qu'est-ce que vous pouvez (allez) faire?
Nous pouvons ... On peut...
Nous allons .... On va...

NOM ______________________ DATE ______________________

N. Renseignez-vous. Voici le prix des locations *(rentals)* de voitures pour le week-end offertes par France-Cars, une grande agence de location de voitures. Votre voiture doit être réparée et vous avez besoin de louer une voiture pendant le temps de la réparation. Vous êtes le (la) client(e) et votre partenaire qui est le vendeur (la vendeuse) représente France-Cars. Demandez-lui tous les renseignements nécessaires pour louer votre voiture.

Voici quelques questions possibles: Quelles sortes de voitures sont disponibles *(available)?* La voiture est-elle assez grande pour cinq personnes? Est-elle automatique? A-t-elle une galerie, un toit *(roof)* ouvrant? L'assurance *(insurance)* est-elle comprise? Quand est-ce qu'on peut prendre la voiture? Quand est-ce qu'il faut la rendre? Quel est le prix? Ce prix couvre-t-il un nombre de kilomètres illimité? La TVA (taxe sur la valeur ajoutée) est-elle incluse? etc.

Votre partenaire trouve les réponses à ces questions dans le tableau reproduit ici.

France-Cars

UN WEEK-END EN FRANCE

(1) Le véhicule doit être pris le vendredi à partir de 14 H et restitué au plus tard le lundi suivant avant 10 H ou pris le samedi à partir de 14 H et restitué au plus tard le mardi suivant avant 10 H, à la station de départ, sinon le tarif de base jour et kilomètre sera appliqué.

(2) Le véhicule doit être pris le vendredi à partir de 14 H et restitué au plus tard le mardi suivant avant 10 H, à la station de départ, sinon le tarif de base jour et kilomètre sera appliqué.

- Les kilomètres supplémentaires sont facturés selon le tarif de base.
- Les modèles de voitures sont modifiables selon disponibilité.

TARIF F. TTC Assurance rachat de franchise incluse		(1) Du vendredi 14 h au lundi 10 h/ou du samedi 14 h au mardi 10 h	(2) Du vendredi 14 h au mardi 10 h
Cat.	Modèles ou similaire.	1 000 km inclus	. 1 300 km inclus
A	**FORD FIESTA SUPER FESTIVAL** RENAULT SUPER 5 FIVE PEUGEOT 205 JUNIOR UNO 45 FIRE OPEL CORSA GL	555	777
B	RENAULT SUPER 5 SL PEUGEOT 205 GL	595	840
C	**FORD ESCORT 1.6 CL** OPEL KADETT 1 200 PEUGEOT 309 GL PROFIL RENAULT 11 GTL	645	900
D	**FORD SIERRA 1800 CL** PEUGEOT 405 GR RENAULT 21 GTS BMW 316	730	1 020
E	**FORD SCORPIO 2.0 GLI "ABS"** RENAULT 25 GTS OPEL OMEGA 2 0 I GL	860	1 200
F	**FORD ESCORT 1600 CL** RENAULT 11 [A] OPEL ASCONA	860	1 200
G	MERCEDES 190 E [A] BMW 320 IA T.O.	1 285	1 800
H	MERCEDES 260 E [A]	1 720	2 400
I	RENAULT ESPACE 2000 GTS T.O.	1 285	1 800
J	**FORD TRANSIT** (9 places)	1 120	1 560

TVA 28 %. ·,·. Galerie - TO : Toit ouvrant - [A] Automatique

O. La voiture de mes rêves! Décrivez la voiture de vos rêves avec autant de détail que possible. De quelle marque *(brand/type)* est-elle? Qu'est-ce qu'elle a comme extras *(options)?* etc.

____

____

____

____

____

____

SUPPLÉMENT

P. À votre tour. Voici une pause-sur-image du **Gros plan.** Expliquez avec autant de détail que vous pouvez l'utilisation de cette voiture. Qui s'en sert *(Who uses it)?* Quand? Où? Pourquoi? Seul(e) ou avec quelqu'un d'autre? Gratuitement *(Free)?* Donnez tous les renseignements que vous pouvez.

____
____
____
____
____
____
____
____
____
____

Q. Le sens des numéros. Regardez le Module VIII dans sa totalité. Décidez d'abord si les numéros suivants sont prononcés par les personnages ou le narrateur ou sont visibles à l'image. Indiquez votre réponse avec un **x** dans la colonne convenable. Ensuite, regardez la vidéo une deuxième fois et expliquez le sens de ces numéros.

	PRONONCÉ	**VU**	**SENS**
3513RH61	______	x	plaque d'immatriculation *(license plate)*
98	______	______	______________________
150	______	______	______________________
2	______	______	______________________
46	______	______	______________________
130	______	______	______________________
200	______	______	______________________
13	______	______	______________________
12	______	______	______________________
90	______	______	______________________
5.59	______	______	______________________
400	______	______	______________________
97	______	______	______________________
9292ZT77	______	______	______________________
37.52.70.87	______	______	______________________

NOM ________________________________ DATE ________________________

MODULE IX AU CENTRE POMPIDOU

MISE EN SCÈNE

Yves et Moustafa, deux amis de Bruno et Alissa, arrivent au Centre Pompidou, pour faire des recherches à la Bibliothèque publique.

PRÉPARATION

A. Beaubourg. Lisez la description suivante et décidez si les phrases qui suivent sont vraies ou fausses.

Conçu *(Conceived)* en 1969, mais ouvert seulement en 1977, le Centre Pompidou a toujours été un sujet de controverse, car il a été bâti *(built)* au centre du vieux Paris dans un style ultramoderne. Néanmoins *(Nevertheless)*, le Centre Pompidou (que les Parisiens appellent souvent simplement Beaubourg, car *[for]* il se trouve sur le plateau Beaubourg) attire *(attracts)* beaucoup de monde à sa Bibliothèque publique d'information (BPI), à son musée national d'Art moderne (MNAM) et à plusieurs autres activités, y compris la musique constamment présente sur l'esplanade (= la place devant un grand monument).

V F 1. Le Centre Pompidou a été construit dans un style ultramoderne.

V F 2. Le Centre Pompidou se trouve dans un quartier très moderne.

V F 3. Les Parisiens appellent le Centre Pompidou «Beaubourg» parce que la rivière à côté s'appelle Beaubourg.

V F 4. Il y a une bibliothèque et un musée dans le Centre Pompidou.

B. La BPI. Maintenant, lisez les renseignements dans le catalogue de la Bibliothèque publique d'information et répondez aux questions.

1. Comment est-ce qu'on consulte le catalogue de la BPI?

2. Est-ce qu'il est nécessaire d'avoir une connaissance des ordinateurs pour consulter le catalogue?

3. Si on veut consulter un film, un journal, une revue ou un enregistrement *(recording)*, que faut-il faire?

4. Pendant quelles heures la bibliothèque est-elle la plus fréquentée?

5. Quand est-elle la plus calme?

6. Pendant quelle saison de l'année est-elle particulièrement calme?

7. Quelle sorte de bibliothèques y a-t-il dans la région parisienne?

8. Quelles bibliothèques prêtent à domicile *(are lending libraries)*?

LE CATALOGUE DE LA BPI

Le catalogue de tous les documents de la BPI est consultable sur 60 écrans disposés sur les trois niveaux de la bibliothèque. Son mode d'emploi est décrit très précisément dans les premières pages des menus.
Ces systèmes peuvent être consultés sans aucune connaissance informatique.
Les recherches sont possibles à partir de l'auteur, du titre (ou des mots de ce titre), du libellé complet du sujet (ou de mots significatifs de ce sujet) des documents désirés.
Les films, les périodiques et les documents sonores parlés de langue française font l'objet de répertoires imprimés disponibles auprès des bureaux d'informations.

Evitez les périodes d'affluence :

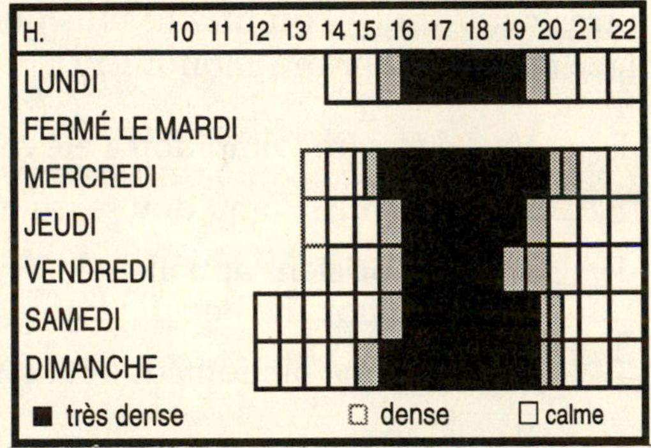

De manière générale, évitez les périodes des vacances de la Toussaint, de février et de Pâques.
Meilleure période : du 15 juin au 15 septembre.
Nous vous rappelons qu'il existe aussi à Paris et dans la région parisienne :

- Les bibliothèques municipales, qui prêtent à domicile.
- Les bibliothèques universitaires, réservées aux étudiants.
- De nombreuses bibliothèques spécialisées dans tous les domaines (vous pouvez en consulter la liste dans les bureaux d'information de la BPI).

NOM ______________________________ DATE ______________________

VISIONNEMENT

C. Que voyez-vous? Regardez la première partie du Module IX **«Au Centre Pompidou»** sans le son et répondez aux questions suivantes.

1. Où se trouvent Yves et Moustafa?

   ____

2. Comment est-ce qu'ils montent au deuxième étage?

   ____

3. Dans quelle partie du bâtiment vont-ils?

   ____

4. À votre avis, Yves connaît-il déjà le jeune homme assis *(seated)* à côté de lui? Sur quoi basez-vous votre jugement? ______________________________

   ____

5. À votre avis, pourquoi Moustafa est-il venu au Centre Pompidou?

   ____

6. À votre avis, pourquoi Moustafa est-il allé regarder une vidéo?

   ____

D. Qu'entendez-vous? Maintenant, regardez la vidéo avec le son. Écoutez bien la conversation et complétez les expressions suivantes.

1. MOUSTAFA: ... Bruno et Alissa seront là dimanche pour la fête de ______ ______________________.
2. YVES: ... ils ont eu ______ ______________________ de voiture.
3. MOUSTAFA: C'est un truc *(project, thing)* ______________________ l'architecture.
4. YVES: ... je commence à ______________________ tout de suite.
5. MOUSTAFA: Je vais ______________________ ______ ______________________ dont j'ai besoin.
6. YVES: Il s'agit de *(It's about)* ______________________?
7. MOUSTAFA: ... un rapport sur la ______________________ ______________________.
8. YVES: ... je commence ______ ______________________ dans le dictionnaire.
9. MOUSTAFA: J'ai fait toute ______ ______________________ des projets récents ______ ______________________.
10. YVES: Par exemple, la pyramide ______ ______________________.
11. MOUSTAFA: ... ______ ______________________ du Louvre a été construite en 1989.
12. YVES: C'est ______________________! Tu ne ______________________ pas?

APPLICATION

E. Comment trouver un livre? Ces pages vous expliquent ce qu'il faut faire pour trouver un livre à la BPI. Lisez les instructions, puis répondez aux questions.

1. À quel étage *(floor)* se trouvent les livres sur la peinture *(painting)* et l'architecture?

____

____

2. Quelle partie de la bibliothèque se trouve au deuxième étage?

____

____

3. Quelle est la cote *(call number)* des livres sur les relations internationales?

____

____

4. Où est-ce qu'on peut consulter le catalogue?

____

____

5. Si vous devez faire un rapport sur Napoléon 1er, à quel étage irez-vous?

____

____

6. Si vous voulez lire les œuvres *(works)* de Descartes, Voltaire ou Sartre, vous devrez aller à quel étage?

____

____

DES CHIFFRES ET DES LETTRES

Tous les documents de la Bibliothèque sont classés ensemble par discipline. Chaque discipline est représentée par un chiffre (ph. 1).

0 documentation générale, **2e étage**
1 philosophie, **1er étage**
2 religions, **1er étage**
3 sciences sociales, **3e étage**
5 sciences exactes, **3e étage**
6 techniques, **3e étage**
7 arts, sports, loisirs, tourisme, **1er étage**
8 langue et littérature, **1er étage**
9 histoire, géographie, **3e étage**
Ce classement va du général au particulier : le 1er chiffre indique la discipline dont fait partie le document, les chiffres suivants précisent son sujet (ph. 2 et 3).

3	Droit. Economie. Sciences sociales
3 2	Politique
32 7	Relations internationales
327 .2	Organisations internationales
327.2 1	O.N.U.

Donc, plus le sujet est précis, plus il y a de chiffres (ph. 3)
Plusieurs documents traitant d'un même sujet sont désignés par le même ensemble de chiffres et regroupés sur les rayons (ph. 4).
Sous les chiffres, il y a des lettres, en général les trois premières lettres du nom de l'auteur, ce qui permet de différencier les documents (ph. 4).
La combinaison de ces chiffres et de ces lettres constitue la cote, qui est inscrite aussi bien sur le document (ph.4) que sur les catalogues.
Le catalogue de tous les documents de la BPI est consultable sur 60 écrans disposés sur les trois niveaux de la bibliothèque.

Pour en savoir plus...
Des séances gratuites de formation — le jeudi soir — sont proposées au public.

NOM ______________________ DATE ______________________

GROS PLAN L'ARCHITECTURE À PARIS

PRÉPARATION

F. Visitez Paris! Regardez bien ce plan qui montre quelques monuments importants à Paris et la liste qui donne leurs dates de construction. Ensuite, répondez aux questions.

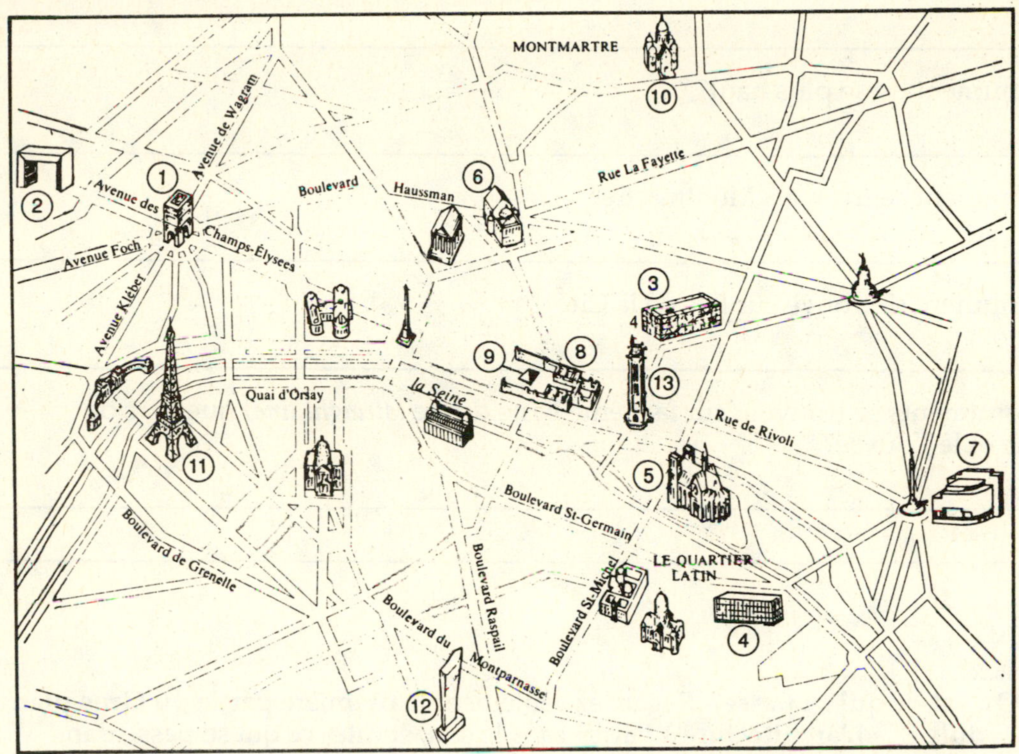

1. Arc de Triomphe (1806–1836)
2. Arche de la Défense (1983–1989)
3. Centre Pompidou (1977)
4. Institut du monde arabe (1987)
5. Notre-Dame de Paris (1163–1345)
6. Opéra de Paris (1862–1874)
7. Opéra de la Bastille (1989)
8. Palais du Louvre (1200–1870)
9. Pyramide du Louvre (1989)
10. Sacré-Cœur (1876–1912)
11. Tour Eiffel (1887–1889)
12. Tour Montparnasse (1972)
13. Tour Saint-Jacques (début du 16e siècle)

1. Quel monument a été commencé le premier? ______________________
2. Quel monument a pris le plus de temps à achever? ______________________
3. Quels sont les quatre monuments les plus récents? ______________________

   ____
4. Quel monument a été construit pour le centenaire *(hundreth anniversary)* de la Révolution française (1789)? ______________________
5. Quel monument a été construit sous le règne de Napoléon 1er (1804–1815)?

   ____
6. Quel monument a été commencé sous le règne de Napoléon III (1848–1852)?

   ____

G. Et quoi d'autre? Qu'est-ce que vous savez d'autre sur ces monuments? Essayez de répondre aux questions suivantes.

1. Quel édifice s'appelle aussi Beaubourg?

   ____

2. Dans quel édifice vivait Quasimodo le bossu *(hunchback)?*

   ____

3. Quel monument est le plus haut?

   ____

4. Quel monument se trouve à Montmartre?

   ____

5. Quel monument se trouve sur l'île de la Cité?

   ____

6. Quels monuments se trouvent sur la même ligne droite *(straight line)* que l'arc de Triomphe et le Louvre?

   ____

   ____

VISIONNEMENT

H. Qu'est-ce qui se passe? Regardez seulement la première partie du **Gros plan** du Module IX **«L'architecture à Paris»** sans le son, et dites ce qui se passe dans chacun des endroits suivants.

1. dans les rues autour *(around)* du Centre Pompidou

   ____

2. sur l'esplanade du Centre Pompidou

   ____

3. au musée national d'Art moderne

   ____

4. à la Bibliothèque publique d'information

   ____

NOM ______________________ DATE ______________________

I. Les monuments de Paris. Regardez le reste du **Gros plan** sans le son. Combien de monuments parisiens reconnaissez-vous (à part le Centre Pompidou)? Écrivez leurs noms.

1. ______________________ 5. ______________________
2. ______________________ 6. ______________________
3. ______________________ 7. ______________________
4. ______________________ 8. ______________________

J. Le Centre Pompidou. Lisez les questions suivantes. Regardez le **Gros plan** en entier avec le son. Ensuite, répondez aux questions.

1. Quand est-ce que le Centre Pompidou a été mis en service?

   ____

2. Où se trouve le Centre Pompidou?

   ____

3. Qui va au musée national d'Art moderne?

   ____

4. Est-ce que beaucoup de gens viennent à la bibliothèque du Centre Pompidou?

   ____

5. Quel monument mentionné par le narrateur est visible de l'Escalator du Centre Pompidou? ______________________

6. Quel mélange *(mixture)* caractérise les monuments de Paris?

   ____

PROBLÈME!   FERMÉ LE MARDI

PRÉPARATION

K. Le Louvre. Lisez la brochure *Louvre: guide d'orientation* à la page suivante, puis répondez aux questions.

1. Si vous voulez écrire au Louvre (par exemple pour dire que vous avez oublié votre manteau), quelle adresse faut-il employer?

   ____

2. En fin de matinée ou l'après-midi, il y a souvent beaucoup de visiteurs au Louvre. Si vous voulez être devant les portes du Louvre quand il ouvre afin de *(in order to)* pouvoir entrer avant la foule *(crowd)*, à quelle heure faut-il arriver?

   ____

3. À quelle heure le musée ferme-t-il le lundi? le jeudi?

   ____

4. Est-ce que le hall Napoléon (sous la pyramide du Louvre) a les mêmes heures d'ouverture que le musée?

   ____

5. Les caisses *(cashiers)* ferment-elles en même temps que le musée et le hall? Sinon, précisez la différence.

   ____

6. Qu'est-ce qu'il faut faire pour avoir des informations?

   ____

7. Les visites guidées sont-elle possibles? Comment?

   ____

8. Au Louvre on peut voir des œuvres d'art, bien entendu. Mais que peut-on faire d'autre?

   ____

VISIONNEMENT

L. La déception *(disappointment)* **de Moustafa.** Regardez le **Problème** du Module IX avec le son. Ensuite, répondez aux questions suivantes.

1. Qu'est-ce que Moustafa veut mettre dans son rapport?

   ____

2. Où est-ce qu'il a eu cette idée? ______________________________

3. Où se trouve l'entrée du musée? ______________________________

4. Pourquoi Yves et Moustafa n'entrent-ils pas au musée?

   ____

LOUVRE
guide d'orientation

Musée du Louvre
34-36, quai du Louvre
75058 Paris Cedex 01

Informations
Tél. : 40 20 51 51 - 40 20 53 17

Entrée principale
Pyramide (cour Napoléon)

Autres entrées
- passage réservé aux Amis du Louvre et aux groupes (entre la place du Palais-Royal et la cour Napoléon)
- Porte Jaujard

Heures d'ouverture du musée
jeudi, vendredi, samedi et dimanche : **ouvert de 9 h à 18 h.** Fermeture des caisses : 17 h 15. Lundi et mercredi : **ouvert de 9 h à 21 h 45.** Fermeture des caisses : 21 h 15.
Le musée est fermé le mardi.

Heures d'ouverture du hall Napoléon
sont ouverts tous les jours de 9 h à 22 h - sauf le mardi : le restaurant le Grand Louvre, le Café du Louvre, la Librairie du musée (à partir de 9 h 30), l'Auditorium du Louvre, les salles de l'Histoire du Louvre, les fossés du Louvre médiéval et les expositions temporaires (de 12 h à 22 h).

Fermeture des caisses à 21 h 15 pour l'Auditorium du Louvre, les salles d'Histoire du Louvre, les fossés du Louvre médiéval et les expositions temporaires.

Informations des visiteurs
Au niveau accueil du hall Napoléon, les écrans vidéo des deux murs d'information indiquent chaque jour :
- **les programmes de l'Auditorium du Louvre, des visites-conférences et des activités en ateliers**
- **les expositions temporaires en cours et leur localisation**
- **les collections accessibles ce même jour**

Auditorium du Louvre
Conférences, colloques, films, concerts... Le programme du jour est indiqué sur les murs d'information au niveau d'accueil.
Réservations : 40 20 52 29
Informations : 40 20 52 99

Expositions temporaires
Elles sont organisées :
- dans le hall Napoléon
- au Pavillon de Flore, Denon 10, 2ᵉ étage, porte Jaujard
- exceptionnellement, dans d'autres salles du musée

Acoustiguides
Disponibles en 6 langues (50 minutes), hall Napoléon, niveau mezzanine.

Boutiques du musée du Louvre
Livres d'art, reproductions d'œuvres, objets-cadeaux sont disponibles à la Librairie du musée (hall Napoléon) ainsi qu'en divers points de vente dans le Louvre.
Informations : 40 20 52 06.
Chalcographie du Louvre, niveau accueil : consultation et vente de gravure.

Restaurants
Restaurant, café, cafétéria sont accessibles dans le hall Napoléon, niveau accueil et niveau mezzanine.

Amis du Louvre
La société des Amis du Louvre propose à ses adhérents des avantages et des services :
entrée gratuite par le passage réservé, information privilégiée...
Information et adhésion : hall Napoléon, niveau accueil.
Tél. : 40 20 53 34.

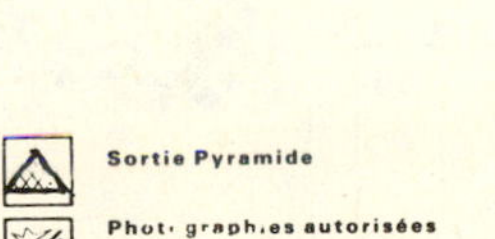

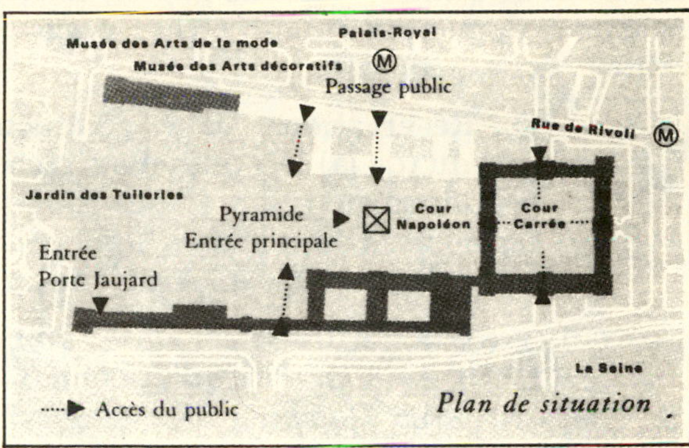

Plan de situation

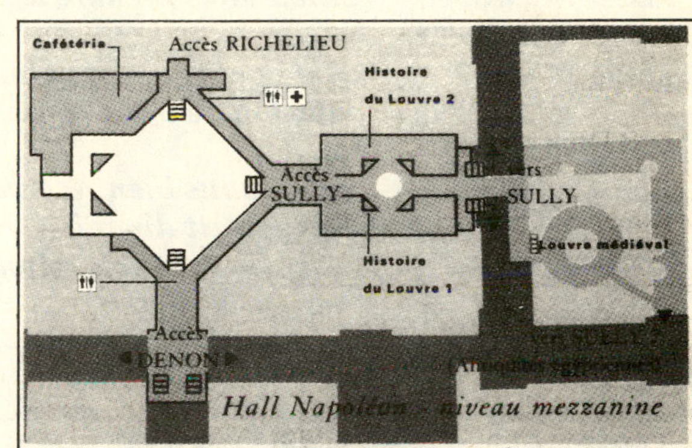

Hall Napoléon - niveau mezzanine

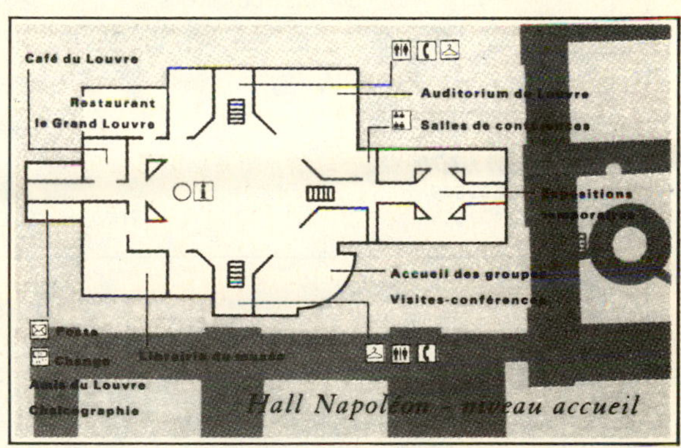

Hall Napoléon - niveau accueil

APPLICATION

M. À vous de jouer. Avec un(e) partenaire, jouez les rôles d'Yves et Moustafa. Considérez les diverses façons de résoudre *(solve)* leur dilemme et déterminez ce que vous allez faire.

SUPPLÉMENT

N. La colonie de vacances *(Summer camp).* Vous êtes moniteur (monitrice) *(counselor)* dans une colonie de vacances. Vous voulez amener votre groupe au musée national d'Art moderne ou au Louvre. Sur une autre feuille de papier, écrivez la lettre que vous envoyez au directeur du Musée pour demander un tarif réduit *(reduced rate).* N'oubliez pas de donner tous les détails de la visite prévue *(planned).*

O. Réservations. Faites cette activité avec un(e) partenaire. Une personne joue le rôle du (de la) réceptionniste au Select Hôtel; l'autre personne est le (la) client(e) au téléphone qui réserve une chambre et qui demande des renseignements sur les restaurants dans le quartier. Le (La) client(e) demande au (à la) réceptionniste de réserver une table à l'Ardelène ou au Paris-Dakar.

❖ RÉCEPTIONNISTE: ***Allô, Select Hôtel, bonjour.***
CLIENT(E): ***Oui, bonjour. Je voudrais réserver une chambre, s'il vous plaît.***
RÉCEPTIONNISTE: ***Combien de personnes?***
CLIENT(E): ***Pour ... personnes.***
RÉCEPTIONNISTE: ***Avec salle de bains? (douche, grand lit,* etc.)**
CLIENT(E): **...**
RÉCEPTIONNISTE: ***Voulez-vous prendre le petit déjeuner?* (etc.)**
CLIENT(E): **...**
RÉCEPTIONNISTE: ***Votre nom, s'il vous plaît?***
CLIENT(E): ***... Y a-t-il de bons restaurants dans le quartier?***
RÉCEPTIONNISTE: ***Oui, il y a...***
CLIENT(E): ***Voulez-vous bien réserver une table pour ... personnes à ... (restaurant). On voudrait dîner à 20 heures.***
RÉCEPTIONNISTE: ***D'accord. À ce soir, Monsieur (Madame).***
CLIENT(E): ***Merci, à ce soir.***

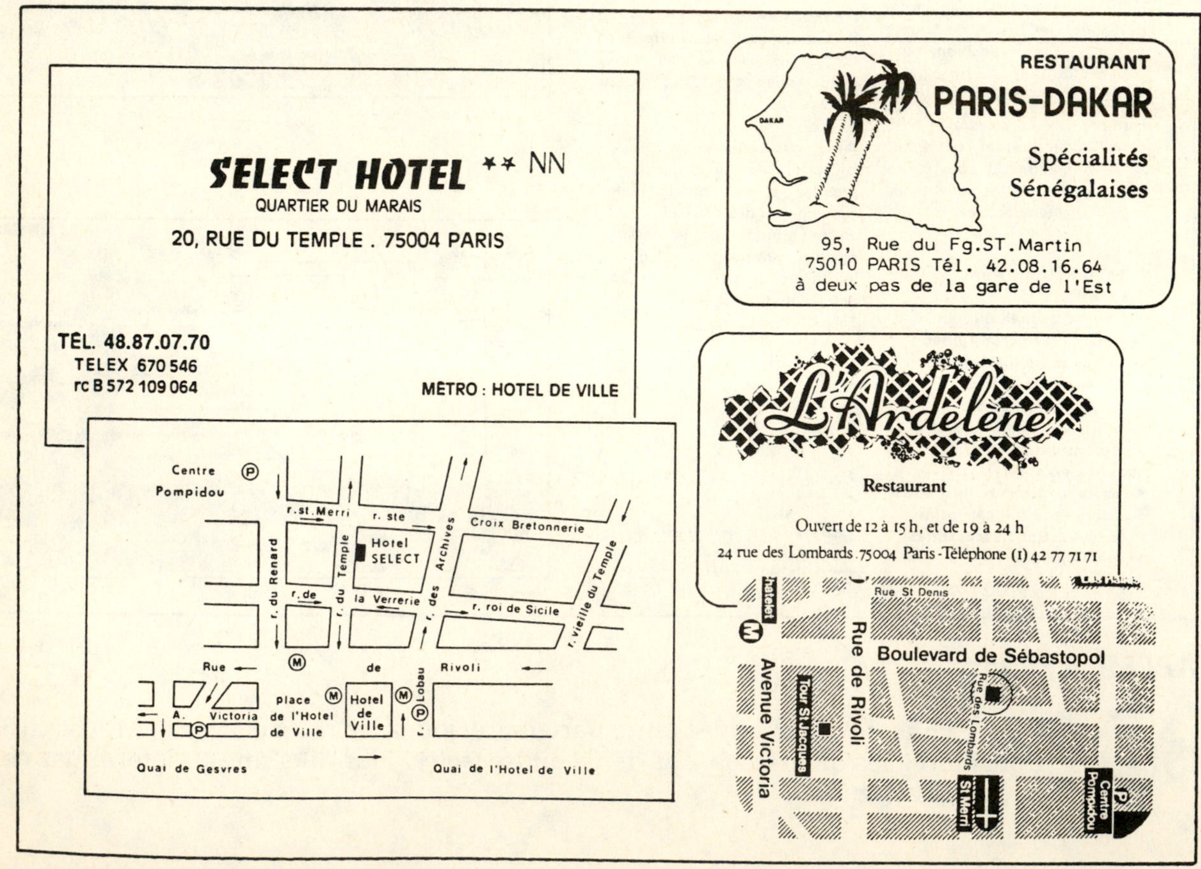

NOM _______________________________ DATE _______________________

MODULE X AU MARCHÉ, RUE MOUFFETARD

MISE EN SCÈNE

C'est bientôt l'anniversaire d'Yves. Pour fêter *(To celebrate)* ses 21 ans, Yves a décidé de préparer un repas pour ses amis. Malgré *(Despite)* le mauvais temps, il se rend au marché de la rue Mouffetard, dans le 5ème arrondissement, pour faire ses courses.

PRÉPARATION

A. Faisons le marché! Regardez bien ce plan de l'Intermarché à Nogent-le-Rotrou et répondez aux questions suivantes.

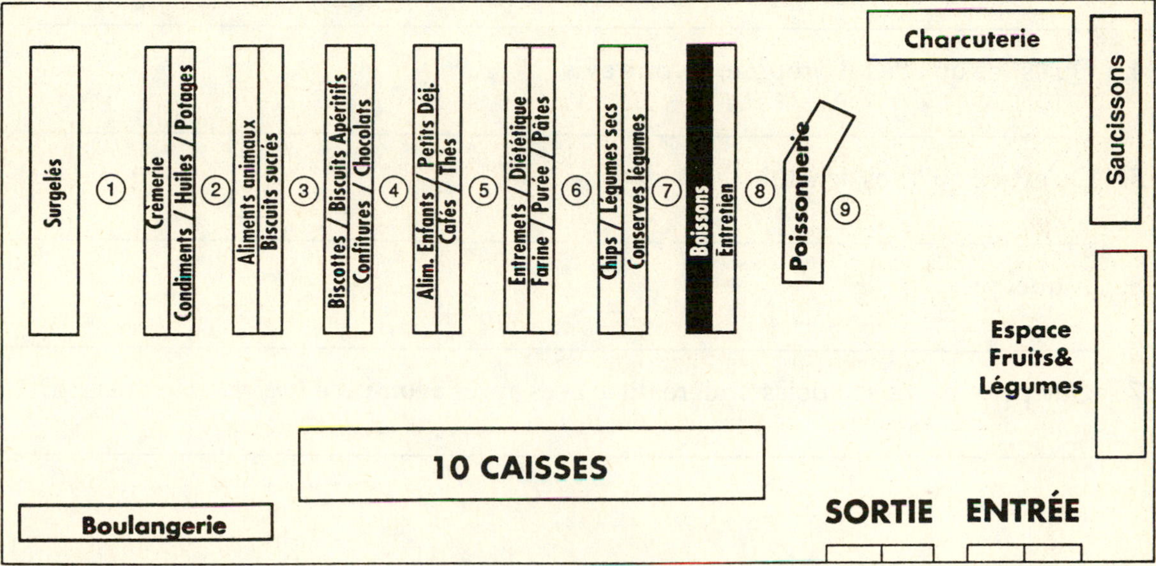

1. Dans quelle allée *(aisle)* le beurre se trouve-t-il?

____

2. Le café se trouve dans la même allée que quel autre produit?

____

3. Où trouve-t-on les saucisses *(sausages)?*

____

4. Si on veut acheter du saumon, du thon ou de la truite *(trout)*, où faut-il aller?

____

5. À votre avis, où se trouve le riz *(rice)?*

____

6. Où trouve-t-on les gâteaux?

____

VISIONNEMENT

B. Que voyez-vous? Regardez la première partie du Module X **«Au marché, rue Mouffetard»** sans le son. Ensuite, répondez aux questions suivantes.

1. Dans quel arrondissement est-ce qu'Yves fait ses courses aujourd'hui?

   ____

2. Quel temps fait-il?

   ____

3. À votre avis, que demande Yves à la poissonnière *(fish merchant)?*

   ____

4. Qu'est-ce qu'elle lui propose, à votre avis?

   ____

5. Qu'est-ce qu'Yves achète?

   ____

6. À quel prix?

   ____

7. Que pensez-vous la poissonnière dit à Yves après avoir pesé *(weighed)* le poisson?

   ____

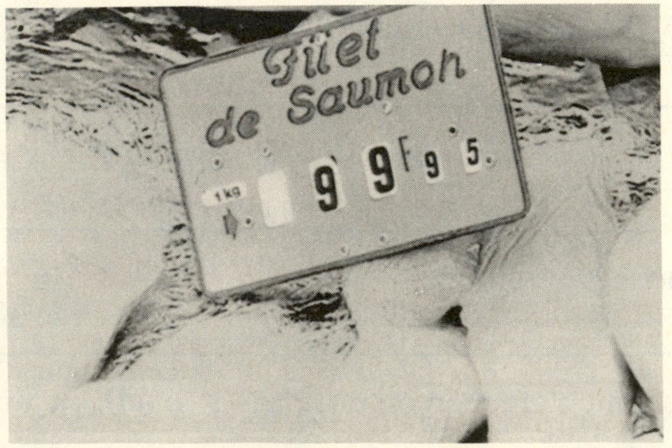

NOM ________________________________ DATE ________________________

C. Écoutez! Regardez encore une fois la première partie du Module X, cette fois-ci avec le son. Ensuite, répondez aux questions suivantes.

1. Pourquoi Yves veut-il préparer un repas pour ses amis?

   ____

2. Quelle sorte de recette *(recipe)* Yves cherche-t-il pour le poisson qu'il va acheter?

   ____

3. Comment la poissonnière propose-t-elle de préparer les différents poissons? Indiquez si c'est au four *(oven)*, au barbecue ou à la poêle *(frying pan)*.

   des truites: ____

   ____

   des tranches *(slices, steaks)* de thon: ______________________________

   ____

   des filets de saumon: ______________________________________

   ____

4. Combien coûte le poisson qu'Yves a acheté?

   ____

D. Faisons la cuisine! Reconstituez ici la recette donnée par la poissonnière pour préparer le saumon. Entourez d'un cercle chaque élément que vous entendez dans la vidéo.

Ingrédients

du vin	du sel	des filets
de l'ail *(garlic)*	du poivre	des oignons *(onions)*

Ustensiles

un plat en terre *(earthenware)*
une poêle

Préparations à faire avant de mettre au four

salez *(salt)*	sucrez	poivrez	mélangez *(mix)*
mettez du vin blanc	mettez du vin rouge	ajoutez *(add)*	

Température de cuisson *(cooking)*

à four chaud	à four moyen *(medium)*	au gril

Temps de cuisson

dix minutes	douze minutes	deux minutes

APPLICATIONS

E. La politesse. Même au marché, les Français sont toujours extrêmement polis. Ils disent «Bonjour, Madame» ou «Monsieur, bonjour» avant de commander *(ordering)*. Quand ils finissent, ils disent «Merci bien, bonne journée» ou «Merci beaucoup, à la semaine prochaine». Avec un(e) partenaire, imaginez que vous êtes au marché et que vous voulez faire les achats *(purchases)* suivants. L'un(e) joue le rôle du (de la) client(e); l'autre joue le rôle du (de la) marchand(e). N'oubliez pas les formules de politesse.

❖ une livre *(pound)* de fraises

LE (LA) CLIENT(E): ***Bonjour, Monsieur (Madame). Une livre de fraises, s'il vous plaît.***
LE (LA) MARCHAND(E): ***Voici. Ça fait dix francs.***
LE (LA) CLIENT(E): ***Voilà dix francs. Merci bien, bonne journée.***

1. quatre artichauts et un kilo de tomates
2. trois kilos de pommes de terre
3. deux truites et un litre de moules *(mussels)*
4. une tranche de pâté de campagne

NOM ______________________________ DATE ______________________

F. Une recette spéciale. Avez-vous une recette préférée? Écrivez-la ici. Si vous n'avez pas de recette préférée, expliquez comment on prépare des œufs brouillés *(scrambled eggs)*.

MOTS UTILES

une poêle *frying pan*
une casserole *pot*
une cuillère en bois *wooden spoon*
une tasse *cup*
un bol *bowl*
mettez *put*
ajoutez *add*
mélangez *mix*
mettez au four *put in the oven*

RECETTE

______________________________ (plat)

TEMPÉRATURE: ________
(en degrés Fahrenheit)

MODE DE CUISSON: ______________________

INGRÉDIENTS: ______________________

____

____

____

USTENSILES: ______________________

____

INSTRUCTIONS À SUIVRE: ______________________

____

____

____

____

PRÉSENTATION À TABLE: ______________________

____

GROS PLAN

PRÉPARATION

G. Catégories. Mettez chacun des aliments de la liste suivante dans la catégorie appropriée.

le fromage	**la banane**	**la pomme de terre**	**la fraise**
la pomme	**le pâté**	**le beurre**	**la crème**
la tomate	**la carotte**	**le poulet**	**le rosbif**

LÉGUMES	**FRUITS**	**PRODUITS LAITIERS**	**CHARCUTERIE ET VIANDE**
______________	______________	______________	______________
______________	______________	______________	______________
______________	______________	______________	______________

VISIONNEMENT

H. À table! Regardez les gens qui sont à table dans la première partie du Module X et répondez aux questions suivantes (en anglais, si nécessaire).

1. Que voyez-vous de différent entre le couvert *(place setting)* que vous voyez dans la vidéo et un couvert américain?

   ____

   ____

2. Remarquez-vous quelque chose de différent entre la façon française et la façon américaine de tenir l'argenterie *(hold the silverware)?*

   ____

   ____

3. Dessinez ici le couvert que vous voyez dans la vidéo et écrivez le nom de chaque objet.

NOM ______________________________ DATE ______________________

I. Avec les yeux ou avec les oreilles? Regardez le **Gros plan** du Module X **«Le marché»** avec le son. Dans les listes suivantes, *encerclez* les noms de légumes, de fruits et d'autres aliments que vous voyez. Ensuite, regardez le **Gros plan** encore une fois et *soulignez* les noms des articles qui sont prononcés par la narratrice.

des artichauts	des pommes
des concombres	des fraises
des tomates	des bananes
des pommes de terre	des framboises
des carottes	des radis
le fromage	le pâté
le beurre	des saucisses
le lait	un poulet rôti
la crème	

J. D'un endroit à l'autre. Dans ce **Gros plan,** comment s'appellent les divers endroits que vous voyez?

1. ______________________________
2. ______________________________
3. ______________________________
4. ______________________________
5. ______________________________
6. ______________________________

APPLICATION

K. Votre table est prête. Si Madame veut bien prendre place. Si Monsieur veut bien s'asseoir. Vous êtes dans un petit restaurant de quartier, dont voici le menu. Passez votre commande.

Menu à 55 francs

Salade de tomates ou oeuf dur mayonnaise
ou pâté de campagne

Bifteck frites ou côtelette de porc à la crème
ou moules marinière

Fromage ou dessert

1/4 vin ou eau minérale

bifteck frites = *steak with French fries*
côtelette de porc = *pork chop*
moules marinière = *mussels with wine sauce*
œuf dur = *hard-boiled egg*

PROBLÈME! PAS DE RIZ

PRÉPARATION

L. Les achats. Un(e) touriste qui ne connaît pas le système en France va dans les mauvais *(wrong)* magasins. Imaginez que vous êtes le vendeur (la vendeuse). Expliquez-lui que vous n'avez pas ce qu'il (elle) veut, et envoyez-le (la) dans le bon magasin ou la bonne boutique.

❖ (dans une crémerie) CLIENT(E): ***Je voudrais trois saucisses* (sausages) *de Toulouse, s'il vous plaît.***
CRÉMIER (CRÉMIÈRE): ***Je regrette, mais nous n'avons pas de saucisses. Il faut aller dans une charcuterie.***

1. (dans une boucherie) CLIENT(E): Donnez-moi s'il vous plaît un kilo de pêches *(peaches).*

   BOUCHER (BOUCHÈRE): ______________________________

   ____

2. (dans une épicerie) CLIENT(E): Est-ce que vous avez du bifteck haché *(chopped, ground)?*

   ÉPICIER (ÉPICIÈRE): ______________________________

   ____

3. (dans une charcuterie) CLIENT(E): J'aimerais deux parts de gâteau au chocolat.

   CHARCUTIER (CHARCUTIÈRE): ______________________________

   ____

4. (dans une pâtisserie) CLIENT(E): Un kilo de riz *(rice)*, s'il vous plaît.

   PÂTISSIER (PÂTISSIÈRE): ______________________________

   ____

5. (dans une pharmacie) CLIENT(E): J'ai besoin de trois tranches *(slices)* de thon.

   PHARMACIEN (PHARMACIENNE): ______________________________

   ____

VISIONNEMENT

M. Que voyez-vous? Regardez le **Problème** du Module X sans le son et répondez aux questions suivantes.

1. Quel temps fait-il?

   ____

2. Où est Yves?

   ____

3. Que vend le vendeur?

   ____

4. Qu'est-ce que le vendeur a dans la main?

   ____

5. Yves, trouve-t-il ce qu'il cherche chez ce vendeur?

   ____

6. Yves, achète-t-il quelque chose?

   ____

N. Que disent-ils? Regardez le **Problème** du Module X avec le son et complétez le dialogue.

YVES (à lui-même): Bon. Avec le ____________________ il me faut du riz.

VENDEUR: ____.

YVES: Bonjour, ____________________. Bon, ben, est-ce que __________

____________________ du riz?

VENDEUR: Ah non. Je regrette. __________ ne faisons __________ le riz __________. Nous ne

____________________ que *(only)* __________ légumes.

YVES: Vous ne vendez __________ de __________?

VENDEUR: Non, nous ne faisons __________ les ____________________ seulement.

YVES: (à la caméra): Qu'est-ce que __________ __________ faire?

APPLICATION

O. Qu'est-ce qu'il va faire? Voici l'agenda d'Yves pour aujourd'hui. Remplissez-le *(Fill it in)* avec toutes les activités montrées ou mentionnées dans le Module X. Ajoutez d'autres activités selon votre imagination.

8 h	
9 h	
10 h	
11 h	
12 h	
13 h	
14 h	
15 h	
16 h	
17 h	
18 h	
19 h	
20 h	
21 h	
22 h	

NOM ______________________________ DATE ______________________

SUPPLÉMENT

P. Le menu. Vous êtes propriétaire *(owner)* d'un restaurant. Ce matin vous êtes allé(e) au marché où vous avez acheté tout ce qu'il y a sur votre liste. Regardez la liste ci-dessous et établissez votre menu pour aujourd'hui. N'hésitez pas à utiliser toute votre imagination.

LISTE D'ACHATS

des tomates
des carottes
un chou *(cabbage)* rouge
de la salade *(lettuce)*
du pâté de campagne *(country pork pâté)*
des moules
un thon
des truites *(trout)*
du filet de bœuf
des saucisses *(sausages)* de Morteau

des côtelettes d'agneau *(lamb chops)*
des œufs
de la crème
du fromage de chèvre *(goat cheese)*
un brie
deux camemberts
des fraises
deux tartes
un gâteau aux framboises *(raspberries)*

Menu à 88 francs

Hors-d'œuvre
______________________ ou
______________________ ou
____

Entrées
______________________ ou
______________________ ou
____

Fromages
______________________ ou
______________________ ou
____

Desserts
______________________ ou
______________________ ou
____

Q. Commandez *(Order)* **votre repas.** Votre partenaire est client(e) dans votre restaurant. Il (Elle) commande son repas dans le menu ci-dessus. Ensuite, changez de rôle.

NOM ______________________ DATE ______________________

MODULE XI LE PAPILLON

MISE EN SCÈNE

Une voiture dans une grande ville n'est pas sans problèmes. D'abord, il faut chercher à se garer *(to park)*. Et si jamais *(ever)* on reste trop longtemps, on risque de trouver un papillon *(parking ticket)* sous son essuie-glace *(windshield wiper)*.

PRÉPARATION

A. Connaissez-vous l'Europe? Étudiez la carte de l'Europe de l'Ouest ci-dessous. D'abord, fournissez *(provide)* les informations qui manquent *(are missing)* dans le tableau ci-dessous. Ensuite, entourez d'un cercle le nom des pays où on parle français.

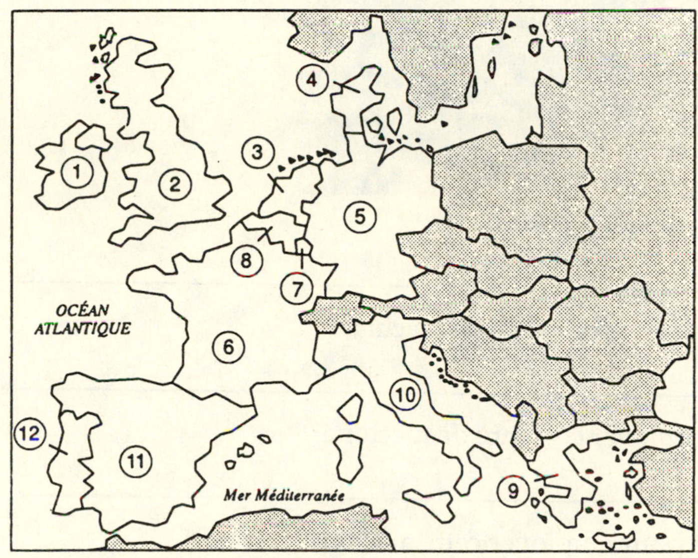

	Pays	Habitants Homme/Femme	Langue
1.	______	un Irlandais/une Irlandaise	l'anglais
2.	______	un Anglais/______	______
3.	la Hollande	______/______	le hollandais
4.	______	un Danois/Une Danoise	le danois
5.	l'Allemagne	______/______	______
6.	la France	______/une Française	______
7.	______	un Luxembourgeois/______	le français, l'allemand
8.	______	un Belge/une Belge	le français, le flamand
9.	la Grèce	______/______	______
10.	______	un Italien/______	______
11.	l'Espagne	______/une Espagnole	l'espagnol
12.	______	un Portugais/______	le portugais

B. Une machine intéressante. Voici la photo d'une machine courante *(common)* en France. Regardez bien la photo et essayez de répondre aux questions.

1. À quoi sert *(is used)* cette machine?

____

2. Où est-ce qu'on trouve ce genre de machine?

____

3. Quand faut-il employer ce genre de machine?

____

4. Que faut-il faire pour employer cette machine?

____

5. Quelles pièces *(coins)* peut-on introduire dans cette machine?

____

6. Qu'est-ce qui se passe *(happens)* si on oublie de se servir de cette machine?

____

7. Expliquez ce petit ticket:

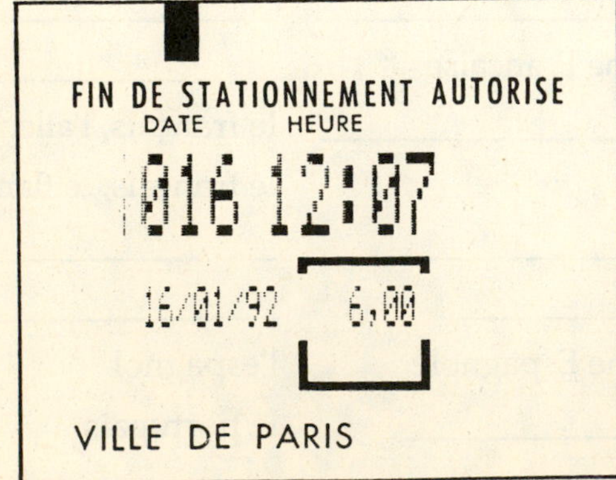
FIN DE STATIONNEMENT AUTORISE
DATE HEURE
016 12:07
16/01/92 6,00
VILLE DE PARIS

____

____

____

NOM ______________________________ DATE ______________________

VISIONNEMENT

C. Les yeux travaillent. Regardez le dialogue du Module XI **«Le papillon»** sans le son. Ensuite, répondez aux questions suivantes.

1. Pour qui travaille la femme en bleu?
____
2. Qu'est-ce qu'elle fait?
____
3. À votre avis, que dit le monsieur qui parle avec la femme en bleu?
____
4. À quoi les hommes jouent-ils?
____
5. Qu'est-ce que le monsieur en costume a trouvé sur le pare-brise *(windshield)* de sa voiture?
____
6. Qu'est-ce que c'est que la machine avec un grand «P»?
____
7. Quel mot le grand «P» représente-t-il?
____

D. Quelques mots importants. Maintenant regardez le dialogue du Module XI avec le son. Avec l'aide du contexte visuel et du dialogue, expliquez le sens des mots suivants et leur importance dans ce dialogue.

1. le papillon ______________________________
2. le parcmètre ______________________________
3. la Belgique ______________________________
4. le bureau de tabac ______________________________
5. le timbre ______________________________
6. la contravention ______________________________

APPLICATION

E. Le papillon. Étudiez le papillon que vous voyez ici et répondez aux questions.

VOLET A CONSERVER PAR LE CONTREVENANT POUR JUSTIFICATIF DU PAIEMENT

CONTRAVENTION LE 120697 A 14 h 10 — 29419051

AGENT — SERVICE

COLLER ICI LA PARTIE DU TIMBRE-AMENDE A CONSERVER

CONTRAVENTION AU STATIONNEMENT

LIEU D'INFRACTION — DÉPT. — COMMUNE — NATURE DE L'INFRACTION

INTERDIT MATÉRIALISÉ

UNILATÉRAL NON OBSERVÉ MATÉRIALISÉ

DOUBLE FILE

ARRÊT AUTOBUS

STATION DE TAXIS

PASSAGE PIÉTONS

SUR TROTTOIR

PROLONGÉ DE PLUS D'UNE HEURE

DÉFAUT DE DISQUE

TEMPS DÉPASSÉ

STATIONNEMENT NON PAYÉ

RENAULT 1	CITROEN 2	PEUGEOT 3
VW 4	FIAT 5	OPEL 6	FORD 7
AUTRES 8	GENRE OU MODÈLE	

IMMATRICULATION: CHIFFRES — LETTRES — DÉPT. — ÉTRANGER

Cas n° 1

POUR LE RÈGLEMENT DE CETTE CONTRAVENTION, SUIVEZ LES INDICATIONS PORTÉES SUR LA CARTE-LETTRE

1. Quand est-ce que ce papillon a été posé (jour et heure)?

2. Pourquoi le papillon a-t-il été posé?

3. Ce papillon a été mis sur quelle marque *(make)* de voiture?

4. Où est-ce que cette voiture est immatriculée *(registered)?*

5. Pour payer l'amende, qu'est-ce que la personne peut acheter et coller sur le papillon?

NOM ______________________________ DATE ______________________

GROS PLAN LE TABAC

PRÉPARATION

F. Partout *(Everywhere)* **en France.** Lisez le texte suivant sur un projet d'établissement *(establishment)* d'une nouvelle agence. Puis, répondez aux questions.

PROJET pour une présence active de l'administration française dans chaque village en France

Mesdames et messieurs, je m'adresse à vous *(I'm speaking to you)* aujourd'hui pour vous convaincre *(convince)* que le gouvernement français a besoin d'être directement représenté partout en France. Pensez à ceci: notre gouvernement limite la vente de certains produits (les timbres, les cigarettes et les allumettes *[matches]*, par exemple).

Qui surveillera la vente de ces produits? La poste n'est ouverte qu'en semaine *(only during the week)*, et seulement pendant la journée. Les notaires *(lawyer-notaries)* et les mairies *(town halls)* ont déjà trop à faire. Les épiceries n'offrent pas la sécurité nécessaire.

Et qui plus est, mes chers collègues, il faut songer à *(consider)* la vente des timbres fiscaux *(tax stamps)* pour payer les contraventions, les taxes et les impôts. Qui s'en occupera *(will take care of this)?* Qui vendra la vignette automobile *(annual automobile registration)?* Et qui—mesdames et messieurs, je vous le demande—assurera la vente des billets de loto *(lottery tickets)*, ainsi que le paiement des prix?

C'est évident, mesdames et messieurs, nous avons besoin d'un représentant du gouvernement dans chaque ville, dans chaque quartier, dans chaque village. De cela nous sommes persuadés. Je vous pose donc aujourd'hui la question suivante: comment assurer cette présence?

1. Qui parle ici?

   ____

2. Qu'est-ce qu'il (elle) veut?

   ____

3. Pourquoi?

   ____

4. À quoi sert *(is used)* un timbre fiscal?

   ____

5. Qu'est-ce que l'agence suggérée doit vendre?

   ____

VISIONNEMENT

G. Dans les cafés-tabac. Regardez le **Gros plan** du Module XI **«Le tabac»** sans le son et faites une liste des activités que vous voyez dans les cafés-tabac représentés à l'écran *(screen)*.

____

____

____

____

____

____

H. Descriptions. Regardez bien cette pause-sur-image. Expliquez tout ce que vous voyez dans cette photo.

____

____

____

I. On peut tout y trouver. D'abord, regardez le **Gros plan** avec le son et faites une liste de tous les articles vendus dans un tabac qui sont mentionnés par le narrateur. Ensuite, regardez le **Gros plan** encore une fois et faites une liste des articles vendus dans un tabac que vous voyez à l'image.

Articles vendus dans un tabac qui sont...

mentionnés par le narrateur	**visibles à l'image**
____________________	____________________
____________________	____________________
____________________	____________________
____________________	____________________
____________________	____________________
____________________	____________________

NOM ______________________ DATE ______________________

APPLICATION

J. S'il vous plaît, Monsieur. Regardez tous les articles représentés ici, tous vendus dans les bureaux de tabac. Imaginez que vous êtes dans un bureau de tabac et écrivez ce que vous diriez pour acheter chacun de ces articles.

EXPRESSIONS UTILES

S'il vous plaît...	
Pourriez-vous me donner...?	*May I have . . . ?*
Je voudrais...	*I would like . . .*
J'aimerais...	*I would like . . .*
C'est combien...?	*How much is it (the . . .)?*

1. ____

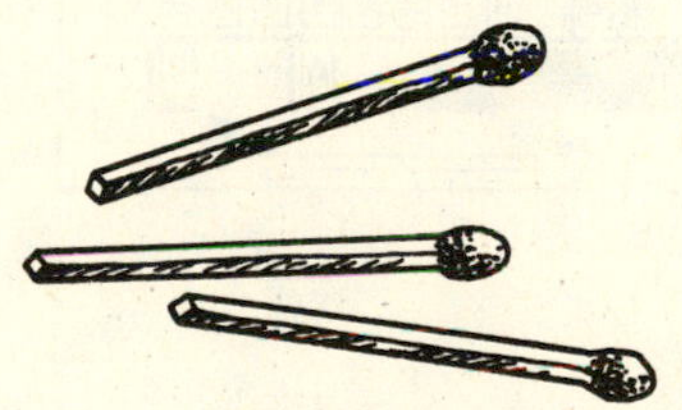

2. ____

3. ____

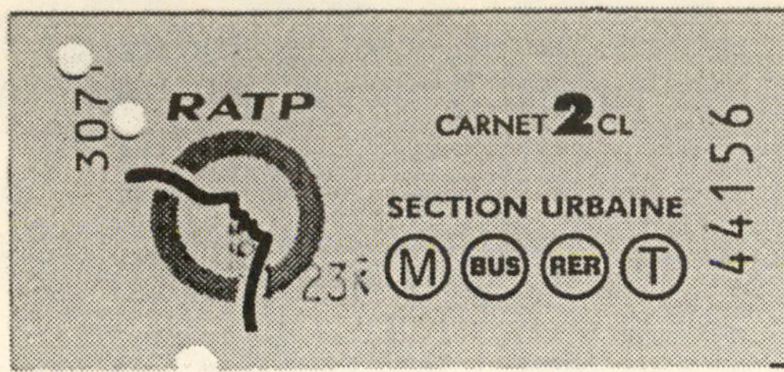
RATP
CARNET 2 CL
SECTION URBAINE
M BUS RER T
44156

4.

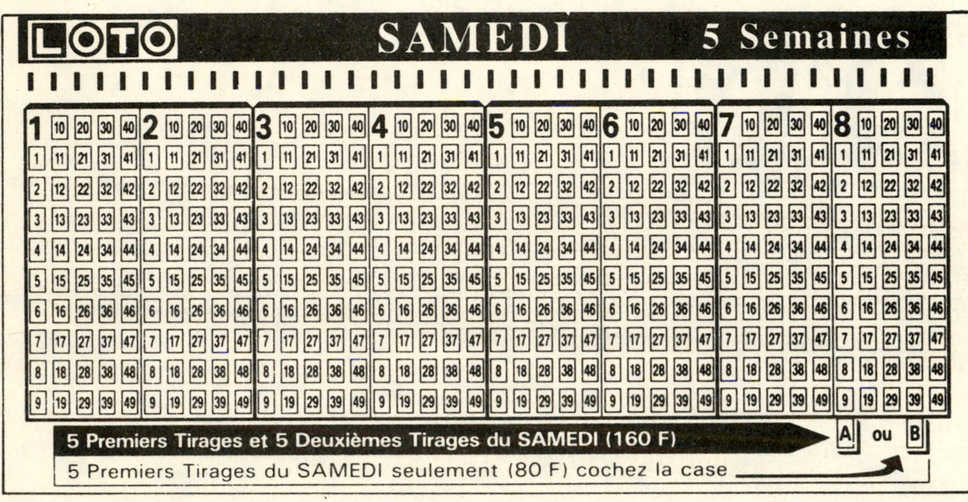
LOTO
SAMEDI
5 Semaines
5 Premiers Tirages et 5 Deuxièmes Tirages du SAMEDI (160 F)
A ou B
5 Premiers Tirages du SAMEDI seulement (80 F) cochez la case

5.

TAPIS VERT
Gagnez 1000 fois la mise !
TABLE À 2 F
TABLE À 10 F
TABLE À 50 F
TABLE À 5 F
TABLE À 20 F
TABLE À 100 F
Nombre de tirages consécutifs : 1 3 7 (Un tirage chaque jour)
La mise de chaque table est indiquée pour 1 tirage.
Elle est multipliée par le nombre de jours auquel vous participez.
COMMENT JOUER :
1. Choisissez une ou plusieurs tables de jeu (à chaque table correspond la mise indiquée).
2. Sur les tables choisies, COCHEZ 4 CARTES : un seul pique, un seul cœur, un seul carreau, un seul trèfle.
3. Cochez le nombre de tirages auquelvousvoulezparticiper.
RÉSULTATS :
– Tirage chaque jour en direct à la télévision.
GAINS :
– Si vous avez coché sur une table les 4 cartes tirées, vous gagnez 1000 fois la mise journalière de cette table.
– 3 des cartes tirées : 30 fois la mise.
– 2 des cartes tirées : 2 fois la mise.

6.

NOM ______________________ DATE ______________________

PROBLÈME! LA POSTE EST FERMÉE

PRÉPARATION

K. La poste, s'il vous plaît. Imaginez que, dans la rue, un homme vous a posé la question suivante: «Elle se trouve *(is located)* où la poste, s'il vous plaît?» Comment répondriez-vous dans les cas suivants?

❖ La poste est fermée, parce que c'est dimanche.
Je regrette, Monsieur, mais la poste est fermée aujourd'hui.

1. La poste est fermée depuis un quart d'heure.

   ____

2. La poste se trouve derrière le bâtiment devant vous.

   ____

3. La poste est dans la rue où vous vous trouvez, mais elle va fermer dans quelques minutes. ______________________

4. Vous n'avez aucune idée *(no idea)* où se trouve la poste.

   ____

VISIONNEMENT

L. Pas de chance. Regardez le **Problème** du Module XI avec le son et répondez aux questions suivantes.

1. Décrivez l'endroit où se trouve Moustafa.

   ____

2. Selon Moustafa, où se trouve la poste?

   ____

3. Pourquoi Moustafa dit-il «Vous n'avez pas de chance»?

   ____

4. La poste ferme à cinq heures. Quelle heure est-il?

   ____

5. Quelle est la réaction du monsieur qui cherche la poste?

   ____

M. Quelques solutions. Imaginez que vous êtes le passant qui cherche la poste dans le **Problème** du Module XI. Donnez quatre solutions possibles à votre dilemme.

1. ______________________
2. ______________________
3. ______________________
4. ______________________

APPLICATIONS

N. Un télégramme. Imaginez que vous êtes le chauffeur belge que vous avez vu dans le dialogue du Module XI. Vous venez de recevoir une contravention *(ticket)* de 450 francs. Vous n'avez pas assez d'argent pour payer cette contravention. Écrivez ici le télégramme que vous envoyez en Belgique pour demander l'argent nécessaire. N'oubliez pas de remplir *(fill out)* toutes les parties du formulaire qui vous concernent.

N° 698 **TÉLÉGRAMME**

Étiquettes

N° d'appel :

INDICATIONS DE TRANSMISSION

Ligne de numérotation

ZCZC

N° télégraphique

Taxe principale.

Timbre à date

Taxes accessoires

N° de la ligne du P.V. :

Ligne pilote

Bureau de destination | Département ou Pays

Total . .

Bureau d'origine	Mots	Date	Heure	Mentions de service

Services spéciaux demandés : (voir au verso)

Inscrire en **CAPITALES** l'adresse complète (rue, n° bloc, bâtiment, escalier, etc...), le texte et la signature (une lettre par case ; **laisser une case blanche entre les mots**).

Nom et adresse

TEXTE et éventuellement signature très lisible

Nom et adresse de l'expéditeur :

Pour avis en cas de non remise. - Indications transmises et taxées sur demande expresse de l'expéditeur.

O. À la poste. Vous avez écrit votre télégramme et vous arrivez à la poste. Que dites-vous au guichet de la poste? Comment est-ce que le guichetier (la guichetière) vous répond? Écrivez ici votre dialogue à la poste. Inventez tous les détails nécessaires.

SUPPLÉMENT

P. Vos réactions. Êtes-vous fâché(e) *(angry)?* Êtes-vous content(e)? Donnez votre réaction dans les situations suivantes.

Je suis ravie(e) *delighted*
Je suis fâché(e)
Je suis content(e)
Je suis heureux(-euse)
Je suis frustré(e) *frustrated*

1. Vous venez de recevoir une contravention de 75 francs.

 ____

2. Vous avez gagné 14.000 francs au loto *(lottery).*

 ____

3. Vous avez besoin d'un timbre et vous venez d'apprendre que la poste est fermée.

 ____

4. Vous arrivez à votre voiture juste avant de recevoir un papillon.

 ____

5. Vous avez eu une contravention de 900 francs.

 ____

6. Vous avez gagné 100 francs au Tapis vert, mais vous avez failli *(just missed)* gagner 10.000 francs. ______________________________

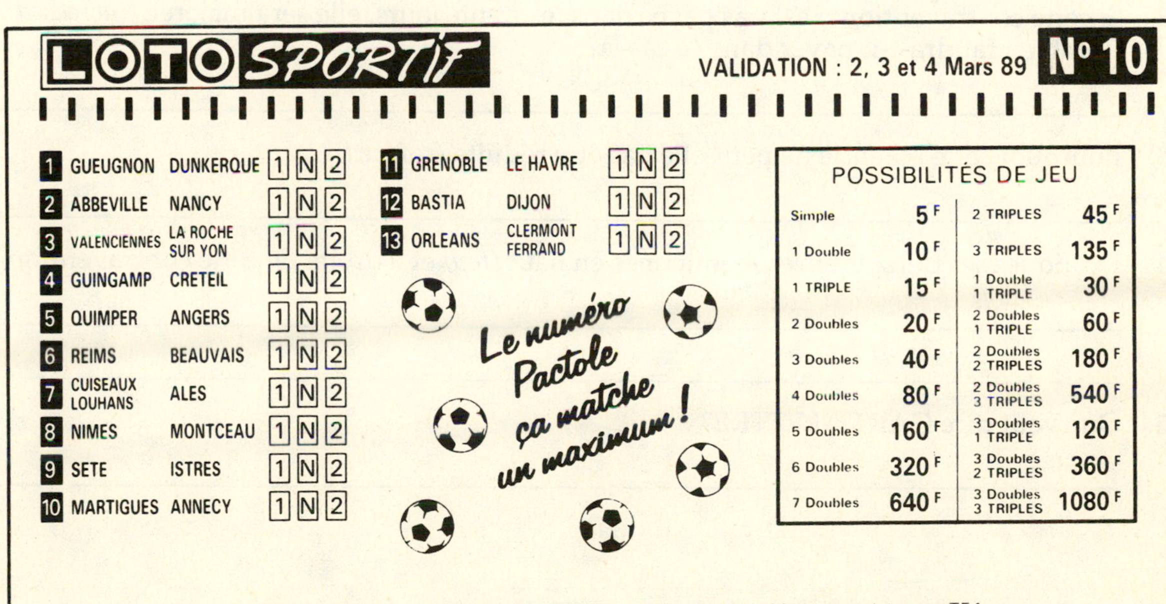

LOTO SPORTIF

VALIDATION : 2, 3 et 4 Mars 89 Nº 10

1	GUEUGNON	DUNKERQUE	1 N 2
2	ABBEVILLE	NANCY	1 N 2
3	VALENCIENNES	LA ROCHE SUR YON	1 N 2
4	GUINGAMP	CRETEIL	1 N 2
5	QUIMPER	ANGERS	1 N 2
6	REIMS	BEAUVAIS	1 N 2
7	CUISEAUX LOUHANS	ALES	1 N 2
8	NIMES	MONTCEAU	1 N 2
9	SETE	ISTRES	1 N 2
10	MARTIGUES	ANNECY	1 N 2
11	GRENOBLE	LE HAVRE	1 N 2
12	BASTIA	DIJON	1 N 2
13	ORLEANS	CLERMONT FERRAND	1 N 2

Le numéro Pactole ça matche un maximum!

POSSIBILITÉS DE JEU

Simple	5 F	2 TRIPLES	45 F
1 Double	10 F	3 TRIPLES	135 F
1 TRIPLE	15 F	1 Double 1 TRIPLE	30 F
2 Doubles	20 F	2 Doubles 1 TRIPLE	60 F
3 Doubles	40 F	2 Doubles 2 TRIPLES	180 F
4 Doubles	80 F	2 Doubles 3 TRIPLES	540 F
5 Doubles	160 F	3 Doubles 1 TRIPLE	120 F
6 Doubles	320 F	3 Doubles 2 TRIPLES	360 F
7 Doubles	640 F	3 Doubles 3 TRIPLES	1080 F

Résultats et tirage du NUMERO PACTOLE : le dimanche 5 Mars en soirée sur TF1
Renseignements et informations complémentaires sur minitel **36.15 LOTO**

Ce bulletin est uniquement destiné à la lecture de votre jeu sur un terminal du Loto National. Il permet d'obtenir un reçu contre le versement de la mise. Ce reçu devra être présenté pour le paiement des gains.

Q. Les amendes *(Fines).* Voici la première partie du papillon reçu par notre ami belge. Regardez bien cette contravention et répondez aux questions suivantes.

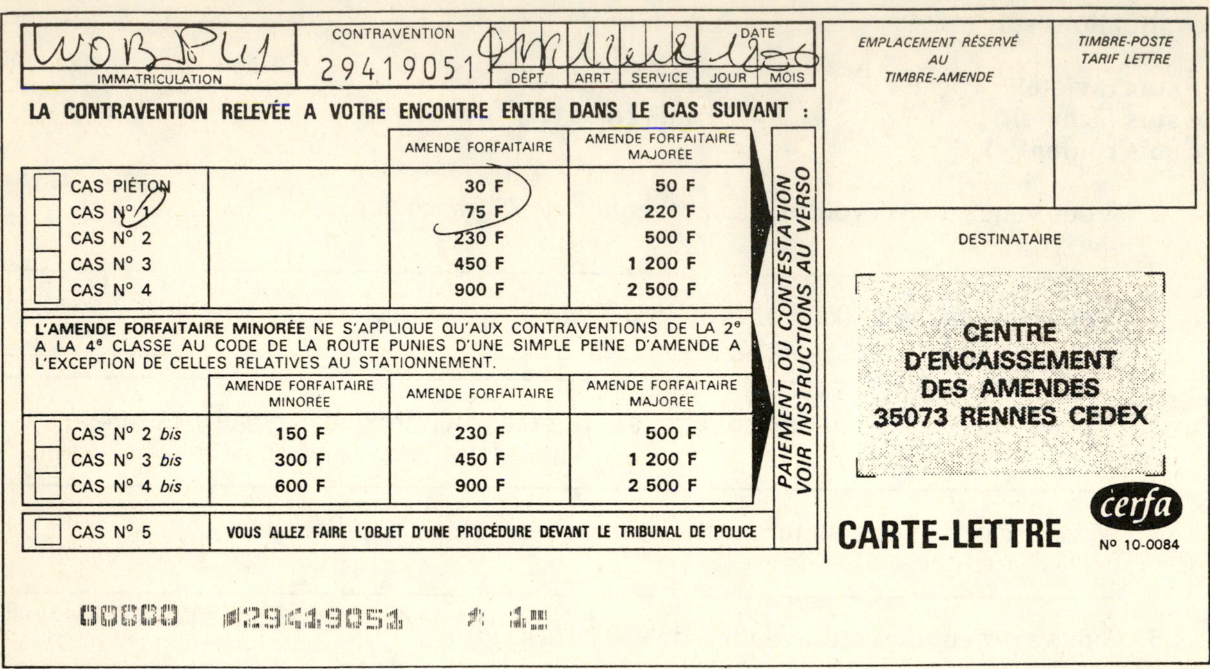

IMMATRICULATION | CONTRAVENTION 29419051 | DÉPT | ARRT | SERVICE | DATE JOUR | MOIS

EMPLACEMENT RÉSERVÉ AU TIMBRE-AMENDE

TIMBRE-POSTE TARIF LETTRE

LA CONTRAVENTION RELEVÉE A VOTRE ENCONTRE ENTRE DANS LE CAS SUIVANT :

		AMENDE FORFAITAIRE	AMENDE FORFAITAIRE MAJORÉE
CAS PIÉTON		30 F	50 F
CAS N° 1		75 F	220 F
CAS N° 2		230 F	500 F
CAS N° 3		450 F	1 200 F
CAS N° 4		900 F	2 500 F

L'AMENDE FORFAITAIRE MINORÉE NE S'APPLIQUE QU'AUX CONTRAVENTIONS DE LA 2e A LA 4e CLASSE AU CODE DE LA ROUTE PUNIES D'UNE SIMPLE PEINE D'AMENDE A L'EXCEPTION DE CELLES RELATIVES AU STATIONNEMENT.

	AMENDE FORFAITAIRE MINORÉE	AMENDE FORFAITAIRE	AMENDE FORFAITAIRE MAJORÉE
CAS N° 2 *bis*	150 F	230 F	500 F
CAS N° 3 *bis*	300 F	450 F	1 200 F
CAS N° 4 *bis*	600 F	900 F	2 500 F

CAS N° 5 — VOUS ALLEZ FAIRE L'OBJET D'UNE PROCÉDURE DEVANT LE TRIBUNAL DE POLICE

PAIEMENT OU CONTESTATION VOIR INSTRUCTIONS AU VERSO

DESTINATAIRE

CENTRE D'ENCAISSEMENT DES AMENDES 35073 RENNES CEDEX

cerfa

CARTE-LETTRE N° 10-0084

1. L'amende prévue *(prescribed)* par cette contravention s'élève *(mounts up)* à quelle somme?

   ____

2. Si cette contravention n'est pas payée dans les trente jours, elle sera majorée *(increased)*. Combien faudra-t-il payer dans ce cas-là?

   ____

3. Pourquoi cette amende ne peut-elle pas être réduite *(reduced)?*

   ____

4. Expliquez les deux timbres mentionnés en haut *(top)* et à droite de cette contravention.

   ____

   ____

5. Que veut dire CARTE-LETTRE?

   ____

NOM ____________________ DATE ____________________

MODULE XII LA FÊTE DE LA MUSIQUE

MISE EN SCÈNE

Tous les ans, au mois de juin, Paris fait la fête à la musique. Partout (*Everywhere*), pendant deux jours, il y a de la musique de toutes sortes. Ce soir, Marie-Christine et Jean-François, Bruno et Alissa, Yves et Moustafa se rendent tous à la fête de la Musique. Yves et Moustafa doivent y rencontrer leur amie Betty.

PRÉPARATION

A. Toutes sortes de musique. Lisez le programme suivant. Ensuite, répondez aux questions.

Mercredi 12 juin
ORCHESTRE DE CHAMBRE JEAN-FRANÇOIS PAILLARD. "Les Quatre Saisons" de Vivaldi. Église Saint-Germain-des-Près. 21h. *Places 100 et 120 francs.*

Jeudi 13 juin
YVES DUTEIL. Chante ses propres compositions. 21h. Gymnase Robert Desnos. *Places 80 à 120 francs.*

Vendredi 14 juin
RHODA SCOTT. Orgue jazz. À partir de 21 heures. Le Bilboquet. Couvert (*Cover charge)* 30 francs, avec consommation *(drink included).*

ORCHESTRE NATIONAL DE FRANCE. Oeuvres de Debussy, Ravel, Poulenc. Salle Pleyel. 20 h 30. *Places 50 à 100 francs.* Concert télévisé.

Samedi 15 juin
LES TROMPETTES DE VERSAILLES. Oeuvres de Haendel, Vivaldi, Purcell, Telemann. 21h. Église Saint-Julien-le-Pauvre. *Places: 90 à 150 francs.*

FESTIVAL BAROQUE DE VERSAILLES. Opéra. CARMEN de Bizet. Château de Versailles. 19 h 30. Places: *100 à 1 000 francs.*

Dimanche 16 juin
ENSEMBLE ARS ANTIQUA DE PARIS. Musique au temps des troubadours et des trouvères; musique de la cour de Bourgogne (XVème siècle). 18 h 45 et 21 h. Sainte Chapelle. *Places: 75 et 110 francs.*

Mardi 18 juin
KING PLEASURE AND THE BISCUIT BOYS. Rock rétro. À partir de 22 heures. Slow-club de Paris. Consommation.

1. Si vous voulez entendre de la musique rock, où faut-il aller? À quelle heure?

   ____

2. Quel est le concert le plus cher? Quelle sorte de concert est-ce?

   ____

3. Où peut-on écouter de la musique médiévale?

   ____

4. Quels concerts ont lieu *(take place)* dans les églises parisiennes?

   ____

5. Quel concert ne se passe pas à Paris?

   ____

6. Quel concert peut-on voir et entendre sans quitter son appartement?

   ____

7. Quel soir peut-on écouter un chansonnier français?

   ____

8. Quels concerts offrent uniquement de la musique française?

   ____

VISIONNEMENT

B. De la musique partout! Regardez le dialogue avec le son et reliez les mots qui conviennent pour compléter les phrases suivantes.

1. Il y a du jazz...	à la République.
2. On peut entendre Joe Cocker...	à l'Hôtel de Sully.
3. Il y a de la musique Amérique latine...	partout.
4. Il y a des groupes de rock...	au musée Picasso.

C. Extra! Regardez le dialogue du Module XII **«La fête de la Musique»** avec le son. Vous entendrez beaucoup d'expressions populaires, très courantes parmi *(among)* les jeunes en France. D'abord, identifiez la personne qui a employé l'expression mentionnée. Ensuite, expliquez le sens de l'expression (en anglais, si nécessaire). Si vous ne connaissez pas le sens exact de l'expression, laissez-vous guider par le contexte: qu'est-ce que vous diriez dans une situation semblable?

1. Super: ____________________
   sens: ____
2. D'où tu sors?: ____________________
   sens: ____
3. Sympa: ____________________
   sens: ____
4. Qu'est-ce que tu fous dans le coin?: ____________________
   sens: ____
5. Tchao les mecs: ____________________
   sens: ____
6. Bisous: ____________________
   sens: ____

Maintenant, écrivez sur une autre feuille un dialogue avec un(e) partenaire en employant au moins trois de ces expressions.

D. Les verbes. Écoutez bien les verbes dans le dialogue du Module XII. Trouvez au moins une forme verbale utilisée dans la vidéo à chacun des temps ci-dessous.

1. présent de l'indicatif: ____
2. subjonctif: ____
3. passé composé: ____
4. imparfait: ____

NOM ______________________________ DATE ______________________

APPLICATION

E. Les concerts. Voici plusieurs affiches *(posters)* pour des concerts extrêmement variés. Étudiez bien ces affiches et répondez aux questions qui suivent. Commencez vos réponses par le mot **si** et faites attention aux temps des verbes.

❖ Si votre ami(e) aimait le jazz, quel concert lui proposeriez-vous?
Si mon ami(e) aimait le jazz, je lui proposerais le programme au Jazz Club.

1. Si vous n'aimiez pas la musique sacrée, quel concert ne faudrait-il pas choisir?

   Réponse: Si ______________________________

2. Si vous êtes à Montpellier le 18 juillet, qu'est-ce que vous pourrez entendre?

   Réponse: Si ______________________________

3. Si vous n'aviez pas de voiture, serait-il possible d'aller à l'Opéra le 13 octobre?

   Réponse: Si ______________________________

4. Si vous aimiez la musique espagnole, quel numéro de téléphone devriez-vous appeler?

   Réponse: Si ______________________________

5. Si votre ami(e) n'était libre qu'à *(not free until)* dix heures et demie du soir, quel concert faudrait-il choisir?

   Réponse: Si mon ______________________________

PROBLÈME! COMMENT SAVOIR À QUELLE HEURE?

PRÉPARATION

F. Qu'est-ce qu'on va regarder? Voici une liste partielle des programmes de la télévision pour le 22 septembre, au soir. Lisez ce guide puis répondez aux questions. Vous n'avez pas besoin de comprendre chaque mot pour trouver les réponses aux questions.

20h00
TF1/F2/F3 JOURNAL
20h30
Canal+ FOOTBALL: Caen/Marseille
M6 ***Mission Impossible, 20 ans après.*** FEUILLETON AMÉRICAIN.
20h40
TF1/F2 MÉTÉO
20h45
TF1 ***L'Étudiante,*** FILM de Claude Pinoteau. Pour Valentine, seule compte *(the only thing that matters)* l'agrégation *(competitive examination)* de lettres classiques qu'elle prépare avec ardeur. Cependant *(Nevertheless)*, un événement imprévu *(unforseen)* va perturber sa vie si bien organisée. Elle tombe amoureuse d'Édouard, qui est tout son contraire: musicien de rock sans organisation aucune. COMÉDIE.

20h45
F3 ***Les Aventures de Tintin: L'Île noire,*** DESSIN ANIMÉ d'après Hergé, réalisé par Stéphane Bernasconi. Au cours *(During)* d'une promenade en campagne, Tintin aperçoit *(sights)* un avion en difficulté; mais quand il s'en approche, il est accueilli *(welcomed)* par des coups de feu (gunshots). Ses aventures le conduisent jusqu'en Écosse *(Scotland)*. POUR ENFANTS.
20h50
F2 ***La Révolution française,*** FILM de Robert Enrico. Mars 1789: face au mécontentement *(discontent)* du peuple et aux problèmes de trésorerie *(financial problems)* du pays, Louis XVI convoque *(convokes)* les États généraux. Le 23 juin, le tiers état *(Third Estate)* se constitue en Assemblée nationale. Le 14 juillet le peuple s'empare *(takes over)* de la Bastille. GRANDE FRESQUE HISTORIQUE.

22h35
F3 JOURNAL
22h45
TF1 ***Le Point sur la Table,*** DÉBAT POLITIQUE avec Anne Sinclair. Discussion de la position de la France dans l'Europe d'après Maastricht.
23h30
F2 ***Prénom Marianne,*** document de Djamila Sahraoui. La France, lorsqu'elle *(when it)* est représentée sur un tableau, une place publique ou dans une mairie, est toujours représentée sous les traits d'une femme. Mais depuis quand? Depuis que l'on ne dit plus le royaume *(kingdom)* de France mais la République française. DOCUMENTAIRE HISTORIQUE.

1. Si vous vous intéressez à l'avenir de l'Europe, quel programme aurez-vous envie de voir ce soir? ______________________________

2. Des trois films qui passent entre huit heures et demie et neuf heures, lequel préférez-vous? Pourquoi? ______________________________

____

3. Si vous êtes particulièrement intéressé(e) par les sports, quel programme regarderez-vous, à quelle heure et sur quelle chaîne? ______________________________

____

4. Qui est Marianne? Depuis quand existe-t-elle? Pour en savoir plus, peut-on se coucher tôt? Pourquoi (pas)? ______________________________

____

NOM ______________________ DATE ______________

5. Voyez-vous une différence entre cet exemple de la programmation télévisuelle en France et la programmation de la télévision américaine? Les sujets sont-ils différents? À quoi attribuez-vous cette différence? ______________________

____

____

VISIONNEMENT

G. Les temps du verbe. Regardez le **Problème** du Module XII avec le son. Dans l'espace de seulement quelques phrases, les personnages emploient beaucoup de différents temps de verbes. D'abord, trouvez dans la vidéo un verbe conjugué à chaque temps mentionné. Ensuite, écrivez la phrase dans laquelle ce verbe est employé.

❖ futur proche: on va faire
phrase: ***Mais on va bientôt faire une émission sur la musique pour les jeunes.***

1. présent: ______________
   phrase: ______________________
2. imparfait: ______________
   phrase: ______________________
3. infinitif: ______________
   phrase: ______________________
4. conditionnel: ______________
   phrase: ______________________
5. passé composé: ______________
   phrase: ______________________

H. Comprenez-vous? Regardez encore une fois le **Problème** et répondez aux questions suivantes.

1. Que pense Betty du guitariste? ______________________

   ____
2. Qu'est-ce qu'elle lui demande? ______________________
3. Comment répond-il? ______________________
4. Quel est le problème de Betty à la fin de cette séquence? ______________________

   ____
5. Comment peut-elle résoudre *(solve)* son problème? Donnez au moins deux solutions possibles.

   a. ______________________

   b. ______________________

GROS PLAN LE MONDE FRANCOPHONE

PRÉPARATION

I. La francophonie. Dans le monde, il y a des dizaines de pays où on parle français. Regardez bien cette carte sur laquelle huit pays ou régions francophones sont indiqués par des numéros. Écrivez le nom de chaque pays ou région à côté du numéro correspondant. Choisissez dans la liste fournie.

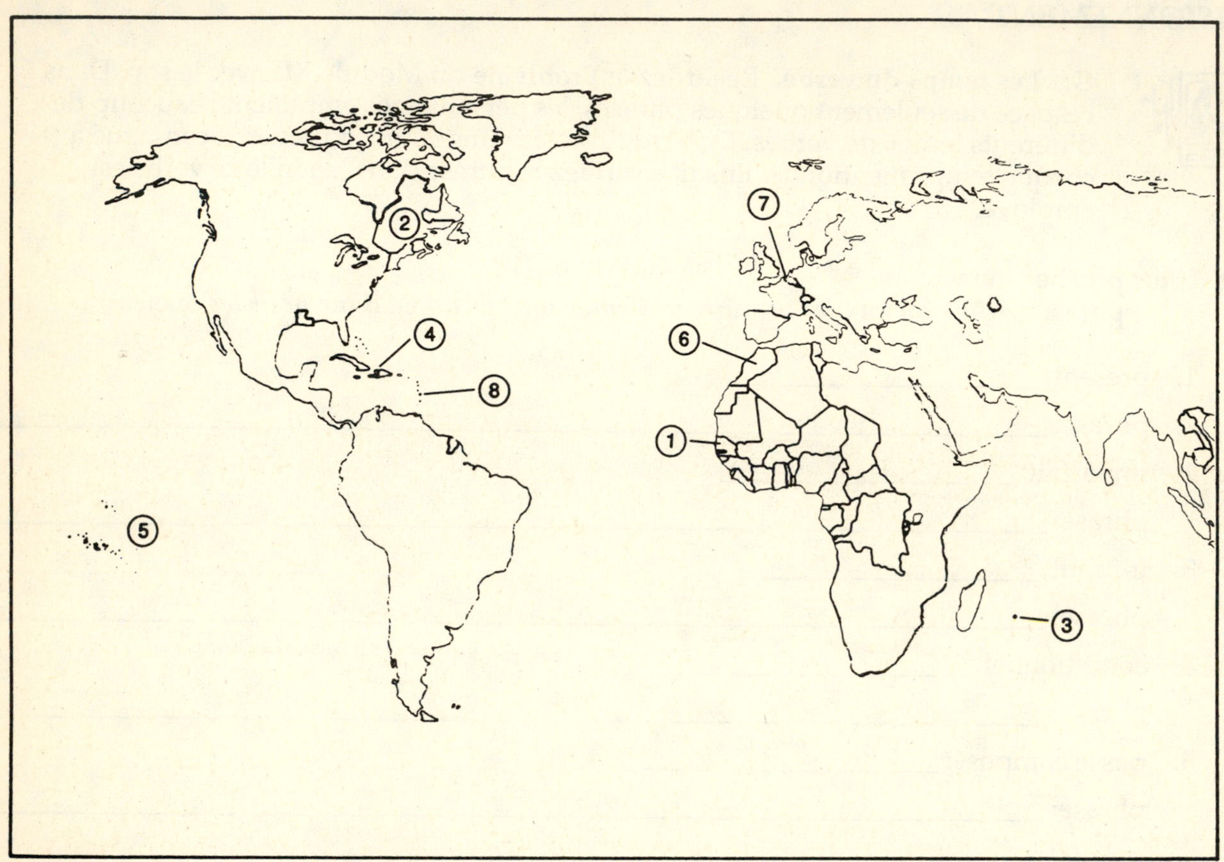

la Belgique	**le Québec**
Haïti	**la Réunion**
le Maroc	**le Sénégal**
la Martinique	**Tahiti**

1. ______________________
2. ______________________
3. ______________________
4. ______________________
5. ______________________
6. ______________________
7. ______________________
8. ______________________

NOM ______________________ DATE ______________________

J. Les capitales. Voici une liste de quelques pays où on parle français et le nom de leurs capitales. Tracez une ligne entre chaque pays et sa capitale.

la Guyane française	Ouagadougou
le Canada	Alger
la France	Bruxelles
la Belgique	Ottawa
l'Algérie	Rabat
le Burkina-Faso	Tunis
le Maroc	Paris
la Nouvelle-Calédonie	Berne
la Suisse	Nouméa
la Tunisie	Cayenne

VISIONNEMENT

K. Vive la différence! Regardez le **Gros plan** du Module XII **«Le monde francophone».** Indiquez dans le tableau les caractéristiques particulières de chaque endroit représenté.

	Québec	**Martinique**	**Sénégal**	**Tahiti**
climat				
végétation				
habits				
architecture				
activités				
musique				

APPLICATIONS

L. Êtes-vous fort(e) en maths? Regardez bien cette carte de l'Afrique du Nord et de l'Ouest et lisez les statistiques qui l'accompagnent. D'abord, utilisez les informations données et écrivez le pourcentage de Francophones dans chaque pays dans la colonne à droite. Ensuite, classez les 17 pays du plus francophone au moins francophone (le pays le plus francophone = 1; le pays le moins francophone = 17) dans la colonne à gauche.

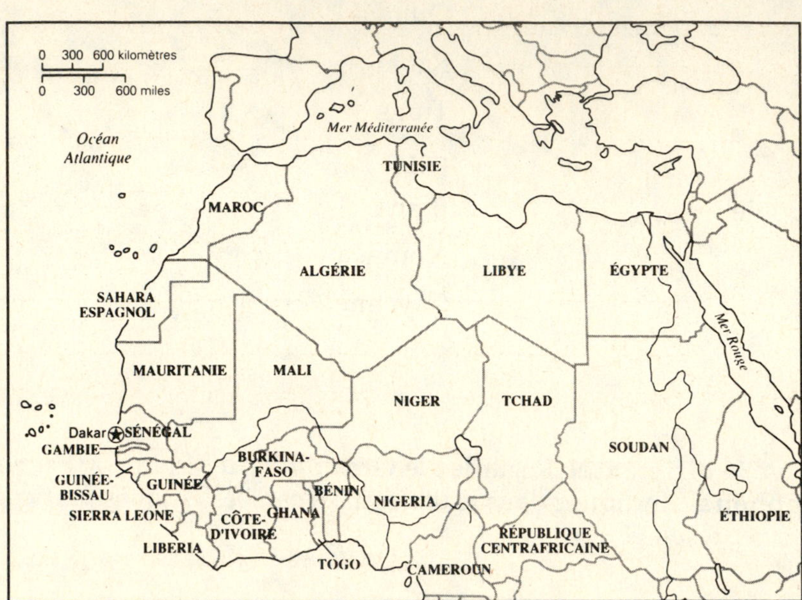

Classification	Pays d'Afrique du Nord et de l'Ouest	Francophones (en millions)	Population (en millions)	Pourcentage
________	l'Algérie	6,650	27,3	24,4
________	le Bénin	0,620	4,8	_____
________	le Burkina-Faso	0,410	10,0	_____
________	le Cameroun	1,460	12,8	_____
________	la République Centrafricaine	0,310	3,1	_____
________	la Côte d'Ivoire	2,650	13,4	_____
________	l'Égypte	0,205	58,3	_____
________	la Guinée	0,515	7,5	_____
________	la Libye	0,006	4,9	0,12
________	le Mali	0,610	8,9	_____
________	le Maroc	4,130	28,0	_____
________	la Mauritanie	0,108	2,1	_____
________	le Niger	0,315	8,5	_____
________	le Sénégal	0,760	7,9	_____
________	le Tchad	0,310	5,4	_____
________	le Togo	0,515	4,1	_____
________	la Tunisie	2,270	8,4	_____

NOM ______________________ DATE ______________________

M. L'Afrique francophone. Maintenant utilisez la carte de l'Afrique du Nord et de l'Ouest et les statistiques que vous avez trouvées pour répondre aux questions suivantes.

1. Quels sont les pays de l'Afrique qui sont les plus près de la France?

 ____

 ____

2. Quels sont les pays où plus de dix pour cent de la population parlent français?

 ____

 ____

3. Y a-t-il des pays où plus de vingt pour cent de la population parlent français? Si oui, indiquez lesquels. ______________________

 ____

4. Dans quelle partie de l'Afrique les pays les plus francophones se trouvent-ils?

 ____

5. Avez-vous jamais *(ever)* étudié l'histoire des Européens en Afrique? Pouvez-vous suggérer *(suggest)* pourquoi il y a une forte présence de la langue française en Afrique du Nord et en Afrique de l'Ouest? ______________________

 ____

 ____

SUPPLÉMENT

N. À vous maintenant! À la page suivante, vous trouverez le programme de la fête de la Musique pour Nogent-le-Rotrou. Lisez bien le programme et avec un(e) partenaire planifiez votre dimanche. Vous voulez consacrer toute la journée à la musique. D'abord, établissez vos préférences en musique. Puis, mettez-vous d'accord sur un emploi du temps. Ensuite, écrivez vos sélections.

EXPRESSIONS UTILES

Quel genre de musique aimes-tu?
Moi, je préfère...
As-tu envie *(Do you feel like)* **d'écouter...?**
Qu'est-ce que tu penses de la musique classique? du rock? du jazz? etc.
Est-ce que tu aimes...?
Et l'après-midi, qu'est-ce que tu préfères?
Qu'est-ce qu'on fait le soir?

Programme de la Fête de la Musique

1 ÉGLISE NOTRE-DAME
11 heures : Messe avec la participation de Jean-Louis SPRAUEL (violoncelle) et Josette CAUCHEFER-BLIN (orgue), professeurs à l'École Municipale de Musique.

2 KIOSQUE A MUSIQUE (place Winston-Churchill)
11 heures - 13 heures : Sons of Scotland

3 CAFÉ SAINT-POL - Scène ouverte aux musiciens
11 heures : Gérard DEBONO, Claude DUCHET et leurs élèves
16 heures : Duo Marie-Christine et Muriel ROUILLON
18 h 30 : Le Théâtre Buissonnier

4 LE THÉÂTRE BUISSONNIER
sera en ballade dans les rues de la ville avec des chansons sur la mer et les marins. Passage à **11 heures** au centre commercial des Gauchetières.

5 GRILL DE LA GARE - LA HULOTTE
A partir de 14 - 15 heures : The Nad, The Raid Dogs, Blues en Sol, K'Rolls Brothers, Alain CADIOU, Jean-Pierre MARAIS,... avec une scène ouverte toutes les demi-heures.

6 BAR "LE RAIL"
15 heures : Les élèves du Centre d'Expression Musicale
15 h 30 : Rodrigue JANOIS

7 HARMONIE MUNICIPALE (remorque itinérante)
15 heures : Kiosque à musique - Rond Point Rémi-Belleau
15 h 20 : La Charmille
15 h 50 : Place Winston Churchill
16 h 30 : Centre Commercial des Gauchetières
17 heures : Place de la Gare

8 LES PERCHERONS
Ballade hippomobile au travers de la ville à partir de **15 heures**
Lieux de passage :
Place Winston Churchill
La Charmille
Les Gauchetières
Place de la Gare (retrouvailles avec le Théâtre Buis sonnier entre **17 h 30** et **18 h 30**)
Place Saint-Pol entre **21 heures** et **23 heures**

9 ABBAYE SAINT-DENIS
15 h 30 : Chorale Syrinx de Brunelles - Flûte et orgue

10 ÉGLISE SAINT-JEAN BAPTISTE - Les Gauchetières
15 h 30 : Les Majorettes de l'Avenir et les Étoiles Nogentaises
Départ du défilé devant la salle des sports Jean-Macé à **14 h 30** et spectacle devant l'église
20 h 30 - 21 h 30 : Les Ménestrels du Perche

11 THÉÂTRE DE VERDURE (en cas de pluie : salle polyvalente)
Scène ouverte à tous les musiciens
16 heures : Atelier de la Danse
17 h 30 : Danse de l'ASJ

12 ÉCOLE MUNICIPALE DE MUSIQUE
16 h 30 : Josette CAUCHEFER-BLIN et ses élèves avec le concours de Rhoda SCOTT et Sophie-Véronique CHOPLIN-CAUCHEFER en présence d'anciens élèves
Participation de Gérard DEBONO, Claude DUCHET et ses élèves

13 MAISON DE RETRAITE DES TEMPS BLEUS
17 heures : Les Ménestrels du Perche

14 PUB SAINT-JEAN
A partir de 17 heures : Scène ouverte à tous les musiciens
21 heures : Rock Punk "Suspense"

15 SALLE SIMONE-SIGNORET
18 heures - 18 h 30 : Nogent-Accordéon
18 h 30 - 19 h 30 : Les Étoiles du Perche

16 RIVER CAFÉ
20 heures : Sons of Scotland, K'Rolls Brothers, Les Incognitos,...

17 PUB SAINTE-ANNE
20 heures : "Les Quasars" Rock des années 70

18 CINÉMA LE REX
20 heures - 21 heures : Mlle ROMET et ses élèves

19 LE CENTRE D'EXPRESSION MUSICALE ET SES ÉLÈVES
seront dans différents endroits de la ville

20 SAMEDI 20 JUIN - CAFÉ "LA RENAISSANCE"
21 heures : Les élèves du Centre d'Expression Musicale

EMPLOI DU TEMPS—dimanche 21 juin

matin: ____________________

____

après-midi: ____________________

____

soir: ____________________

____

NE RESTEZ PAS SEULEMENT SPECTATEUR.
PRENEZ VOTRE INSTRUMENT!

ANSWER KEYS

WORKBOOK ANSWER KEY

Unité 1

LEÇON 1

1. Au club international
1. André, Philippe
2. Thérèse, Suzanne
3. Pierre, Jacques
4. Hélène, Jérôme
5. Luc, Jean-Louis
6. Monique, Cécile
7. Véronique, Brigitte
8. Henri, Antoine

2. Dans le foyer de la cité universitaire
(Some suggested answers)
1. Oui, ça va bien.
2. Comme ci, comme ça.
3. Je m'appelle Jean-Charles.
4. À demain!
5. Enchanté.
6. Salut! Bonjour!
7. À bientôt!

3. Rencontres (Answers will vary.)

Communication
(Some suggested answers)
1. Au revoir, Jean-Marc.
2. À bientôt, Monique!
3. Ça va?
4. Comment vous appelez-vous? (Comment t'appelles-tu?)
5. Je m'appelle Éric.
6. Maman, je te présente Élise.
7. Comme ci, comme ça.

LEÇON 2

1. Mon quartier (Answers will vary.)

2. Rencontres
(Some suggested answers)
1. Comment vas-tu?
2. De rien.
3. Merci bien.
4. Je vais bien, merci. Et vous?
5. Ça va?
   Ça va pas mal.

3. Ça va?
(Some suggested answers)
1. Comme ci, comme ça.
2. Ça va bien.
3. Ça va mal.
4. Ça va très bien.
5. Ça va pas mal.

4. Au café (Answers will vary.)

5. Présentations
1. Nicolas Duval
2. Daniel Renard
3. Élisabeth Aveline
4. Michèle Camus
5. Louis Beaufort
6. Bruno Maréchal
7. Bernard Colas
8. Denise Martinot
9. Rémi Andrieux
10. Charles Malec

6. Les accents
1. André
2. Félix
3. Michèle
4. Marlène
5. Joël
6. François
7. Raphaël

Communication
(Some suggested answers)
1. Bonjour, Monsieur! Comment allez-vous?
2. Salut, Corinne! Ça va?
3. Merci. / Merci bien!
4. Un café, s'il vous plaît.
5. De rien.

LEÇON 3

1. **Qui est-ce?**
   1. Voilà Tuyen, une copine vietnamienne.
   2. Voilà Roger, un copain suisse.
   3. Voici France, une copine québécoise.
   4. Voici Léopold, un poète sénégalais.
   5. Voilà Ricardo, un architecte mexicain.
   6. Voici Raïssa, une amie marocaine.

2. **Mais non!**
   1. Non, elle est française.
   2. Non, il est anglais.
   3. Non, il est martiniquais.
   4. Non, elle est mexicaine.
   5. Non, il est suisse.
   6. Non, il est canadien.
   7. Non, elle est américaine.

3. **Une rue en ville**
   1. Voici (Voilà) l'hôpital.
   2. Voici (Voilà) la discothèque.
   3. Voici (Voilà) la pharmacie.
   4. Voici (Voilà) le garage.
   5. Voici (Voilà) le cinéma.
   6. Voici (Voilà) le parc.

4. **À Paris**
   1. The doctor is phoning the hospital.
   2. Thomas is dining at the restaurant.
   3. Daniel is inviting Monica to the movies.
   4. The tourists visit the museum.
   5. The taxi is arriving at the airport.
   6. The bus passes along Avenue Victor-Hugo.

5. **Préférences** (Answers will vary.)

Communication

(Some suggested answers)
1. Qui est-ce?
2. C'est Mme Leblanc.
3. Voici Notre-Dame.
4. Voilà le musée d'Orsay.
5. Je déteste les spaghetti et je préfère la salade.
6. J'aime le cinéma et j'adore danser.
7. Hassan, je te présente mon ami Olivier.

Unité 2

LEÇON 4

1. **Au travail**
   1. Ils travaillent
   2. Vous travaillez
   3. Tu travailles
   4. Nous travaillons
   5. Ils travaillent
   6. Il travaille
   7. Je travaille
   8. Elles travaillent

2. **Activités**
   1. jouer; jouons
   2. regarder; regardent
   3. dîner; dînez
   4. téléphoner; téléphones
   5. travailler; travaille
   6. visiter; visitent

3. **Dialogues**
   1. parlez / ne parlons pas anglais.
   2. jouent / ne jouent pas au tennis.
   3. étudiez / n'étudions pas la géographie.
   4. écoute / n'écoute pas la radio.
   5. aiment / n'aiment pas Paul.
   6. téléphones / ne téléphone pas à Caroline.

4. **Les maths**
   1. neuf
   2. douze
   3. onze
   4. six
   5. sept
   6. cinq
   7. quatre
   8. six

5. **Ponctualité**
   1. cinq heures
   2. une heure
   3. onze heures
   4. midi
   5. minuit
   6. neuf heures

Communication
1. Oui, je parle anglais. / Non, je ne parle pas anglais.
2. Oui, je parle italien. / Non, je ne parle pas italien.
3. Oui, j'habite à San Francisco. / Non, je n'habite pas à San Francisco.

4. Oui, je regarde la télé française. / Non, je ne regarde pas la télé française.
5. Oui, je joue au bridge. / Non, je ne joue pas au bridge.
6. Oui, j'étudie la biologie. / Non, je n'étudie pas la biologie.
7. Oui, j'aime Paris. / Non, je n'aime pas Paris.

LEÇON 5

1. Où?

1. Nous sommes à Montréal.
2. Vous êtes à Genève.
3. Ils sont à Tours.
4. Elle est à Paris.
5. Je suis à Dakar.
6. Tu es à Québec.

2. Préférences

1. Vous aimez voyager.
2. Tu n'aimes pas voyager.
3. J'aime nager.
4. Elle n'aime pas téléphoner.
5. Nous aimons danser.
6. Ils n'aiment pas étudier.
7. Vous n'aimez pas écouter la radio.

3. Rencontres

1. Oui, je suis en cours maintenant. / Non, je ne suis pas en cours maintenant.
2. Oui, j'étudie beaucoup. / Non, je n'étudie pas beaucoup.
3. Oui, je voyage souvent. / Non, je ne voyage pas souvent.
4. Oui, je nage. / Non, je ne nage pas.
5. Oui, je nage bien. / Non, je ne nage pas bien.
6. Oui, je chante bien. / Non, je ne chante pas bien.
7. Oui, j'aime voyager. / Non, je n'aime pas voyager.
8. Oui, j'aime danser. / Non, je n'aime pas danser.

4. Questions

1. Est-ce que Robert nage / nage souvent
2. Est-ce que tu chantes / ne chante pas bien
3. Est-ce que Paul et André étudient / étudient beaucoup
4. Est-ce que vous regardez / ne regardons pas souvent la télévision

5. Les nombres

1. 28	7. 92
2. 31	8. 66
3. 52	9. 43
4. 85	10. 14
5. 15	11. 80
6. 71	12. 57

6. À quelle heure?

1. neuf heures moins dix
2. neuf heures dix
3. sept heures moins vingt
4. huit heures et quart
5. deux heures et demie
6. cinq heures moins le quart

Communication

1. Est-ce que vous nagez souvent?
2. Est-ce que tu veux jouer au tennis?
3. Est-ce que vous voulez jouer?
4. Est-ce que tu peux téléphoner à François?
5. Je ne peux pas dîner avec vous.
6. Je dois étudier.

LEÇON 6

1. Quand on est étudiant

1. Oui, on regarde souvent la télé. / Non, on ne regarde pas souvent la télé.
2. Oui, on dîne souvent au restaurant. / Non, on ne dîne pas souvent au restaurant.
3. Oui, on est idéaliste. / Non, on n'est pas idéaliste.
4. Oui, on est toujours d'accord avec les professeurs. / Non, on n'est pas toujours d'accord avec les professeurs.

2. Rencontres

(Answers will vary.)

3. Une interview

1. Où est-ce que tu étudies?
2. Qu'est-ce que tu étudies?
3. Avec qui est-ce que tu voyages?
4. Comment est-ce que tu voyages?
5. Quand est-ce que tu rentres au Canada?

6. Pourquoi est-ce que tu visites les États-Unis?

4. **Vraiment?**
   1. Elle est avec lui?
   2. Elle habite avec elles?
   3. Il étudie avec elle?
   4. Elle travaille pour lui?
   5. Elle est avec eux?
   6. Il voyage avec eux?

5. **Réciprocité**
   1. Ils étudient avec moi.
   2. Elle danse avec toi.
   3. Il travaille pour vous.
   4. Nous étudions avec eux.
   5. Tu rentres avec elles.
   6. Elles habitent avec nous.

6. **Quand?**
   1. Nous arrivons à Genève le deux septembre.
   2. Vous rentrez à Québec le quinze février.
   3. Jean-Pierre invite Suzanne le vingt et un août.
   4. Je dîne au restaurant le premier juin.

Communication

1. Est-ce que tu parles français? / Est-ce qu'on parle français
2. Qu'est-ce que tu étudies? / Est-ce qu'on étudie beaucoup
3. Qu'est-ce que tu écoutes? / Est-ce que je peux écouter la radio avec toi?
4. À quelle heure est-ce que tu dînes? / Est-ce que tu veux dîner avec moi demain?

Unité 3

LEÇON 7

1. ***Être* et *avoir***

1. est / a	4. sommes / avons
2. êtes / avez	5. sont / ont
3. suis / ai	6. es/ as

2. **Présentations**
   1. Philippe est un cousin.
   2. Louise est une cousine.
   3. Jacqueline est une amie.
   4. Nicolas et Paul sont des copains.
   5. Thomas et Denis sont des amis.
   6. Anne et Véronique sont des copines.

3. **Est-ce que ça marche?**
   1. Voici deux motos. Elles marchent.
   2. Voici une montre. Elle ne marche pas.
   3. Voici deux stylos. Ils ne marchent pas.
   4. Voici une voiture. Elle marche.

4. **On ne peut pas tout avoir.**
   1. Marie a une machine à écrire, mais elle n'a pas d'ordinateur.
   2. Jean-Jacques a un VTT, mais il n'a pas de voiture.
   3. Nous avons une chaîne stéréo, mais nous n'avons pas de disques.
   4. Louise et Marc ont un caméscope, mais ils n'ont pas de magnétophone.
   5. J'ai une moto, mais je n'ai pas de vélomoteur.
   6. Tu as un ordinateur, mais tu n'as pas d'imprimante.

5. **La chambre de Caroline**
   1. Non, il n'y a pas de téléviseur.
   2. Non, il n'y a pas de sac à dos.
   3. Non, il n'y a pas de compact disques.
   4. Oui, il y a un appareil-photo.
   5. Non, il n'y a pas d'ordinateur.
   6. Non, il n'y a pas de cassettes.

6. **Expression personnelle**
   (Answers will vary.)

Communication

(Answers will vary.)

LEÇON 8

1. **Shopping**
   1. Regarde l'appareil-photo.
   2. Regarde la radio.
   3. Regarde les montres.
   4. Regarde les livres.
   5. Regarde le stylo.

2. **Mes amis**
   1. Il (n')est (pas) blond.
      Elle (n')est (pas) blonde.
   2. Il (n')est (pas) grand.
      Elle (n')est (pas) grande.

3. Il (n')est (pas) optimiste.
   Elle (n')est (pas) optimiste.
4. Il (n')est (pas) indépendant.
   Elle (n')est (pas) indépendante.
5. Il (n')est (pas) réservé.
   Elle (n)est (pas) réservée.
6. Il (n')est (pas) égoïste.
   Elle (n')est (pas) égoïste.
7. Il (n')est (pas) poli.
   Elle (n')est (pas) polie.

3. Non!
1. ne sont pas petits. Ils sont grands.
2. ne sont pas mariées. Elles sont célibataires.
3. n'est pas sympathique. Il est désagréable.
4. n'est pas heureuse. Elle est triste.

4. Le tour du monde
1. une minichaîne japonaise
2. une guitare espagnole
3. des montres suisses
4. des disques allemands
5. un vélo anglais
6. des CD français

5. Une question de personnalité
1. Paul est amusant. Il a des amies amusantes.
2. Annie est petite. Elle a une petite auto.
3. Sylvie et Catherine sont françaises. Elles ont une voiture française.
4. Pauline est grande. Elle a un grand appartement.
5. Mme Lenoir est compétente. Elle a un assistant compétent.
6. Le professeur est brillant. Il a des étudiants brillants.

6. Descriptions
1. Il est / C'est / Il est
2. C'est / Elle est / C'est
3. C'est / C'est / Elle est
4. Il est / C'est / Il est

Communication

A. Vos amis
(Answers will vary.)

B. Vos possessions
(Answers will vary.)

LEÇON 9

1. Généralisations
1. Les étudiants (ne) respectent (pas) les professeurs.
2. Les étudiants américains (n')aiment (pas) le cinéma.
3. Les Américains (ne) détestent (pas) la violence.
4. Les personnes indépendantes (ne) sont (pas) pour l'autorité.

2. Qu'est-ce qu'ils font?
1. Je reste à l'université.
2. On parle du match de tennis.
3. Vous jouez du piano.
4. Tu téléphones à l'étudiante canadienne.
5. Le président parle aux journalistes.
6. Vous rentrez des magasins.

3. Le verbe exact
1. sommes / avons / allons
2. a / va /est
3. sont / vont / ont
4. êtes / Avez / Allez

4. Activités
1. allons à la bibliothèque. Nous allons étudier.
2. vas au stade. Tu vas jouer au football.
3. va au bureau. Elle va travailler.
4. allez à la piscine. Vous allez nager.
5. vais à l'aéroport. Je vais voyager.
6. vont au musée. Ils vont regarder des tableaux.

5. Samedi soir
1. Je reste chez moi.
2. Tu restes chez toi.
3. Nous ne restons pas chez nous.
4. Ils restent chez eux.
5. Il ne reste pas chez lui.

6. Questions
1. téléphone-t-elle
2. travaillent-ils
3. voyage-t-elle
4. est-il au restaurant
5. jouent-elles au tennis
6. va-t-on à la piscine

Communication

1. Aimes-tu le sport?
2. Joues-tu aux échecs?
3. Joues-tu de la guitare?
4. Vas-tu souvent au cinéma?
5. Vas-tu aller au théâtre samedi?
6. Veux-tu aller au restaurant avec moi dimanche?

Unité 4

LEÇON 10

1. Combien?

1. deux mille trois cents
2. trois mille deux cents
3. cinq mille quatre cents
4. trente mille
5. deux cent mille

2. Activités

1. envoyons
2. nettoie
3. paient
4. emploie
5. payez
6. nettoie
7. emploies
8. paie

3. À qui est-ce?

1. est à Éric
2. est à nous
3. est à Annette
4. est à vous
5. est à moi
6. est à toi
7. sont aux étudiants

4. Emprunts

1. le vélo de Philippe.
2. la machine à écrire de Sylvie.
3. la mobylette d'Élisabeth.
4. les livres du professeur.
5. les cassettes des étudiants anglais.
6. l'ordinateur des voisins.
7. le budget du copain de Janine.

5. Les relations familiales

1. Robert est le fils d'Alain Vasseur.
2. Jacques Vasseur est le père d'Éliane.
3. Monique Vasseur est la tante de Suzanne.
4. Robert est le frère de Suzanne.
5. Suzanne est la sœur de Robert.
6. Éliane est la cousine de Suzanne.
7. Robert est le cousin d'Éliane.
8. Robert et Suzanne sont les petits-enfants de M. Dumas.
9. Mme Dumas est la femme de M. Dumas.
10. Jacques Vasseur est le mari de Monique Vasseur.

6. À l'aéroport

1. son / son
2. son / son / son
3. son / sa
4. ses / son
5. leurs / leur
6. leurs / leur
7. ton / les
8. nos / notre
9. vos / votre

Communication

(Answers will vary.)

LEÇON 11

1. Quels vêtements?

(Answers will vary.)

2. Activités

1. achètent
2. amènes
3. célèbrent
4. possède
5. espérons
6. répète
7. préfère

3. La publicité

1. Ces chaussures sont jolies.
2. Ce livre est intéressant.
3. Cet anorak est bon marché.
4. Ces disques sont bons.
5. Cet appareil-photo est excellent.
6. Cette veste est élégante.
7. Ces raquettes de tennis sont chères.

4. Dialogues

1. Quelles chaussures / J'achète ces chaussures-ci.
2. Quel manteau / Elle va acheter ce manteau-ci.
3. Quelle cravate / Il va porter cette cravate-ci.
4. Quelles chaussettes / Nous préférons ces chaussettes-ci.

5. Comparaisons

1. M. Simon est moins riche que Mme Dumas.
2. La Ferrari est plus rapide que l'Alfa Roméo.
3. L'imperméable est aussi cher que le costume.

4. En français, Robert est meilleur que Paul.
5. Jacqueline est aussi jeune que sa cousine.
6. Les Yankees sont meilleurs que les Red Sox.

6. À votre avis
(Answers will vary.)

Communication
(Answers will vary.)

LEÇON 12

1. Attention!
1. Nous faisons attention.
2. Tu ne fais pas attention.
3. Vous faites attention.
4. Ils ne font pas attention.
5. Je fais attention.
6. Elle ne fait pas attention.

2. Qu'est-ce qu'ils font?
1. Nous faisons le ménage.
2. Ils font leurs devoirs.
3. Je fais la vaisselle.
4. Vous faites des économies.
5. Tu fais une promenade.
6. Il fait un voyage.

3. Où est-ce?
1. devant l'
2. entre le
3. à gauche du
4. derrière la
5. à droite du
6. à gauche de l'

4. Descriptions
1. nouvel / nouvelle
2. vieux / vieux / vieilles
3. belle / beau
4. belle / belles
5. nouvelle / nouveaux / nouveau
6. vieux / vieil

5. Les Oscars (Answers will vary.)
1. Le comédien le plus drôle est...
2. Le professeur le plus intéressant est...
3. Le meilleur film est...
4. La ville la plus jolie est...
5. Les voitures les plus confortables sont...
6. Le meilleur restaurant est...

6. Quel temps fait-il?
(Answers will vary.)
1. Il fait mauvais. Il pleut. Il fait du vent.
2. Il fait beau. Il fait chaud. Il fait ... degrés.
3. Il neige. Il fait froid. Demain, il ne va pas neiger.

Communication
(Answers will vary.)

Unité 5

LEÇON 13

1. Pourquoi?
1. a chaud
2. as soif
3. a dix-huit ans
4. ai sommeil
5. avez faim
6. a tort
7. ai froid

2. Activités
1. choisissent
2. réussissez
3. finissent
4. réfléchissez
5. grossit
6. maigris

3. D'autres activités
1. attendent
2. rend
3. perdez
4. vend
5. entend
6. réponds
7. rendent

4. Des conseils
1. Va
2. Nettoie
3. Fais
4. Finis
5. Réponds
6. Sois
7. Aie
8. Choisis

5. Le club de théâtre
1. Restez
2. Faites
3. Réfléchissez
4. Répétez
5. Répondez
6. Ne perdez pas
7. Ne soyez pas
8. N'ayez pas

Communication
A. Le week-end
(Answers will vary.)
B. Les économies
(Answers will vary.)

LEÇON 14

1. Le week-end

1. avons regardé / a regardé
2. avez nagé / ai nagé
3. a étudié / as étudié
4. ont dîné / avez dîné
5. ont joué / a joué

2. Oui ou non?

1. Nous avons visité Paris. Nous avons rendu visite à nos amis français.
2. Philippe a mangé beaucoup de spaghetti. Il n'a pas maigri.
3. Tu as maigri. Tu n'as pas grossi.
4. J'ai perdu patience. Je n'ai pas attendu mes amis.
5. Vous avez gagné le match. Vous n'avez pas perdu.
6. Hélène et Suzanne ont étudié. Elles n'ont pas rendu visite à leur oncle.

3. En vacances

1. Est-ce que ces étudiants ont travaillé?
2. Est-ce que vous avez rendu visite à vos grands-parents?
3. Est-ce que M. Lamblet a maigri?
4. Est-ce que tu as voyagé en train?

4. Précisions

1. Avec qui ont-ils dîné au restaurant?
2. Dans quel magasin a-t-elle acheté une robe?
3. À qui a-t-il vendu sa mobylette?
4. Où ont-elles nagé?
5. Quand ont-ils rendu les livres?

5. Le mois dernier

1. Oui, j'ai été malade. / Non, je n'ai pas été malade.
2. Oui, j'ai été invité(e) chez des amis. / Non, je n'ai pas été invité(e) chez des amis.
3. Oui, j'ai eu un accident. / Non, je n'ai pas eu d'accident.
4. Oui, j'ai eu une aventure extraordinaire. / Non, je n'ai pas eu d'aventure extraordinaire.
5. Oui, j'ai fait des économies. /Non, je n'ai pas fait d'économies.
6. Oui, j'ai fait une promenade à bicyclette. / Non, je n'ai pas fait de promenade à bicyclette.

6. Zut alors!

1. n'avons pas gagné
2. n'ai pas répondu
3. a fait
4. n'ont pas été
5. a eu

Communication

(Answers will vary.)

LEÇON 15

1. Activités

1. partons
2. dors
3. sentez
4. sortent
5. pars
6. sens
7. dort

2. Hier soir

1. Nous sommes resté(e)s chez nous.
2. Elle n'est pas restée chez elle.
3. Je suis resté(e) chez moi.
4. Ils sont restés chez eux.
5. Tu n'es pas resté(e) chez toi.
6. Elles ne sont pas restées chez elles.
7. Il est resté chez lui.
8. Vous n'êtes pas resté(e)(s) chez vous.

3. Questions et réponses

1. sont nés
2. sont arrivés
3. est restée
4. est tombée
5. est mort
6. sont montés
7. sont descendus
8. est partie
9. sont sorties
10. sont entrés

4. En vacances

1. est allée / a visité
2. a fait / est sorti
3. ont eu / sont restés
4. sommes descendus / avons voyagé
5. as quitté / est parti(e)

5. **Dates de naissance**
(Answers will vary.)

6. **Quand?** (Answers will vary.)
   1. J'ai nagé il y a...
   2. Je suis allé(e) à la bibliothèque il y a...
   3. J'ai rendu visite à mes amis il y a...
   4. J'ai envoyé une lettre à mes grands-parents il y a...
   5. J'ai nettoyé ma chambre il y a...

7. **La belle vie**
   1. j'ai peu étudié.
   2. j'ai beaucoup nagé.
   3. je suis souvent allé au cinéma.
   4. j'ai trop dormi.
   5. j'ai bien joué au tennis.
   6. j'ai très souvent voyagé.
   7. je suis rarement resté chez moi.
   8. j'ai vraiment aimé mon voyage.

Communication
(Answers will vary.)

Unité 6

LEÇON 16

1. **Activités**
   1. devenons
   2. reviens
   3. venez
   4. devient
   5. sont venus
   6. est devenue
   7. est revenu
   8. sont devenues

2. **D'où viennent-ils?**
(Answers will vary.)
   1. reviennent du café. Elles viennent de...
   2. reviens d'un magasin de vêtements. Tu viens de...
   3. reviennent de la bibliothèque. Ils viennent de...
   4. revenons de la discothèque. Nous venons de...

3. **Un peu de géographie?**
   1. le Vietnam et le Japon
   2. L'Algérie, le Maroc et le Sénégal
   3. Le Canada, les États-Unis et le Venezuela
   4. L'Allemagne, la France et le Luxembourg

4. **Quel pays?**
   1. passe l'été aux États-Unis.
   2. rentre de Chine.
   3. étudie en Suisse.
   4. reviennent du Brésil.
   5. arrivons d'Espagne.

5. **Depuis combien de temps?**
   1. Tu téléphones depuis quarante-cinq minutes.
   2. Vous êtes à la bibliothèque depuis trois heures.
   3. J'ai la grippe depuis cinq jours.
   4. Nous étudions le français depuis quatre mois.
   5. M. Rimbaud habite à Paris depuis dix ans.

6. **Depuis quand?**
(Answers will vary.)

Communication
(Answers will vary.)

LEÇON 17

1. **Activités**
   1. apprend / apprennent
   2. prenez / prenons
   3. comprends / comprends
   4. a appris / ai appris
   5. avez compris / avons compris
   6. as pris / ai pris

2. **Le menu**
(Answers will vary.)

3. **Au régime**
   1. Vous prenez de la viande.
   2. Tu prends du poisson.
   3. Anne et Denise ne prennent pas de fromage.
   4. Mme Mirault prend de la salade.
   5. Nous ne prenons pas de tarte.
   6. Je ne prends pas de glace.

4. **À la fête**
Buvez
bois
boit / boivent
buvons

5. Qu'est-ce qu'ils font?

1. faisons du camping
2. font des maths
3. faites de la gymnastique
4. font du français
5. fais du théâtre
6. fait de l'espagnol

6. Chez le médecin

1. Oui, faites du ski.
2. Non, ne buvez pas de bière!
3. Oui, buvez de l'eau minérale.
4. Non, ne mangez pas de glace!
5. Oui, mangez du yaourt.
6. Non, ne prenez pas de crème avec le café!
7. Oui, prenez du thé.
8. Non, ne mangez pas de pâtes.

Communication

(Answers will vary.)

LEÇON 18

1. Les vêtements (Answers will vary.)

1. je mets...
2. nous mettons...
3. Ils mettent...
4. Tu mets...
5. Il a mis...
6. Vous avez mis...

2. Préférences personnelles

1. J'aime le riz. Je mange souvent du riz. / Je n'aime pas le riz. Je ne mange pas (souvent) de riz.
2. J'aime la bière. Je bois souvent de la bière. / Je n'aime pas la bière. Je ne bois pas (souvent) de bière.
3. J'aime le vin. J'achète souvent du vin. / Je n'aime pas le vin. Je n'achète pas (souvent) de vin.
4. J'aime la glace. Je prends souvent de la glace. / Je n'aime pas la glace. Je ne prends pas (souvent) de glace.
5. J'aime le pain. Je mange souvent du pain. / Je n'aime pas le pain. Je ne mange pas (souvent) de pain.
6. J'aime l'eau minérale. Je commande souvent de l'eau minérale. / Je n'aime pas l'eau minérale. Je ne commande pas (souvent) d'eau minérale.

3. Au restaurant français

1. du / de la
2. le / un
3. le / de la
4. la / le
5. le / une
6. de la / la
7. Le / du
8. une / une

4. À l'université

1. Oui, j'étudie beaucoup. / Non, je n'étudie pas beaucoup.
2. Oui, j'ai beaucoup d'examens. / Non, je n'ai pas beaucoup d'examens.
3. Oui, il y a beaucoup d'étudiants français à mon université. / Non, il n'y a pas beaucoup d'étudiants français à mon université.
4. Oui, je voyage beaucoup. / Non, je ne voyage pas beaucoup.
5. Oui, les étudiants ont beaucoup de vacances. / Non, les étudiants n'ont pas beaucoup de vacances.
6. Oui, je fais beaucoup de jogging. / Non, je ne fais pas beaucoup de jogging.

5. Des plaintes!

1. Je fume trop.
2. Je ne maigris pas assez.
3. Je n'ai pas assez de loisirs.
4. Je dépense trop d'argent.
5. Je ne fais pas assez d'économies.
6. Je ne gagne pas assez d'argent.

6. Comparaisons

1. Roland fait plus de sport qu'Henri.
2. M. Martin gagne autant d'argent que son frère.
3. Marthe achète plus de vêtements que Sylvie.
4. Philippe boit moins d'eau minérale que Charles.

Communication

(Answers will vary.)

Unité 7

LEÇON 19

1. Oui ou non?

1. suivez
2. ne suivons pas

3. suit
4. ne suivent pas
5. ne suis pas
6. suis
7. n'avez pas suivi
8. ont suivi

2. **Désirs et possibilités**
   1. veux / ne peux pas
   2. veulent / peuvent
   3. veut / ne peut pas
   4. veux / peux
   5. voulez / ne pouvez pas
   6. voulons / pouvons

3. **Pour réussir à l'examen**
   1. dois
   2. ne dois pas
   3. devons
   4. devez
   5. doit
   6. doivent

4. **Non!**
   1. Il ne faut pas avoir peur.
   2. Il ne faut pas être impatient(e).
   3. Il ne faut pas perdre son temps.
   4. Il ne faut pas grossir.
   5. Il ne faut pas rater ses examens.

5. **Qu'est-ce qu'il faut faire?**
   (Answers will vary.)

6. **Une classe de français très difficile**
   1. Tout le monde
   2. Chaque
   3. de nombreux
   4. un autre
   5. plusieurs
   6. toutes les

Communication
(Answers will vary.)

LEÇON 20

1. **Les spectacles**
   1. voyons
   2. voient
   3. voyez
   4. vois
   5. vois
   6. voit
   7. a vu
   8. avons vu

2. **L'intrus**
   1. d
   2. b
   3. b
   4. c
   5. b

3. **Questions personnelles**
   1. Oui, je le connais. / Non, je ne le connais pas.
   2. Oui, je les connais. / Non, je ne les connais pas.
   3. Oui, ils les connaissent. / Non, ils ne les connaissent pas.
   4. Oui, je les étudie. / Non, je ne les étudie pas.
   5. Oui, je la regarde souvent. / Non, je ne la regarde pas souvent.
   6. Oui, je les regarde. / Non, je ne les regarde pas.
   7. Oui, je les aide. / Non, je ne les aide pas.
   8. Oui, je l'achète. / Non, je ne l'achète pas.
   9. Oui, je la nettoie souvent. / Non, je ne la nettoie pas souvent.

4. **Relations personnelles**
   (Answers will vary.)

5. **Oui ou non?**
   1. Il la trouve intéressante.
   2. Nous les connaissons bien.
   3. Il ne les aide pas.
   4. Ils l'écoutent.
   5. Il ne l'oublie pas.
   6. Je ne les comprends pas.

6. **Ce soir**
   1. Oui, je vais l'inviter. / Non, je ne vais pas l'inviter.
   2. Oui, je vais l'acheter. / Non, je ne vais pas l'acheter.
   3. Oui, je vais la regarder. / Non, je ne vais pas la regarder.
   4. Oui, je veux les écouter. / Non, je ne veux pas les écouter.
   5. Oui, je dois les faire. Non, je ne dois pas les faire.
   6. Oui, je dois la nettoyer. / Non, je ne dois pas la nettoyer.

7. **Le cancre**
   1. Oui, il l'a invitée.
   2. Non, il ne les a pas finis.
   3. Oui, il les a écoutées.
   4. Non, il ne l'a pas apprise.
   5. Oui, il l'a mise.
   6. Non, il ne l'a pas étudiée.

Communication
(Answers will vary.)

LEÇON 21

1. **À la bibliothèque**
   1. écris / lisent
   2. écrivons / lis
   3. écrivez / lisons

4. écrivent / lisent
5. as écrit / avez lu

2. **Des excuses**
   1. Je dis que je suis malade.
   2. Nous disons que nous avons une entrevue professionnelle.
   3. Vous dites que vous devez aller chez le dentiste.
   4. Henri dit qu'il doit aider ses parents.
   5. Mes amis disent qu'ils vont chez le médecin.
   6. Tu dis que tu as la grippe.

3. **Rapports personnels**
   1. Oui, je lui téléphone souvent. / Non, je ne lui téléphone pas souvent.
   2. Oui, je lui demande des conseils. / Non, je ne lui demande pas de conseils.
   3. Oui, je leur dis toujours la vérité. / Non, je ne leur dis pas toujours la vérité.
   4. Oui, je lui parle de mes problèmes. / Non, je ne lui parle pas de mes problèmes.
   5. Oui, je leur écris pendant les vacances. / Non, je ne leur écris pas pendant les vacances.

4. **Bons et mauvais rapports**
   1. la / lui
   2. lui / lui
   3. lui / lui
   4. leur / leur
   5. leur / leur
   6. les / les

5. **Merci!**
   1. nous prêtent
   2. vous aide
   3. me montrent
   4. te rendons visite
   5. m'ont invité(e)
   6. t'ai prêté
   7. nous a répondu
   8. lui ai envoyé

6. **Au bureau de tourisme**
   1. aidez-la!
   2. ne lui téléphonez pas!
   3. ne le prêtez pas!
   4. répondez-leur!
   5. écrivez-lui!
   6. ne l'envoyez pas!

7. **Oui et non**
   1. Ne me téléphone pas après dix heures. Téléphone-moi demain matin.
   2. Ne nous sers pas de viande. Sers-nous des légumes.
   3. Rends-moi visite lundi. Ne me rends pas visite samedi.
   4. Ne nous donne pas de conseils. Donne-nous 200 francs.

Communication
(Answers will vary.)

Unité 8

LEÇON 22

1. **Leurs talents**
   1. Elle sait danser.
   2. Nous savons parler français.
   3. Je ne sais pas jouer au bridge.
   4. Tu ne sais pas nager.
   5. Ils savent jouer du piano.
   6. Vous savez bien faire la cuisine.

2. **Dans notre quartier**
   1. connais / connais
   2. connais / sais
   3. connaissons / savons
   4. savez / savez
   5. connaissent / savent

3. **Opinions personnelles**
   1. Boston et San Francisco sont des villes qui (ne) sont (pas) très agréables.
   2. Les Américains sont des gens qui (ne) sont (pas) idéalistes.
   3. Le président est un homme qui (n')a (pas) beaucoup d'idées.
   4. Les professeurs sont des gens qui (ne) gagnent (pas) bien leur vie.
   5. Les Renault sont des voitures qui (ne) consomment (pas) beaucoup d'essence.

4. **Oui ou non?** (Answers will vary.)
   1. Oui, c'est une ville que je connais bien. / Non, c'est une ville que je ne connais pas bien.
   2. Oui, c'est un homme que j'admire beaucoup. / Non, c'est un homme que je n'admire pas beaucoup.

3. Oui, ce sont des personnes que je respecte beaucoup. / Non, ce sont des personnes que je ne respecte pas beaucoup.
4. Oui, c'est un magazine que je lis souvent. / Non, c'est un magazine que je ne lis pas souvent.
5. Oui, c'est une langue que je parle bien. / Non, c'est une langue que je ne parle pas bien.
6. Oui, ce sont des gens que j'invite souvent. / Non, ce sont des gens que je n'invite pas souvent.

5. *Qui* ou *que?*

1. qui a téléphoné?
   que tu attends?
   qui t'a prêté sa voiture?
   qui passe dans la rue?
   que tu invites chez toi?
2. qui sont amusants?
   qui vont à l'université avec vous?
   que vous trouvez sympathiques?
   qui vous invitent?
   que vous n'aimez pas?
3. que j'ai acheté?
   que tu as lu?
   qui parle de l'accident?
   qui montre des photos extraordinaires?
   que vous avez trouvé sur la table?
4. qui viennent de France.
   que j'écoute souvent.
   que mes parents détestent.
   qui coûtent dix francs.
   qui sont extraordinaires.

6. À Paris

1. qui / que
2. qui / qu'
3. qui / qui
4. qu' / que

7. C'est évident!

1. Je ne bois rien.
2. Nous n'invitons personne.
3. Il ne parle à personne.
4. Tu n'achètes rien.
5. Elle ne connaît personne.
6. Il n'oublie rien.
7. Ils n'aident personne.

8. Non!

1. Nous n'avons rien fait.
2. Vous n'avez rencontré personne.
3. Je n'ai rien appris.
4. Tu n'as invité personne.
5. Gisèle n'a téléphoné à personne.
6. Pierre n'a fait la connaissance de personne.

Communication

(Answers will vary.)

LEÇON 23

1. La bonne vie

1. vit bien.
2. ne vivons pas bien.
3. ne vis pas bien.
4. vis bien.
5. ont bien vécu.
6. n'a pas bien vécu.

2. Non!

1. ne parle pas encore
2. ne travaille plus
3. n'aidez jamais
4. n'habitons plus
5. n'ai pas encore

3. C'est faux!

1. Paul n'a jamais pris le caméscope de Mélanie!
2. Nous ne sommes jamais partis sans payer!
3. Henri n'est jamais sorti avec la fiancée de Georges!
4. Vous n'avez jamais écrit cette lettre d'insulte!

4. Les jobs

1. Ils avaient des jobs. Ils travaillaient
2. Elle avait un job. Elle travaillait
3. Nous avions des jobs. Nous travaillions
4. Vous n'aviez pas de job. Vous ne travailliez pas.
5. Je n'avais pas de job. Je ne travaillais pas.
6. Tu n'avais pas de job. Tu ne travaillais pas.

5. Hier à midi

1. était / choisissait
2. étais / envoyais
3. étais / attendais
4. étaient / rendaient
5. étions / déjeunions
6. était / finissait

6. **En 1900**
   1. La pollution n'était pas un problème sérieux.
   2. Les femmes ne pouvaient pas voter.
   3. On n'allait pas au cinéma.
   4. Les gens travaillaient le samedi.
   5. On ne voyageait pas en avion.
   6. Les gens ne regardaient pas la télévision.
   7. Les appartements n'avaient pas l'air conditionné.

7. **Une fois n'est pas coutume.**
   1. jouions / nous avons joué
   2. téléphonait / il a téléphoné
   3. dormais / j'ai dormi
   4. allais / tu es allé(e)
   5. retrouviez / vous avez retrouvé
   6. sortait / elle est sortie
   7. faisions / nous avons fait

8. **À Paris**
   1. suivions
   2. déjeunais
   3. a dîné
   4. a rencontré
   5. alliez
   6. prenais
   7. a fait
   8. communiquais

Communication
(Answers will vary.)

LEÇON 24

1. **La soucoupe volante**
   1. étudiait.
   2. dormions.
   3. lisiez le journal.
   4. jouais aux cartes.
   5. dînaient.
   6. finissais une lettre.
   7. rendions visite à un ami.
   8. faisait la cuisine.
   9. attendiez votre frère.

2. **Pourquoi?**
   1. Nous sommes allés au café parce que nous avions soif.
   2. Vous avez mis un manteau parce que vous aviez froid.
   3. Jacqueline est restée chez elle parce qu'elle était malade.
   4. Mes cousins sont allés en Espagne parce qu'ils voulaient apprendre l'espagnol.
   5. Ma sœur a vendu sa voiture parce qu'elle avait besoin d'argent.
   6. Tu as pris de l'aspirine parce que tu avais une migraine terrible.

3. **Un événement**
   1. était
   2. était
   3. faisait
   4. avais
   5. suis sorti(e)
   6. ai fait
   7. passais / ai remarqué / regardaient
   8. ai regardé
   9. ai vu / faisait
   10. portait
   11. est arrivée / a arrêté
   12. a demandé / faisait
   13. a répondu / voulait

4. **Le premier jour à l'université**
   (Answers will vary.)

5. **C'est arrivé hier.**
   1. étaient / est entré
   2. avons vu / allaient
   3. allait / a arrêté
   4. a téléphoné / déjeunais
   5. travaillait / dormais
   6. a étudié / est sortie

6. **Et avant?**
   1. avais rencontré
   2. étions allés
   3. avais étudié
   4. était sortie
   5. avaient suivi
   6. n'avaient pas visité

Communication (Answers will vary.)
   1. Il était sept heures et demie.
   2. Il pleuvait.
   3. Il est sorti par la fenêtre.
   4. Il portait un pull et un pantalon.
   5. Il a passé le sac à une jeune femme.
   6. Elle portait un imperméable et des lunettes de soleil. Elle était blonde.
   7. Ils sont partis à motocyclette.
   8. (Answers will vary.)

Unité 9

LEÇON 25

1. **Dans la course**
   1. courez.

2. ne cours pas.
3. courent.
4. ne cours pas.
5. courait.
6. ne courions pas.
7. a couru.
8. n'avez pas couru.

2. Oui ou non?

1. Oui, j'y vais souvent. / Non, je n'y vais pas souvent.
2. Oui, j'y dîne souvent. / Non, je n'y dîne pas souvent.
3. Oui, j'y habite. / Non, je n'y habite pas.
4. Oui, j'y passe mes week-ends. / Non, je n'y passe pas mes week-ends.
5. Oui, j'y joue souvent. / Non, je n'y joue pas souvent.
6. Oui, j'y ai déjeuné samedi soir. / Non, je n'y ai pas déjeuné samedi soir.
7. Oui, j'y suis allé(e). / Non, je n'y suis pas allé(e).
8. Oui, je vais y aller. / Non, je ne vais pas y aller.

3. Des conseils

1. Vas-y!
2. N'y assiste pas!
3. Écris-lui!
4. Ne leur téléphone pas!
5. Réponds-y!
6. Réponds-leur!

4. Les loisirs

1. fait du patinage / en fait
2. faites de la voile / en faisons
3. avez fait du camping / n'en avons pas fait
4. ont fait de la planche à voile / en ont fait

5. Au régime

1. Oui, ils en font.
2. Non, elle n'en boit pas.
3. Oui, ils en mangent.
4. Oui, il en a fait.
5. Non, elle n'en a pas commandé.
6. Non, elle n'en a pas mis.

6. Les statistiques
(Answers will vary.)

7. En quelles quantités?
(Answers will vary.)

Communication
(Answers will vary.)

LEÇON 26

1. L'anatomie

1. On écoute avec les oreilles.
2. On parle avec la bouche.
3. On joue de la guitare avec les doigts.
4. On joue au basket avec les mains.
5. On joue au football avec les pieds.
6. On sent les odeurs avec le nez.
7. On court avec les jambes.
8. On mâche du chewing-gum avec les dents.

2. Le repos

1. Nous ne nous reposons pas.
2. Vous vous reposez.
3. Je me repose.
4. Elle ne se repose pas.
5. Tu te reposes.
6. Ils ne se reposent pas.
7. Ils se reposent.
8. Elle ne se repose pas.
9. Je me repose.

3. Les activités de la journée

1. te réveilles
2. se rase
3. nous lavons
4. me brosse les dents
5. se promènent
6. m'habille
7. vous reposez
8. se couche

4. Quel pronom?

1. se
2. le
3. le
4. s'
5. la
6. le

5. Quand?

1. Tu vas te raser
2. Nous allons nous promener
3. Elle va se reposer
4. Vous allez vous laver les mains
5. Je vais me brosser les dents
6. Ils vont se lever

6. Activités

1. souffre
2. offres
3. ouvrent
4. découvre
5. avons ouvert
6. a offert
7. a souffert
8. ont découvert

Communication
(Answers will vary.)

LEÇON 27

1. **Activités**
   1. nous préparons
   2. me souviens
   3. vous excusez
   4. se dépêche
   5. nous arrêtons
   6. s'occupe
   7. vous appelez
   8. s'amusent
   9. s'intéresse
   10. se met en colère
   11. nous asseyons
   12. se trompe

2. **Expression personnelle**
   (Answers will vary.)

3. **Encouragements**
   1. Amuse-toi!
   2. Ne t'impatiente pas!
   3. Ne te préoccupe pas inutilement!
   4. Ne te mets pas en colère!
   5. Entends-toi avec tes parents!
   6. Ne te dispute pas avec tes amis!

4. **Des conseils**
   1. Reposez-vous!
   2. Excusons-nous!
   3. Ne t'énerve pas!
   4. Ne vous amusez pas!
   5. Dépêchons-nous!
   6. Couchez-vous!

5. **L'amitié?**
   1. nous entendons / ne nous disputons pas
   2. ne vous comprenez pas / ne vous parlez pas
   3. se connaissent / s'invitent

6. **Samedi**
   1. Tu t'es amusée
   2. Vous vous êtes promenés
   3. Elles se sont levées
   4. Ils se sont couchés
   5. Elle s'est disputée
   6. Je me suis préparé
   7. Elles se sont habillées
   8. Ils se sont reposés

7. **Pauvre Juliette!**
   1. ne s'est pas levée
   2. ne s'est pas dépêchée
   3. s'est trompée
   4. s'est impatientée
   5. ne s'est pas amusée
   6. s'est couchée

Communication
(Answers will vary.)

Unité 10

LEÇON 28

1. **La personnalité**
   1. Elle est ponctuelle.
   2. Elle est amoureuse.
   3. Ils sont libéraux.
   4. Elles sont paresseuses.
   5. Elle est travailleuse.
   6. Ils sont loyaux.
   7. Elles sont étrangères.
   8. Elle est ennuyeuse.
   9. Elle est créatrice.
   10. Elle est conservatrice.
   11. Elle est inquiète.
   12. Ils sont actifs.

2. **Questions**
   1. rousse
   2. jalouse
   3. gentille
   4. favorite
   5. grosse
   6. longue
   7. folle

3. **Commentaires personnels**
   (Answers will vary.)

4. **Des conseils**
   1. Étudie consciencieusement!
   2. Parle calmement!
   3. Parlez discrètement!
   4. Attends patiemment!
   5. Joue prudemment!
   6. Habille-toi élégamment!
   7. Parle franchement!

5. **L'interview**
   1. Jacques est le premier.
   2. Sylvie est la deuxième.
   3. Henri est le septième.
   4. Brigitte est la huitième.
   5. Paul est le dixième.
   6. Suzanne est la douzième.
   7. Hélène est la quinzième.

8. Marylène est la vingtième.
9. Roger est le vingt et unième.
10. Marc est le vingt-deuxième.

6. Des personnalités
1. Ils commencent à travailler à neuf heures.
2. Elle apprend à faire du ski nautique.
3. Je ne m'arrête pas d'étudier.
4. Tu ne cherches pas à avoir des responsabilités.
5. Vous n'oubliez pas de faire vos devoirs.
6. Ils n'essaient pas de faire des progrès.
7. Elle ne cesse pas d'avoir des idées originales.
8. Nous hésitons à prendre des décisions.

Communication
(Answers will vary.)

LEÇON 29

1. Sur les Champs-Élysées
1. apercevons
2. aperçois
3. aperçoit
4. aperçoivent
5. ai aperçu
6. avons aperçu

2. Vouloir, c'est pouvoir!
1. Il gagnera beaucoup d'argent.
2. Il se mariera.
3. Nous voyagerons.
4. Je réussirai dans mes études.
5. Ils choisiront une profession intéressante.
6. Elle apprendra le russe.
7. Ils maigriront.
8. J'écrirai un roman.
9. Vous vivrez à Paris.
10. Tu t'amuseras.
11. Il partira pour Tahiti.

3. Cet été
1. travaillerons / ne nous reposerons pas
2. étudieras / n'apprendras pas
3. resterez / ne partirez pas
4. passerai / connaîtrai
5. suivront / ne grossiront pas
6. achètera / se promènera

4. Des projets
1. ferons / irons
2. sera / aura
3. auront / feront
4. serai / aurai
5. irez / ferez

5. Quand? (Answers will vary.)
1. J'irai à la bibliothèque...
2. Je ferai les courses...
3. J'aurai un examen...
4. Je verrai mes parents...
5. J'obtiendrai mon diplôme...
6. Je saurai piloter un avion...
7. Je recevrai une lettre...
8. Je courrai dans une course...

6. Plus tard!
1. Tu viendras chez moi
2. Elle verra ses amis
3. Elle enverra cette lettre
4. Ils devront étudier
5. Il voudra se reposer
6. Je pourrai t'aider
7. Il saura nager

7. Si...
(Answers will vary.)

8. Conséquences
1. gagnerai de l'argent quand je travaillerai.
2. maigrirez quand vous ferez de l'exercice.
3. cherchera du travail quand elle aura son diplôme.
4. enverras cette lettre quand tu iras à la poste.
5. enverrons un télégramme quand nous saurons la date de notre départ.
6. aura des responsabilités quand elle sera la présidente de sa compagnie.

Communication
(Answers will vary.)

LEÇON 30

1. Les vacances
1. Oui, j'étudierais. / Non, je n'étudierais pas.
2. Oui, je lirais des livres français. / Non, je ne lirais pas de livres français.
3. Oui, je jouerais au tennis. / Non, je ne jouerais pas au tennis.
4. Oui, je sortirais souvent. / Non, je ne sortirais pas souvent.

5. Oui, je dormirais beaucoup. / Non, je ne dormirais pas beaucoup.
6. Oui, j'irais à la piscine. / Non, je n'irais pas à la piscine.
7. Oui, je ferais des promenades. / Non, je ne ferais pas de promenades.
8. Oui, je serais de mauvaise humeur. / Non, je ne serais pas de mauvaise humeur.
9. Oui, j'aurais beaucoup de rendez-vous. / Non, je n'aurais pas beaucoup de rendez-vous.
10. Oui, je verrais vos cousins. / Non, je ne verrais pas vos cousins.
11. Oui, je enverrais des lettres à mes amis. / Non, je n'enverrais pas de lettres à mes amis.
12. Oui, je courrais tous les jours. / Non, je ne courrais pas tous les jours.

2. Avec plus d'argent

1. Jacques irait en Italie pendant les vacances.
2. Anne et Nicole seraient généreuses avec leurs amies.
3. Je ferais des économies.
4. Tu voudrais voyager souvent.
5. Alain aurait un appartement à Paris.
6. Vous enverriez de l'argent à vos parents.
7. Mes parents pourraient s'acheter une nouvelle voiture.
8. Nous verrions toutes les merveilles du monde.
9. Antoine deviendrait un mécène.
10. M. Richard devrait payer plus d'impôts.

3. Commentaires personnels

(Answers will vary.)

4. Si...

1. Si Paul avait une voiture, il irait à la plage.
2. Si nous étions en vacances, nous nous reposerions.
3. Si je travaillais, je gagnerais de l'argent.
4. Si Sylvie se reposait, elle serait en bonne santé.
5. Si vous travailliez, vous réussiriez.
6. Si Jacques suivait un régime, il maigrirait.

5. Annonces

1. Mes cousins ont téléphoné qu'ils viendraient demain.
2. J'ai dit que je répondrais à ta lettre.
3. Jacques et Émilie ont annoncé qu'ils se marieraient en juin.
4. Antoine a écrit qu'il irait en Suisse pendant les vacances.

6. Conditions

1. reste
2. gagnais
3. louerons
4. étudierais
5. faisiez
6. irions
7. a
8. étiez

7. Activités

1. traduisent
2. construis
3. produit
4. conduisez
5. conduisent
6. détruis

Communication

(Answers will vary.)

Unité 11

LEÇON 31

1. Obligations personnelles?

1. Il faut que j'étudie ce soir. / Il ne faut pas que j'étudie ce soir.
2. Il faut que je travaille pendant les vacances. / Il ne faut pas que je travaille pendant les vacances.
3. Il faut que je maigrisse. / Il ne faut pas que je maigrisse.
4. Il faut que je réussisse à l'examen de français. / Il ne faut pas que je réussisse à l'examen de français.
5. Il faut que je perde mon temps. / Il ne faut pas que je perde mon temps.
6. Il faut que je rende visite à mes cousins cet été. / Il ne faut pas que je rende visite à mes cousins cet été.
7. Il faut que je réfléchisse à l'avenir. / Il ne faut pas que je réfléchisse à l'avenir.
8. Il faut que je m'impatiente. / Il ne faut pas que je m'impatiente.
9. Il faut que je me repose. / Il ne faut pas que je me repose.

2. Les bons conseils

1. Il faut / finisses
2. Il ne faut pas / dorment

3. Il faut / écrive
4. Il faut / disions
5. Il ne faut pas / partent
6. Il ne faut pas / lises
7. Il faut / conduise
8. Il faut / offrions

3. Les conseils

1. buvez / boivent
2. obtienne / obtenions
3. appreniez / apprennent
4. voies / voyions

4. Oui ou non?

1. Il (n')est (pas) bon que nous buvions du thé chaud.
2. Il (n')est (pas) indispensable que vous obteniez un «A».
3. Il (n')est (pas) nécessaire qu'elle voie un médecin.
4. Il (n')est (pas) essentiel qu'ils maintiennent leurs traditions.

5. L'interview

1. Il faut que Paul ait une photo. Il faut qu'il soit à l'heure.
2. Il faut que Marc et Robert aient leurs diplômes. Il ne faut pas qu'ils soient arrogants.
3. Il faut que nous ayons les résultats des examens. Il faut que nous soyons polis avec l'interviewer.
4. Il faut que vous ayez vos notes. Il ne faut pas que soyez timides.
5. Il faut que tu aies une lettre de recommandation. Il ne faut pas que tu sois nerveux (nerveuse).
6. Il faut que j'aie mon curriculum vitae. Il faut que je sois sûr(e) de moi.

6. Non!

1. Non, je ne veux pas que tu prennes mon auto.
2. Non, je ne veux pas que tu voies mes photos.
3. Non, je ne veux pas que tu viennes chez moi après le dîner.
4. Non, je ne veux pas que tu boives cette bière.

7. Des souhaits

1. Mes parents souhaitent que j'aie un bon travail.
2. Je préfère que vous veniez chez moi jeudi soir.
3. Mme Dupont permet que son fils prenne la voiture.
4. Charles désire que ses copains sortent avec lui dimanche.

Communication

(Answers will vary.)

LEÇON 32

1. Des convictions

1. croyons
2. a cru
3. crois
4. croyais
5. croient
6. croirez
7. a cru

2. Oui ou non?

1. Il est nécessaire que je fasse des progrès en français. / Il n'est pas nécessaire que je fasse des progrès en français.
2. Il est utile que j'aille à l'université. / Il n'est pas utile que j'aille à l'université.
3. Il est indispensable que je puisse gagner beaucoup d'argent. / Il n'est pas indispensable que je puisse gagner beaucoup d'argent.
4. Il est essentiel que je sache jouer au tennis. / Il n'est pas essentiel que je sache jouer au tennis.
5. Il est normal que je veuille être indépendant(e). / Il n'est pas normal que je veuille être indépendant(e).

3. Votre opinion

1. Oui, je crois que la France est une grande puissance. / Non, je crois pas que la France soit une grande puissance.
2. Oui, je crois que les Américains sont très patriotes. / Non, je ne crois pas que les Américains soient très patriotes.
3. Oui, je crois que le président sait ce qu'il fait. / Non, je ne crois pas que le président sache ce qu'il fait.
4. Oui, je crois que les Martiens veulent conquérir le monde. / Non, je ne crois pas que les Martiens veuillent conquérir le monde.
5. Oui, je crois qu'on va vers une dépression économique. / Non, je ne crois pas qu'on aille vers une dépression économique.

6. Oui, je crois qu'on peut arrêter le progrès. / Non, je ne crois pas qu'on puisse arrêter le progrès.

4. Réactions
1. de passer l'été au Canada. / qu'elle passe l'été au Canada.
2. de partir en vacances. / qu'il parte en vacances.
3. d'avoir un accident. / qu'il ait un accident.
4. de partir. / que je parte.
5. de faire des progrès en français. / que tu fasses des progrès en français.
6. d'être malade. / qu'il soit malade.

5. Pourquoi?
1. pour que j'aille en ville.
2. pour que vous achetiez ce livre.
3. pour que leurs enfants aillent à l'université.
4. pour que tu fasses la connaissance de mon copain allemand.
5. pour que vous rencontriez mes amis.
6. pour qu'il fasse une promenade.
7. pour qu'ils aient des nouvelles.

6. La correspondance
1. Nous écrivons au professeur pour qu'il nous écrive des lettres de recommandation.
2. J'écris à mes cousins avant qu'ils (ne) partent en vacances.
3. Tu écris à ta cousine parce qu'elle vient de se marier.
4. Vous écrivez à vos amis pendant qu'ils sont à Paris.
5. M. Martin écrit à sa fille depuis qu'elle est étudiante à Paris.
6. Janine écrit à ses cousines pour qu'elles viennent chez elle pendant les vacances.

7. Les attitudes
1. vas
2. veniez
3. fassions
4. sont
5. connaît
6. puissiez
7. veuille
8. dites
9. (ne) partes
10. sachiez

Communication
(Answers will vary.)

LEÇON 33

1. Des relations personnelles
1. les / les
2. l' / lui
3. lui / l'
4. les / leur
5. m' / me
6. te / t'

2. Des services
1. Prête-lui
2. Donne-leur
3. Ne lui rends pas visite.
4. Ne les écoute pas.
5. Ne l'attends pas.
6. Aide-moi.
7. Ne nous critique pas.
8. Ne me donne pas

3. Bonnes vacances!
1. Jacques la lui donne.
2. Tu le leur envoies.
3. Francine le lui donne.
4. Nous les lui rendons.
5. Marc la lui vend.
6. Le professeur le leur rend.
7. Vous les leur envoyez.
8. Jean-Pierre les leur explique.

4. Votre meilleur(e) ami(e)
1. Oui, il (elle) me la prête. / Non, il (elle) ne me la prête pas.
2. Oui, il (elle) me le prête. / Non, il (elle) ne me le prête pas.
3. Oui, il (elle) me les donne. / Non, il (elle) ne me les donne pas.
4. Oui, il (elle) me la dit toujours. / Non, il (elle) ne me la dit pas toujours.
5. Oui, il (elle) me la demande. / Non, il (elle) ne me la demande pas.
6. Oui, il (elle) me la raconte. / Non, il (elle) ne me la raconte pas.
7. Oui, il (elle) me les montre. / Non, il (elle) ne me les montre pas.

5. S'il te plaît!
1. Prête-le-moi, s'il te plaît!
2. Montre-le-moi, s'il te plaît!
3. Montre-les-moi, s'il te plaît!
4. Donne-le-moi, s'il te plaît!
5. Vends-les-moi, s'il te plaît!
6. Vends-la-moi, s'il te plaît!

6. Qu'est-ce qu'il doit faire?
1. montre-les-lui.
2. rends-le-lui.

3. dis-la-leur.
4. vends-le-lui.
5. prête-la-leur.

7. Oui ou non?

1. Oui, il leur en vend.
2. Non, il ne lui en donne pas.
3. Non, elle ne leur en sert pas.
4. Oui, il nous en a donné.
5. Oui, ils m'en ont envoyé.

Communication

(Answers will vary.)

RÉVISION ANSWER KEY

Révision 1: Leçons 1–9

Partie A. Structures

Test 1. Les pronoms sujets et les pronoms accentués

1. Tu
2. vous
3. lui
4. eux
5. moi
6. nous
7. elle
8. elle

Test 2. La forme des adjectifs

1. brillantes
2. bonne
3. canadiennes
4. mauvais
5. individualiste
6. mariées
7. polies
8. égoïstes

Test 3. L'article défini: formes simples et formes contractées

1. Je vais parler au professeur.
2. Je vais inviter les amies de Claudine.
3. Je vais utiliser le caméscope de Philippe.
4. Le train va arriver à la gare dans dix minutes.
5. Nathalie va jouer au tennis avec nous.
6. Le professeur va parler aux étudiants.
7. Les étudiants vont arriver du laboratoire.
8. Jeanne aime parler des copains de Michèle.

Test 4. La négation

1. Non, Paul ne regarde pas la télévision.
2. Non, Sylvie n'a pas de compact disques.
3. Non, Christine n'aime pas parler français.
4. Non, Georges ne va pas aller à Paris.

Test 5. Descriptions

1. Paul et Antoine sont des garçons sympathiques.
2. Jacqueline et Hélène sont des amies françaises.
3. Les Rolling Stones sont des musiciens anglais.
4. Jane Fonda est une actrice américaine.
5. Les Ford et les Chevrolet sont des voitures américaines.
6. Les Renault sont de bonne voitures.
7. M. Dupont est un professeur intéressant.
8. Christine et Florence sont de vraies amies.

Test 6. Autres structures

1. b
2. c
3. a
4. c
5. d
6. d
7. c
8. b
9. d
10. c

Partie B. Verbes

Test 7. Les verbes en *-er*

1. habitons
2. visite
3. dînes
4. étudiez
5. danse
6. invitent

Test 8. Les verbes *être, avoir* et *aller*

1. sommes; avons; allons
2. êtes; avez; allez
3. sont; ont; vont
4. es; as; vas

Test 9. Verbes

1. joue au
2. joue du
3. écoute
4. regarde
5. téléphone à
6. pense à
7. entre dans
8. passe

Partie C. Vocabulaire

Test 10. Qu'est-ce que c'est?

1. une montre
2. un appareil-photo
3. un crayon
4. un ordinateur
5. une maison
6. une piscine
7. un disque
8. un stylo

Test 11. Les contraires

1. mauvais
2. fort
3. lent
4. célibataire
5. brun
6. heureux

Test 12. Logique!

1. d
2. b
3. b
4. d
5. a
6. c
7. a
8. b

Révision 2: Leçons 10–18

Partie A. Structures

Test 1. Les adjectifs possessifs

1. nos
2. ma
3. tes
4. leur
5. votre
6. leurs
7. son
8. ton
9. vos
10. notre

Test 2. L'article partitif: formes et emplois

1. du lait, de la limonade
2. de l'eau minérale, le jus d'orange
3. des pâtes, de la salade
4. du sucre, de la crème
5. le poisson, de la sole
6. de l'ambition, de courage
7. le pain, le fromage
8. de champagne, Le vin

Test 3. Les articles et les prépositions avec les pays

1. La France, l'Italie, le Portugal
2. aux États-Unis, au Canada
3. du Japon, au Venezuela, en Argentine

Test 4. Autres structures

1. a
2. b
3. d
4. a
5. d
6. b
7. d
8. c
9. b

Partie B. Verbes

Test 5. Le présent des verbes comme *payer, acheter* et *préférer*. Le présent des verbes en *-ir* et *-re*

1. envoie
2. finissent
3. réussissons
4. attend
5. possède
6. vends
7. amène
8. achètes
9. répondez
10. célèbre

Test 6. Le présent des verbes irréguliers

1. sors
2. part
3. buvez
4. comprennent
5. faites
6. viens
7. apprennent
8. mets
9. reviennent

Test 7. Le passé composé avec *avoir:* verbes réguliers

1. a téléphoné
2. n'ai pas téléphoné
3. ont joué
4. n'avons pas visité
5. avez acheté
6. n'a pas vendu
7. avons rendu
8. n'ont pas fini
9. as maigri
10. n'ai pas perdu

Test 8. Les participes passés irréguliers

1. a eu
2. a été
3. a bu
4. a fait
5. a pris
6. a appris
7. a mis
8. a dormi
9. a servi

Test 9. *Être* ou *avoir?*

1. a visité; est allée
2. sont sortis; sont allés
3. sommes allé(e)s; sommes rentré(e)s
4. ai invité; est venu
5. avez voyagé; êtes arrivés
6. ont étudié; sont devenues

Test 10. Verbes et expressions verbales

1. grossit
2. attend
3. nettoie
4. rend visite à
5. fait
6. fait les courses / du shopping
7. fait la cuisine
8. sort
9. porte
10. met
11. commande
12. apporte
13. déjeune
14. loue
15. rencontre / retrouve
16. oublie
17. cherche
18. trouve

Partie C. Vocabulaire

Test 11. Qu'est-ce que c'est?

1. un chapeau
2. des lunettes
3. un costume
4. des chaussettes
5. un bureau
6. un fauteuil
7. une valise
8. un gâteau
9. un œuf
10. une cerise
11. une fraise
12. une poire

Test 12. Logique!

1. b
2. d
3. c
4. a
5. d
6. a
7. b
8. a
9. b
10. a
11. d
12. c

RÉVISION 3: Leçons 19–27

Partie A. Structures

Test 1. Les pronoms compléments d'objet direct

1. Philippe la regarde.
2. Nous les invitons.
3. Je l'aide.
4. Nous les écoutons.
5. François la regarde.
6. Je ne la veux pas.
7. Je ne les connais pas.
8. Invite-la.
9. Ne les invite pas.
10. Je les ai écoutés.
11. Il ne l'a pas aidée.
12. Nous allons la regarder.

Test 2. Quel pronom?

1. le
2. en
3. lui
4. y
5. en
6. la
7. les
8. leur
9. y
10. en

Test 3. *Qui* ou *que?*

1. qui
2. qui
3. que
4. que
5. que, qui
6. que, que

Test 4. Les constructions négatives

1. Non, je n'ai rien entendu.
2. Non, personne n'a téléphoné.
3. Non, je n'habite plus à Paris.
4. Non, il n'est pas encore parti.
5. Non, rien n'est arrivé.
6. Non, je n'ai rien fait ce week-end.

Partie B. Verbes

Test 5. Le présent des verbes irréguliers

1. connaissons
2. suis
3. écrivez
4. peuvent
5. dites
6. lisent
7. ouvre
8. dois
9. court
10. voyons

Test 6. Le passé composé des verbes irréguliers

1. avons dû
2. a vécu
3. as pu
4. a ouvert
5. ai vu
6. avez lu
7. as su
8. a couru
9. as connu
10. as voulu

Test 7. La forme de l'imparfait

1. habitais, habitions
2. finissiez, finissait
3. rendais, rendaient
4. avais, avions
5. faisions, faisaient
6. étiez, étais
7. apprenais, apprenait
8. buvaient, buvais
9. voyais, voyait
10. lisais, lisiez

Test 8. L'emploi de l'imparfait

1. a visité
2. parlait
3. a parlé
4. a joué
5. jouait
6. est entré, jouaient
7. étais, j'ai rencontré
8. avons pris, jouaient
9. était, est arrivé
10. est allé, faisait
11. était, a eu
12. est resté, avait

Test 9. La forme des verbes réfléchis

1. me lave; me suis lavé(e)

2. ne se rase pas; s'est rasé
3. ne vous levez pas; vous êtes levé(e)(s)
4. se lève tard; ne s'est pas levée
5. nous promenons; ne nous sommes pas promené(e)s
6. s'amusent; ne se sont pas amusées
7. s'arrêtent; ne se sont pas arrêtés

Test 10. Quelques verbes pronominaux (présent, infinitif, impératif)

1. se réveille
2. se lève
3. se couche
4. nous habillons
5. se rase
6. me reposer
7. te souvenir
8. nous promener
9. lève-toi
10. ne vous impatientez pas
11. ne t'arrête pas
12. Dépêchons-nous

Partie C. Vocabulaire

Test 11. Logique!

1. d	5. d	9. d
2. c	6. d	10. b
3. b	7. a	11. b
4. a	8. b	12. d

Test 12. Le mot exact

1. régime	6. météo
2. note	7. siècle
3. droit	8. natation
4. écrivain	9. rendez-vous
5. vérité	10. tête

RÉVISION 4: Leçons 28–33

Partie A. Structure

Test 1. Adjectifs irréguliers

1. franche	4. ponctuelle
2. gentilles	5. sérieux
3. folle	6. paresseuses

Test 2. L'emploi de l'infinitif après les verbes, les adjectifs et les noms

1. à	6. de	10. à
2. à	7. à	11. —
3. de	8. de	12. de
4. —	9. de	13. de
5. de		

Test 3. Les pronoms compléments d'objet direct et indirect

1. la, lui	3. les, leur	5. m', me
2. lui, l'	4. les, leur	6. nous, nous

Test 4. L'ordre des pronoms compléments

1. Je les lui prête.
2. Paul la lui vend.
3. Jacqueline les leur donne.
4. Anne la leur dit.
5. Charles me la prête.
6. Montre-le-lui!
7. Prête-la-leur.
8. Donnez-le-moi.
9. Je les y invite.
10. Nous leur en donnons.
11. Nous t'y amenons.
12. Je vous en montre.

Partie B. Verbes

Test 5. Les formes du futur

1. habiterai, habiterons
2. réussiras, réussiront
3. vendra, vendrez
4. sortirai, sortirons
5. serez, serai
6. aura, aurez
7. ferai, feras
8. irons, iront
9. viendras, viendront
10. recevrai, recevrez
11. pourront, pourrai
12. courront, courras

Test 6. Le conditionnel

1. achèterais, achèterait, achèteriez
2. réussirions, réussirais, réussiraient
3. serait
4. irions
5. aurais
6. ferais
7. pourriez
8. voudrions

Test 7. L'emploi des temps avec *quand* et *si*

1. travaillera
2. travaille
3. travaillait
4. travaillerait
5. travaille
6. travaillerait
7. travaillait
8. travaille
9. travaillera
10. travaillait

Test 8. Le subjonctif des verbes réguliers

1. étudient, réussissent
2. mange, maigrisse
3. finisse, choisisse
4. trouviez, réussissiez
5. téléphonions, rendions
6. vende, achète
7. répondent, oublient
8. finissent, joues

Test 9. Le subjonctif: formation régulière, verbes à deux radicaux

1. apprennes, apprennent
2. veniez, viennent
3. buvions, boive
4. voie, voyiez
5. reçoivent, receviez

Test 10. Des subjonctifs irréguliers

1. sois, soyez
2. ayons, aie
3. aille, allions
4. fasse, fassiez
5. puisses, puissent
6. sachiez, sache
7. veuille, vouliez

Test 11. Indicatif ou subjonctif?

1. est
2. soit
3. soit
4. soit
5. soit
6. est
7. soit
8. soit
9. est
10. soit
11. est
12. soit

Test 12. Des verbes irréguliers

1. croyons
2. ai cru
3. conduis
4. as conduit / emmené
5. reçoivent
6. as reçu

Partie C. Vocabulaire

Test 13. Logique!

1. c
2. a
3. d
4. c
5. d
6. c
7. d
8. a

DICTÉE (Lab Program) ANSWER KEY

Unité 1

LEÇON 1

Activité 8. Salut!

—Salut! Ça va?
—Oui, ça va bien.
—Jean-Paul, je te présente mon amie Clara.
—Enchanté.
—Au revoir. À demain!

LEÇON 2

Activité 13. Salutations

—Bonjour, Mademoiselle.
—Bonjour, Monsieur.
—Comment allez-vous?
—Je vais très bien. Et vous?
—Je vais comme ci, comme ça.

LEÇON 3

Activité 12. Bonjour!

—Voici Annie et Nicole. Et voilà Pascal, un copain suisse.
—Bonjour, Annie.
—Bonjour, Nicole.
—Qui est-ce?
—C'est Pascal.
—Au revoir, Annie. À bientôt.

LEÇON 4

Activité 16. Au Canada

Vous habitez à Paris? J'habite à Québec avec Paul et Jacques. Nous habitons à Québec, mais nous ne travaillons pas à Québec. Je travaille à Montréal. Paul et Jacques étudient à l'Université Laval.

LEÇON 5

Activité 17. Les voyages

J'aime voyager. Je voyage assez souvent. Maintenant je suis à Québec. Je veux aussi visiter Montréal. Est-ce que vous voyagez souvent? Est-ce que vous aimez voyager?

LEÇON 6

Activité 16. Le tennis

Avec qui est-ce que tu joues au tennis? Tu joues avec Paul et Philippe, n'est-ce pas? Pourquoi est-ce que tu joues avec eux? Pourquoi est-ce que tu ne joues pas avec moi? Moi aussi, je joue bien!

LEÇON 7

Activité 17. Jacqueline

Voici Jacqueline. C'est une amie. Elle a des disques, mais elle n'a pas de chaîne stéréo. Moi, j'ai une minichaîne, mais elle ne marche pas. Et toi, est-ce que tu as une chaîne stéréo?

LEÇON 8

Activité 13. Suzanne

Suzanne est une grande fille brune. Elle habite à Paris, mais elle n'est pas française. Elle est américaine. Elle a un copain. C'est un étudiant anglais. Et vous, est-ce que vous avez des amis anglais?

LEÇON 9

Activité 17. Le temps libre

Où allez-vous? Moi, je vais à la piscine avec Jean-Michel. Nous allons nager et jouer au volley. À quatre heures, nous allons aller chez lui et nous allons jouer aux cartes. Aimez-vous le bridge?

LEÇON 10

Activité 15. Mes voisins

Mes voisins ont deux enfants. Leur fils Robert est étudiant. C'est mon copain. Leur fille Alice est professeur. Elle est mariée. Son mari travaille au laboratoire de l'université.

LEÇON 11

Activité 14. Au magasin

Je vais acheter cette cravate rouge. Elle coûte soixante-dix francs. Elle n'est pas très bon marché, mais elle est jolie. Je vais aussi acheter cette chemise bleue et ces chaussures noires. Et toi, quelles chaussures préfères-tu?

LEÇON 12

Activité 16. Le week-end

Qu'est-ce que vous faites le week-end?

Quand il pleut, je fais le ménage. Mais quand il fait beau, je ne reste pas chez moi. Ce week-end, je vais faire une promenade à bicyclette. Je vais aller chez Roger, mon nouvel ami. Il habite un bel appartement dans une vieille maison.

LEÇON 13

Activité 15. Sylvestre

Mon cousin Sylvestre a dix-neuf ans. Il a l'intention d'aller en France. Il a besoin d'argent. Voilà pourquoi il vend son auto. Avez-vous envie d'acheter cette auto? Réfléchissez à ma question!

LEÇON 14

Activité 16. Samedi dernier

Qu'est-ce que vous avez fait samedi dernier? Moi, j'ai téléphoné à Julien. L'après-midi, nous avons joué au tennis. Le soir, nous avons dîné dans un restaurant italien. Après, nous avons rendu visite à un copain. Vraiment, nous n'avons pas perdu notre temps!

LEÇON 15

Activité 16. Au Canada

L'année dernière, Georges est allé au Canada avec sa cousine Sylvie. Ils sont partis de Paris le dix juillet. Ils ont visité Québec où ils sont restés deux semaines. Là-bas, Georges a rencontré une étudiante canadienne avec qui il est souvent sorti.

LEÇON 16

Activité 14. Catherine

Je viens de téléphoner à Catherine. Elle vient de passer une semaine à Québec. Maintenant, elle est à Montréal. Elle est là-bas depuis samedi. Elle revient aux États-Unis le premier juillet.

LEÇON 17

Activité 16. Au restaurant

Guillaume et Suzanne sont au restaurant. Guillaume regarde le menu. Il va prendre du poulet et de la salade. Il va boire du vin. Suzanne va prendre de la salade, mais elle ne va pas prendre de poulet. Elle va prendre du jambon et boire de l'eau minérale.

LEÇON 18

Activité 15. Au restaurant

Nous déjeunons souvent dans ce restaurant. La viande et les légumes sont toujours très bons. François va commander du poulet avec des frites. Moi, je vais prendre de la sole parce que je suis au régime.

LEÇON 19

Activité 20. Ce soir

Ce soir, mes amis veulent aller au cinéma. Je veux sortir avec eux, mais je ne peux pas. Demain, j'ai un examen très difficile. Je dois rester chez moi. À mon université, il faut beaucoup étudier si on ne veut pas rater ses examens.

LEÇON 20

Activité 17. Monique et Henri

Connais-tu Monique? Moi, je la connais bien. Je l'ai rencontrée l'année dernière à Paris. Je vais l'inviter à la fête. Elle va venir avec son cousin Henri. Je ne le connais pas, mais ses amis le trouvent très sympathique. Il fait des études d'ingénieur à l'Université de Grenoble.

LEÇON 21

Activité 16. J'ai besoin de mon livre.

Tu connais Christine, n'est-ce pas? Elle m'a parlé de toi quand je lui ai rendu visite hier. Je lui ai prêté un livre, et maintenant j'ai besoin de ce livre. Je veux lui téléphoner. Donne-moi son numéro de téléphone, s'il te plaît!

LEÇON 22

Activité 15. Ma voisine

J'habite dans un immeuble qui n'est pas très moderne mais que je trouve confortable. Je connais tous mes voisins. J'ai une voisine qui est très sympathique et que j'invite souvent chez moi. C'est une étudiante qui a passé plusieurs années dans une université américaine.

LEÇON 23

Activité 16. Le fils des voisins

Quand j'avais douze ans, j'habitais dans un petit village. Je passais tous mes week-ends avec Henri, le fils des voisins. C'était mon meilleur ami. Nous allions souvent à la plage et parfois nous faisions des promenades à bicyclette.

LEÇON 24

Activité 13. Hier soir

Hier soi, je suis sorti avant le dîner. Il faisait un temps épouvantable. Il neigeait et la visibilité était très mauvaise. Quand je suis rentré, j'ai vu quelqu'un qui attendait un taxi, mais il n'y avait pas de taxi. J'ai reconnu mon ami Jean-Claude. Je l'ai invité chez moi et nous avons dîné ensemble.

LEÇON 25

Activité 14. À la mer

Allez-vous souvent à la mer? Quand j'étais jeune, j'y allais tous les étés. C'est là que j'ai appris à faire de la voile. J'en faisais très souvent. Maintenant, je n'en fais plus parce que je n'ai pas de bateau. Si j'ai de l'argent, je vais en acheter un cet été.

LEÇON 26

Activité 15. Le dimanche

À quelle heure est-ce que vous vous levez le dimanche? Moi, je ne me lève jamais avant dix heures. Je me rase, je me lave, je m'habille et j'écoute la radio. L'après-midi, je me promène avec mon amie Marie-Laure. Nous nous promenons souvent à la campagne. Et vous, est-ce que vous vous promenez avec vos amis?

LEÇON 27

Activité 16. Guy et Suzanne

Aujourd'hui, Guy s'est levé tôt. Il s'est rasé et il s'est habillé. Après, il a téléphoné à Suzanne. Ils se sont donné rendez-vous au café de l'université pour trois heures. Guy est arrivé un peu en retard, mais Suzanne ne s'est pas impatientée. Guy et Suzanne se sont promenés jusqu'à sept heures. Est-ce qu'ils s'aiment? C'est possible.

LEÇON 28

Activité 16. Étienne et ses sœurs

Connais-tu Étienne? C'est un garçon très travailleur et très ambitieux. Ses sœurs sont assez différentes. Christine est une fille très sportive, mais elle n'est pas très intellectuelle. Catherine est une fille très idéaliste et très généreuse. Voilà pourquoi elle a beaucoup d'amis loyaux.

LEÇON 29

Activité 17. Voyage en Italie

Si j'ai de l'argent cet été, je ferai un voyage en Italie avec mon ami Charles. Nous irons d'abord à Rome. Quand nous serons là-bas, nous verrons mes cousins. J'espère qu'ils pourront nous trouver un hôtel bon marché. Je leur enverrai un télégramme quand je saurai la date de notre départ.

LEÇON 30

Activité 14. Après l'université

Qu'est-ce que je ferais si je n'étais pas étudiant? Je ne resterais pas ici. Si j'avais de l'argent, je ferais un grand voyage. Je verrais de nouveaux pays. J'irais au Japon ou en Chine. Je reviendrais en France après deux ou trois ans.

LEÇON 31

Activité 17. Les courses

Je vais aller au supermarché. Il faut que j'achète de la bière. Ensuite, je veux passer à la bibliothèque. Il faut que je prenne un livre. Non, il n'est pas nécessaire que vous veniez avec moi. Mais, j'aimerais bien que vous me prêtiez votre voiture.

LEÇON 32

Activité 20. Visite à Genève

Je suis content que tu ailles à Genève cet été, mais j'ai peur que tu ne puisses pas rencontrer mon frère. Je sais qu'il voyage beaucoup et je doute qu'il soit chez lui en juillet.

LEÇON 33

Activité 14. Mon vélo

Je n'ai pas mon vélo. Je l'ai prêté à Thomas. Demande-le-lui. S'il ne te le donne pas, dis-lui que je vais le chercher demain.

Internet Connections

CONNECTING WITH FRENCH INTERNET SITES

The Internet allows you to access up-to-date information about the French-speaking world. Moreover, by surfing the many French sites on the Web, you will quickly realize how useful your French skills can be. French is, after all, the second most common Internet language.

NOTE: Websites are modified frequently, and even addresses are subject to change. The following list is provided as a point of departure. If a site has been changed or is no longer accessible, just browse till you find another one.

GETTING STARTED

- The American Association of Teachers of French has a home page that will direct you to Internet options.
  http://www.utsa.edu/aatf/
  In particular, visit the AATF Internet "surfing" page.
  http://www.utsa.edu/aatf/surfing.html

- Another place to get started is via Tennessee Bob's Famous French Links.
  http://www.utm.edu/departments/french/french.html

- You may prefer to go directly to France via the following home pages:
  http://www.FranceWeb.fr
  http://www.imaginet.fr
  http://www.cocorico.com/
  http://www.france.diplomatie.fr
  http://www.franceguide.com

- There are also interesting French-speaking sites in Canada that you can access.
  http://www.matin.qc.ca

EXPANDING ON THE *VIVRE EN FRANCE* TOPICS

The Internet lets you expand on the themes of the *Vivre en France* sections at the end of each unit in the Student Text.

- Unité 1. Pendant le cours
  Use the computer to consult an electronic map of France.
  http://web.urec.fr/france/france.html

- Unité 2. L'identité
  Use the Web to meet French students looking for international pen pals.
  http://www.libul.com

- Unité 3. En ville
  Try to find your way around on the Paris metro.
  http://www.paris.org.:80/Metro/

- Unité 4. La vie à Paris
  Visit the Louvre.
  http://www.louvre.fr/
  Or check on today's weather.
  http://www.meteo.fr/

- Unité 5. À l'hôtel
  Find a hotel.
  http://www.franceguide.com
  http://www.paris.org/ then go to **hotels**

- Unité 6. Au café
  Check out the Paris cafés and restaurants.
  http://www.paris.org/ then go to **cafés** or **restaurants**

- Unité 7. Le courrier
  Find a French pen pal and begin a correspondence.
  http://www.libul.com

- Unité 8. Les sorties
  Find out what is happening in Paris.
  http://pariscope.fr/
  http://www.paris.org/ then go to **calendar**

- Unité 9. Le sport et la santé

tennis:	**http://www.fft.fr/**	
skiing:	**http://skiin.com/**	then search under **France**
sports events:	**http://www.FranceWeb.fr/**	then go to **grands événements sportifs**

- Unité 10. En voyage

train schedules:	**http://www.sncf.fr**
touring France:	**http://www.franceguide.com**

- Unité 11. L'achat des vêtements
  Check out the catalogues of French mail-order houses.
  http://www.redoute.fr/
  http://www.trois-suisses.fr/